Supporting Digital Mental Health in Educational Environments

Shafiq Ul Rehman
https://orcid.org/0000-0003-2266-218X
Kingdom University, Bahrain

IGI Global
Scientific Publishing
Publishing Tomorrow's Research Today

Vice President of Editorial	Melissa Wagner
Director of Acquisitions	Mikaela Felty
Director of Book Development	Jocelynn Hessler
Production Manager	Mike Brehm
Cover Design	Jose Rosado

Published in the United States of America by
IGI Global Scientific Publishing
701 East Chocolate Avenue
Hershey, PA, 17033, USA
Tel: 717-533-8845 | Fax: 717-533-7115
Website: https://www.igi-global.com E-mail: cust@igi-global.com

Library of Congress Cataloging-in-Publication Data

LCCN: 2025040078 (CIP Data Pending)
ISBN13: 9798337350073
Isbn13Softcover: 9798337350080
EISBN13: 9798337350097
British Cataloguing in Publication Data
A Cataloguing in Publication record for this book is available from the British Library.

Table of Contents

Detailed Table of Contents

We are living in an age of rapid digital tranformation where technological innovations are shaping nearly every aspect of human interaction, learning, and lifestyle. At the heart of this revolution lies social media, which has moved far beyond being a casual communication tool to becoming an essential component of modern existence. For students, who represent one of the most digitally active populations, social media is not merely a platform for recreation—it is embedded in their academic endeavors, social exchanges, identity formation, and even professional aspirations. Platforms such as Facebook, Instagram, Twitter (now X), TikTok, YouTube, and Snapchat have revolutionized how young people connect with knowledge, peers, and opportunities. YouTube tutorials support academic study, LinkedIn facilitates early professional networking, and WhatsApp groups are used for collaborative assignments. This digital ecosystem has created unprecedented avenues for growth and inclusion, offering students a sense of belonging in global virtual communities.

An expanding constellation of commercial and open-source learning-analytics (LA) platforms—Canvas "New Analytics," Blackboard Predict, Purdue's Course Signals, Civitas Illume, Moodle Learning Analytics, and the On Task intervention engine—promise to flag students who are academically or psychologically "at risk." Yet their effectiveness, ethical soundness, and transferability remain unevenly documented. Rather than designing a novel tool.Through a systematic literature review, and cross-case analysis of five institutional implementations, the chapter distils a research-backed, privacy-preserving, human-in-the-loop workflow that institutions can adopt with the technology they already own or can licence. The chapter outcome is a pragmatic, evidence-based roadmap that shows where current systems excel, where they falter, and how policy, practice, and organisational culture can close the gap between algorithmic alerts and meaningful student support.

Student mental health is an urgent concern across all levels of education, with stress, anxiety, and depression often fueled by academic pressures, peer competition, and digital overload. Traditional counseling typically intervenes late, highlighting the need for AI-driven technologies that enable early detection and timely support. This chapter explores how machine learning, natural language processing, wearable sensors, and learning analytics can monitor academic, behavioral, linguistic, and physiological data to detect signs of distress. AI tools may provide personalized assistance through chatbots, adaptive learning, and predictive analytics for intervention, particularly valuable where resources are scarce. Yet, challenges such as privacy, bias, transparency, and consent demand responsible frameworks. Human-centered AI, participatory design, ethical audits, and governance structures are essential to ensure trust and accountability. Done responsibly, AI can transform student well-being, enabling proactive support and resilient educational communities.

The supercharged pace of online learning has rendered it more essential than ever before to respond to students' mental health needs. An increasing number of students are experiencing anxiety, depression, and burnout in both K–12 and higher-education contexts, and traditional ways of managing them are not keeping up. Digital learning platforms can help care for students' health in new ways by drawing on the information they collect. Through predictive analytics, schools can detect early warning signs of emotional problems, disengagement, and isolation. These early warning systems must support teachers, counselors, and school administrators to intervene before issues become more entrenched. This paper delves into how AI technologies can be used to predict mental health problems, avoid crises, and emotionally shield students. It also discusses how ethical, individualized, and team-based methods need to be employed to construct systems that honor the dignity of students and establish their trust.

Preface

The rapid digital transformation of educational environments has reshaped not only how students learn, but also how they experience school, community, and self. As the Editor of *Supporting Digital Mental Health in Educational Environments*, I am honored to introduce a volume that addresses one of the most urgent and complex challenges of our time: ensuring that digital learning ecosystems support—not compromise—the mental health and well-being of learners and educators.

In recent years, innovations such as virtual classrooms, learning management systems, adaptive learning technologies, and mobile applications have expanded access, flexibility, and personalization across educational contexts. Yet, as these technologies have become embedded in daily academic life, we have witnessed new psychological pressures emerge. Digital fatigue, social isolation, information overload, academic inequities, and limited access to mental health care have intensified stress for students, educators, and institutions alike. The COVID-19 pandemic magnified these challenges dramatically, exposing vulnerabilities but also inspiring new models of digital care and community support. As the boundaries between online and offline learning environments grow increasingly porous, addressing mental health within digitally mediated education has become an indispensable priority.

This volume brings together scholars, practitioners, technologists, and policymakers committed to building educational systems that are not only technologically advanced but also emotionally attuned, culturally inclusive, and ethically grounded. Our aim is to bridge disciplinary divides and create a shared knowledge base that empowers stakeholders to design, implement, and evaluate digital mental health supports that are effective, equitable, and sustainable.

Each chapter in this book contributes to this mission by offering interdisciplinary insights, case studies, and evidence-based practices. Readers will encounter explorations of AI-driven mental health tools, virtual counseling models, digital well-being programs, teletherapy integration, wearable technologies, learning analytics, and the ethical use of student data. These contributions highlight the immense potential of digital tools to enhance early detection, prevention, and intervention—while also addressing issues of accessibility, privacy, stigma, and cultural responsiveness.

This book is written for a broad yet deeply invested audience: researchers, educators, mental health professionals, EdTech developers, policy leaders, and graduate students who share an interest in improving mental health outcomes in digitally enriched educational environments. Whether you seek to conduct research, design digital solutions, craft institutional policies, or support students directly, this volume provides both conceptual grounding and practical guidance.

As Editor, my hope is that this book will inspire thoughtful innovation, encourage cross-sector collaboration, and spark new conversations about the future of mental health in education. Digital technologies will continue to evolve at an extraordinary pace—but so too must our commitment to fostering learning environments where every individual can thrive emotionally as well as academically.

By advancing a vision of holistic, supportive, and ethically responsible digital learning ecosystems, this book invites all of us to participate in shaping an educational future that is resilient, humane, and responsive to the mental health needs of our communities.

ORGANIZATION OF THE BOOK

Chapter 1: Designing Resilient Educational Ecologies for Mental Health in Techno-Social Learning Environments

The opening chapter establishes a conceptual and practical foundation for understanding digital mental health within today's complex techno-social learning ecosystems. It introduces a forward-thinking framework—rooted in bioecology, universal design, trauma literacy, privacy-preserving computation, and dialogic humanization—that reimagines how educational systems can embed care into their digital architectures. By translating principles such as cognitive ergonomics, inclusion by default, and bounded caregiving into actionable rules for instruction, assessment, platform design, and governance, the chapter provides a systemic grammar for building resilient learning environments. Its operational matrices and distribution-sensitive auditing tools demonstrate how well-being can be measured, equity strengthened, and learning made durable. This chapter sets the tone for the volume by showing that mental health support must be embedded into the very infrastructure of digital education.

Chapter 2: Empowering Through Care — Mental Health and Counseling in Student Well-being

Chapter 2 examines the evolving role of mental health and counseling services within higher education, highlighting how emotional well-being has become central to academic success. Through a close look at academic pressures, peer dynamics, and misalignment between personal interests and degree paths, the chapter illustrates the emotional burdens many students face. In response, institutions are expanding their support ecosystems with counseling centers, mentor–mentee programs, mindfulness practices, wellness curricula, psychometric evaluations, and coordinated communication between faculty, families, and students. By showcasing how these supports cultivate resilience and emotional competence, the chapter paints a picture of educational environments increasingly committed to holistic student development—preparing learners for both academic demands and the broader challenges of adulthood.

Chapter 3: Mental Health Support in Digital Education in the Current Scenario

This chapter reflects on the profound digital shift catalyzed by the COVID-19 pandemic and its implications for student mental health. While digital education expanded accessibility and flexibility, it also introduced heightened risks: excessive screen time, reduced social interaction, academic strain, and deepening feelings of isolation and fatigue. The authors argue that mental health support must be integral to any effective digital-education system, not an optional add-on. By detailing the psychological challenges faced by students and educators during and after the pandemic, the chapter underscores the need for mental-health-informed digital pedagogies, improved support structures, and intentional well-being practices in online learning environments.

Chapter 4: Procrastination in the Digital Age — Examining Internet Addiction Among Pre-Service English Teachers

Chapter 4 presents a mixed-methods study exploring the relationship between internet addiction and academic procrastination among pre-service English teachers. Its findings reveal a clear positive correlation, with internet addiction accounting for a notable proportion of procrastinatory behavior. By integrating quantitative analyses with qualitative insights, the chapter illustrates how digital habits intersect with emotional well-being, academic self-regulation, and identity formation. The research challenges assumptions about gender-based differences and aligns with broader literature on digital behavior's impact on academic functioning. Ultimately, the chapter calls for intentional curricular efforts to strengthen digital literacy, time-management skills, and self-regulation to support the next generation of educators.

Chapter 5: Social Media's Impact on Student Mental Health and Digital Literacy

This chapter investigates the multifaceted role of social media in students' academic, social, and emotional lives. Moving beyond the idea of social media as a leisure activity, the authors highlight its centrality in modern education—from YouTube tutorials that scaffold learning to platforms like LinkedIn and WhatsApp that enable collaboration and professional growth. While social media creates opportunities for belonging and global connectivity, it also heightens exposure to comparison, misinformation, cognitive overload, and emotional strain. The chapter emphasizes the dual necessity of digital literacy and mental-health literacy, urging educators to recognize both the empowering and destabilizing effects of social media on student identity, motivation, and psychological well-being.

Chapter 6: Synthesising Learning-Analytics Systems for Early Identification of At-Risk Students

Chapter 6 evaluates a wide range of commercial and open-source learning-analytics tools designed to identify students who may be academically or psychologically at risk. Through a systematic review and multi-institutional analysis, the authors illuminate the strengths, limitations, and ethical complexities of current systems. Rather than proposing new software, the chapter offers a clear, research-grounded workflow that institutions can implement using existing technologies. By integrating privacy-preserving methods, human-in-the-loop decision processes, and evidence-based interventions, it provides a pragmatic roadmap for closing the gap between algorithmic alerts and authentic student support. The chapter contributes a vital perspective on how learning-analytics systems can become more just, transparent, and genuinely helpful.

Chapter 7: AI-Driven Early Detection and Monitoring of Student Mental Health

This chapter explores the transformative potential of artificial intelligence in detecting early signs of student mental distress. It outlines how machine learning, natural language processing, wearable technologies, and learning analytics can work together to monitor behavioral, academic, linguistic, and physiological data—enabling earlier intervention when students experience anxiety, depression, or stress. The authors highlight both the promise and the pitfalls of AI-driven mental health tools, noting challenges such as bias, consent, opacity, and fairness. By advocating for human-centered design, ethical governance structures, participatory development, and clear accountability measures, the chapter underscores how responsible AI can enhance well-being and strengthen educational resilience.

Chapter 8: Predict, Prevent, Protect — AI-Driven Early Warning Systems for Student Mental Health

Building on the technological insights of earlier chapters, Chapter 8 focuses on AI-enabled early warning systems that help educators identify distress before it escalates. The authors examine how predictive analytics can surface patterns of disengagement, emotional strain, or social withdrawal within digital learning environments. They argue that effective early warning systems must support—not replace—teachers, counselors, and administrators, and must be designed to uphold dignity, autonomy, and trust. The chapter calls for ethical, individualized, and team-based practices that ensure interventions are proactive and compassionate. In doing so, it positions AI as an instrument of care when integrated thoughtfully and responsibly.

Chapter 9: Pulse of the Mind — Wearable Devices for Emotional and Physiological Monitoring

Chapter 9 investigates the rising use of wearable devices to monitor physiological and emotional indicators relevant to student mental health. From heart-rate variability to sleep patterns and electrodermal activity, wearables offer continuous, real-time insight into stress, fatigue, and cognitive load. When combined with machine learning, these signals can inform early interventions and personalized support strategies. The chapter provides an overview of sensor technologies, real-world school and university applications, and illustrative case studies. It also addresses pressing ethical concerns—particularly around privacy, consent, and equity for vulnerable student populations. The chapter concludes by describing how wearables may integrate with institutional policies and digital mental-health systems to strengthen resilience and academic success.

Chapter 10: Virtual Counselling and Teletherapy Platforms for Students and Educators

This chapter examines the expanding role of virtual counselling and teletherapy within digitally transforming educational environments. With mental health challenges rising among both students and educators, virtual platforms—ranging from AI chatbots to professional teletherapy—have become essential components of contemporary support ecosystems. The authors discuss their benefits, including accessibility, flexibility, and scalability, while also acknowledging limitations related to privacy, technological disparities, and clinical effectiveness. Real-world case studies illustrate successful models of implementation. The chapter concludes by offering strategies for sustainable adoption and integration, presenting virtual counselling as a compassionate and necessary extension of the modern educational landscape.

Chapter 11: Sustaining Digital Mental Health Services in South African Higher Education

The final chapter offers a regionally specific yet globally relevant exploration of sustaining digital mental health services in South African higher education institutions. While e-health tools have the potential to transform staff well-being, long-term adoption is hindered by intertwined social, economic, environmental, and technological barriers. This chapter proposes a strategic sustainability framework that addresses these obstacles through inclusive design, leadership commitment, data governance, and cross-sector partnerships. By providing a practical blueprint for policymakers, the chapter advances the goal of equitable, resilient, and culturally informed mental health support systems. In doing so, it contributes meaningfully to global conversations about sustainable development and digital well-being in higher education.

CONCLUSION

As editor of *Supporting Digital Mental Health in Educational Environments*, I close this preface with a shared conviction: the future of education depends not only on technological innovation, but on our collective ability to center human well-being within these rapidly evolving digital landscapes. Across the chapters in this volume, our contributors illuminate the complex interplay between pedagogy, technology, psychology, and ethics, offering a multidimensional understanding of what it means to design emotionally supportive learning ecosystems in the digital age.

Together, these chapters show that supporting mental health in educational environments is neither the responsibility of a single discipline nor the outcome of any one tool. Rather, it is a collaborative endeavor that spans policy and practice, design and data, counseling and curriculum, research and lived experience. Whether exploring AI-driven early detection, virtual counseling platforms, learning analytics systems, wearables, or the everyday stressors faced by students and educators, the authors in this volume consistently call for digital solutions that are responsible, inclusive, transparent, and rooted in care.

This book affirms that digital technologies can be powerful allies in strengthening mental health—when implemented with intention, guided by ethical principles, and shaped through participatory collaboration. The work presented here challenges educators, developers, institutional leaders, and policymakers to imagine learning environments where technological advancement and emotional well-being reinforce one another rather than exist in tension. It encourages us to build systems that not only respond to distress, but also cultivate resilience, connection, and belonging.

As the boundaries between physical and digital learning continue to blur, the imperative to safeguard mental health becomes ever more urgent. We hope this volume serves as both a roadmap and an invitation—an invitation to re-envision educational ecosystems that honor the whole person and a roadmap for integrating digital tools that meaningfully support psychological flourishing. By engaging with these insights, we believe stakeholders across the globe can contribute to more compassionate, equitable, and mentally healthy educational futures.

With this vision in mind, we offer this book as a resource and catalyst for ongoing dialogue, innovation, and action.

Shafiq Ul Rehman

Kingdom University, Bahrain

Chapter 1
Designing Resilient Educational Ecologies for Mental Health in Techno-Social Learning Environments:
Neurodigital Pedagogies and Architectonics of Care

Ashraf Alam
https://orcid.org/0000-0001-6178-1187
Alliance University, Bengaluru, India

ABSTRACT

Educating at scale now unfolds within techno social ecologies where cognition, affect, equity, and infrastructure co-determine outcomes. This chapter advances a dignitarian architecture of digital care that integrates bioecology, universal design, dialogic humanization, trauma literacies, and privacy preserving computation into actionable grammars for classrooms, platforms, and policy. The study specifies cognitive ergonomics, inclusion by default, contestable inference, and bounded caregiving as system invariants, and translate them into cadence rules, authentic assessment, accessibility fidelity, and governance with enforceable remedies. Compact matrices operationalize risks, assets, competencies, and product checks, while distribution sensitive auditing secures subgroup parity under real world constraints. The result is a programmatic synthesis that renders wellbeing measurable, equity buildable, and learning durable across diverse contexts.

DOI: 10.4018/979-8-3373-5007-3.ch001

1. INTRODUCTION

1.1 Problem Framing and Rationale

Hybrid and online provisions have reconstituted schooling into a techno social ecology in which cognition, affect, motivation, and equity co determine learning outcomes. The instructional milieu now traverses domestic spaces, cloud platforms, and institutional rules, which together modulate attention, arousal, and self-regulation (Taylor et al., 2024; Severes et al., 2025; Davies et al., 2021). Continuous telepresence compresses recovery cycles and multiplies micro stressors that accumulate into fatigue and disengagement when left unmanaged. The instructional transaction therefore requires an explicit architecture of care that treats mental health as a design variable rather than an aftercare service (Badawi et al., 2023; Costardi et al., 2023; Daisy, 2025). This chapter positions digital care as a criterion of educational quality, foregrounds a grammar of inclusion that anticipates heterogeneity by default, and proposes programmatic mechanisms that bind pedagogy, technology, and governance into a coherent system. The argument proceeds from ecological first principles, specifies actionable design constraints for classrooms and platforms, and aligns institutional procurement and policy with rights-based norms. The resulting synthesis is intended to serve academics who seek conceptual clarity, policy makers who need decision frameworks, workforce leaders who require operational guardrails, and technologists who build the tools that now mediate instruction at scale.

1.2 Techno-Social Learning Ecologies and Cognitive Ergonomics

The digital classroom functions as a coupled human machine system governed by resource limits that include bandwidth, device capability, visual field constraints, and working memory capacity. Cognitive ergonomics in this setting prioritizes load budgeting across synchronous and asynchronous mixes, structured alternation between focused attention and diffuse recovery, and stable routines that dampen avoidable arousal (Ludlow et al., 2024; Rheinberger et al., 2023). Camera norms, chat cadence, and notification regimes shape social presence and attentional fragmentation, while interface friction and latency influence frustration and dropout. The physiological substrate is not peripheral, because sleep architecture, visual strain, and musculoskeletal load fluctuate with timetable density and task design. These conditions can be engineered through explicit cadence rules, predictable micro breaks, and multimodal representation that reduces decoding effort for multilingual and neurodiverse learners (Pine, 2021; Smith et al., 2023; Hugh-Jones et al., 2022). Educators operate as bounded caregivers who require analytic cues without surveillance excess, and platforms must present interpretable signals that aid formative decisions while preserving dignity. Table 1 in Section 2 consolidates the anchoring frameworks that structure these design moves and clarifies how each framework translates into classroom routines, interface criteria, and institutional policy levers.

1.3 Equity Externalities and Risk Stratification

Digital delivery amplifies pre-existing stratifications through device scarcity, unstable connectivity, crowded housing, gendered privacy risks, and disability accessibility gaps. The resulting pattern produces uneven participation, higher absence of voice for learners who lack quiet space or private screens, and increased cognitive cost for those who translate across languages or modalities in real time. Risk accumulation is nonlinear, because multiple small disadvantages interact to reduce self-efficacy and elevate stress long before failure becomes visible in grades (Bergin et al., 2020; Chen et al., 2025; Harith et al., 2022). Equity sensitive course design therefore cannot remain an accommodation mindset, it must adopt universal design principles that normalize multiple means of engagement and demonstration of competence without special pleading. Assessment logistics require recalibration that reduces dependence on continuous video presence and invasive identity checks and instead foregrounds authentic tasks, open resource reasoning, and staged submissions with feedback. Procurement and support models must integrate low-cost offline access paths and consistent assistive technology compatibility. The institutional aim becomes resilience at the learner edge rather than maximal functionality for the median user, which aligns with a public health view of harm prevention and produces system level gains in belonging, agency, and persistence.

1.4 Operational Definitions and Scope

The chapter treats digital care as the integrated set of pedagogical routines, platform affordances, and institutional rules that minimize avoidable stress, protect privacy, and enlarge agency for learners and educators. Mental health within instruction denotes the capacity to sustain attention, regulate arousal, engage in prosocial interaction, and recover from setbacks in ways that support learning goals and civic development (Wani et al., 2024; Graham et al., 2020; Balcombe & De Leo, 2021). Inclusion denotes anticipatory design that removes structural impediments for disability, language, geography, and socioeconomic status, rather than episodic accommodations after a mismatch is discovered. Privacy denotes purpose limited data practices, minimal collection, short retention, transparent inference, and the separation of care functions from discipline. Fairness denotes the reduction of disparate error and access gaps across subgroups through evaluation protocols that account for variations in context and embodiment. The scope spans K to 12 and higher education and includes formal instruction, assessment, and student support delivered through learning platforms, communication tools, and institutional data systems. The chapter does not adjudicate individual clinical protocols, it concentrates on educational design choices that influence population level wellbeing within routine teaching and learning.

1.5 Chapter Thesis and Structure

The central thesis states that psychosocially sustainable learning emerges when ecological theory, humanizing pedagogy, universal design, trauma informed practice, and privacy preserving computation are operationalized together through concrete rules for classrooms, interfaces, and governance. Section 2 distills the conceptual scaffolds that guide design decisions and presents Table 1 synthesizing frameworks, design moves, and risk consequences. Section 3 maps the mental health landscape of platform mediated classrooms across students and educators and introduces Table 2 which enumerates risks, protective factors, and interventions across ecological layers. Section 4 professionalizes educator care through a competency taxonomy, training modalities, and workload protections and offers Table 3 that aligns competencies with observable behaviors and assessment rubrics. Section 5 translates inclusion and privacy principles into implementable product criteria and supplies Table 4 which functions as a compact checklist for digital mental health interventions across accessibility, privacy, fairness, and participation. Section 6 embeds the architecture of care through curriculum, policy, procurement, finance, and accountability, supported by Table 5 that sequences workstreams, owners, milestones, and metrics. Section 7 concludes with a synthesis that foregrounds feasibility, fidelity, and durability for diverse systems and settings.

2. THEORETICAL FRAMEWORKS AND EDUCATIONAL FOUNDATIONS

2.1 Bioecological Systems for Platformed Learning

A bioecological optic conceptualizes learning as nested person in context couplings that operate concurrently at device, household, institutional, and cultural scales. The digital microsystem comprises interface friction, notification cadence, audiovisual density, and privacy affordances that calibrate arousal, working memory, and conversational turn taking (Wies et al., 2021; Xu et al., 2023; Jackson et al., 2024). The mesosystem links home and school through schedules, caregiving logistics, and shared bandwidth that reallocate time and attention across siblings and multigenerational households. The exosystem encodes assessment templates, retention windows, and vendor practices whose rules shape opportunity structures without direct learner input. The macrosystem stabilizes narratives about productivity, dignity, visibility, and surveillance tolerance which in turn govern camera norms and inference acceptance. The chronosystem tracks cumulative exposure to telepresence and the transition from emergency pivot to durable routine that crystallizes habits and expectations. Intervention therefore targets multiple levers rather than exhorting willpower in a vacuum. A crosswalk that binds framework to design move and monitoring signal is essential for timely course correction. Table 1 synthesizes these correspondences so that educators, designers, and leaders can align pedagogy, interface, and governance while detecting stress before it hardens into disengagement.

2.2 Critical Humanization and Dialogic Praxis

Critical humanization advances learning quality through power transparency, reciprocal authorship of norms, and interpretability that privileges inquiry over discipline. Dialogic praxis converts these values into structured participation rules that legitimize multilingual expression, contextualized reasoning, and respectful critique across chat, polls, breakout rooms, and asynchronous feedback. Analytics become prompts to converse rather than cudgels to coerce, which lowers defensive compliance and increases voluntary disclosure when confusion or overload arises (Xi et al., 2025; Lattie et al., 2022; Yeo et al., 2024). Consent rituals for recording, negotiated visibility protocols, and narrative assignments that privilege situated understanding reduce reputational threat while incentivizing intellectual risk taking. Time protected reflection enables metacognitive consolidation and reduces the volatility that arises when busy weeks compress feedback cycles. Boundary clarity around educator availability conserves empathic bandwidth and keeps care within sustainable limits. The operational grammar cannot remain aspirational, it must be rendered into concise heuristics that busy instructors can enact under routine pressure. Table 1 encodes these heuristics alongside sentinel indicators that surface trust erosion, muted participation, or unequal voice distribution early enough for corrective action that preserves dignity and rigor.

2.3 Universal Design for Learning as Anticipatory Inclusion

Universal Design for Learning functions as anticipatory inclusion that normalizes heterogeneity and prevents avoidable friction before accommodations are required. Multiple means of engagement, representation, and action are delivered as defaults rather than exceptions, which lowers decoding effort for multilingual learners, improves navigability for assistive technologies, and preserves autonomy through structured choice without diluting outcomes (Khanna & Carper, 2022; Bassilios et al., 2022; Liu & Schueller, 2023). Caption integrity, transcript accuracy, alt text fidelity, and keyboard operability cease to be decorative checkboxes and become reliability properties of instruction. Predictable cadence rules with planned micro breaks stabilize attention and reduce visual and musculoskeletal strain, while low bandwidth pathways and offline caching protect participation at the network edge. Choice among products, scaffolded pacing, and exemplar rich rubrics increase agency while maintaining comparability. These principles must connect to auditable routines and measurable signals to avoid drift. Table 1 operationalizes this connection by pairing each framework archetype with concrete moves and compact indicators that can be observed within ordinary course logistics.

Table 1. Crosswalk of Frameworks to Operational Design Heuristics Matrix

Framework Archetype	Defining Construct	Actionable Pedagogy and Interface Moves	Systemic Risks if Neglected	Sentinel Indicators for Monitoring
Bioecological Systems	Nested person in context coupling	Load budgeting across sync and async, bandwidth tiering, family schedule harmonization, routine micro breaks	Accretive fatigue, inequitable voice loss, volatility driven attrition	Attendance volatility, turn taking dispersion, recovery adherence
Critical Humanization and Dialogue	Reciprocal meaning making with power transparency	Negotiated camera norms, consent rituals, dialogic feedback, narrative assessments	Defensive compliance, surveillance threat, muted participation	Sentiment balance, question latency, voluntary disclosure rate
Universal Design for Learning	Anticipatory multimodality with choice architecture	Caption integrity, alt text fidelity, choice among products, scaffolded pacing	Decoding overload, modality exclusion, accommodation stigma	Accessibility pass rate, modality uptake mix, late work clustering
Social and Emotional Learning	Competency development in self and social regulation	Emotional check ins, peer accountability, constructive critique scripts, repair routines	Dysregulated discourse, peer isolation, brittle collaboration	Norm adherence, peer help frequency, conflict closure ratio
Trauma Informed Pedagogy	Safety, predictability, and empowerment	Transparent agendas, opt in visibility, escalation maps, educator self-care boundaries	Trigger spirals, trust erosion, caregiver burnout	Predictability adherence, help seeking latency, staff strain signals
Privacy Preserving Governance and Ethics	Data minimization and dignitarian safeguards	Purpose limitation, short retention, contestable inference, accessible grievance	Purpose creep, disparate error, reputational harm	Consent comprehension, audit pass rate, inference reversal usage

The matrix anchors principle to practice and reduces ambiguity during high workload periods when good intentions tend to degrade under time pressure. By tracking dispersion of turn taking, latency of questions after prompts, or clustering of late work by modality, educators can infer rising friction and adjust cadence, exemplars, or support windows. Accessibility integrity measured through caption accuracy and alt text quality signals whether the course remains navigable for assistive technologies. Privacy preserving governance aligns with UDL because the right to control one's visibility remains compatible with deep participation through alternative modalities. The outcome is a system that scales dignity and rigor together by treating inclusion and privacy as invariants rather than add ons.

2.4 Social and Emotional Learning in Hybrid Ecologies

Social and Emotional Learning in platform mediated classrooms organizes daily practice around five interdependent competencies that stabilize motivation, attention, and relationship quality. Self-awareness and self-management are trained through forecast reflect cycles where learners anticipate effort, select strategies, and appraise outcomes without stigma (Torous et al., 2025; Leo et al., 2022; Ludlow et al., 2023). Social awareness and relationship skills are cultivated through structured critique that pairs explanation with justification and rewards repair after rupture, which maintains elasticity in collaboration when errors occur in public. Responsible decision making is rehearsed through scenario analysis where students weigh externalities of choices such as camera use, chat frequency, or file sharing, thereby practicing civic reasoning inside the micro polity of the class (Balcombe & De Leo, 2022; Riboldi et al., 2023; Balcombe et al., 2022). Table 1 situates SEL alongside UDL and humanization and specifies compact indicators such as peer help frequency, norm adherence, and conflict closure ratio so that caring practice becomes observable and improvable. Consistency across weeks matters more than episodic enthusiasm, which requires that routines be scripted, rehearsed, and insulated from assessment pressure so that psychosocial safety does not evaporate when deadlines converge.

2.5 Trauma Informed Practice for Psychosocial Safeguarding

Trauma informed practice recognizes that unpredictability and involuntary exposure are potent triggers that can collapse participation even in learners with intact academic capacity. Transparent agendas, opt in visibility, and quiet escalation maps allow learners to regulate arousal and seek support without public disclosure (Venning et al., 2021; Kaur et al., 2025; Schuler & Raknes, 2022). Repair rituals that legitimize apology and reset rebuild trust after missteps and convert conflict into learning rather than lingering rancor. The approach protects educators through workload engineering, collegial consultation, and boundary clarity that prevent heroic overextension and distribute affective labor. Camera policies, breakout allocations, and cold call protocols are treated as powerful stimuli that require consent architectures rather than default imposition. Cultural display rules are respected so that silence is not misread as defiance and eye contact is not universalized as engagement. Table 1 codifies these commitments by naming risks such as trigger spirals and caregiver burnout and by listing sentinel signals such as help seeking latency and predictability adherence that allow timely redirection without escalation.

2.6 Metacognition, Self-Regulation, and Cognitive Ergonomics

Metacognition and self-regulation provide the intrapersonal machinery that enables deliberate effort allocation under fluctuating cognitive load. Implementation intentions convert intentions into executable scripts that specify when and where to act, which reduces procrastination by shrinking choice sets (Venning et al., 2021; Kaur et al., 2025; Schuler & Raknes, 2022). Cognitive offloading through checklists, exemplars, and templates reduces working memory strain and frees capacity for reasoning. Interleaved practice and spaced retrieval stabilize long term retention without dramatic expansion of study time. Cognitive ergonomics complements these strategies by aligning task design with human limits, such as capping synchronous density, interspersing micro breaks, and sequencing from novelty to consolidation to mitigate fatigue. Interfaces that surface progress, allow frictionless resubmission, and enable discreet questions lower the social cost of help seeking. The indicators in Table 1 support calibration, for example recovery adherence shows whether planned breaks occur, while question latency reveals whether prompts elicit thoughtful engagement or signal overload. The aim is an ecology where effort is invested purposefully rather than defensively and where progress remains legible to both learner and instructor.

2.7 Needs Hierarchy Privacy and Safety as Precondition for Learning

A reframed needs hierarchy for digital learning places cyber safety, informational privacy, and social dignity immediately after physiological requirements because these determinants govern whether learners can participate without fear of reputational or bodily harm. Privacy as control over personal data, appearance, and network location reduces anticipatory anxiety and unlocks candid formative error which is essential for growth (Stiles-Shields et al., 2025; Taylor et al., 2024; Dederichs et al., 2021). Safety includes predictable moderation, clear recourse against harassment, and response mechanisms that do not penalize disclosure. Belonging emerges through routines that validate multiple literacies and invite cultural resources into problem solving, which increases epistemic agency. Esteem is built through feedback that distinguishes performance from worth and that pinpoints growth trajectories without euphemism. Self-actualization takes the form of contributory agency when students co design criteria or build resources for peers, which internalizes civic responsibility and stabilizes motivation. The ethics row in Table 1 links these needs to procurement and data practices such as purpose limitation, short retention, and contestable inference so that protections remain durable across personnel changes and vendor updates.

2.8 Governance Standards and Rights Based Procurement

Governance translates values into durable operations by binding institutions to standards, audits, and contracts that survive leadership turnover and budget shocks. Accessibility governance requires periodic third-party validation of caption accuracy, keyboard navigation, and color contrast rather than reliance on vendor attestations (Palermo et al., 2023; Kanuri et al., 2020; Min et al., 2022). Privacy governance mandates data minimization, explicit retention windows, and mechanisms to challenge or reverse algorithmic inferences, which reduces chilled speech and reputational harm. Fairness management demands distribution sensitive evaluation so that error rates across groups are measured and mitigated rather than assumed equal. Procurement embeds these expectations into tenders with measurable milestones and consequences for noncompliance. Finance migrates from pilot enthusiasm to stable operations and maintenance that covers updates, training, and evaluations so that gains do not decay after grant cycles (Linardon et al., 2022; Song et al., 2024; Fleming et al., 2023). Accountability practices such as transparency reports, student representation with voting rights, and enforceable grievance pathways convert rights into lived experience. The governance line in Table 1 crystallizes these moves and the associated indicators so that leaders can steer decisively and educators can trust that ethical decisions will be institutionally supported.

3. MAPPING THE MENTAL HEALTH LANDSCAPE IN DIGITALLY MEDIATED CLASSROOMS

3.1 Student Phenomena in Platformed Classrooms

Student experience in digitally mediated classrooms emerges from the coupling of cognitive load, arousal regulation, and socio spatial constraints that operate at multiple scales. At the immediate interface, self-view magnification, gaze fixation, and notification storms amplify self-consciousness and fragment attention, which degrades working memory fidelity and raises error propensity during complex reasoning (Bassi et al., 2024; Tomičić & Gjorgjioska, 2024; Abura-Meerdink & Albright, 2024). Household density, device sharing, and acoustic spillover impose covert costs on participation that manifest as strategic silence, camera avoidance, and shortened interventions even among highly motivated learners. Linguistic hierarchies privilege default language codes and suppress translanguaging practices, which elevates decoding effort and constricts epistemic agency for bilingual and multilingual students. Over a term, cumulative screen exposure, irregular sleep timing, and unbuffered assessment clusters accrue into fatigue states that mimic apathy yet reverse when cadence is reengineered (Mindu et al., 2023; O'Dea et al., 2021; Stern et al., 2023). These dynamics require ecological rather than individual remedies, since the same student oscillates across contexts that alternately impair and enable learning. The cross-scale patterning of risks and assets is summarized in Table 2, which converts diffuse phenomena into tractable levers so that instructors can stabilize participation without intrusive monitoring and technologists can redesign interfaces that lower arousal without suppressing social presence.

3.2 Educator Affective Labor and Attrition Risk

Educators operate as bounded caregivers within techno social ecologies that reward immediacy and penalize delay, which intensifies affective labor and threatens role drift from teacher to perpetual counselor. Continuous telepresence compresses recovery, multiplies micro escalations, and inflates message triage, while analytics dashboards invite over interpretation of noisy signals that conflate struggle with disengagement (Lukka & Palva, 2023; Schueller & Torous, 2020; Bevan Jones et al., 2020). Without workload engineering and boundary clarity, empathic availability becomes unbounded and generates compassion fatigue that is easily misread as indifference by students and administrators. Surveillance oriented tools heighten moral stress by recruiting teachers into roles that conflict with dignitarian commitments, especially when proctoring or forced visibility triggers student distress (Borghouts et al., 2021; Vial et al., 2022; Park et al., 2022). A sustainable model requires redistribution of care through peer consultation, clear escalation maps, and protected time for reflection, along with procurement policies that separate instructional analytics from discipline. Educator wellbeing therefore depends on structural safeguards rather than exhortation, with priority levers identified explicitly in Table 2, where exosystem and macrosystem rows surface policy instruments that reduce moral injury while preserving instructional efficacy.

3.3 Stratified Vulnerabilities across Context and Identity

Vulnerability stratification arises when context and identity interact to amplify friction and mute voice in ways that simple averages conceal. Gendered harassment and reputational harm pressures increase the cost of visibility for many students, which suppresses spontaneous inquiry and reduces willingness to iterate publicly (Liverpool et al., 2020; Kozelka et al., 2024; Gibson et al., 2024). Disability access gaps and neurodiversity misreads convert neutral tasks into repeated demonstrations of grit, which drains cognitive resources that should fund learning. Rural connectivity volatility and prepaid data ceilings impose stochastic absences that are misclassified as disinterest, while linguistic monocultures compress expressive range and induce avoidance of complex argumentation (Lim et al., 2024; Muchamore et al., 2024; Ridout et al., 2024). These disadvantages do not accumulate linearly, they compound into sudden disengagement when assessment density peaks or when household demands spike. The analytic task is to render these patterns legible through compact constructs that decision makers can act upon immediately. The eco layered risk asset mapping in Table 2 operationalizes this requirement by pairing each ecological stratum with dominant risks, protective assets, evidence signals, and intervention levers that are implementable within routine constraints.

Table 2. Matrix of Eco Layered Risk Asset Signals and Intervention

Ecological Stratum	Dominant Psychosocial Risks	Contextual Protective Assets	Observable Evidence Signals	Priority Intervention Levers
Microsystem	self-view hypervigilance, notification overload, cramped space, acoustic spill	ergonomic placement, caption integrity, low bandwidth mode, self-view off	off camera persistence, latency spikes, error bursts, rapid task switching	cap sync density, scripted micro breaks, noise shaping, interface declutter
Mesosystem	caregiver conflict, device sharing, time poverty, sibling competition	family schedule harmonization, offline caching, asynchronous windows	attendance volatility, mid-session exits, clustered deadline failures	flexible deadlines, bandwidth tiering, staggered releases, household alignment
Exosystem	punitive assessment, invasive proctoring, long retention, opaque inference	authentic assessment, purpose limitation, grievance channels	privacy tickets, appeal surges, camera refusal waves	retire proctoring, shorten retention, contestable inference, alternative verification
Macrosystem	surveillance tolerance, language hierarchy, gendered harassment, stigma	dignity norms, multilingual policies, anti-harassment enforcement	toxicity reports, language switching suppression, chilled speech	moderated forums, multilingual rubrics, consequence clarity, restorative protocols

continued on following page

Table 2. Continued

Ecological Stratum	Dominant Psychosocial Risks	Contextual Protective Assets	Observable Evidence Signals	Priority Intervention Levers
Chronosystem	cumulative load, sleep drift, burnout creep, crisis normalization	pacing maps, recovery intervals, rotational staffing	rising strain self-reports, sick leave climb, help seeking latency	workload caps, recovery adherence audits, schedule deintensification
Cross Cutting Determinants	disability access gaps, rural volatility, neurodiversity misreads, disparate error	WCAG conformance, low tech channels, choice of visibility, inference reversal	accessibility failures, subgroup error gaps, disproportionate flags	third party audits, low bandwidth defaults, co design boards, fairness testing

The matrix functions as a decision scaffold that compresses complex interactions into minimally sufficient cues for action without reducing individuals to stereotypes. Evidence signals such as attendance volatility, help seeking latency, or clustered deadline failures can be monitored with low intrusiveness and used to trigger adjustments in cadence, modality, or assessment structure before distress consolidates into withdrawal. Protective assets like offline caching and multilingual rubrics expand the feasible set of demonstrations of competence while preserving outcome comparability. Intervention levers such as workload caps, moderated forums, and inference reversal convert normative commitments into operational routines that endure during busy periods and leadership turnover. By concentrating on strata rather than traits, Table 2 prevents pathologizing students and reframes the problem as an engineering and governance task that institutions can own collectively.

3.4 Measurement and Methodological Pluralism for Decision Quality

High stakes decisions about support and remediation require instrumentation that respects context while resisting false precision. Surveys provide broad coverage but underreport distress when stigma and surveillance fears are salient, therefore they must be complemented by experience sampling that captures temporal dynamics and by qualitative diaries that expose situational triggers (Porche et al., 2022; Zhang et al., 2022; Hicks et al., 2025). Learning analytics reveal participation rhythms and error bursts yet carry construct validity risks when proxies for attention or emotion are overinterpreted, which necessitates distribution sensitive evaluation that checks subgroup error rates before any automated triage. Accessibility audits detect friction that dashboards miss, such as caption drift or keyboard traps that block screen reader navigation (Nwaogu et al., 2021; Cameron et al., 2025; Brotherdale et al., 2024). Policy ethnography uncovers institutional rules that inadvertently magnify risk, for example retention windows that deter candid inquiry. Mixed method ensembles become most powerful when keyed to the signals enumerated in Table 2 so that each indicator has a corroborating measure from a different modality, which reduces misclassification and increases the legitimacy of subsequent interventions for both students and staff.

3.5 Help Seeking, Stigma, and Algorithmic Misclassification

Help seeking in digital classrooms is shaped by perceived reputational cost, fear of surveillance, and prior experiences of dismissal, which jointly depress early disclosure and raise the probability of crisis presentations. Anonymous channels and asynchronous queries reduce exposure yet can delay feedback if staffing and workflows are not tuned, while public forums accelerate resolution but heighten risk of ridicule or misinterpretation (Maqsood et al., 2024; Pendse et al., 2022; Knapp et al., 2023). Algorithmic triage promises efficiency but can entrench disparity when proxies for engagement encode access gaps rather than motivation, which inflates false positives for some groups and false negatives for others. Contestability mechanisms and human in the loop review mitigate harm only when accessible within the same interface where flags appear and when reversal has no downstream penalty. Stigma reduction requires visible norms that separate competence from composure and that normalize repair after rupture so that students can reenter discussions without residue (Krisher et al., 2024; Stanger & Lucas, 2024; Hornstein et al., 2023). The design of these channels and norms should align with the matrix in Table 2, where grievance pathways, inference reversal, and moderated forums are treated as core infrastructure rather than optional extras.

3.6 Synthesis to Intervention and Programmatic Prioritization

A coherent intervention portfolio translates ecological diagnosis into sequenced actions that deliver relief quickly while building durable capacity. Immediate moves include cadence reengineering that caps synchronous density, inserts scripted micro breaks, and staggers deadlines to prevent load spikes, along with deployment of low bandwidth modes and offline caching to stabilize participation for households with volatile connectivity. Medium horizon work establishes authentic assessment in place of punitive surveillance, implements purpose limitation and short retention to restore dignity, and operationalizes multilingual rubrics that expand expressive range without diluting rigor (Adu et al., 2024; Brown et al., 2022; Shen et al., 2022). Long horizon investment builds rotational staffing, third party accessibility audits, and distribution sensitive evaluation pipelines that monitor subgroup error rates and trigger corrective redesign when gaps widen. Program governance assigns owners to the intervention levers specified in Table 2 and publishes sentinel indicators so that accountability is ambient rather than episodic (Hornstein et al., 2021; Lal et al., 2024; Brooks et al., 2023). By aligning pedagogy, interface, and policy around the same signals, institutions convert caring intent into measurable practice that survives stress cycles and leadership change, thereby converting digital classrooms into psychosocially sustainable ecologies.

4. TRAINING AND SUPPORTING EDUCATORS AS BOUNDED CAREGIVERS

4.1 Rationale for Professionalization of Educator Care

Educators sustain the psychosocial metabolism of digitally mediated classrooms through continuous calibration of arousal, attention, and trust, yet this labor often remains tacit and unresourced. Professionalization requires an explicit competency architecture, experiential training pipelines, and verification regimes that convert invisible care into observable craft (Balcombe, 2023; Lo et al., 2022; Costescu et al., 2022). The risk asset cartography in Table 2 from Section 3 identified strata where distress concentrates and where protective routines yield outsized returns. Translating that diagnosis into durable practice demands role clarity, consent aligned analytics, and workload protections that prevent empathic depletion. The goal is not to expand pastoral obligations indefinitely but to bound caregiving within a principled scope that preserves instructional focus while enabling timely triage. A standards informed vocabulary of care improves handoffs to counselors, reduces misclassification of struggle as disengagement, and inoculates against surveillance drift by codifying dignitarian safeguards (Mota et al., 2022; Soubutts et al., 2024; Nogueira-Leite et al., 2024). Professionalization also anchors equity, since consistent routines reduce reliance on discretionary goodwill that can vary with bias and fatigue. The present section specifies scope, competencies, training modalities, verification evidence, and drift control, with core elements consolidated in Table 3, so that institutions can scale humane practice without sacrificing feasibility during the most demanding phases of the academic calendar.

4.2 Role Delineation and Scope of Bounded Caregiving

Bounded caregiving delineates an educator's remit as sentinel detection, low intensity stabilization, and ethically governed referral while explicitly excluding clinical diagnosis and coercive surveillance. The sentinel function relies on interpretable signals such as turn taking dispersion, question latency, and clustering of late work rather than opaque affect scores (Rosenberg et al., 2022; Ruzek et al., 2024; Schneider et al., 2024). Stabilization privileges consent driven visibility, predictable cadences, and repair rituals that reconstitute belonging after rupture. Referral proceeds along transparent pathways that protect privacy and avoid punitive externalities, accompanied by documentation that records patterns without stigmatizing labels (Kumar et al., 2022; Balcombe & De Leo, 2020; Zainal et al., 2025). The scope includes the cultivation of SEL aligned discourse norms, trauma sensitive choice architectures, and privacy preserving participation options that uphold agency for students who cannot disclose constraints. It also includes protection of educators through boundary rules for availability, capped synchronous density, and collegial backup during spikes in demand. Institutions express commitment by embedding these expectations into job descriptions, evaluation rubrics, and procurement criteria. The competency taxonomy that operationalizes this remit appears in Table 3 within Section 4.3, which aligns high fidelity behaviors with preferred training modalities and mastery evidence so that role clarity is matched by concrete enactment in daily practice.

4.3 Competency Taxonomy for Bounded Caregiving

Competency grows where theory meets rehearsal under conditions that approximate classroom volatility. The taxonomy presented here clusters the craft into six mutually reinforcing domains that map onto the ecological levers surfaced earlier. Affective attunement organizes perception of stress signals without pathologizing difference (Naslund & Deng, 2021; Cross et al., 2022; Sakellari et al., 2021). Technopedagogical interpretation trains data humility so that proxy metrics are read in context. Ethical empathy binds care to dignity and consent. Crisis stabilization structures de-escalation and escalation with minimal exposure. Boundary setting preserves educator viability through availability rules and cadence engineering. Reflective inquiry institutionalizes learning loops through collegial review. The matrix that follows compresses these domains into high density prompts for design of training, verification, and drift control (Machado et al., 2024; Meyerhoff et al., 2023; Merry et al., 2020). It functions as a living scaffold that leadership can adopt wholesale or adapt locally without diluting the invariants of dignity, privacy, and equity. As with Table 2, the intention is to provide minimally sufficient structure that enables decisive action while resisting technocratic overreach.

Table 3. Competency Matrix for Bounded Caregiving in Digital Classrooms

Competency Domain	High Fidelity Behaviors	Preferred Training Modality	Verification and Mastery Evidence	Maintenance and Drift Control
Affective Attunement and Trauma Literacies	calibrates tone, anticipates triggers, uses repair scripts, normalizes opt in visibility	mixed reality simulations, spaced microlearning, guided rehearsals	debrief transcripts, fidelity checklists, learner sentiment balance	peer observation cycles, booster modules, trigger audits
Technopedagogical Interpretation and Data Humility	contextualizes analytics, rejects facile proxies, triangulates signals, protects consent	case based clinics, dashboard sandboxes, red teaming	rubric aligned interpretations, reversal justifications, error analyses	model card reviews, subgroup drift scans, contestation logs
Ethical Empathy and Dignitarian Practice	separates person from performance, preserves agency, uses accessible language	role play with reflective journaling, narrative assessment studios	student voice artifacts, grievance resolution quality, consent comprehension	transparency reports, language accessibility audits, rights refreshers
Crisis Stabilization and Escalation Navigation	de-escalates calmly, documents minimally, activates supports, preserves confidentiality	tabletop exercises, interdisciplinary drills, checklists	incident closure quality, time to support, exposure minimization	after action reviews, escalation map tests, confidentiality drills
Boundary Setting and Workload Engineering	defines availability windows, caps sync density, engineers recovery intervals	workload design workshops, calendaring labs, manager coaching	schedule compliance, response latency norms, recovery adherence	rota systems, protected time enforcement, load dashboards
Reflective Inquiry and Peer Consultation	conducts structured debriefs, shares anonymized cases, iterates routines	communities of practice, supervision huddles, micro case rounds	improvement cycles, action research memos, norm adherence	supervision calendars, knowledge base updates, drift alarms

The matrix operationalizes an ethic of care that is concrete, teachable, and auditable without resorting to intrusive micromanagement. By foregrounding verification and maintenance columns, Table 3 prevents the common decay pattern where initial enthusiasm fades into ad hoc practice once schedules compress. The verification artifacts are deliberately lightweight, such as fidelity checklists, reversal justifications, and improvement cycles, so that evidence of mastery does not become another source of burnout. Drift control positions peer observation, audit routines, and rota systems as structural supports rather than discretionary extras, which distributes affective labor and preserves empathic bandwidth. Institutions can embed this matrix into professional review by asking for two or three curated artifacts per domain each term, accompanied by a short reflective memo on lessons learned and next adjustments, which keeps the craft cumulative without bureaucratic excess.

4.4 Andragogical Architectures for High Velocity Skill Acquisition

Adult learning in high tempo educational environments benefits from designs that are modular, job embedded, and performance anchored. Mixed reality simulations compress months of experience into short scenarios that surface common pitfalls such as overinterpretation of analytics or inadvertent shaming during public critique (Ratheesh & Alvarez-Jimenez, 2022; Malla & Joober, 2021; Mabil-Atem et al., 2024). Spaced microlearning packages core ideas into brief, recurrent episodes that sustain recall under workload. Coaching protocols tether new moves to live classes through side-by-side planning, in situ observation, and rapid debriefs that close the loop while details remain fresh. Communities of practice stabilize momentum by turning isolated hacks into shared patterns, while case libraries prevent reinvention by cataloging what to try when a familiar failure mode reappears. Training intensity aligns with the domains in Table 3 so that cognitive effort targets high leverage routines rather than scattered tips. Verification evidence then flows naturally from practice, since artifacts like debrief transcripts or schedule compliance are generated during normal work (Faria et al., 2023; Sasaki et al., 2021; Gan et al., 2022). This architecture respects educator time, accelerates mastery, and positions care competencies as core pedagogy rather than peripheral enrichment.

4.5 Workload Engineering and Protective Arrangements for Staff Viability

Care collapses when time and attention are saturated, which makes workload design a primary prevention strategy rather than a convenience. Schedules that cap synchronous density, insert predictable recovery intervals, and cluster administrative tasks away from peak teaching demand reduce micro error rates and enhance patience during challenging interactions (Gratzer et al., 2021; Kozelka et al., 2023; Mendes-Santos et al., 2022). Availability windows that are public and enforceable mitigate guilt driven overwork and clarify expectations for students who might otherwise escalate through multiple channels. Rotational coverage models distribute high strain duties such as triage of anonymous queries or moderation of heated forums, which prevents the emergence of hidden specialists who silently absorb the most stressful work (Good, 2020; Balcombe & De Leo, 2020; van Grunsven, 2021). Managerial coaching ensures alignment between pedagogical commitments and institutional metrics so that staff are not punished for protecting dignity, for example by retiring invasive proctoring in favor of authentic assessment. The boundary setting domain in Table 3 provides concrete levers and evidence streams that leaders can adopt immediately, including schedule compliance checks and recovery adherence audits that make wellbeing visible and actionable without medicalization.

4.6 Supervision, Peer Consultation, and Reflective Informatics

Supervision institutionalizes reflective practice by creating predictable spaces where educators surface near misses, analyze failure modes, and propose redesigns without fear. Short huddles focused on one anonymized case produce higher signal density than sprawling meetings and generate actionable knowledge that feeds the shared case library (Dallinger et al., 2022; Aboujaoude & Gega, 2020; Musakuro & Gie, 2025). Reflective informatics complements supervision by offering private dashboards that visualize cadence, response patterns, and workload against agreed standards so that staff can adjust without external policing. Peer consultation mitigates isolation by pairing colleagues for reciprocal observation and micro feedback on one agreed move per cycle, which reduces cognitive load and increases follow through (Martinez-Martin et al., 2020; Bhatt, 2025; Lipschitz et al., 2023). These routines protect against drift by embedding learning into the pulse of the week rather than relying on sporadic workshops. The reflective inquiry domain in Table 3 names simple artifacts such as action research memos and improvement cycles that evidence growth while reinforcing a culture of collective competence. When supervision and informatics are aligned, care becomes both communal and data literate without sacrificing trust.

4.7 Evaluation, Credentialing, and Continuous Improvement with Equity Guardrails

Evaluation must reward the right things, otherwise staff will game what is measured and neglect what matters. Credentialing that recognizes mastery in the domains listed in Table 3, verified through compact artifacts and observed behaviors, signals that care is core scholarship rather than invisible labor (Burchert et al., 2024; Lukka et al., 2023; Renfrew et al., 2021). Distribution sensitive analytics ensure that gains are not purchased at the expense of minoritized groups and that error rates across subgroups are monitored and corrected. Student voice artifacts such as grievance resolution quality and consent comprehension become standard inputs to performance conversations alongside course outcomes. Continuous improvement cycles require small, frequent adjustments that accumulate, which aligns with short reflective memos and micro experiments documented in the knowledge base (Balcombe & De Leo, 2022; Himle et al., 2022; Cross et al., 2023). Institutional review boards for teaching tools should include educators and students who have demonstrated competence in dignitarian practice so that procurement aligns with classroom realities. When evaluation, credentialing, and procurement pull in the same direction, systems retain coherence under stress, and educators can invest in care with confidence that leadership will sustain the enabling conditions over multiple terms.

5. DESIGNING INCLUSIVE AND PRIVACY PRESERVING DIGITAL MENTAL HEALTH TOOLS

5.1 Integrative Design Stance for Ethical Toolmaking

Inclusive digital mental health tooling emerges from an integrative design stance that fuses ecological theory, universal design, trauma literacies, social and emotional learning, and privacy preserving computation into a single engineering grammar. The stance treats dignity as an invariant constraint, frames cognitive ergonomics as non-negotiable, and operationalizes fairness as error parity rather than aspiration (Opie et al., 2024; Hopkin et al., 2024; Staples et al., 2023). Interfaces are sculpted to lower arousal without muting social presence through decluttered layouts, caption parity, and consent aware visibility. Data pipelines are thinned to the minimum viable granularity and routed through short retention windows that foreclose purpose creep. Evaluation is distribution sensitive, which means error and access are checked across language, disability, and connectivity strata before release and at each update (Cross & Alvarez-Jimenez, 2024; Vicary et al., 2025; Yin et al., 2024). This chapter has sequenced enabling conditions across roles and strata through Tables 1 to 3, which together motivate a compact checklist for product teams. Table 4 distills this checklist into minimalist rules, implementation patterns, failure modes, and verification tests that product owners, procurement leads, and institutional auditors can adopt without delay. The goal is a coherent grammar that scales across tools, protects staff from moral injury, and expands learner agency under routine constraints.

5.2 Inclusion Grammar for Multilingual and Disability Justice

Inclusion grammar codifies anticipatory multimodality, linguistic hospitality, and assistive technology fidelity as reliability properties of instructional software. Multimodality reduces decoding load through high quality captions, semantic transcripts, and alt text that preserves conceptual content for charts and diagrams (Leo et al., 2022; Hamdoun et al., 2023; Kurki et al., 2021). Linguistic hospitality legitimizes translanguaging through interface options for plural scripts, input method editors that respect local norms, and rubric language that evaluates reasoning quality rather than accent or idiom. Assistive technology fidelity requires keyboard navigability, focus order integrity, and live region semantics for screen readers so that blind and low vision users traverse content with parity (Kim et al., 2023; Thomson et al., 2024; Taher et al., 2024). Low bandwidth resilience, offline caching, and progressive enhancement protect participation at the network edge and prevent volatility driven attrition. These properties are not cosmetic add ons, they are infrastructural commitments that enable equitable cognition. The implementation layer must therefore surface explicit checks aligned with the verification tests in Table 4, which treat accessibility pass rates, caption accuracy, and modality uptake as continuous quality metrics rather than episodic compliance rituals.

5.3 Privacy by Design and Data Minimization

Privacy by design converts dignitarian principles into architectural safeguards that limit data collection, shrink inference scope, and keep care functions separate from discipline. The pipeline begins with purpose limitation that enumerates the smallest useful signals and excludes proxies that tempt surveillance, for example posture or gaze when learning goals require comprehension only (Borghouts et al., 2023; Ftanou et al., 2025; Graham et al., 2020). Collection is mediated by on device preprocessing where feasible, differential privacy budgets when aggregation is required, and short retention with cryptographic erasure that can be attested in audits. Inference remains contestable through model cards and user facing explanations that enable challenge and reversal without stigma. Grievance channels are accessible within the same interface where flags appear, which collapses friction and normalizes due process (Owen et al., 2025; Magomedova & Fatima, 2025; Masri et al., 2024). Institutional procurement encodes these requirements into contracts with measurable acceptance criteria. The compact rule set in Table 4 assembles these safeguards into a product ready matrix that shortens translation time between policy and code while protecting instructional trust.

Table 4. Checklist for inclusive and ethical digital care toolmaking

Principle Domain	Minimalist Engineering Rule	Implementation Patterns	Common Failure Modes	Verification and Audit Tests
Accessibility and Multimodality	design for caption parity and keyboard primacy	semantic transcripts, alt text, focus order, low bandwidth modes	decorative captions, keyboard traps, contrast debt	WCAG pass rates, caption accuracy, assistive device traversal
Privacy and Data Minimization	collect the least, retain the shortest, explain inferences	on device preprocessing, short retention, model cards, consent logs	purpose creep, opaque scoring, runaway retention	data flow diagrams, retention attestations, contestation resolution time
Fairness and Disparity Auditing	measure subgroup error and access, correct before scale	stratified evaluation, reweighting, counterfactual testing	disparate error, language bias, disability exclusion	subgroup error parity, language coverage, accessibility variance
Safety and Harm Reduction	reduce arousal triggers and exposure risk	self-view off by default, moderated forums, opt in visibility	hypervigilance, harassment spill, chilled speech	toxicity incidence, report closure quality, visibility choice uptake
Participation and Co-Governance	embed user voice with decision rights	youth boards, educator councils, grievance pathways	token feedback, delayed remedies, governance opacity	decision logs, remedy timeliness, participation quorum
Reliability and Resilience	degrade gracefully under strain without data loss	progressive enhancement, offline caching, circuit breakers	crash loops, sync conflicts, phantom submissions	failure injection, recovery integrity, data reconciliation audits

The matrix supplies a compact program of work that turns abstract norms into testable properties. Minimalist rules reduce speculative data appetite and resist metric inflation, while implementation patterns give engineers concrete templates that remain robust in diverse contexts. Failure modes name common pathologies such as decorative captions or opaque scoring so that teams can preempt regression rather than relearn. Verification couples human judgment with automation through accessibility passes, retention attestations, subgroup error parity, and failure injection so that quality is systemic rather than heroic. Institutions can embed this matrix into tenders and acceptance testing, while teams can integrate the checks into continuous delivery pipelines. When procurement, engineering, and classroom practice reference the same artifact, drift between policy language and shipped behavior narrows and trust becomes observable.

5.4 Algorithmic Validity, Fairness, and Model Governance

Algorithmic validity demands that constructs align with phenomena rather than marketing proxies, which means attention, engagement, and emotion must be inferred only when the learning objective requires them and when signals have defensible links to cognition. Fairness requires that error rates be checked across disability, language, skin tone, and bandwidth strata before deployment and after updates, with corrective actions logged and auditable (Obikane et al., 2022; Balcombe & De Leo, 2021; Zhu et al., 2025; Lehtimaki et al., 2021). Governance insists on model documentation that specifies training data, known failure cases, mitigation strategies, and performance envelopes, along with mechanisms to disable features that drift out of bounds. Interfaces must present contestable explanations and enable reversal without social penalty, which protects student dignity and teacher judgment (Wang et al., 2025; Taher et al., 2023; Sit et al., 2022). The fairness and privacy rows in Table 4 encode the leanest possible rules that still deliver substantive protection, while the verification tests provide operational handles such as subgroup parity thresholds and contestation resolution time. The result is a model lifecycle that is intelligible to educators, compliant for auditors, and corrigible when unexpected interactions surface in live classrooms.

5.5 Participation Safeguards and Consentful Interaction Architectures

Participation safeguards position consent as a daily practice rather than a one-time click, which shifts architectures toward visibility choice, muted self-view, and granular control of recordings and transcript distribution. Moderated forums with configured civility thresholds and escalation paths reduce harassment risk without suppressing dissent, while narrative prompts and rubric language separate critique of ideas from judgment of persons (Han et al., 2020; Baka et al., 2025; Dambi et al., 2022). Anonymous question queues and asynchronous inquiry reduce reputational risk and increase equity of voice when combined with service level guarantees on response time. Grievance pathways located where harm occurs rather than on distant portals shrink friction and increase remedy timeliness. Co governance bodies with student and educator voting rights review policy changes, feature launches, and audit findings so that legitimacy is shared (Bennett-Levy et al., 2021; Tremain et al., 2020; Gonsalves et al., 2025). The participation and safety lines in Table 4 translate these principles into specific tests such as remedy timeliness and report closure quality, which convert civility into measurable reliability rather than etiquette.

5.6 Evaluation, Fidelity, and Distribution Sensitive Monitoring

Evaluation strategy must bind fidelity to both pedagogy and rights so that tools support learning without eroding dignity. Distribution sensitive monitoring tracks accessibility, error, and uptake across strata to prevent global averages from masking local failures (Topooco et al., 2022; Kodish et al., 2023; Cohen & Schleider, 2022). Fidelity audits compare promised features against shipped behavior through structured walkthroughs and failure injection so that graceful degradation and data reconciliation are verified in practice. Continuous delivery integrates accessibility passes, retention checks, and subgroup error scans into build pipelines, which converts compliance into routine hygiene. Post deployment reviews publish transparency summaries that include decision logs, coverage maps, and grievance statistics to sustain accountability (Zhao et al., 2023; Khatib et al., 2022; Fabian et al., 2023). The reliability row in Table 4 specifies resilience tests that catch sync conflicts and phantom submissions before they damage trust, while the fairness row anchors corrective loops when parity drifts. When institutions treat these checks as table stakes and vendors accept them as routine, digital mental health tools become safer, more legible, and more effective for educators and learners who operate under real world constraints.

6. INSTITUTIONAL EMBEDDING FOR CURRICULUM POLICY PROCUREMENT AND FINANCE

6.1 Curricular Mainstreaming and Cognitive Ergonomics

Curricular mainstreaming operationalizes digital care by encoding inclusion, privacy, and cognitive ergonomics into course blueprints, timetable logic, and assessment grammars. Program committees translate universal design into mandatory templates that specify caption integrity, transcript fidelity, multilingual rubrics, and keyboard navigability as reliability properties rather than optional refinements (Andrews et al., 2023; Bernard et al., 2023; Petrovic & Gaggioli, 2020). Assessment reform replaces punitive proctoring with authentic tasks that reward reasoning transparency and iterative improvement, which lowers arousal while heightening epistemic rigor. Timetable engineering caps synchronous density, prescribes micro recovery intervals, stages deadlines to avoid load spikes, and aligns practical windows with local bandwidth cycles. Faculty development pairs micro credentials with observed behaviors so that mastery is evidenced through fidelity checklists, artifact curation, and recovery adherence rather than passive attendance (Braun et al., 2023; Potts et al., 2023; Lyon et al., 2020). Accreditation dossiers then surface accessibility pass rates, subgroup parity checks, and grievance resolution quality to demonstrate institutional maturity. These moves require cross functional choreography that links curriculum boards, platform teams, registrars, and counseling units. Table 5 in Section 6.2 consolidates this choreography into a compact roadmap that names policy anchors, process reconfiguration, accountable owners, and sentinel metrics so that mainstreaming survives leadership turnover and budget variability.

6.2 Governance Architectures and Norm Entrepreneurship

Governance translates principles into enforceable guarantees through standards, audits, contracts, and transparent remedies. Accessibility governance mandates periodic third party validation of captions, contrast, focus order, and screen reader traversal, while privacy governance limits collection, shortens retention, and requires contestable inferences with in interface reversal (Song & Song, 2023; Gbollie et al., 2023; Boucher & Raiker, 2024). Fairness management institutionalizes distribution sensitive evaluation so that subgroup error gaps trigger corrective redesign. Contracts embed these invariants with measurable acceptance criteria and penalties for nonconformance. Norm entrepreneurship then diffuses dignitarian habits through exemplar repositories, recognition programs, and student teacher co governance so that compliance evolves into culture. The cross functional cadence required to hold these pieces together is made explicit in Table 5, which functions as a navigational artifact for councils and deans who must coordinate curriculum, procurement, finance, and student affairs without drift.

Table 5. Roadmap for Institution Wide Digital Care Operational Mainstreaming

Strategic Workstream	Policy and Standard Anchor	Process and Infrastructure Reconfiguration	Accountable Owner and Cadence	Milestones and Sentinel Metrics
Curriculum and Assessment	UDL baseline, WCAG adoption, proctoring retirement	template mandate, cadence rules, authentic tasks, multilingual rubrics	program chair, registrar, term sprints	accessibility pass rate, deadline dispersion, late work clustering
Governance and Compliance	privacy charter, retention limits, contestable inference	audit cycles, consent logs, model cards, grievance portals	data officer, legal counsel, quarterly boards	audit pass trend, reversal usage, remedy timeliness
Procurement and Vendor Oversight	rights based clauses, parity thresholds, portability	conformance testing, failure injection, exit ramps	CIO, purchasing lead, release gates	subgroup error parity, crash recovery integrity, contract remedies

continued on following page

Table 5. Continued

Strategic Workstream	Policy and Standard Anchor	Process and Infrastructure Reconfiguration	Accountable Owner and Cadence	Milestones and Sentinel Metrics
Finance and Operations	sustained O and M, evaluation reserve, accessibility line	life cycle budgeting, audit funding, uptime SLOs	CFO, platform ops, annual plan	uptime reliability, audit coverage, cost per learner stability
Human Resources and Workload	bounded care policy, recovery protections, rota norms	schedule caps, protected time, supervision calendars	HR director, department heads, monthly reviews	recovery adherence, response latency norms, staff retention
Student Voice and Accountability	co governance charter, grievance enforceability	decision logs, participation quorums, transparency reports	student union, ombud office, term forums	participation rate, closure quality, trust sentiment balance

The matrix compresses a multi-year institutional change program into five columns that can be monitored without onerous bureaucracy. Policy anchors define non-negotiable. Process reconfiguration translates these anchors into daily workflows and platform settings. Accountable owners and cadences fix responsibility and tempo. Milestones and sentinel metrics render progress legible through a small set of ratios and rates that are difficult to game. By embedding this artifact in council agendas and tender packs, institutions keep governance intelligible and adaptable, which sustains legitimacy across cohorts and staffing cycles.

6.3 Finance and Operating Models for Durability and Scale

Durability requires that finance graduate from pilot episodics to steady state operations. Life cycle budgeting provisions for maintenance, accessibility audits, distribution sensitive evaluation, and failure injection so that quality does not decay after grant sunsets. Operating models align platform uptime objectives with teaching calendars and include capacity buffers for peak assessment weeks, which reduces error cascades and reputational damage (Gómez Bergin et al., 2023; Mohr et al., 2021; Rudd & Beidas, 2020). Evaluation reserves fund third party audits and subgroup error scans that vendors cannot self-certify without conflict. Cost per learner stability depends on portability and exit ramps that reduce lock in and enable renegotiation when parity drifts. Internal chargebacks must not penalize programs that admit higher proportions of rural or disabled learners, therefore subsidies target equity rather than enrollment volume. Finance committees reference the procurement and operations rows in Table 5 to negotiate service levels that protect dignity and inclusion while remaining fiscally prudent. When budgets, contracts, and release gates encode the same invariants, classroom practice ceases to be hostage to heroic improvisation and becomes a property of the system.

6.4 Overcoming Inertia and Platform Fragmentation in Complex Systems

Institutional inertia and platform sprawl amplify cognitive load, obscure accountability, and slow remedy cycles. Consolidation without monoculture becomes the design target. Architecture councils standardize a small set of interoperable tools that pass accessibility audits, offer low bandwidth modes, and expose clear observability so that failures surface early (Rodriguez-Villa et al., 2021; Phang et al., 2023; Ayobi et al., 2021). Migration plans prioritize high harm reductions first, such as retiring invasive proctoring and tools that block assistive technologies. Sandboxes allow controlled trials of privacy enhancing features with public artifacts that document outcomes for community scrutiny. Change management treats staff time as a scarce asset, therefore migrations occur in semester aligned waves with opt in pilots, rehearsals, and rollback contingencies. The governance and procurement lines in Table 5 provide the choreography for these moves through conformance testing, failure injection, and exit ramps that reduce fear and increase adoption. When simplification and accountability move together, platform ecology becomes legible, and instructional energy shifts from tool wrangling to learning design.

6.5 Workload Engineering and Staff Protections with Accountability

Workload engineering converts wellbeing from aspiration into compliance. Departments implement schedule caps for synchronous activity, fixed recovery intervals, and transparent availability windows that students can rely upon. Rota systems distribute high strain duties such as anonymous query triage and heated forum moderation, which prevents silent concentration of affective labor (Ellis et al., 2022; Amin et al., 2025; Stiles-Shields et al., 2023). Supervision calendars guarantee reflective huddles and micro case rounds that transform near misses into institutional learning. Managerial scorecards measure recovery adherence and response latency norms rather than raw message counts, aligning incentives with care rather than performance theater. Human resources references the HR row in Table 5 to institutionalize bounded care policies and to link professional review with artifact-based evidence from Section 4, which keeps recognition tethered to practice. When protections are encoded in calendars, dashboards, and reviews, empathy becomes sustainable and role clarity reduces moral stress. The result is a workforce that can offer presence without erosion and that models dignitarian norms for students who will carry these habits into civic and workplace contexts.

6.6 Accountability and Student Voice for Durable Legitimacy

Accountability legitimizes power by making decisions reviewable and remedies real. Co governance bodies with student and educator voting rights review audits, policy changes, and major feature launches, and they publish decision logs that document rationale and dissent. Grievance pathways live where harm occurs rather than on distant portals, and they measure remedy timeliness and closure quality to prevent procedural exhaustion. Transparency reports summarize accessibility coverage, subgroup parity, and contestation outcomes in language that the community can scrutinize. Participation quorums guard against tokenism and ensure that those most affected have a seat that counts (Zhang et al., 2021; Smith et al., 2024; Stein et al., 2021). The student voice and governance rows in Table 5 provide the minimum viable scaffolding for this regime. When legitimacy is renewed each term through visible responsiveness and enforceable rights, classrooms retain psychological safety and policy retains consent. Institutions then possess a repeatable method to adapt tools and norms as technologies evolve, which future proofs the architecture of care without sacrificing speed or rigor.

7. CONCLUSION

7.1 Synthesis of Architecture and Praxis

The chapter has articulated a unified architecture of digital care that fuses ecological theory, humanizing pedagogy, universal design, trauma literacies, and privacy preserving computation into a practicable grammar for institutions that teach at scale. The synthesis translates values into routines, interfaces, and rules that withstand timetable pressure and leadership churn. Section 2 codified anchoring frameworks and converted them into heuristics and indicators that are auditable in ordinary course logistics, as consolidated in Table 1. Section 3 mapped risks and assets across ecological strata and offered a signals to levers matrix in Table 2 that lets educators intervene early without intrusive surveillance. Section 4 professionalized educator care through a competency matrix in Table 3 that aligns observable behaviors with training, verification, and drift control. Section 5 reframed tooling as ethical infrastructure and supplied a checklist in Table 4 that binds accessibility, privacy, fairness, safety, participation, and resilience to testable properties. Section 6 embedded the whole grammar through a roadmap in Table 5 that aligns curriculum, governance, procurement, finance, human resources, and student voice with milestones and sentinel metrics. The result is an operational synthesis where dignity and rigor cohere and where equity, privacy, and learning move together.

7.2 Final Commitment to Dignitarian Design

A dignitarian settlement for platformed education requires durable commitments that bind pedagogy, engineering, and policy to the same invariants. Institutions commit by mainstreaming universal design as reliability property, by retiring invasive proctoring in favor of authentic assessment, by shortening retention and contesting inference, and by auditing accessibility and subgroup error as routine hygiene. Product teams commit by implementing low bandwidth resilience, caption parity, keyboard primacy, model documentation, and failure injection so that quality remains robust under strain. Educators commit by practicing bounded caregiving, by rehearsing repair, by reading analytics with humility, and by protecting their availability and recovery through visible schedules. Students commit by participating in co governance, by exercising consent, and by building resources that lift peers. Progress remains legible through compact indicators that appear across this chapter such as recovery adherence, modality uptake mix, remedy timeliness, subgroup parity, and crash recovery integrity. When these measures improve together, classrooms become psychosocially sustainable ecologies that are safer, fairer, and more effective. The path is incremental yet cumulative, and the grammar provided here allows any institution to begin now, iterate deliberately, and hold its tools and practices to the same humane standard that it holds its scholarship.

REFERENCES

Aboujaoude, E., & Gega, L. (2020). From digital mental health interventions to digital "addiction": Where the two fields converge. *Frontiers in Psychiatry, 10*, 1017. DOI: 10.3389/fpsyt.2019.01017 PMID: 32038336

Abura-Meerdink, G. A., & Albright, D. L. (2024). Effectiveness of adolescent school-based digital mental health interventions: A systematic review. *Research on Social Work Practice, 34*(6), 701–710. DOI: 10.1177/10497315231201140

Adu, M., Banire, B., Dockrill, M., Ilie, A., Lappin, E., McGrath, P., Munro, S., Myers, K., Obuobi-Donkor, G., Orji, R., Pillai Riddell, R., Wozney, L., & Yisa, V. (2024). Centering equity, diversity, and inclusion in youth digital mental health: Findings from a research, policy, and practice knowledge exchange workshop. *Frontiers in Digital Health, 6*, 1449129. DOI: 10.3389/fdgth.2024.1449129 PMID: 39544986

Amin, A., Hong, Y., & Mazhar, B. (2025). Enhancing AI-Driven Mental Health Solutions: The Role of Social Support in Wysa's Effectiveness for Stress Management and Anxiety Reduction among International Medical Students in China. *International Journal of Human-Computer Interaction*, •••, 1–16. DOI: 10.1080/10447318.2025.2537788

Andrews, B., Klein, B., Corboy, D., McLaren, S., & Watson, S. (2023). Therapist training in video chat technology for use in an adaptive digital mental health intervention: Challenges, facilitators and implications for training models. *Counselling & Psychotherapy Research, 23*(3), 818–829. DOI: 10.1002/capr.12667

Ayobi, A., Grimes, A., Mackinnon, S., Soubutts, E., Eardley, R., Banks Gross, Z., & O'Kane, A. A. (2021, June). Designing visual cards for digital mental health research with ethnic minorities. In *Proceedings of the 2021 ACM Designing Interactive Systems Conference* (pp. 942-954). DOI: 10.1145/3461778.3462085

Badawi, E., Coursaris, C. K., Sénécal, S., & Léger, P. M. (2023). Facilitating engagement of universal school-based digital mental health solutions through user experience: A qualitative exploration. *Frontiers in Digital Health, 5*, 1040739. DOI: 10.3389/fdgth.2023.1040739 PMID: 37035481

Baka, E., Tan, Y. R., Wong, B. L. H., Xing, Z., & Yap, P. (2025). A scoping review of digital interventions for the promotion of mental health and prevention of mental health conditions for young people. *Oxford Open Digital Health, 3*, oqaf005. DOI: 10.1093/oodh/oqaf005 PMID: 40230873

Balcombe, L. (2023, October). AI chatbots in digital mental health. [). MDPI.]. *Informatics (MDPI), 10*(4), 82. DOI: 10.3390/informatics10040082

Balcombe, L., & De Leo, D. (2020). An integrated blueprint for digital mental health services amidst COVID-19. *JMIR Mental Health*, *7*(7), e21718. DOI: 10.2196/21718 PMID: 32668402

Balcombe, L., & De Leo, D. (2020). Psychological screening and tracking of athletes and digital mental health solutions in a hybrid model of care: Mini review. *JMIR Formative Research*, *4*(12), e22755. DOI: 10.2196/22755 PMID: 33271497

Balcombe, L., & De Leo, D. (2021). Athlete psychological resilience and integration with digital mental health implementation amid Covid-19. In *Anxiety, uncertainty, and resilience during the pandemic period-anthropological and psychological perspectives*. IntechOpen. DOI: 10.5772/intechopen.97799

Balcombe, L., & De Leo, D. (2021). Digital mental health challenges and the horizon ahead for solutions. *JMIR Mental Health*, *8*(3), e26811. DOI: 10.2196/26811 PMID: 33779570

Balcombe, L., & De Leo, D. (2022). Evaluation of the use of digital mental health platforms and interventions: Scoping review. *International Journal of Environmental Research and Public Health*, *20*(1), 362. DOI: 10.3390/ijerph20010362 PMID: 36612685

Balcombe, L., & De Leo, D. (2022, February). Human-computer interaction in digital mental health. [). MDPI.]. *Informatics (MDPI)*, *9*(1), 14. DOI: 10.3390/informatics9010014

Balcombe, L., De Leo, D., & Turner, M. J. (2022). Athlete psychological resilience and digital mental health implementation. *Frontiers in Psychology*, *13*, 1082998. DOI: 10.3389/fpsyg.2022.1082998 PMID: 36532980

Bassi, E. M., Bright, K. S., Norman, L. G., Pintson, K., Daniel, S., Sidhu, S., Gondziola, J., Bradley, J., Fersovitch, M., Stamp, L., Moskovic, K., LaMonica, H. M., Iorfino, F., Gaskell, T., Tomlinson, S., Johnson, D. W., & Dimitropoulos, G. (2024). Perceptions of mental health providers of the barriers and facilitators of using and engaging youth in digital mental-health-enabled measurement based care. *Digital Health*, *10*, 20552076241253093. DOI: 10.1177/20552076241253093 PMID: 38726214

Bassilios, B., Ftanou, M., Tan, A., Morgan, A., Machlin, A., Mangelsdorf, S., & Pirkis, J. (2022). *Environmental scan of digital mental health services*. Australian Government Department of Health and Aged Care.

Bennett-Levy, J., Singer, J., Rotumah, D., Bernays, S., & Edwards, D. (2021). From digital mental health to digital social and emotional wellbeing: How Indigenous community-based participatory research influenced the Australian government's digital mental health agenda. *International Journal of Environmental Research and Public Health*, *18*(18), 9757. DOI: 10.3390/ijerph18189757 PMID: 34574678

Bergin, A. D., Vallejos, E. P., Davies, E. B., Daley, D., Ford, T., Harold, G., Hetrick, S., Kidner, M., Long, Y., Merry, S., Morriss, R., Sayal, K., Sonuga-Barke, E., Robinson, J., Torous, J., & Hollis, C. (2020). Preventive digital mental health interventions for children and young people: A review of the design and reporting of research. *NPJ Digital Medicine*, *3*(1), 133. DOI: 10.1038/s41746-020-00339-7 PMID: 33083568

Bernard, A., de Ossorno Garcia, S., Salhi, L., John, A., & DelPozo-Banos, M. (2023). Patterns of engagement in a digital mental health service during COVID-19: A cohort study for children and young people. *Frontiers in Psychiatry*, *14*, 1143272. DOI: 10.3389/fpsyt.2023.1143272 PMID: 37575580

Bevan Jones, R., Stallard, P., Agha, S. S., Rice, S., Werner-Seidler, A., Stasiak, K., Kahn, J., Simpson, S. A., Alvarez-Jimenez, M., Rice, F., Evans, R., & Merry, S. (2020). Practitioner review: Co-design of digital mental health technologies with children and young people. *Journal of Child Psychology and Psychiatry, and Allied Disciplines*, *61*(8), 928–940. DOI: 10.1111/jcpp.13258 PMID: 32572961

Bhatt, S. (2025). Digital mental health: Role of artificial intelligence in psychotherapy. *Annals of Neurosciences*, *32*(2), 117–127. DOI: 10.1177/09727531231221612 PMID: 39544658

Borghouts, J., Eikey, E., Mark, G., De Leon, C., Schueller, S. M., Schneider, M., Stadnick, N., Zheng, K., Mukamel, D., & Sorkin, D. H. (2021). Barriers to and facilitators of user engagement with digital mental health interventions: Systematic review. *Journal of Medical Internet Research*, *23*(3), e24387. DOI: 10.2196/24387 PMID: 33759801

Borghouts, J., Pretorius, C., Ayobi, A., Abdullah, S., & Eikey, E. V. (2023). Factors influencing user engagement with digital mental health interventions. *Frontiers in Digital Health*, *5*, 1197301. DOI: 10.3389/fdgth.2023.1197301 PMID: 37143934

Boucher, E. M., & Raiker, J. S. (2024). Engagement and retention in digital mental health interventions: A narrative review. *BMC Digital Health*, *2*(1), 52. DOI: 10.1186/s44247-024-00105-9

Braun, P., Schwientek, A. K., Angerer, P., Guthardt, L., Icks, A., Loerbroks, A., & Apolinário-Hagen, J. (2023). Investigating information needs and preferences regarding digital mental health services among medical and psychology students in Germany: A qualitative study. *Digital Health*, *9*, 20552076231173568. DOI: 10.1177/20552076231173568 PMID: 37256006

Brooks, H., Irmansyah, I., Syarif, A. K., Pedley, R., Renwick, L., Rahayu, A. P., Manik, C., Prawira, B., Hann, M., Brierley, H., Lovell, K., & Bee, P. (2023). Evaluating a prototype digital mental health literacy intervention for children and young people aged 11–15 in Java, Indonesia: A mixed methods, multi-site case study evaluation. *Child and Adolescent Psychiatry and Mental Health*, *17*(1), 79. DOI: 10.1186/s13034-023-00608-9 PMID: 37365594

Brotherdale, R., Berry, K., Branitsky, A., & Bucci, S. (2024). Co-producing digital mental health interventions: A systematic review. *Digital Health*, *10*, 20552076241239172. DOI: 10.1177/20552076241239172 PMID: 38665886

Brown, P., Prest, B., Miles, P., & Rossi, V. (2022). The development of national safety and quality digital mental health standards. *Australasian Psychiatry*, *30*(2), 154–157. DOI: 10.1177/10398562211042361 PMID: 34569321

Burchert, S., Alkneme, M. S., Alsaod, A., Cuijpers, P., Heim, E., Hessling, J., Hosny, N., Sijbrandij, M., van't Hof, E., Ventevogel, P., & Knaevelsrud, C.STRENGTHS Consortium. (2024). Effects of a self-guided digital mental health self-help intervention for Syrian refugees in Egypt: A pragmatic randomized controlled trial. *PLoS Medicine*, *21*(9), e1004460. DOI: 10.1371/journal.pmed.1004460 PMID: 39250521

Cameron, G., Mulvenna, M., Ennis, E., O'Neill, S., Bond, R., Cameron, D., & Bunting, A. (2025). Effectiveness of digital mental health interventions in the workplace: Umbrella review of systematic reviews. *JMIR Mental Health*, *12*(1), e67785. DOI: 10.2196/67785 PMID: 39854722

Chen, X., Chen, L., Song, D., Wang, Y., & Ryoo, J. (2025). *Digital mental health for young people: sustainably managing stress and anxiety*. Mental Health and Digital Technologies.

Cohen, K. A., & Schleider, J. L. (2022). Adolescent dropout from brief digital mental health interventions within and beyond randomized trials. *Internet Interventions : the Application of Information Technology in Mental and Behavioural Health*, *27*, 100496. DOI: 10.1016/j.invent.2022.100496 PMID: 35257001

Costardi, C. G., D'agostini, A. C. C., Pan, P. M., & Bressan, R. A. (2023). Digital mental health interventions for school teachers–A narrative review. *Early Intervention in Psychiatry*, *17*(8), 749–758. DOI: 10.1111/eip.13431 PMID: 37041728

Costescu, C., Podina, I. R., & Voinescu, A. (2022). Digital mental health: Interventions and assessment. *Frontiers in Psychology*, *13*, 1014527. DOI: 10.3389/fpsyg.2022.1014527 PMID: 36506981

Cross, S. P., & Alvarez-Jimenez, M. (2024). The digital cumulative complexity model: A framework for improving engagement in digital mental health interventions. *Frontiers in Psychiatry*, *15*, 1382726. DOI: 10.3389/fpsyt.2024.1382726 PMID: 39290300

Cross, S. P., Karin, E., Staples, L. G., Bisby, M. A., Ryan, K., Duke, G., Nielssen, O., Kayrouz, R., Fisher, A., Dear, B. F., & Titov, N. (2022). Factors associated with treatment uptake, completion, and subsequent symptom improvement in a national digital mental health service. *Internet Interventions : the Application of Information Technology in Mental and Behavioural Health*, *27*, 100506. DOI: 10.1016/j.invent.2022.100506 PMID: 35242587

Cross, S. P., Nicholas, J., Bell, I. H., Mangelsdorf, S., Valentine, L., Thompson, A., Gleeson, J. F., & Alvarez-Jimenez, M. (2023). Integrating digital interventions with clinical practice in youth mental health services. *Australasian Psychiatry*, *31*(3), 302–305. DOI: 10.1177/10398562231169365 PMID: 37072342

Daisy, A. (2025). Digital mental health education: alleviating stigma and enhancing well-being in schools. In *Advancing sustainable development goals with educational technology* (pp. 143–180). IGI Global Scientific Publishing.

Dallinger, V. C., Krishnamoorthy, G., du Plessis, C., Pillai-Sasidharan, A., Ayres, A., Waters, L., Groom, Y., Alston, O., Anderson, L., & Burton, L. (2022). Utilisation of digital applications for personal recovery amongst youth with mental health concerns. *International Journal of Environmental Research and Public Health*, *19*(24), 16818. DOI: 10.3390/ijerph192416818 PMID: 36554700

Dambi, J., Norman, C., Doukani, A., Potgieter, S., Turner, J., Musesengwa, R., Verhey, R., & Chibanda, D. (2022). A digital mental health intervention (Inuka) for common mental health disorders in Zimbabwean adults in response to the COVID-19 pandemic: Feasibility and acceptability pilot study. *JMIR Mental Health*, *9*(10), e37968. DOI: 10.2196/37968 PMID: 35960595

Davies, S. M., Jardine, J., Gutridge, K., Bernard, Z., Park, S., Dawson, T., Abel, K. M., & Whelan, P. (2021). Preventive digital mental health for children in primary schools: Acceptability and feasibility study. *JMIR Formative Research*, *5*(12), e30668. DOI: 10.2196/30668 PMID: 34898446

Dederichs, M., Weber, J., Pischke, C. R., Angerer, P., & Apolinário-Hagen, J. (2021). Exploring medical students' views on digital mental health interventions: A qualitative study. *Internet Interventions : the Application of Information Technology in Mental and Behavioural Health*, *25*, 100398. DOI: 10.1016/j.invent.2021.100398 PMID: 34026567

Ellis, D. M., Draheim, A. A., & Anderson, P. L. (2022). Culturally adapted digital mental health interventions for ethnic/racial minorities: A systematic review and meta-analysis. *Journal of Consulting and Clinical Psychology*, *90*(10), 717–733. DOI: 10.1037/ccp0000759 PMID: 36227330

Fabian, K. E., Foster, K. T., Chwastiak, L., Turner, M., & Wagenaar, B. H. (2023). Adapting a transdiagnostic digital mental health intervention for use among immigrant and refugee youth in Seattle: A human-centered design approach. *Translational Behavioral Medicine*, *13*(11), 867–875. DOI: 10.1093/tbm/ibad041 PMID: 37418614

Faria, M., Zin, S. T. P., Chestnov, R., Novak, A. M., Lev-Ari, S., & Snyder, M. (2023). Mental health for all: The case for investing in digital mental health to improve global outcomes, access, and innovation in low-resource settings. *Journal of Clinical Medicine*, *12*(21), 6735. DOI: 10.3390/jcm12216735 PMID: 37959201

Fleming, T., Poppelaars, M., & Thabrew, H. (2023). The role of gamification in digital mental health. *World Psychiatry; Official Journal of the World Psychiatric Association (WPA)*, *22*(1), 46–47. DOI: 10.1002/wps.21041 PMID: 36640378

Ftanou, M., Machlin, A., Mangelsdorf, S. N., Morgan, A., & Bassilios, B. (2025). Australian digital mental health services: Consumer perceptions of their usability and acceptability. *Journal of Technology in Behavioral Science*, *10*(2), 320–335. DOI: 10.1007/s41347-024-00431-9

Gan, D. Z., McGillivray, L., Larsen, M. E., Christensen, H., & Torok, M. (2022). Technology-supported strategies for promoting user engagement with digital mental health interventions: A systematic review. *Digital Health*, *8*, 20552076221098268. DOI: 10.1177/20552076221098268 PMID: 35677785

Gbollie, E. F., Bantjes, J., Jarvis, L., Swandevelder, S., Du Plessis, J., Shadwell, R., Davids, C., Gerber, R., Holland, N., & Hunt, X. (2023). Intention to use digital mental health solutions: A cross-sectional survey of university students attitudes and perceptions toward online therapy, mental health apps, and chatbots. *Digital Health*, *9*, 20552076231216559. DOI: 10.1177/20552076231216559 PMID: 38047161

Gibson, K., Trnka, S., Jonas, M., Pomare, P., Thompson, S., Tiatia-Siau, J., Aimiti Ma'ia'i, K. D., Aoake, M., Bouttier-Esprit, T., Spray, I., & Vyas, S. (2024). Digital mental health strategies used by young people in Aotearoa New Zealand during the COVID-19 pandemic:'Just do it yourself, DIY'. *Digital Health, 10,* 20552076241260116. DOI: 10.1177/20552076241260116 PMID: 39070892

Gómez Bergin, A. D., Valentine, A. Z., Rennick-Egglestone, S., Slade, M., Hollis, C., & Hall, C. L. (2023). Identifying and categorizing adverse events in trials of digital mental health interventions: Narrative scoping review of trials in the international standard randomized controlled trial number registry. *JMIR Mental Health, 10,* e42501. DOI: 10.2196/42501 PMID: 36811940

Gonsalves, P. P., Ansari, S., Berry, C., Gonsalves, F., Iyengar, S., Kashyap, P., Mittal, D., Pal, S., Razdan, E., & Michelson, D. (2025). Co-designing digital mental health interventions with young people: 10 recommendations from lessons learned in low-and-middle-income countries. *Health Education Journal, 84*(4), 373–384. DOI: 10.1177/00178969241297821

Good, S. (2020). *Evaluating the Effectiveness of a Digital Mental Health Literacy Intervention for Children and Young People Within a School Setting* (Doctoral dissertation, Royal Holloway, University of London).

Graham, A. K., Greene, C. J., Powell, T., Lieponis, P., Lunsford, A., Peralta, C. D., Orr, L. C., Kaiser, S. M., Alam, N., Berhane, H., Kalan, O., & Mohr, D. C. (2020). Lessons learned from service design of a trial of a digital mental health service: Informing implementation in primary care clinics. *Translational Behavioral Medicine, 10*(3), 598–605. DOI: 10.1093/tbm/ibz140 PMID: 32766862

Graham, A. K., Lattie, E. G., Powell, B. J., Lyon, A. R., Smith, J. D., Schueller, S. M., Stadnick, N. A., Brown, C. H., & Mohr, D. C. (2020). Implementation strategies for digital mental health interventions in health care settings. *The American Psychologist, 75*(8), 1080–1092. DOI: 10.1037/amp0000686 PMID: 33252946

Gratzer, D., Torous, J., Lam, R. W., Patten, S. B., Kutcher, S., Chan, S., Vigo, D., Pajer, K., & Yatham, L. N. (2021). Our digital moment: Innovations and opportunities in digital mental health care. *Canadian Journal of Psychiatry, 66*(1), 5–8. DOI: 10.1177/0706743720937833 PMID: 32603188

Hamdoun, S., Monteleone, R., Bookman, T., & Michael, K. (2023). AI-based and digital mental health apps: Balancing need and risk. *IEEE Technology and Society Magazine, 42*(1), 25–36. DOI: 10.1109/MTS.2023.3241309

Han, S. Y. S., Tomasik, J., Rustogi, N., Lago, S. G., Barton-Owen, G., Eljasz, P., Cooper, J. D., Ozcan, S., Olmert, T., Farrag, L. P., Friend, L. V., Bell, E., Cowell, D., Thomas, G., Tuytten, R., & Bahn, S. (2020). Diagnostic prediction model development using data from dried blood spot proteomics and a digital mental health assessment to identify major depressive disorder among individuals presenting with low mood. *Brain, Behavior, and Immunity*, *90*, 184–195. DOI: 10.1016/j.bbi.2020.08.011 PMID: 32861718

Harith, S., Backhaus, I., Mohbin, N., Ngo, H. T., & Khoo, S. (2022). Effectiveness of digital mental health interventions for university students: An umbrella review. *PeerJ*, *10*, e13111. DOI: 10.7717/peerj.13111 PMID: 35382010

Hicks, L. J., Toombs, E., Lund, J., Kowatch, K. R., Hopkins, C., & Mushquash, C. J. (2025). Expanding our understanding of digital mental health interventions for Indigenous youth: An updated systematic review. *Journal of Telemedicine and Telecare*, *31*(7), 919–960. DOI: 10.1177/1357633X241239715 PMID: 38584397

Himle, J. A., Weaver, A., Zhang, A., & Xiang, X. (2022). Digital mental health interventions for depression. *Cognitive and Behavioral Practice*, *29*(1), 50–59. DOI: 10.1016/j.cbpra.2020.12.009

Hopkin, G., Branson, R., Campbell, P., Coole, H., Cooper, S., Edelmann, F., & Salmon, M. (2024). Considerations for regulation and evaluation of digital mental health technologies. *Digital Health*, *10*, 20552076241293313. DOI: 10.1177/20552076241293313 PMID: 39502489

Hornstein, S., Forman-Hoffman, V., Nazander, A., Ranta, K., & Hilbert, K. (2021). Predicting therapy outcome in a digital mental health intervention for depression and anxiety: A machine learning approach. *Digital Health*, *7*, 20552076211060659. DOI: 10.1177/20552076211060659 PMID: 34868624

Hornstein, S., Zantvoort, K., Lueken, U., Funk, B., & Hilbert, K. (2023). Personalization strategies in digital mental health interventions: A systematic review and conceptual framework for depressive symptoms. *Frontiers in Digital Health*, *5*, 1170002. DOI: 10.3389/fdgth.2023.1170002 PMID: 37283721

Hugh-Jones, S., Pert, K., Kendal, S., Eltringham, S., Skelton, C., Yaziji, N., & West, R. (2022). Adolescents accept digital mental health support in schools: A co-design and feasibility study of a school-based app for UK adolescents. *Mental Health & Prevention*, *27*, 200241. DOI: 10.1016/j.mhp.2022.200241

Jackson, H. M., Gulliver, A., Hasking, P., Leach, L., Batterham, P. J., Calear, A. L., & Farrer, L. M. (2024). Exploring student preferences for implementing a digital mental health intervention in a university setting: Qualitative study within a randomised controlled trial. *Digital Health, 10*, 20552076241277175. DOI: 10.1177/20552076241277175 PMID: 39224795

Kanuri, N., Arora, P., Talluru, S., Colaco, B., Dutta, R., Rawat, A., Taylor, B. C., Manjula, M., & Newman, M. G. (2020). Examining the initial usability, acceptability and feasibility of a digital mental health intervention for college students in India. *International Journal of Psychology, 55*(4), 657–673. DOI: 10.1002/ijop.12640 PMID: 31867730

Kaur, I., Kamel, R., Sultanik, E., Tan, J., Mazefsky, C. A., Brookman-Frazee, L., McPartland, J. C., Goodwin, M. S., Pennington, J., Beidas, R. S., Mandell, D. S., & Nuske, H. J. (2025). Supporting emotion regulation in children on the autism spectrum: Co-developing a digital mental health application for school-based settings with community partners. *Journal of Pediatric Psychology, 50*(1), 129–140. DOI: 10.1093/jpepsy/jsae078 PMID: 39441712

Khanna, M. S., & Carper, M. (2022). Digital mental health interventions for child and adolescent anxiety. *Cognitive and Behavioral Practice, 29*(1), 60–68. DOI: 10.1016/j.cbpra.2021.05.003

Khatib, A., Abo-Rass, F., & Gelkopf, M. (2022). Theory of planned behavior: Exploring the use of digital mental health interventions in Israel. *The Journal of Nervous and Mental Disease, 210*(7), 504–509. DOI: 10.1097/NMD.0000000000001459 PMID: 34966111

Kim, J., Aryee, L. M., Bang, H., Prajogo, S., Choi, Y. K., Hoch, J. S., & Prado, E. L. (2023). Effectiveness of digital mental health tools to reduce depressive and anxiety symptoms in low-and middle-income countries: Systematic review and meta-analysis. *JMIR Mental Health, 10*, e43066. DOI: 10.2196/43066 PMID: 36939820

Knapp, A. A., Hersch, E., Wijaya, C., Herrera, M. A., Kruzan, K. P., Carroll, A. J., Lee, S., Baker, A., Gray, A., Harris, V., Simmons, R., Kour Sodhi, D., Hannah, N., Reddy, M., Karnik, N. S., Smith, J. D., Brown, C. H., & Mohr, D. C. (2023). "The library is so much more than books": Considerations for the design and implementation of teen digital mental health services in public libraries. *Frontiers in Digital Health, 5*, 1183319. DOI: 10.3389/fdgth.2023.1183319 PMID: 37560198

Kodish, T., Schueller, S. M., & Lau, A. S. (2023). Barriers and strategies to improve digital mental health intervention uptake among college students of color: A modified Delphi study. *Journal of Behavioral and Cognitive Therapy*, *33*(1), 10–23. DOI: 10.1016/j.jbct.2022.12.002

Kozelka, E. E., Acquilano, S. C., Al-Abdulmunem, M., Guarino, S., Elwyn, G., Drake, R. E., & Carpenter-Song, E. (2023). Documenting the digital divide: Identifying barriers to digital mental health access among people with serious mental illness in community settings. *SSM. Mental Health*, *4*, 100241. DOI: 10.1016/j.ssmmh.2023.100241

Kozelka, E. E., Acquilano, S. C., Al-Abdulmunem, M., Guarino, S., Elwyn, G., Drake, R. E., & Carpenter-Song, E. (2024). Digital mental health and its discontents: Assumptions about technology that create barriers to equitable access. *Psychiatric Services (Washington, D.C.)*, *75*(3), 299–302. DOI: 10.1176/appi.ps.20230238 PMID: 38050440

Krisher, L., Boeldt, D. L., Sigmon, C. A. N., Rimel, S. E., & Newman, L. S. (2024). Pragmatic approach to the assessment and use of digital mental health interventions for health workers. *American Journal of Public Health*, *114*(S2), 171–179. DOI: 10.2105/AJPH.2023.307505 PMID: 38354345

Kumar, M., Macharia, P., Nyongesa, V., Kathono, J., Yator, O., Mwaniga, S., McKay, M., Huang, K. Y., Shidhaye, R., Njuguna, S., & Saxena, S. (2022). Human-centered design exploration with Kenyan health workers on proposed digital mental health screening and intervention training development: Thematic analysis of user preferences and needs. *Digital Health*, *8*, 20552076221090035. DOI: 10.1177/20552076221090035 PMID: 35444811

Kurki, M., Gilbert, S., Mishina, K., Lempinen, L., Luntamo, T., Hinkka-Yli-Salomäki, S., Sinokki, A., Upadhyaya, S., Wei, Y., & Sourander, A. (2021). Digital mental health literacy-program for the first-year medical students' wellbeing: A one group quasi-experimental study. *BMC Medical Education*, *21*(1), 563. DOI: 10.1186/s12909-021-02990-4 PMID: 34742258

Lal, S., Gleeson, J. F., D'Alfonso, S., Lepage, M., Joober, R., Lee, H., Abdel-Baki, A., Lecomte, T., & Alvarez-Jimenez, M. (2024). Digital mental health intervention for schizophrenia spectrum and psychotic disorders: Protocol for a pragmatic feasibility study of Horyzons-Canada. *Digital Health*, *10*, 20552076241282231. DOI: 10.1177/20552076241282231 PMID: 39372808

Lattie, E. G., Stiles-Shields, C., & Graham, A. K. (2022). An overview of and recommendations for more accessible digital mental health services. *Nature Reviews Psychology, 1*(2), 87–100. DOI: 10.1038/s44159-021-00003-1 PMID: 38515434

Lehtimaki, S., Martic, J., Wahl, B., Foster, K. T., & Schwalbe, N. (2021). Evidence on digital mental health interventions for adolescents and young people: Systematic overview. *JMIR Mental Health, 8*(4), e25847. DOI: 10.2196/25847 PMID: 33913817

Leo, A. J., Schuelke, M. J., Hunt, D. M., Metzler, J. P., Miller, J. P., Areán, P. A., Armbrecht, M. A., & Cheng, A. L. (2022). A digital mental health intervention in an orthopedic setting for patients with symptoms of depression and/or anxiety: Feasibility prospective cohort study. *JMIR Formative Research, 6*(2), e34889. DOI: 10.2196/34889 PMID: 35039278

Leo, A. J., Schuelke, M. J., Hunt, D. M., Miller, J. P., Areán, P. A., & Cheng, A. L. (2022). Digital mental health intervention plus usual care compared with usual care only and usual care plus in-person psychological counseling for orthopedic patients with symptoms of depression or anxiety: Cohort study. *JMIR Formative Research, 6*(5), e36203. DOI: 10.2196/36203 PMID: 35507387

Lim, C. T., Fuchs, C., & Torous, J. (2024). Integrated digital mental health care: A vision for addressing population mental health needs. *International Journal of General Medicine, 17*, 359–365. DOI: 10.2147/IJGM.S449474 PMID: 38318335

Linardon, J., Westrupp, E. M., Macdonald, J. A., Mikocka-Walus, A., Stokes, M. A., Greenwood, C. J., Youssef, G. J., Teague, S., Hutchinson, D., Sciberras, E., & Fuller-Tyszkiewicz, M. (2022). Monitoring Australian parents' shifting receptiveness to digital mental health interventions during the COVID-19 pandemic. *The Australian and New Zealand Journal of Psychiatry, 56*(11), 1503–1514. DOI: 10.1177/00048674211065985 PMID: 34963330

Lipschitz, J. M., Pike, C. K., Hogan, T. P., Murphy, S. A., & Burdick, K. E. (2023). The engagement problem: A review of engagement with digital mental health interventions and recommendations for a path forward. *Current Treatment Options in Psychiatry, 10*(3), 119–135. DOI: 10.1007/s40501-023-00297-3 PMID: 38390026

Liu, M., & Schueller, S. M. (2023). Moving evidence-based mental health interventions into practice: Implementation of digital mental health interventions. *Current Treatment Options in Psychiatry, 10*(4), 333–345. DOI: 10.1007/s40501-023-00298-2

Liverpool, S., Mota, C. P., Sales, C. M., Čuš, A., Carletto, S., Hancheva, C., Sousa, S., Cerón, S. C., Moreno-Peral, P., Pietrabissa, G., Moltrecht, B., Ulberg, R., Ferreira, N., & Edbrooke-Childs, J. (2020). Engaging children and young people in digital mental health interventions: Systematic review of modes of delivery, facilitators, and barriers. *Journal of Medical Internet Research, 22*(6), e16317. DOI: 10.2196/16317 PMID: 32442160

Lo, B., Pham, Q., Sockalingam, S., Wiljer, D., & Strudwick, G. (2022). Identifying essential factors that influence user engagement with digital mental health tools in clinical care settings: Protocol for a Delphi study. *Digital Health, 8*, 20552076221129059. DOI: 10.1177/20552076221129059 PMID: 36249478

Ludlow, K., March, S., Russell, J. K., Ryan, B., Brown, R. L., Hides, L., Donovan, C., Spence, S. H., Saxby, J., & Cobham, V. E. (2024). Co-designing a new digital mental health platform,'momentum', with caregivers of young people aged 7–17. *Digital Health, 10*, 20552076241263693. DOI: 10.1177/20552076241263693

Ludlow, K., Russell, J. K., Ryan, B., Brown, R. L., Joynt, T., Uhlmann, L. R., Smith, G. E., Donovan, C., Hides, L., Spence, S. H., March, S., & Cobham, V. E. (2023). Co-designing a digital mental health platform,"Momentum", with young people aged 7–17: A qualitative study. *Digital Health, 9*, 20552076231216410. DOI: 10.1177/20552076231216410 PMID: 38033517

Lukka, L., & Palva, J. M. (2023). The development of game-based digital mental health interventions: Bridging the paradigms of health care and entertainment. *JMIR Serious Games, 11*(1), e42173. DOI: 10.2196/42173 PMID: 37665624

Lukka, L., Salonen, A., Vesterinen, M., Karhulahti, V. M., Palva, S., & Palva, J. M. (2023). The qualities of patients interested in using a game-based digital mental health intervention for depression: A sequential mixed methods study. *BMC Digital Health, 1*(1), 37. DOI: 10.1186/s44247-023-00037-w

Lyon, A. R., Dopp, A. R., Brewer, S. K., Kientz, J. A., & Munson, S. A. (2020). Designing the future of children's mental health services. *Administration and Policy in Mental Health, 47*(5), 735–751. DOI: 10.1007/s10488-020-01038-x PMID: 32253634

Mabil-Atem, J. M., Gumuskaya, O., & Wilson, R. L. (2024). Digital mental health interventions for the mental health care of refugees and asylum seekers: Integrative literature review. *International Journal of Mental Health Nursing, 33*(4), 760–780. DOI: 10.1111/inm.13283 PMID: 38291740

Machado, A. S., Ferreira, B., Pereira, C. Y., Carrola, C., de Melo, B. B. V., & Campos, C. (2024). Digital mental health interventions for children and youth. In *Handbook of Research on Advances in Digital Technologies to Promote Rehabilitation and Community Participation* (pp. 20–47). IGI Global Scientific Publishing.

Magomedova, A., & Fatima, G. (2025). Mental health and well-being in the modern era: A comprehensive review of challenges and interventions. *Cureus, 17*(1). Advance online publication. DOI: 10.7759/cureus.77683 PMID: 39974249

Malla, A., & Joober, R. (2021). COVID-19 and the future with digital mental health: Need for attention to complexities. *Canadian Journal of Psychiatry, 66*(1), 14–16. DOI: 10.1177/0706743720957824 PMID: 32885686

Maqsood, A., Gul, S., Zahra, T., Noureen, N., & Khattak, A. (2024). From face-to-face to screen-to-screen: Exploring the multifaceted dimensions of digital mental health care. *Frontiers in Psychiatry, 15*, 1413127. DOI: 10.3389/fpsyt.2024.1413127 PMID: 39564463

Martinez-Martin, N., Dasgupta, I., Carter, A., Chandler, J. A., Kellmeyer, P., Kreitmair, K., Weiss, A., & Cabrera, L. Y. (2020). Ethics of digital mental health during COVID-19: Crisis and opportunities. *JMIR Mental Health, 7*(12), e23776. DOI: 10.2196/23776 PMID: 33156811

Masri, D., Jaber, L., Mashal, R., Albourini, F., Alsaoud, M. A., & Al-Tarawneh, A. M. (2024, February). The Role of Wearables & Technology in Mental Health. In *2024 2nd International Conference on Cyber Resilience (ICCR)* (pp. 1-5). IEEE. DOI: 10.1109/ICCR61006.2024.10532880

Mendes-Santos, C., Nunes, F., Weiderpass, E., Santana, R., & Andersson, G. (2022). Understanding mental health professionals' perspectives and practices regarding the implementation of digital mental health: Qualitative study. *JMIR Formative Research, 6*(4), e32558. DOI: 10.2196/32558 PMID: 35412459

Merry, S. N., Cargo, T., Christie, G., Donkin, L., Hetrick, S., Fleming, T., Holt-Quick, C., Hopkins, S., Stasiak, K., & Warren, J. (2020). Debate: Supporting the mental health of school students in the COVID-19 pandemic in New Zealand–a digital ecosystem approach. *Child and Adolescent Mental Health, 25*(4), 267–269. DOI: 10.1111/camh.12429 PMID: 33025729

Meyerhoff, J., Kornfield, R., Lattie, E. G., Knapp, A. A., Kruzan, K. P., Jacobs, M., Stamatis, C. A., Taple, B. J., Beltzer, M. L., Berry, A. B. L., Reddy, M., Mohr, D. C., & Graham, A. K. (2023). From formative design to service-ready therapeutic: A pragmatic approach to designing digital mental health interventions across domains. *Internet Interventions : the Application of Information Technology in Mental and Behavioural Health, 34*, 100677. DOI: 10.1016/j.invent.2023.100677 PMID: 37808416

Min, W., Jun, G., & Feng, L. (2022). How psychological wellbeing and digital mental health services intervene the role of self-efficacy and affective commitment of university students in their performance? *Frontiers in Psychiatry, 13*, 946793. DOI: 10.3389/fpsyt.2022.946793 PMID: 35873249

Mindu, T., Mutero, I. T., Ngcobo, W. B., Musesengwa, R., & Chimbari, M. J. (2023). Digital mental health interventions for young people in rural South Africa: Prospects and challenges for implementation. *International Journal of Environmental Research and Public Health, 20*(2), 1453. DOI: 10.3390/ijerph20021453 PMID: 36674209

Mohr, D. C., Kwasny, M. J., Meyerhoff, J., Graham, A. K., & Lattie, E. G. (2021). The effect of depression and anxiety symptom severity on clinical outcomes and app use in digital mental health treatments: Meta-regression of three trials. *Behaviour Research and Therapy, 147*, 103972. DOI: 10.1016/j.brat.2021.103972 PMID: 34600398

Mota, N. B., Pimenta, J., Tavares, M., Palmeira, L., Loch, A. A., Hedin-Pereira, C., & Dias, E. C. (2022). A Brazilian bottom-up strategy to address mental health in a diverse population over a large territorial area–an inspiration for the use of digital mental health. *Psychiatry Research, 311*, 114477. DOI: 10.1016/j.psychres.2022.114477 PMID: 35245744

Muchamore, I., Karanikolas, P., & Gooding, P. M. (2024). How lived experience expertise shapes research and development in digital mental health. *Available at SSRN* 4932039. DOI: 10.2139/ssrn.4932039

Musakuro, R. N., & Gie, L. (2025). Strategies for sustainable adoption of e-health tools for digital mental health services. *SA Journal of Human Resource Management, 23*, 11. DOI: 10.4102/sajhrm.v23i0.3053

Naslund, J. A., & Deng, D. (2021). Addressing mental health stigma in low-income and middle-income countries: A new frontier for digital mental health. *Ethics, Medicine, and Public Health, 19*, 100719. DOI: 10.1016/j.jemep.2021.100719 PMID: 35083375

Nogueira-Leite, D., Marques-Cruz, M., & Cruz-Correia, R. (2024). Individuals' attitudes toward digital mental health apps and implications for adoption in Portugal: Web-based survey. *BMC Medical Informatics and Decision Making*, *24*(1), 99. DOI: 10.1186/s12911-024-02488-1 PMID: 38637866

Nwaogu, J. M., Chan, A. P., Naslund, J. A., Hon, C. K., Belonwu, C., & Yang, J. (2021). Exploring the barriers to and motivators for using digital mental health interventions among construction personnel in Nigeria: Qualitative study. *JMIR Formative Research*, *5*(11), e18969. DOI: 10.2196/18969 PMID: 34751652

O'Dea, B., King, C., Achilles, M. R., Calear, A. L., & Subotic-Kerry, M. (2021). Delivering a digital mental health service in Australian secondary schools: Understanding school counsellors' and parents' experiences. *Health Services Insights*, *14*, 11786329211017689. DOI: 10.1177/11786329211017689 PMID: 34045867

Obikane, E., Sasaki, N., Imamura, K., Nozawa, K., Vedanthan, R., Cuijpers, P., Shimazu, T., Kamada, M., Kawakami, N., & Nishi, D. (2022). Usefulness of Implementation Outcome Scales for Digital Mental Health (iOSDMH): Experiences from six randomized controlled trials. *International Journal of Environmental Research and Public Health*, *19*(23), 15792. DOI: 10.3390/ijerph192315792 PMID: 36497867

Opie, J. E., Vuong, A., Welsh, E. T., Gray, R., Pearce, N., Marchionda, S., Mutch, R., & Khalil, H. (2024). Outcomes of best-practice guided digital mental health interventions for youth and young adults with emerging symptoms: Part I. A systematic review of socioemotional outcomes and recommendations. *Clinical Child and Family Psychology Review*, *27*(2), 424–475. DOI: 10.1007/s10567-024-00469-4 PMID: 38489101

Owen, J. E., Kuhn, E., Jamison, A. L., Ramsey, K. M., Taylor, K., Heinz, A., ... & Rosen, C. S. (2025). The National Center for PTSD Model for Digital Mental Health: A public sector approach to development, evaluation, implementation, and optimization of resources for helping trauma survivors. *Psychological Trauma: Theory, Research, Practice, and Policy*.

Palermo, E. H., Young, A. V., Deswert, S., Brown, A., Goldberg, M., Sultanik, E., Tan, J., Mazefsky, C. A., Brookman-Frazee, L., McPartland, J. C., Goodwin, M. S., Pennington, J., Marcus, S. C., Beidas, R. S., Mandell, D. S., & Nuske, H. J. (2023). A digital mental health app incorporating wearable biosensing for teachers of children on the autism spectrum to support emotion regulation: Protocol for a pilot randomized controlled trial. *JMIR Research Protocols*, *12*(1), e45852. DOI: 10.2196/45852 PMID: 37358908

Park, S. Y., Sigmon, C. N., Boeldt, D., & Sigmon, C. A. N. (2022). A framework for the implementation of digital mental health interventions: The importance of feasibility and acceptability research. *Cureus*, *14*(9). Advance online publication. DOI: 10.7759/cureus.29329 PMID: 36277565

Pendse, S. R., Nkemelu, D., Bidwell, N. J., Jadhav, S., Pathare, S., De Choudhury, M., & Kumar, N. (2022, April). From treatment to healing: envisioning a decolonial digital mental health. In *Proceedings of the 2022 CHI Conference on Human Factors in Computing Systems* (pp. 1-23).

Petrovic, M., & Gaggioli, A. (2020). Digital mental health tools for caregivers of older adults—A scoping review. *Frontiers in Public Health*, *8*, 128. DOI: 10.3389/fpubh.2020.00128 PMID: 32411643

Phang, Y. S., Heaukulani, C., Martanto, W., Morris, R., Tong, M. M., & Ho, R. (2023). Perceptions of a Digital Mental Health platform among participants with depressive disorder, anxiety disorder, and other clinically diagnosed Mental disorders in Singapore: Usability and acceptability study. *JMIR Human Factors*, *10*, e42167. DOI: 10.2196/42167 PMID: 36989020

Pine, R. (2021). Teachers' and health professionals' attitudes towards adolescent mental health and digital mental health interventions. *Advances in Mental Health*, *19*(3), 295–305. DOI: 10.1080/18387357.2020.1814160

Porche, M. V., Folk, J. B., Tolou-Shams, M., & Fortuna, L. R. (2022). Researchers' perspectives on digital mental health intervention co-design with marginalized community stakeholder youth and families. *Frontiers in Psychiatry*, *13*, 867460. DOI: 10.3389/fpsyt.2022.867460 PMID: 35530032

Potts, C., Lindström, F., Bond, R., Mulvenna, M., Booth, F., Ennis, E., Parding, K., Kostenius, C., Broderick, T., Boyd, K., Vartiainen, A.-K., Nieminen, H., Burns, C., Bickerdike, A., Kuosmanen, L., Dhanapala, I., Vakaloudis, A., Cahill, B., MacInnes, M., & O'Neill, S. (2023). A multilingual digital mental health and well-being Chatbot (ChatPal): Pre-post multicenter intervention study. *Journal of Medical Internet Research*, *25*, e43051. DOI: 10.2196/43051 PMID: 37410537

Ratheesh, A., & Alvarez-Jimenez, M. (2022). The future of digital mental health in the post-pandemic world: Evidence-based, blended, responsive and implementable. *The Australian and New Zealand Journal of Psychiatry*, *56*(2), 107–109. DOI: 10.1177/00048674211070984 PMID: 34996319

Renfrew, M. E., Morton, D. P., Morton, J. K., & Przybylko, G. (2021). The influence of human support on the effectiveness of digital mental health promotion interventions for the general population. *Frontiers in Psychology, 12*, 716106. DOI: 10.3389/fpsyg.2021.716106 PMID: 34489818

Rheinberger, D., Baffsky, R., McGillivray, L., Zbukvic, I., Dadich, A., Larsen, M. E., Lin, P.-I., Gan, D. Z. Q., Kaplun, C., Wilcox, H. C., Eapen, V., Middleton, P. M., & Torok, M. (2023). Examining the feasibility of implementing digital mental health innovations into hospitals to support youth in suicide crisis: Interview study with young people and health professionals. *JMIR Formative Research, 7*, e51398. DOI: 10.2196/51398 PMID: 37971790

Riboldi, I., Cavaleri, D., Calabrese, A., Capogrosso, C. A., Piacenti, S., Bartoli, F., Crocamo, C., & Carrà, G. (2023). Digital mental health interventions for anxiety and depressive symptoms in university students during the COVID-19 pandemic: A systematic review of randomized controlled trials. *Revista de Psiquiatría y Salud Mental, 16*, 47–58. DOI: 10.1016/j.rpsm.2022.04.005 PMID: 35755491

Ridout, B., Forsyth, R., Amon, K. L., Navarro, P., & Campbell, A. J. (2024). The Urgent Need for an Evidence-Based Digital Mental Health Practice Model of Care for Youth. *JMIR Mental Health, 11*, e48441. DOI: 10.2196/48441 PMID: 38534006

Rodriguez-Villa, E., Rozatkar, A. R., Kumar, M., Patel, V., Bondre, A., Naik, S. S., Dutt, S., Mehta, U. M., Nagendra, S., Tugnawat, D., Shrivastava, R., Raghuram, H., Khan, A., Naslund, J. A., Gupta, S., Bhan, A., Thirthall, J., Chand, P. K., Lakhtakia, T., & Torous, J. (2021). Cross cultural and global uses of a digital mental health app: Results of focus groups with clinicians, patients and family members in India and the United States. *Global Mental Health (Cambridge, England), 8*, e30. DOI: 10.1017/gmh.2021.28 PMID: 34512999

Rosenberg, B. M., Kodish, T., Cohen, Z. D., Gong-Guy, E., & Craske, M. G. (2022). A novel peer-to-peer coaching program to support digital mental health: Design and implementation. *JMIR Mental Health, 9*(1), e32430. DOI: 10.2196/32430 PMID: 35080504

Rudd, B. N., & Beidas, R. S. (2020). Digital mental health: The answer to the global mental health crisis? *JMIR Mental Health, 7*(6), e18472. DOI: 10.2196/18472 PMID: 32484445

Ruzek, J. I., Sadeh-Sharvit, S., Bunge, E. L., Sheperis, D. S., Fitzsimmons-Craft, E., Guinn, V., Joseph, R., Cameron, E., & Taylor, C. B. (2024). Training the psychologist of the future in the use of digital mental health technologies. *Professional Psychology, Research and Practice, 55*(5), 395–404. DOI: 10.1037/pro0000567

Sakellari, E., Notara, V., Lagiou, A., Fatkulina, N., Ivanova, S., Korhonen, J., Kregar Velikonja, N., Lalova, V., Laaksonen, C., Petrova, G., & Lahti, M. (2021). Mental health and wellbeing at schools: Health promotion in primary schools with the use of digital methods. *Children (Basel, Switzerland)*, *8*(5), 345. DOI: 10.3390/children8050345 PMID: 33925744

Sasaki, N., Obikane, E., Vedanthan, R., Imamura, K., Cuijpers, P., Shimazu, T., Kamada, M., Kawakami, N., & Nishi, D. (2021). Implementation Outcome Scales for Digital Mental Health (iOSDMH): Scale development and cross-sectional study. *JMIR Formative Research*, *5*(11), e24332. DOI: 10.2196/24332 PMID: 34817391

Schneider, M. L., Cha, B. S., Borghouts, J., Eikey, E. V., Schueller, S. M., Stadnick, N. A., & Sorkin, D. H. (2024). Individual and organizational outcomes of engaging peers in the cocreation of digital mental health interventions. *Psychological Services*. PMID: 39172398

Schueller, S. M., & Torous, J. (2020). Scaling evidence-based treatments through digital mental health. *The American Psychologist*, *75*(8), 1093–1104. DOI: 10.1037/amp0000654 PMID: 33252947

Schuler, B. R., & Raknes, S. (2022). Does group size and blending matter? Impact of a digital mental health game implemented with refugees in various settings. *International Journal of Migration, Health and Social Care*, *18*(1), 83–94. DOI: 10.1108/IJMHSC-07-2021-0060

Severes, B., Barreto, M., & Esteves, A. (2025). Designing for mental health in higher education: A collaborative approach to digital interventions. *Behaviour & Information Technology*, *44*(10), 2474–2492. DOI: 10.1080/0144929X.2024.2436503

Shen, N., Kassam, I., Chen, S., Ma, C., Wang, W., Boparai, N., Jankowicz, D., & Strudwick, G. (2022). Canadian perspectives of digital mental health supports: Findings from a national survey conducted during the COVID-19 pandemic. *Digital Health*, *8*, 20552076221102253. DOI: 10.1177/20552076221102253 PMID: 35646379

Sit, H. F., Hong, I. W., Burchert, S., Sou, E. K. L., Wong, M., Chen, W., Lam, A. I. F., & Hall, B. J. (2022). A feasibility study of the WHO digital mental health intervention step-by-step to address depression among Chinese young adults. *Frontiers in Psychiatry*, *12*, 812667. DOI: 10.3389/fpsyt.2021.812667 PMID: 35069297

Smith, K. A., Blease, C., Faurholt-Jepsen, M., Firth, J., Van Daele, T., Moreno, C., Carlbring, P., Ebner-Priemer, U. W., Koutsouleris, N., Riper, H., Mouchabac, S., Torous, J., & Cipriani, A. (2023). Digital mental health: Challenges and next steps. *BMJ Mental Health, 26*(1), e300670. DOI: 10.1136/bmjment-2023-300670 PMID: 37197797

Smith, K. A., Hardy, A., Vinnikova, A., Blease, C., Milligan, L., Hidalgo-Mazzei, D., Lambe, S., Marzano, L., Uhlhaas, P. J., Ostinelli, E. G., Anmella, G., Zangani, C., Aronica, R., Dwyer, B., Torous, J., & Cipriani, A. (2024). Digital mental health for schizophrenia and other severe mental illnesses: An international consensus on current challenges and potential solutions. *JMIR Mental Health, 11*, e57155. DOI: 10.2196/57155 PMID: 38717799

Song, M., & Song, Y. M. (2023). Randomized controlled trials of digital mental health interventions on patients with schizophrenia spectrum disorder: A systematic review. *Telemedicine Journal and e-Health, 29*(6), 798–812. DOI: 10.1089/tmj.2022.0135 PMID: 36264184

Song, S., Seo, Y., Hwang, S., Kim, H. Y., & Kim, J. (2024). Digital phenotyping of geriatric depression using a community-based digital mental health monitoring platform for socially vulnerable older adults and their community caregivers: 6-week living lab single-arm pilot study. *JMIR mHealth and uHealth, 12*(1), e55842. DOI: 10.2196/55842 PMID: 38885033

Soubutts, E., Shrestha, P., Davidson, B. I., Qu, C., Mindel, C., Sefi, A., & McNaney, R. (2024, May). Challenges and opportunities for the design of inclusive digital mental health tools: understanding culturally diverse young people's experiences. In *Proceedings of the 2024 CHI Conference on Human Factors in Computing Systems* (pp. 1-16). DOI: 10.1145/3613904.3642641

Stanger, S. B., & Lucas, S. J. (2024). Using indirect service-learning to promote evidence-based digital mental health tools on college campuses. *Teaching of Psychology, 51*(2), 240–247. DOI: 10.1177/00986283221084005

Staples, L. G., Nielssen, O., Dear, B. F., Bisby, M. A., Fisher, A., Kayrouz, R., & Titov, N. (2023). Prevalence and predictors of long COVID in patients accessing a national digital mental health service. *International Journal of Environmental Research and Public Health, 20*(18), 6756. DOI: 10.3390/ijerph20186756 PMID: 37754615

Stein, D. J., Fineberg, N. A., & Chamberlain, S. R. (Eds.). (2021). *Mental health in a digital world.* Academic Press.

Stern, E., Micoulaud Franchi, J. A., Dumas, G., Moreira, J., Mouchabac, S., Maruani, J., Philip, P., Lejoyeux, M., & Geoffroy, P. A. (2023). How can digital mental health enhance psychiatry? *The Neuroscientist*, *29*(6), 681–693. DOI: 10.1177/10738584221098603 PMID: 35658666

Stiles-Shields, C., Gustafson, E. L., Lim, P. S., Bobadilla, G., Thorpe, D., Summersett Williams, F. C., Donenberg, G. R., Julion, W. A., & Karnik, N. S. (2025). Pre-implementation determinants for digital mental health integration in Chicago pediatric primary care. *Journal of Pediatric Psychology*, *50*(1), 86–95. DOI: 10.1093/jpepsy/jsae058 PMID: 39101560

Stiles-Shields, C., Ramos, G., Ortega, A., & Psihogios, A. M. (2023). Increasing digital mental health reach and uptake via youth partnerships. *Npj Mental Health Research*, *2*(1), 9. DOI: 10.1038/s44184-023-00030-1 PMID: 37483392

Taher, R., Hall, C. L., Bergin, A. D. G., Gupta, N., Heaysman, C., Jacobsen, P., Kabir, T., Kalnad, N., Keppens, J., Hsu, C.-W., McGuire, P., Peters, E., Shergill, S., Stahl, D., Stock, B. W., & Yiend, J. (2024). Developing a process for assessing the safety of a digital mental health intervention and gaining regulatory approval: A case study and academic's guide. *Trials*, *25*(1), 604. DOI: 10.1186/s13063-024-08421-1 PMID: 39252100

Taher, R., Hsu, C. W., Hampshire, C., Fialho, C., Heaysman, C., Stahl, D., Shergill, S., & Yiend, J. (2023). The safety of digital mental health interventions: Systematic review and recommendations. *JMIR Mental Health*, *10*(1), e47433. DOI: 10.2196/47433 PMID: 37812471

Taylor, K. V., Garchitorena, L., Scaramutti-Gladfelter, C., Wyrick, M., Grill, K. B., & Seixas, A. A. (2024). A digital mental health solution to improve social, emotional, and learning skills for youth: Protocol for an efficacy and usability study. *JMIR Research Protocols*, *13*(1), e59372. DOI: 10.2196/59372 PMID: 39701588

Taylor, M. E., Liu, M., Abelson, S., Eisenberg, D., Lipson, S. K., & Schueller, S. M. (2024). The reach, effectiveness, adoption, implementation, and maintenance of digital mental health interventions for college students: A systematic review. *Current Psychiatry Reports*, *26*(12), 683–693. DOI: 10.1007/s11920-024-01545-w PMID: 39392547

Thomson, M., Henderson, G., Rogers, T., Locke, B., Vines, J., & MacBeth, A. (2024). Digital mental health and peer support: Building a Theory of Change informed by stakeholders' perspectives. *PLOS Digital Health*, *3*(5), e0000522. DOI: 10.1371/journal.pdig.0000522 PMID: 38814923

Tomičić, A., & Gjorgjioska, M. A. (2024). Epistemic inequality in the digital era: Unpacking biases in digital mental health. *Theory & Psychology*, *34*(6), 777–797. DOI: 10.1177/09593543241279131

Topooco, N., Fowler, L. A., Fitzsimmons-Craft, E. E., DePietro, B., Vázquez, M. M., Firebaugh, M. L., Ceglarek, P., Monterubio, G., Newman, M. G., Eisenberg, D., Wilfley, D. E., & Taylor, C. B. (2022). Digital interventions to address mental health needs in colleges: Perspectives of student stakeholders. *Internet Interventions : the Application of Information Technology in Mental and Behavioural Health*, *28*, 100528. DOI: 10.1016/j.invent.2022.100528 PMID: 35378846

Torous, J., Linardon, J., Goldberg, S. B., Sun, S., Bell, I., Nicholas, J., Hassan, L., Hua, Y., Milton, A., & Firth, J. (2025). The evolving field of digital mental health: Current evidence and implementation issues for smartphone apps, generative artificial intelligence, and virtual reality. *World Psychiatry; Official Journal of the World Psychiatric Association (WPA)*, *24*(2), 156–174. DOI: 10.1002/wps.21299 PMID: 40371757

Tremain, H., McEnery, C., Fletcher, K., & Murray, G. (2020). The therapeutic alliance in digital mental health interventions for serious mental illnesses: Narrative review. *JMIR Mental Health*, *7*(8), e17204. DOI: 10.2196/17204 PMID: 32763881

van Grunsven, J. (2021). Perceptual breakdown during a global pandemic: Introducing phenomenological insights for digital mental health purposes. *Ethics and Information Technology*, *23*(S1, Suppl 1), 91–98. DOI: 10.1007/s10676-020-09554-y PMID: 32905100

Venning, A., Herd, M. C., Oswald, T. K., Razmi, S., Glover, F., Hawke, T., Quartermain, V., & Redpath, P. (2021). Exploring the acceptability of a digital mental health platform incorporating a virtual coach: The good, the bad, and the opportunities. *Health Informatics Journal*, *27*(1), 1460458221994873. DOI: 10.1177/1460458221994873 PMID: 33601947

Vial, S., Boudhraâ, S., & Dumont, M. (2022). Human-centered design approaches in digital mental health interventions: Exploratory mapping review. *JMIR Mental Health*, *9*(6), e35591. DOI: 10.2196/35591 PMID: 35671081

Vicary, E., Brierley, H., Wilkinson, J., Adesina, M., Bee, P., Lovell, K., Uzun, N., Bee, E., & Brooks, H. (2025). Bridging the Gap in Mental Health Literacy: Co-adapting and feasibility testing a digital intervention to improve mental health literacy amongst young people aged 12-14 in the UK. *Frontiers in Psychiatry*, *16*, 1546109. DOI: 10.3389/fpsyt.2025.1546109 PMID: 40761590

Wang, X., Jiang, F., Luo, L., Li, H., Jiang, W., & Shen, X. (2025). Digital Transformation of College Students' Mental Health Education in the Intelligent Era: Model Innovation and Practical Exploration. *health education, 7*(5), 8-18.

Wani, C., McCann, L., Lennon, M., & Radu, C. (2024). Digital mental health interventions for adolescents in low-and middle-income countries: Scoping review. *Journal of Medical Internet Research, 26*, e51376. DOI: 10.2196/51376 PMID: 39471371

Wies, B., Landers, C., & Ienca, M. (2021). Digital mental health for young people: A scoping review of ethical promises and challenges. *Frontiers in Digital Health, 3*, 697072. DOI: 10.3389/fdgth.2021.697072 PMID: 34713173

Xi, Y., Paracha, S., Hands, C., & Angelakis, I. (2025). *Still looking for new ways of promoting children's mental health education through digital technologies: a systematic review*. Mental Health and Digital Technologies.

Xu, Y., Yang, H., Jin, Z., Xiang, J., Xu, H., Pokay, Y. H., Mao, H., Cai, X., Wu, Y., & Wang, D. B. (2023). Application of a Digital Mental Health Clinic in secondary schools: Functionality and effectiveness evaluation. *JMIR Formative Research, 7*(1), e46494. DOI: 10.2196/46494 PMID: 37883144

Yeo, G., Reich, S. M., Liaw, N. A., & Chia, E. Y. M. (2024). The effect of digital mental health literacy interventions on mental health: Systematic review and meta-analysis. *Journal of Medical Internet Research, 26*, e51268. DOI: 10.2196/51268 PMID: 38421687

Yin, R., Martinengo, L., Smith, H. E., Subramaniam, M., Griva, K., & Car, L. T. (2024). The views and experiences of older adults regarding digital mental health interventions: A systematic review ofqualitative studies. *The Lancet. Healthy Longevity, 5*(11), 100638. DOI: 10.1016/j.lanhl.2024.08.007 PMID: 39491881

Zainal, N. H., Wang, V., Garthwaite, B., & Curtiss, J. E. (2025). What factors are related to engagement with digital mental health interventions (DMHIs)? A meta-analysis of 117 trials. *Health Psychology Review*, •••, 1–21. DOI: 10.1080/17437199.2025.2547610 PMID: 40857362

Zhang, X., Lewis, S., Chen, X., Berry, N., & Bucci, S. (2022). Mental health professionals views and the impact of COVID-19 pandemic on implementing digital mental health in China: A nationwide survey study. *Internet Interventions : the Application of Information Technology in Mental and Behavioural Health, 30*, 100576. DOI: 10.1016/j.invent.2022.100576 PMID: 36185346

Zhang, X., Lewis, S., Firth, J., Chen, X., & Bucci, S. (2021). Digital mental health in China: A systematic review. *Psychological Medicine*, *51*(15), 2552–2570. DOI: 10.1017/S0033291721003731 PMID: 34581263

Zhao, X., Stadnick, N. A., Ceballos-Corro, E., Castro, J.Jr, Mallard-Swanson, K., Palomares, K. J., Eikey, E., Schneider, M., Zheng, K., Mukamel, D. B., Schueller, S. M., & Sorkin, D. H. (2023). Facilitators of and barriers to integrating digital mental health into county mental health services: Qualitative interview analyses. *JMIR Formative Research*, *7*(1), e45718. DOI: 10.2196/45718 PMID: 37191975

Zhu, S., Wang, Y., & Hu, Y. (2025). Facilitators and Barriers to Digital Mental Health Interventions for Depression, Anxiety, and Stress in Adolescents and Young Adults: Scoping Review. *Journal of Medical Internet Research*, *27*, e62870. DOI: 10.2196/62870 PMID: 40127430

Chapter 2
Empowering Through Care Mental Health and Counseling in Student Well-Being

Renu Vij
https://orcid.org/0000-0001-9202-8390
Chandigarh University, India

Aashna Narula
https://orcid.org/0009-0002-7761-8573
Pyschopedia Journal, India

ABSTRACT

Mental health has steadily become a defining contributor to student achievement in higher education. This chapter looks at the pressures many students struggle with today—from academic load and peer expectations to studying courses that may not reflect their real interests. In response, universities and colleges are gradually building more supportive environments. Counseling units, mentor–mentee interactions, wellness initiatives, and simple mindfulness practices are becoming part of regular campus life. Courses such as Science of Happiness and Human Values are also being introduced to help young adults understand their emotions and develop personal balance. The chapter further points to the role of psychometric assessments, hostel-based support, and coordinated communication among teachers, parents, and students. Together, these efforts show how institutions are shifting toward building students who are emotionally stronger and better equipped to handle challenges outside the classroom.

DOI: 10.4018/979-8-3373-5007-3.ch002

INTRODUCTION

In higher education, student mental health has emerged as a critical determinant of academic achievement, retention, and overall life satisfaction (Duraku et al., 2024; Olsson et al., 2024). Rates of depression, anxiety, and distress among undergraduates currently range from 25–34%, a concerning trend documented consistently across global studies (Olsson et al., 2024; Duraku et al., 2024).

Academic demands, financial uncertainty, and social isolation are among the primary stressors undermining well-being (Duraku et al., 2024; Rezapour & Elmshaeuser, 2022). These pressures often peak during the transition into university, with first-year students particularly vulnerable (Duraku et al., 2024). Crucially, research links diminished psychological well-being to reduced academic performance and increased dropout risk (Olsson et al., 2024; Duraku et al., 2024).

Traditional university mental health services while effective are often overwhelmed, creating long waits and access barriers (Olsson et al., 2024). To address this, institutions are exploring structural and curricular innovations that integrate psychological resilience into the educational experience, moving beyond reactive counselling to proactive mental health promotion (Olsson et al., 2024).

One of the most researched interventions is the "Science of Happiness" course, pioneered by Laurie Santos at Yale and adapted by the University of Bristol. Evaluations have shown significant improvements in well-being immediately post-course, sustained reductions in anxiety and loneliness at six weeks, and even more compelling 10–15% higher well-being scores maintained over two years by students. Additionally, students who continued practicing, learned techniques like gratitude, kindness, journaling, exercise, and mindfulness (Hobbs et al., 2024; 2021; Neuroscience News, 2024).

Systematic reviews affirm that university-based positive psychology courses produce large effect sizes for reduced anxiety/depression, outperforming alternative psychology instruction (Gander et al., 2023). Likewise, scoping reviews highlight that curricular integration of well-being strategies bolsters resilience and improve mental health (Duraku et al., 2024; Olsson et al., 2024)

Beyond psycho-educational courses, broader structural changes such as inclusive pedagogies, flexible assessments, and learning environment adaptations are gaining traction. These initiatives reflect a shift toward universal design principles aimed at fostering health-promoting academic cultures (Olsson et al., 2024)

BACKGROUND OF THE STUDY

One of the most important issues facing higher education globally in the last ten years has been mental health. A crucial developmental period, the move to university life is characterized by rising academic demands, social adaptation, financial strains, and identity exploration. These changes are frequently accompanied by an increased susceptibility to psychological distress. According to WHO (2024) over one in three students suffer from anxiety or depression symptoms making mental health issues among college students a rising public health concern.

The post pandemic environment has made it even more clear how urgent it is to address mental health in school environments. The OECD (2024) reports that student distress levels are still 25-35% higher than baselines before to 2020, with an increase in loneliness, academic fatigue, and reluctance to seek help. Peer counselling models, institutional well-being framework and digital mental health all saw rapid innovation as a result of COVID-10 pandemic.

Universities are responding by rethinking their strategy, moving away from reactive counselling and towards models of preventative and systemic well-being. This change in perspective places a strong emphasis on socio-emotional learning, resilience and curriculum integrated positive psychology therapies. For example, the "Science of Happiness" course which was developed at Yale and is now being taught all around the world has shown consistent gains in students well-being over time (Hobbs et al., 2024). University participants anxiety symptoms decreased by 34% as a result of structured mindfulness-based cognitive training programs.

This change in the world has been reflected in India's higher education system. Mental health support has been mainstreamed via policy and practice with initiatives like Manodarpan. These programs emphasize the importance of emotional health for both lifelong learning and high quality education. Peer support programs, campus counselling frameworks, and credit based wellness courses have been implemented by various universities.

This integrated approach is supported by recent evidence. According to Raj and Narayan (2025) first year students mental health literacy and help seeking behavior were improved by hybrid counselling systems that combined online and in person modalities. Similarly, it was shown by Hassan and Mukherjee (2024) that including emotional intelligence modules into curricula enhanced student retention and decreased fatigue. These results support the need to integrate academic structure with psychological treatments.

This study is relevant because it supports the Sustainable Development Goals (SDGs 3,4 and 10) of the UN which all place a strong emphasis on equality, high quality education and well-being.

Institutions of higher learning are psychosocial ecosystems that can foster self-awareness, empathy and resilience in addition to being places for learning. Empowering students via mental health care is not a secondary support function but rather a fundamental component of academic achievement and sustainable education as research from both national and international sources continues to confirm. Therefore, this study explores how proactive care and counselling might improve student well-being and institutional resilience, placing itself at the intersection of education, psychology and development policy.

MENTAL HEALTH AND SUSTAINABLE GOAL

SDG 3 Goal focus on Mental Health. The emphasis on student mental health aligns directly with the global policy vision embedded in the United Nations Sustainable Development Goals (SDGs), particularly SDG 3: Ensure healthy lives and promote well-being for all at all ages. This goal, especially Target 3.4, calls for a one-third reduction in premature mortality from non-communicable diseases through prevention, treatment, and promotion of mental health and well-being by 2030 (United Nations, 2015). In the context of higher education, this directive reinforces the responsibility of academic institutions to become active agents in not only preventing mental health crises but also in fostering an environment that nurtures psychological resilience and emotional maturity (UNESCO, 2024).

Higher education systems are now increasingly viewed as key platforms for advancing SDG 3 by embedding mental well-being into core institutional priorities, policies, and student services (Patel et al., 2018). Global and national education policy frameworks, such as India's National Education Policy (NEP) 2020 and UNESCO's Global Education Monitoring Report encourage universities to create inclusive, health-promoting campuses that address the full spectrum of student well-being (Government of India, 2020; UNESCO, 2024). These frameworks explicitly recognize the need to invest in campus mental health infrastructure, including trained counsellors, peer support systems, and preventive education models, to promote both academic excellence and lifelong personal development.

Moreover, the intersection of SDG 3 with SDG 4 (Quality Education) emphasizes that inclusive and equitable quality education must also account for the psychological readiness and emotional health of learners. Students who struggle with mental health issues are less likely to complete their studies, participate in campus life, or transition successfully to employment consequently weakening progress toward SDG 8 (Decent Work and Economic Growth) and SDG 10 (Reduced Inequalities). In this way, the promotion of mental health in university settings is not a siloed concern but rather a foundational cross-cutting issue central to the achievement of multiple SDGs.

The COVID-19 pandemic further amplified this urgency by exposing the fragility of existing support systems and accelerating conversations about institutional accountability in mental health promotion (OECD, 2021; Duraku et al., 2024). Institutions that integrated psychosocial support and flexible pedagogical strategies during the crisis were better able to support student retention and academic continuity strengthening the argument that systemic investment in mental well-being is both ethically essential and developmentally strategic.

INDIA'S UNIQUE EFFORTS TOWARDS ACHIEVING SDG 3: MENTAL HEALTH IN HIGHER EDUCATION

India has taken several pioneering steps to align its national policies with SDG 3, particularly in the realm of youth and student mental well-being. Recognizing that emotional health is critical to learning outcomes and social development, the National Education Policy (NEP) 2020 placed mental health at the heart of institutional reform. The policy mandates the presence of trained counsellors in schools and higher education institutions (HEIs), promotion of well-being through value-based education, and the integration of emotional intelligence and life skills in curricula (Ministry of Human Resource Development, Government of Inida, n.d).

The University Grants Commission (UGC) has also introduced specific guidelines to address student stress and psychological challenges. Its "Manodarpan" initiative, launched under the Atmanirbhar Bharat Abhiyan, is a landmark effort aimed at providing psychosocial support to students during and post-pandemic. It includes a national toll-free helpline, expert mental health resources, and online counseling platforms making support services accessible across socio-economic and geographic divides (Ministry of Education, 2021). The *"Manodarpan"* initiative, launched under the *Atmanirbhar Bharat Abhiyan*, is a transformative mental health program introduced by the Ministry of Education, Government of India. Designed as a direct response to the psychological challenges intensified by the COVID-19 pandemic, it addresses the mental and emotional well-being of students, teachers, and families, with a focused impact on higher education institutions. In line with the United Nations Sustainable Development Goal 3 (Good Health and Well-being), the initiative aims to reduce stress, anxiety, depression, and other psychological issues through accessible counseling services, 24/7 helplines, and digital support platforms. the initiative has led to increased awareness of mental health in university campuses. Regular webinars, online awareness modules, and the availability of trained counselors have enhanced the visibility and acceptance of mental health services in academic spaces (Ministry of Education, 2021). This initiative exemplifies India's policy-level commitment to embedding emotional wellness within educational governance and curriculum reforms. Moreover, it aligns with SDG Target 3.4, which aims to promote mental health and well-being and reduce premature mortality from non-communicable diseases by one-third by 2030. India's integrated approach to preventive mental healthcare in academic institutions, building resilience, reducing stigma, and fostering a student-centric learning environment.

Manodarpan Initiative in Relation to SDG 3 and Higher Education

Table 1. Ministry of Education. (2020). Manodarpan initiative under Atmanirbhar Bharat Abhiyan

Component	*Details*	*Alignment with SDG 3*
Initiative Name	*Manodarpan*	Promotes well-being and mental health awareness
Launched Under	*Atmanirbhar Bharat Abhiyan*	National recovery and resilience program
Target Group	Students, teachers, and families (focus on higher education)	Focus on youth mental health (SDG Target 3.4)
Key Services	National helpline, online counselling, digital resources, webinars	Accessible mental health services
Operational Body	Ministry of Education, Government of India	Policy integration of wellness in education
Tools & Platforms	National helpline: 8448440632, digital outreach programs	Health system strengthening
Reach & Impact	Thousands of calls received and addressed; mental health modules integrated in some universities	Reduces stress, anxiety; promotes early intervention
Contribution to Higher Education	Introduced awareness programs, peer-support systems, and mental health clubs in colleges and universities	Builds institutional resilience for sustainable learning
Relation to SDG 3 (Good Health & Well-being)	Directly supports SDG 3.4: *"Promote mental health and well-being"*	Strengthens India's global commitment to health and education

Government of India. Retrieved from https://manodarpan.education.gov.in

Additionally, the All India Council for Technical Education (AICTE) has mandated wellness centers and peer-support clubs in engineering colleges to encourage open conversations around mental health and reduce stigma. Indian institutions such as IIT Madras and Delhi University have piloted mindfulness-based interventions, emotional resilience training, and "Happiness Curriculum" modules tailored for youth, adapted from state-level innovations in Delhi and Madhya Pradesh schools.

India is also among the first countries to embed value education and emotional wellness into credit-based courses, inspired by models like Yale's "Science of Well-being." Courses such as "Human Values and Professional Ethics" and "Understanding the Self", now offered in many HEIs, are part of the move to integrate well-being with academic learning.

Moreover, the National Institute of Mental Health and Neurosciences (NIMHANS) has partnered with universities to develop campus mental health frameworks and train faculty to identify early signs of distress among students creating a multi-tiered response system rooted in both medical and psychosocial care (NIMHANS, 2022).

These coordinated actions reflect India's evolving understanding that youth mental health is not only a public health priority but a development imperative essential to achieving multiple SDGs. The country's approach merging traditional knowledge systems, digital innovation, and inclusive education policy offers a scalable model for other nations navigating similar challenges.

Mental well-being refers to a balanced psychological state in which individuals can think clearly, manage emotions effectively, form healthy relationships, and face academic and life challenges with resilience. It is not merely the absence of mental illness, but a positive state of mental health where students experience satisfaction, purpose, and emotional stability in daily life. According to The Americal Psychological Association (2023) mental health is a "state of mind characterized by emotional well-being, good behavioural adjustments, relative freedom from anxiety and disabling symptoms, and a capacity to establish constructive relationships and cope with the ordinary demands and stresses of life". Within the higher education landscape, mental well-being plays a central role in shaping a student's academic success, personal growth, and overall life trajectory.

Mental well-being is conceptualized as a proactive and empowering force. The chapter emphasizes that institutions must shift from reactive interventions to a culture of preventive care and emotional support. The goal is to equip students with coping mechanisms, social-emotional skills, and access to counseling services, ensuring their well-being is supported throughout their educational journey.

REVIEW OF LITERATURE

Singh, Menon and Arora (2021) conducted a study to examine the impact of digital mental health tools on university students' emotional well-being. The results revealed that mobile-based mindfulness and cognitive-behavioral therapy (CBT) applications significantly reduced anxiety and stress symptoms among users. Kumar and Sharma (2020) explored the effectiveness of peer counseling programs in Indian higher education institutions. Their findings showed that students who participated in structured peer support groups reported improved emotional resilience and academic engagement compared to those who did not. Thomas and George (2019) conducted a meta-analysis to understand the relationship between mental health literacy and help-seeking behaviour among adolescents and young adults. The analysis indicated a moderate positive correlation, suggesting that improved awareness significantly encourages students to seek professional help. Verma, Nair and Das (2022) studied the role of trauma-informed teaching practices in creating inclusive learning environments for students with mental health challenges. Their research highlighted that schools adopting such practices experienced reduced behavioural issues and better teacher-student relationships.

Patel and Joshi (2023) evaluated the integration of university counselling services (UCS) with academic advisement systems. Their study found that students who regularly used counselling services alongside academic guidance reported greater satisfaction with campus life and demonstrated lower dropout intentions. Reddy (2020) analyzed the barriers to mental health services in Indian universities, focusing on stigma and accessibility. The study concluded that while counselling services are increasingly available, cultural stigma and lack of awareness remain major obstacles to their utilization. Mehra and Kapoor (2021) examined the psychological impact of the COVID-19 pandemic on college students and the role of virtual counselling. Their findings showed that online counselling sessions provided during lockdown periods significantly reduced feelings of isolation and depression among students. Sharma and Iyer (2018) conducted a longitudinal study on the effect of regular group counselling on academic stress in undergraduate students. The results demonstrated a consistent decrease in reported stress levels and improvement in coping strategies over a six-month period.

Gupta and Ahuja (2021) conducted a mixed-method study to evaluate student satisfaction with online counselling services implemented during the COVID-19 lockdown. The findings revealed a moderate level of satisfaction, with students reporting ease of access and emotional relief as major benefits. Bourion-Bédès et al. (2021) investigated the mental health status of university students during the COVID-19 pandemic in a French context. Their results showed high prevalence rates of anxiety and depression, emphasizing the urgent need for preventive counselling services. Rathakrishnan, Hamzah and Arokiasamy (2022) studied the effectiveness of resilience training programs on mental well-being among Malaysian university students. Their study showed that structured resilience training significantly enhanced coping skills and emotional regulation.

Naslund et al. (2022) examined the use of digital platforms to reduce stigma around mental illness in young adults across low- and middle-income countries. Their findings suggested that narrative-based interventions improved student willingness to seek professional help. Wang et al. (2020) carried out a large-scale cross-cultural study in China to explore how coping styles affect psychological well-being among university students. The authors found that adaptive coping mechanisms were positively associated with better academic outcomes and lower stress. Auerbach et al. (2020) explored global mental health challenges faced by students as part of the World Mental Health International College Student (WMH-ICS) initiative. Their data from over 20 countries highlighted the widespread lack of access to formal psychological support despite rising mental health needs.

Subramaniam, Tan and Lim (2023) analysed institutional preparedness for promoting student well-being in Asian universities. Their study concluded that policies focused on inclusive counselling and peer mentoring were more successful in reducing dropout rates and improving student retention.

Why Mental Health in Education

Mental health has emerged as a critical component in the discourse on student well-being, especially in higher education. Institutions are no longer perceived solely as centers of academic instruction but are increasingly expected to contribute to the holistic development of students. Mental health, in this context, refers to the psychological, emotional, and social well-being that enables individuals to manage stress, relate to others, and make constructive decisions. Its relevance in educational settings has become more pronounced due to the growing evidence linking psychological well-being with academic performance, student retention, and life outcomes.

In today's educational discourse, student well-being has grown in importance, with mental health and counselling emerging as essential components that enable students to succeed both personally and intellectually. Vij and Narula (2026) emphasize the critical relevance of care centered educational practises in this setting, especially through the feedback mechanism in online learning environments. The research emphasise how teachers interactions, responses and guidance for students can serve as a kind of daily counselling, impacting psychological resilience, motivations and emotional safety.

The importance of mental health in education has gained significant academic and policy attention in recent years. Mental health, broadly defined as a state of emotional, psychological, and social well-being, plays a fundamental role in how students think, feel, behave, and perform academically. Within higher education, the relevance of mental health extends beyond individual well-being—it directly influences learning outcomes, social relationships, and long-term academic and professional trajectories.

Students in tertiary institutions encounter a complex mix of stressors including academic workloads, financial concerns, peer relationships, family expectations, and the pressure of career uncertainty (Verger et al., 2009; Eisenberg et al., 2007). For many, these challenges can result in emotional exhaustion, anxiety, depression, and disengagement from academic life. Research suggests that untreated mental health issues are a leading cause of absenteeism, low academic performance, and high dropout rates in universities (Kessler et al., 2005).

Educational institutions thus have a responsibility not only to address these issues reactively but also to create proactive mental health ecosystems. This includes accessible counselling services, peer support structures, mental health literacy programs, and inclusive pedagogical practices that promote psychological safety and well-being. The integration of mental health into academic settings contributes to better focus, increased resilience, improved student satisfaction, and the development of life skills critical for future success (Gallagher, 2014).

In addition, attention to mental health in education aligns with global frameworks such as the United Nations Sustainable Development Goal 3, which advocates for ensuring healthy lives and promoting well-being for all at all ages (United Nations, 2015). Institutions that integrate mental health awareness into their curriculum, policy, and culture not only support individual growth but also contribute to more equitable, empathetic, and inclusive learning environments.

Mental health is integral to the mission of education, not only for fostering academic success but for nurturing individuals capable of contributing meaningfully to society. Its inclusion in institutional priorities is essential for building educational ecosystems that are not only intellectually rigorous but also emotionally supportive and socially inclusive.

Importance of Mental Well-being for Student Success in Higher Education

1. **Supports Academic Engagement and Performance**

A sound mental state enables students to concentrate, retain information, and stay motivated. Mental well-being boosts cognitive functioning and helps students manage academic workloads more effectively. When students feel emotionally supported, they are more likely to attend classes, participate actively, and perform better in assessments.

2. **Eases Life Transitions and Reduces Emotional Distress**

Entering higher education often involves major life changes moving away from home, handling financial responsibilities, and adapting to a new social environment. These transitions can trigger stress, anxiety, or feelings of isolation. Prioritizing mental well-being helps students adjust more smoothly and maintain emotional balance during these formative years.

3. **Prevents the Escalation of Mental Health Issues**

College and university years are often the first period when symptoms of mental health conditions such as depression, anxiety, or panic disorders begin to manifest. Providing early support and mental health education creates opportunities for timely intervention, preventing long-term psychological harm.

4. **Fosters a Safe and Inclusive Campus Culture**

A focus on well-being promotes inclusivity, reduces stigma around mental health issues, and encourages students to seek help without fear of judgment. Institutions that embed mental well-being into their policies and campus life create environments where every student feels valued and safe.

5. **Contributes to Global Health Goals (SDG 3)**

Mental well-being aligns closely with Sustainable Development Goal 3, which advocates for the promotion of good health and well-being for all. Higher education institutions play a vital role in achieving this by embedding mental health literacy, peer support systems, and accessible services within the academic setting.

Promoting mental well-being is essential for developing well-rounded students who are capable of succeeding both academically and personally. The higher learning must adopt a comprehensive framework that includes counselling, preventive mental health programs, and resilience training. This ensures that students are not only academically competent but also emotionally equipped to navigate the complexities of modern life. Mental well-being, therefore, is not an optional service—it is a critical component of educational excellence and student empowerment.

Factors Contributing to Student Strain in Higher Education

Students in higher education often encounter multiple stressors that significantly impact their mental well-being. These stressors stem from academic, personal, social, and systemic sources. The transition from adolescence to adulthood, combined with academic expectations and future uncertainties, creates a complex psychological landscape for students. Below are key reasons contributing to mental strain among university students:

1. Peer Pressure

Peer dynamics play a central role in shaping student behaviour and decision-making. The desire to conform, achieve social acceptance, or match the accomplishments of peers can lead students to engage in unhealthy comparisons or overextend themselves academically and socially. Fear of exclusion, coupled with the need to "fit in," can drive anxiety and diminished self-worth.

2. Family Expectations and Pressure

Family pressure remains a profound source of stress, particularly in collectivist cultures where parental aspirations significantly influence student choices. Expectations regarding academic excellence, professional success, and fulfilling roles aligned with family honor can impose an emotional burden. In many cases, the fear of disappointing parents leads to chronic stress, burnout, or emotional withdrawal.

3. Unrealistic Academic and Career Goals

In an increasingly competitive academic landscape, students often set goals that exceed their capacities or fail to consider personal limitations. These goals, while ambitious, can become overwhelming if not matched with adequate support, preparation, and coping skills. Failure to meet such expectations can result in feelings of inadequacy, self-doubt, and reduced motivation.

4. Studying in a Domain Not of Their Choice

A significant number of students pursue academic programs based on parental influence, societal prestige, or perceived job security rather than personal interest or aptitude. When students are misaligned with their academic disciplines, they frequently experience disengagement, underperformance, and emotional distress, which may escalate into anxiety or depression.

5. Lack of Interest or Purpose

A lack of intrinsic motivation or clear sense of purpose in their educational journey can leave students feeling lost or apathetic. This disconnection from learning affects not only academic outcomes but also a student's overall sense of fulfillment and identity. Without meaningful engagement, students may question the value of their efforts, leading to existential stress.

6. High Competition and Performance Pressure

The relentless pressure to excel, secure placements, and outperform peers fosters a cut-throat environment. Ranking systems, grading metrics, and scholarship races amplify stress, especially for students with limited coping mechanisms. Constant competition may also hinder collaboration and create a toxic academic culture that undermines collective well-being.

Table 2. Framework of Mental Strain

```
+------------------------+
| Peer Pressure |
+------------------------+
|
+----------------+ +-----------------------+ +--------------------+
| Family Pressure | ---> | Mental Strain Among | <--- | Unrealistic Goals |
+----------------+ | Higher Ed Students | +--------------------+
|
+---------------------+ +---------------------+ +--------------------+
| Domain Not of Choice | --> | Lack of Interest / | <-- | Competition & |
| | | Motivation | | Performance Pressure|
+---------------------+ +---------------------+ +--------------------+
```

Source-Author

Impact of Mental Well-being on Students in Higher Education

The promotion of mental health and the availability of counselling services within higher education significantly influence students' academic and personal trajectories. The following are key areas where positive mental health interventions yield measurable outcomes:

a) **Reduced Absenteeism**: Students experiencing psychological support and emotional stability are less likely to skip classes. This consistency in attendance directly contributes to improved academic performance and stronger engagement.
b) **Enhanced Cognitive and Emotional Growth**: Mental well-being fosters optimal brain functioning, which supports critical thinking, emotional regulation, and adaptive learning strategies—essential components for success in higher education.
c) **Increase in Happiness Index**: Students who feel mentally supported report higher levels of life satisfaction and subjective well-being. This contributes to a positive academic climate and community culture.
d) **Improved Longevity and Resilience**: Studies show that individuals with good mental health habits in early adulthood develop greater psychological resilience, promoting long-term health and reduced risk of chronic stress-related illnesses.
e) **Greater Knowledge Retention and Application**: Mentally balanced students exhibit stronger memory, better comprehension, and an increased capacity to apply theoretical knowledge in practical or research contexts.
f) **Emergence of Innovative Ideas**: A supportive mental health environment cultivates creativity and divergent thinking, encouraging students to explore interdisciplinary ideas and entrepreneurial ventures.
g) **Higher Levels of Focus and Concentration**: A calm and stable mind enhances attentional control, allowing students to concentrate for longer periods and absorb complex concepts more effectively.

Structures Implemented

Higher education institutions are increasingly aligning their structures and policies with a holistic approach to student development, particularly emphasizing Mental Well-Being (MWB). Recognizing that academic success is deeply intertwined with emotional and psychological health, many universities and colleges—particularly in alignment with the United Nations Sustainable Development Goals (SDG-3: Good Health and Well-being) have initiated comprehensive frameworks that integrate well-being at the institutional, curricular, and co-curricular levels.

1. Sustainable Development Goal (SDG) Centres in Institutions

Many higher education institutions are establishing SDG centre's to drive academic, social, and environmental initiatives aligned with global goals. These centres often embed mental well-being as a thematic focus, organizing awareness campaigns, wellness seminars, and interdisciplinary research on psychological health. These hubs act as both advocacy and implementation arms for integrating MWB across campus life.

2. Centre for Well-being and Wellness

Dedicated Centres for Well-being have emerged as institutional bodies responsible for mental health governance. These centers usually offer a wide array of services ranging from psychological counselling to stress management workshops, peer support groups, and emergency mental health response units. These centers often work in collaboration with academic departments, student unions, and external mental health professionals to create a cohesive well-being ecosystem.

3. Mentor-Mentee Systems

Many universities now adopt structured mentor–mentee systems to provide consistent emotional and academic support throughout a student's academic journey. Each student is assigned a faculty mentor who monitors their academic progress, personal development, and psychosocial adjustment. This model promotes trust, early identification of distress, and the creation of safe spaces for dialogue.

4. Psychometric Testing from Admission to Graduation

Some forward-thinking institutions implement psychometric assessments starting from the admission phase, continuing at regular intervals throughout the academic lifecycle. These assessments evaluate personality traits, emotional stability, aptitude, and stress indicators. The data aids in tailoring personalized interventions, career counselling, and mental health strategies to student needs.

5. Counselling Cells

On-campus counselling cells, usually staffed by trained psychologists, offer confidential one-on-one sessions to students facing emotional, academic, or interpersonal difficulties. These cells often operate alongside faculty referrals and self-initiated student visits, and are integral to crisis management, suicide prevention, and wellness promotion.

6. Specialized Support in Hostels

Recognizing that residential stress contributes significantly to mental strain, several institutions have introduced special seating spaces within hostels, managed by psychologists and wellness crafters. These areas provide non-clinical, informal avenues for students to express concerns, decompress, and engage in therapeutic conversations without stigma or fear.

7. One-to-One Coaching and Counselling

In addition to group workshops, individualized coaching sessions have gained popularity. These are often customized around issues such as time management, self-esteem, conflict resolution, and emotional regulation. Personal counselling helps students navigate complex internal and external challenges with guided psychological tools.

8. Mindfulness, Meditation, and Rewirement Strategies

Mindfulness-based interventions have shown empirical success in reducing anxiety, enhancing focus, and promoting emotional balance. Institutions conduct guided meditation sessions, rewirement exercises (such as journaling, gratitude practices, reflective thinking), and mindful breathing as part of regular student development programs. These are integrated into orientation weeks, examination stress-relief initiatives, and hostel routines. A study by Reetha and Kamble (2025) examined how college students resilience, forgiveness and compassion are affected by gratitude journaling. 180 undergraduate students aged 18 to 24 years participated in randomized controlled experiment. The control group did not receive any intervention, whereas the experimental group was asked to write down three things for which they were thankful for every day. Assessments were done before and after 8 week intervention and the experimental group showed 15% increase in altruism, 12% increase in forgiveness and 20% increase in resilience. The researchers, thus, highlights the potential of journaling as an affordable, useful intervention to promote positive psychological outcomes in educational settings, providing insightful information for mental health programs and therapies catered to college students needs.

9. Yoga and Holistic Practices

Yoga, a traditional Indian practice rooted in mental and physical discipline, has been institutionalized in many universities as part of holistic well-being programs. Regular yoga sessions improve students' sleep quality, emotional stability, and physical energy. Some institutions incorporate yoga in curriculum through electives, or offer certified wellness programs for credit.

CURRICULAR REFORMS: INTEGRATION OF EMERGING SUBJECTS

Across global higher education, and particularly within the Indian context, universities are recognising that academic achievement alone is no longer sufficient to prepare young adults for the pressures of modern life. The dramatic rise in stress, anxiety, burnout, and emotional fatigue among students has compelled institutions to reconsider what is taught and how it is taught. Consequently, curricular reforms now focus on integrating emerging subjects that support emotional intelligence, psychological resilience, value-based learning, and holistic well-being. This shift reflects a wider understanding that student success depends not only on cognitive performance but also on emotional stability, social competencies, and mental balance. By embedding such subjects into structured credit-bearing programs, institutions strengthen the ecosystem of care and counselling and enable preventive mental health practices within the academic environment.

One pivotal inclusion in this reform movement is Workplace Psychology, a field that bridges academic learning with real-world professional functioning. As young graduates enter increasingly volatile and competitive job markets, they face complexities related to interpersonal collaboration, organisational culture, conflict management, and work–life balance. Research in occupational psychology highlights that poor emotional regulation and unmanaged stress can impede decision-making, motivation, and career growth (Schaufeli, 2017; Bakker & Demerouti, 2018). By familiarising students with behavioural dynamics, personality influences, motivation theories, and coping skills, Workplace Psychology enhances their adaptability and prepares them for organisational realities. It also fosters confidence in communication, problem-solving, negotiation, and teamwork—all of which are essential workplace competencies.

Another transformative step in curriculum redesign is the introduction of Science of Well-being and Science of Happiness courses. Rooted in positive psychology, these subjects draw from the foundational work of scholars whose research has consistently shown that practices like gratitude, mindfulness, optimism, and strengths-based engagement contribute to improved mental health outcomes and greater life satisfaction. When universities formalise these courses as credit-bearing requirements, they strengthen student motivation to internalize the teachings rather than treating them as optional add-ons. These courses encourage learners to reflect on their values, practice emotional regulation, nurture social relationships, and develop purpose-driven mindsets—all of which significantly influence mental well-being and academic performance. Studies among Indian university students have shown that structured well-being instruction improves self-esteem, resilience, and academic engagement (Kumar & Tankha, 2021).

A particularly impactful initiative within Indian higher education is the introduction of University Yoga and Human Values (UYH) courses. These modules integrate yogic practices, meditation, reflective writing, ethical reasoning, and experiential activities that cultivate self-awareness and inner equilibrium. Research in contemplative practices indicates that consistent engagement with yoga and meditation helps in reducing perceived stress, improving attention, regulating emotions, and enhancing overall well-being (Telles et al., 2011a). When UYH courses are made mandatory, they signal that emotional health and ethical grounding are integral to the academic mission rather than peripheral interests. These courses also strengthen the link between ancient Indian knowledge systems and contemporary mental health needs, offering students culturally relevant and scientifically validated techniques for personal growth.

Collectively, these curricular developments signal a paradigm shift in higher education—moving from content-heavy, examination-driven learning toward student-centred, holistic education that recognises the interconnectedness of mental, emotional, and academic dimensions. Such reforms complement institutional counselling services, functioning as preventive practices that help reduce psychological strain, enhance coping skills, and promote a culture of well-being across university campuses.

Innovative Practices in Higher Education across Public and Private Universities

Beyond curricular reforms, universities are implementing a range of innovative practices to strengthen emotional care and mental health support. These initiatives highlight growing recognition that student well-being is a shared responsibility across institutional levels—teachers, families, counsellors, peer groups, and external organisations. Many of these practices also align with global sustainability commitments under the Sustainable Development Goals (SDGs), particularly SDG 3 (Good Health and Well-being) and SDG 4 (Quality Education).

1. Teacher–Student–Parent Engagement Models

Several universities have developed structured triangular engagement models that integrate regular communication between teachers, students, and parents. These models typically include scheduled mentoring meetings, academic reviews, parental orientation programs, and early-warning mechanisms for students showing signs of emotional or academic distress. Research indicates that supportive communication between home and institution enhances academic motivation and emotional security among students. Such collaborative relationships ensure that academic challenges are contextualised within familial and emotional realities, allowing for timely interventions. The engagement model also fosters trust, transparency, and a sense of shared accountability for student well-being.

SDG Alignment: SDG 4 – Quality Education; SDG 3 – Good Health and Well-being

2. Counselling and Psychological Support Services

Universities across India are investing substantially in strengthening psychological services. Professional counselling cells now provide comprehensive emotional support that includes personal counselling, psychological assessments, crisis intervention, academic guidance, and career counselling. Many institutions follow a "continuum of care" model where support begins at admission and continues through graduation. Research from higher-education mental health studies confirms that accessible counselling services reduce student stress, improve coping capacities, and enhance academic persistence (Hunt & Eisenberg, 2010; Beiter et al., 2015). The presence of trained psychologists normalises help-seeking behaviour and reduces stigma associated with mental health concerns. Some campuses also employ peer counsellors who extend support within informal student networks.

SDG Alignment: SDG 3 – Good Health and Well-being

3. Use of Psychological Mantras and Cognitive Wellness Tools

A growing number of Indian universities are integrating mantra-based interventions, affirmations, and cognitive wellness tools inspired by both psychological and indigenous knowledge systems. These interventions combine insights from cognitive-behavioural strategies and traditional meditative sound practices. A pilot study conducted on 52 students from STEAM disciplines demonstrated significant emotional improvements when participants listened to self-selected mantras for 40 minutes daily over 60 days (Lolla, 2018). Post-intervention scores indicated reductions in fear, anger, irritation, and nervousness, and improvements in happiness, interest in life, and general mood. Findings of this nature are consistent with neuroscientific research on sound-based meditation, which shows that repetitive auditory stimuli can influence autonomic regulation, attention, and emotional stability (Telles et al., 2011b). Incorporating such practices as part of structured wellness programs offers students easily adoptable techniques that enhance focus, reduce anxiety, and support mental clarity.

SDG Alignment: SDG 3 – Good Health and Well-being

4. Establishment of Art of Living and Value-Based Wellness Centres

Many universities have collaborated with welfare organisations such as the Art of Living Foundation to create value-based wellness centres on campus. These centres provide programs involving mindfulness, yogic breathing techniques, relaxation practices, self-reflection, and group activities. Sudarshan Kriya Yoga (SKY), a rhythmic breathing protocol, has been extensively studied and found to improve emotional balance, psychological resilience, and cognitive functioning (Zope & Zope, 2013). Studies indicate that SKY enhances autonomic regulation, increases positive affect, and reduces stress hormones.

A study by Chauhan (2015) on the Youth Empowerment Seminar (YES+) program reported significant improvements across multiple attributes, including stress management, emotional well-being, confidence, lifestyle awareness, and interpersonal communication. Students experiencing such interventions often report improved self-esteem, better emotional control, and enhanced ability to form supportive social networks. These outcomes are vital for both personal well-being and professional readiness.

SDG Alignment: SDG 3 – Good Health and Well-being; SDG 4 – Quality Education

5. Spiritual Integration through Brahma Kumaris (Om Shanti Centres)

A number of universities have partnered with spiritual organisations such as the Brahma Kumaris to establish Om Shanti Centres on campus. These centres provide guided meditation, reflective dialogue, and sessions on values such as peace, compassion, and ethical living. Spiritual education, when delivered in a non-sectarian manner, helps students cultivate emotional grounding, moral sensitivity, and inner calm. Studies have shown that meditation-based spiritual practices enhance clarity of thought, reduce anxiety, and improve moral reasoning (Worthington & Aten, 2009). Such activities contribute to a peaceful campus culture where students feel supported in their personal and emotional journeys.

SDG Alignment: SDG 3 – Good Health and Well-being; SDG 4 – Quality Education

The reforms and innovations outlined above reflect a significant transformation in higher education, where academic institutions recognize that intellectual development cannot be separated from emotional and psychological well-being. By integrating subjects such as Workplace Psychology, Science of Happiness, and Human Values, universities are enriching academic curricula with life-oriented knowledge. Simultaneously, the adoption of structured counselling services, mantra-based interventions, mindfulness programs, and spiritual wellness centres strengthens support systems that address student needs holistically.

Together, these initiatives represent a shift toward a compassionate, student-centred educational model—one that equips graduates not only for global competitiveness but also for balanced living, responsible citizenship, and lifelong well-being.

Integration of Emerging Subjects for Mental Well-being in Indian Universities

Table 3. Presents a consolidated overview of the universities/institutions that have introduced specialized courses aimed at enhancing student well-being. The Table outlines the course introduced, the nature of the course, the primary focus area and highlights the impact on student's well being.

University/Institution	*Course Introduced*	*Nature of Course*	*Focus Area*	*Impact on Student Well-being*
University of Delhi	Science of Happiness	Credit-based elective	Positive psychology, self-awareness	Enhances optimism, emotional resilience
IIT Kharagpur	Workplace Psychology	UG/PG elective	Organizational behavior, stress management	Prepares students for real-world stress and work dynamics
Banaras Hindu University (BHU)	Human Values & Spiritual Well-being	Mandatory UG foundation	Ethics, mindfulness, values	Builds inner stability and reflective thinking
OP Jindal Global University	Science of Well-being	Interdisciplinary elective	Purpose, gratitude, emotional balance	Improves emotional regulation and life satisfaction
IIT Madras	Wellness and Human Values	Credit-based UG module	Yoga, values, mental peace	Promotes calmness and preventive mental health care
Amity University	Emotional Intelligence and Workplace Psychology	Core & elective options	Self-regulation, motivation, empathy	Strengthens peer relationships and academic performance
Lovely Professional University (LPU)	Happiness and Life Skills	Mandatory life skill course	Positive thinking, mindfulness	Reduces anxiety and enhances engagement
SRM University	Yoga & Human Excellence (UYH)	Foundation course	Holistic wellness, meditation	Encourages balance between academic and personal life

continued on following page

Table 3. Continued

University/Institution	*Course Introduced*	*Nature of Course*	*Focus Area*	*Impact on Student Well-being*
Savitribai Phule Pune University	Value Education & Personality Development	UG course	Self-growth, ethics, community values	Improves self-esteem and social connectedness
Chandigarh University Mohali	Workplace Psychology	PG Course	Organizational behaviour, stress management	Prepares students for real-world stress and work dynamics

Source – websites of Institutions

Limitation

While the chapter offers valuable insights into mental health and counseling practices in Indian higher education, several limitations must be acknowledged. The study is primarily conceptual and grounded in existing literature; thus, it lacks empirical validation through field data or large-scale surveys. Furthermore, the heterogeneity among educational institutions in terms of infrastructure, student demographics, and policy implementation limits the generalizability of the proposed interventions. The focus is largely on higher education contexts, and the mental health needs of school-level students and non-traditional learners are not explored in depth. Additionally, the rapidly evolving digital landscape and its implications for student well-being may require on-going investigation beyond the scope of this chapter.

Future Recommendations

Higher education institutions must keep moving forward towards comprehensive, preventive and inclusive frameworks for mental health support in the future. Establishing sustainable well-being ecosystems that incorporate counseling, emotional literacy and mental health awareness into all facets of academic life must be a top priority for universities. The systemic integration of psychological well-being into curricula, pedagogy and policy rather than considering it as a supplementary service, is the key to future of mental health promotion in education. To provide, professors and staff with skills they need to recognize early indicators of distress, interact with students in an empathic manner, and direct them to the right services, institutions should fund capacity building initiatives.

The next stage of implementation will heavily rely on digital innovations. The creation of online self-assessment tools, mental health applications and AI based counseling tools has potential to democratize access to psychological care, especially for students in underserved or remote areas. To guarantee ethical use, secrecy and emotional authenticity, these technologies must properly combine with human centered methodologies. Creating hybrid models, which combine digital treatments within person counseling can optimize reach and personalization while preserving the therapeutic alliance necessary for quality therapy.

Universities also need to develop a data driven evaluation culture in order to gauge the success of mental health programs. Measurable insights into gaps and progress can be obtained through institutional well-being indicators, student feedback systems and longitudinal research. To share best practices and jointly create regionally adaptable frameworks, partnerships, between national mental health authorities, higher education institutions and international organizations like UNESCO and WHO should be reinforced.

Future policy initiatives should concentrate on integrating mental health as a key performance metric for institutional ranking and certification schemes. This would promote innovation in preventive education in addition to improving institutional accountability. In order to incorporate peer mentoring, wellness advocacy and extra circular involvement into regular governance, universities might also set up student- led mental health councils. Especially in collectivist nations where mental health is still taboo, such participatory approaches would normalize asking for help and eliminate stigma.

Finally, given that student's experience of distress are influenced by a variety of contextual circumstances, future study must look at the interconnectedness of mental health with gender, socio economic position and digital exposure. More comprehensives and long lasting answers may be found by investigating evidence based culturally grounded programs that combine contemporary psychology with indigenous traditions like yoga, mindfulness and compassion based education. Long term, integrating resilience training, emotional intelligence and self-awareness, into the educational process will help create graduates who are not just intellectually strong but also emotionally stable, socially conscious and psychologically robust.

CONCLUSION

The promotion of mental health and counselling in educational settings is fundamental to fostering holistic student development. As academic demands, socio-economic pressures, and digital influences continue to shape student experiences, institutions must evolve in their approach to psychological care. This chapter underscores the need for a systemic, empathetic, and student-centred mental health framework that transcends remedial care and embraces proactive well-being strategies. Aligned with the objectives of national policies such as NEP 2020 and aligned with global sustainable development goals (SDG 3), empowering students through care is both a moral and strategic imperative. Embedding mental health into the core mission of education can transform learning environments into nurturing ecosystems that support resilience, purpose, and lifelong well-being.

REFERENCES

Auerbach, R. P., Mortier, P., Bruffaerts, R., Alonso, J., Benjet, C., Cuijpers, P., & Kessler, R. C. (2020). WHO World Mental Health Surveys International College Student Project: Prevalence and distribution of mental disorders. *Journal of Abnormal Psychology*, *129*(1), 97–110. DOI: 10.1037/abn0000362 PMID: 30211576

Bourion-Bédès, S., Tarquinio, C., Batt, M., Tarquinio, P., Lebreuilly, R., Sorsana, C., & Baumann, C. (2021). Psychological impact of the COVID-19 crisis on French university students: Risk and protective factors. *European Journal of Health Psychology*, *28*(2), 63–72. DOI: 10.1027/2512-8442/a000058

Chauhan, S.Sweta Sharadkumar Chauhan. (2015). Effectiveness of the Art of Living YES+ Programme on College Students. *International Journal of Indian Psychology*, *2*(4). Advance online publication. DOI: 10.25215/0204.070

Duraku, Z. H., Davis, H., Arënliu, A., Uka, F., & Behluli, V. (2024). *Overcoming mental health challenges in higher education: A narrative review*. Frontiers in Psychology. onlinelibrary.wiley.com±2frontiersin.org±2pubmed.ncbi.nlm.nih.gov±2arxiv.orgfrontiersin.orgnews-medical.net±5bristol.ac.uk±5thetimes.co.uk±-5pubmed.ncbi.nlm.nih.gov

Eisenberg, D., Gollust, S. E., Golberstein, E., & Hefner, J. L. (2007). Prevalence and correlates of depression, anxiety, and suicidality among university students. *The American Journal of Orthopsychiatry*, *77*(4), 534–542. DOI: 10.1037/0002-9432.77.4.534 PMID: 18194033

Gallagher, R. P. (2014). *National survey of college counseling centers 2014*. International Association of Counseling Services.

Gander, F., ... (2023). *The Effects of an Online Positive Psychology Course on Happiness, Health, and Well-Being. Psychol Well-Being*, as described in PubMed pubmed.ncbi.nlm.nih.gov

Gupta, N., & Ahuja, K. (2021). Effectiveness and perceptions of online counseling services among Indian university students during COVID-19: A mixed-methods study. *Journal of Psychosomatic Research*, *16*(2), 207–218. DOI: 10.32381/JPR.2021.16.02.9

Hobbs, C., Jelbert, S., Santos, L. R., & Hood, B. (2024). Long-term analysis of a psychoeducational course on university students' mental well-being. *Higher Education*, *2*(6), 2093–2105. bristol.ac.uk. DOI: 10.1007/s10734-024-01202-4

Hunt, J., & Eisenberg, D. (2010). Mental health problems and help-seeking behavior among college students. *The Journal of Adolescent Health*, *46*(1), 3–10. DOI: 10.1016/j.jadohealth.2009.08.008 PMID: 20123251

Kessler, R. C., Berglund, P., Demler, O., Jin, R., Merikangas, K. R., & Walters, E. E. (2005). Lifetime prevalence and age-of-onset distributions of DSM-IV disorders in the National Comorbidity Survey Replication. *Archives of General Psychiatry*, *62*(6), 593–602. DOI: 10.1001/archpsyc.62.6.593 PMID: 15939837

Kumar, M., & Sharma, A. (2020). Effectiveness of peer support counseling in Indian higher education: A psychological well-being perspective. *Asian Journal of Psychiatry*, *54*, 102203. DOI: 10.1016/j.ajp.2020.102203

Kumar, V. V., & Tankha, G. (2021). Nurturing spiritual intelligence in the classroom. In *Leading schools with social, emotional, and academic development (SEAD)* (pp. 187-201). IGI Global. DOI: 10.4018/978-1-7998-6728-9.ch010

Lolla, A. (2018). Mantras help the general psychological well-being of college students: A pilot study. *Journal of Religion and Health*, *57*(1), 110–119. DOI: 10.1007/s10943-017-0371-7 PMID: 28271341

Mehra, A., & Kapoor, R. (2021). Online mental health support for college students during COVID-19: A qualitative study. *Journal of Affective Disorders*, *284*, 42–49. DOI: 10.1016/j.jad.2021.02.012

Ministry of Education. (2021). *Manodarpan – Psychosocial support for mental health and well-being of students*. Government of India. https://manodarpan.education.gov.in/

Ministry of Human Resource Development, Government of India. (n.d.). *National Education Policy 2020*. https://www.education.gov.in/sites/upload_files/mhrd/files/NEP_Final_English_0.pdf

Naslund, J. A., Aschbrenner, K. A., Araya, R., Marsch, L. A., Unützer, J., Patel, V., & Bartels, S. J. (2022). Digital technology for treating and preventing mental disorders in low-income and middle-income countries: A narrative review of the literature. *The Lancet. Psychiatry*, *9*(2), 123–136. DOI: 10.1016/S2215-0366(21)00301-1 PMID: 28433615

Neuroscience News. (2024, March 11). *Happiness Takes Practice - Neuroscience News*. Neuroscience News. https://neurosciencenews.com/happiness-practice-25736/?utm_source=chatgpt.com

OECD. (2021). *The impact of COVID-19 on student well-being*.

Olsson, T. M., Broberg, M., Frisk, S., Wackenhut, A. F., Kjellin, D., Gullstrand, S., Rost, S., & Skoog, T. (2024). Health-promoting learning environments in higher education: A scoping review of structural interventions to protect student mental health. *European Journal of Education*, *59*(4), e12772. DOI: 10.1111/ejed.12772

Patel, D., & Joshi, V. (2023). Integrated counseling and academic guidance services in Indian universities: An outcome-based evaluation. *International Journal of Educational Development*, *98*, 102734. DOI: 10.1016/j.ijedudev.2023.102734

Patel, V., Saxena, S., Lund, C., Thornicroft, G., Baingana, F., Bolton, P., Chisholm, D., Collins, P. Y., Cooper, J. L., Eaton, J., Herrman, H., Herzallah, M. M., Huang, Y., Jordans, M. J. D., Kleinman, A., Medina-Mora, M. E., Morgan, E., Niaz, U., Omigbodun, O., & UnÜtzer, J. Ü. (2018). The Lancet Commission on global mental health and sustainable development. *Lancet*, *392*(10157), 1553–1598. DOI: 10.1016/S0140-6736(18)31612-X PMID: 30314863

Rathakrishnan, B., Hamzah, H. M., & Arokiasamy, L. (2022). Resilience training to improve mental well-being among university students: A Malaysian perspective. *International Journal of Environmental Research and Public Health*, *19*(17), 10751. DOI: 10.3390/ijerph191710751 PMID: 36078463

Reddy, R. (2020). Barriers to mental health service utilization in Indian college students: A cultural and systemic review. *The International Journal of Social Psychiatry*, *66*(5), 457–465. DOI: 10.1177/0020764020931844

Reetha, V., & Kamble, S. V. (2025). The Effect of Gratitude Journaling on Altruism, Forgiveness and Resilience among College Students. *International Journal of Indian Psychology*, *13*(1).

Rezapour, M., & Elmshaeuser, S. K. (2022). *AI-based analysis of COVID-19 impact on student mental health.* ArXiv frontiersin.org+2arxiv.org+2pubmed.ncbi.nlm.nih.gov+2

Sharma, S., & Iyer, P. (2018). Group counseling as a strategy to reduce academic stress among undergraduates. *Journal of College Student Psychotherapy*, *32*(4), 303–317. DOI: 10.1080/87568225.2018.1438477

Singh, R., Menon, V., & Arora, P. (2021). Efficacy of mobile apps in managing student anxiety and depression: A review of randomized controlled trials. *Computers in Human Behavior*, *122*, 106834. DOI: 10.1016/j.chb.2021.106834

Subramaniam, S., Tan, J. Y., & Lim, R. B. (2023). Institutional preparedness in fostering mental well-being: Case studies from Asian higher education. *Asia Pacific Education Review*, *24*(1), 1–15. DOI: 10.1007/s12564-023-09782-4

Telles, S., Maharana, K., Balrana, B., & Balkrishna, A. (2011A). Effects of high-frequency yoga breathing called kapalabhati compared with breath awareness on the degree of optical illusion perceived. *Perceptual and Motor Skills, 112*(3), 981–990. DOI: 10.2466/02.20.22.PMS.112.3.981-990 PMID: 21853784

Telles, S., Sharma, S. K., & Balkrishna, A. (2011B). Blood pressure and heart rate variability during yoga-based alternate nostril breathing. *Journal of Alternative and Complementary Medicine (New York, N.Y.), 17*(2), 109–117. DOI: 10.1089/acm.2010.0140 PMID: 21303197

Thomas, R., & George, L. (2019). Mental health literacy and help-seeking behavior among youth: A meta-analytical study. *Children and Youth Services Review, 100*, 104–112. DOI: 10.1016/j.childyouth.2019.02.035

UNESCO International Institute for Higher Education in Latin America and the Caribbean et al. (2024). *Supporting Student Mental Health and Well-being in Higher Education*, UNESCO: United Nations Educational, Scientific and Cultural Organisation. Venezuela (Bolivarian Republic of). Retrieved from https://coilink.org/20.500.12592/40ycqb3 on 21 Nov 2025. COI: 20.500.12592/40ycqb3.

United Nations. (2015). *Transforming our world: The 2030 Agenda for Sustainable Development*. https://sdgs.un.org/2030agenda

Verger, P., Combes, J. B., Kovess-Masfety, V., Choquet, M., Guagliardo, V., Rouillon, F., & Peretti-Watel, P. (2009). Psychological distress in first year university students: Socioeconomic and academic stressors, mastery and social support in young men and women. *Social Psychiatry and Psychiatric Epidemiology, 44*(8), 643–650. DOI: 10.1007/s00127-008-0486-y PMID: 19096741

Verma, S., Nair, A., & Das, M. (2022). Trauma-informed educational practices and student well-being: Evidence from higher education settings. *Teaching and Teacher Education, 112*, 103638. DOI: 10.1016/j.tate.2022.103638

Vij, R., & Narula, A. (2026). Fostering Effective Feedback and Mental Well-Being: Overcoming Challenges in Digital Education. In *Digital Tools and Platforms for Effective and Personalized Learning* (pp. 437-462). IGI Global Scientific Publishing. DOI: 10.4018/979-8-3373-6013-3.ch016

Wang, C., Pan, R., Wan, X., Tan, Y., Xu, L., Ho, C. S., & Ho, R. C. (2020). Immediate psychological responses and associated factors during the initial stage of the COVID-19 epidemic among the general population in China. *International Journal of Environmental Research and Public Health, 17*(5), 1729. DOI: 10.3390/ijerph17051729 PMID: 32155789

Worthington, E. L., & Aten, J. D. (2009). Psychotherapy with religious and spiritual clients: An introduction. *Journal of Clinical Psychology*, *65*(2), 123–130. DOI: 10.1002/jclp.20561 PMID: 19090533

Zope, S. A., & Zope, R. A. (2013). Sudarshan kriya yoga: Breathing for health. *International Journal of Yoga*, *6*(1), 4–10. DOI: 10.4103/0973-6131.105935 PMID: 23440614

Chapter 3

Role of Mental Health Support in Digital Education in the Current Scenario

Deepa Sharma
https://orcid.org/0000-0003-4374-917X
Maharishi Markandeshwar University, India

Guarav Kumar
Maharishi Markandeshwar University, India

ABSTRACT

During the COVID-19 pandemic, the world witnessed the crucial role of digital media and the internet. This period marked a global digital revolution, with a significant emphasis on digital education facilitated through various online platforms. Students shifted from books to Mobile or Laptop because online education offers accessibility and flexibility but as well as it brings forth a range of psychological challenges for students and educators alike. It also increased screen time, lack of physical interaction, academic pressure, and isolation have contributed to rising cases of anxiety, depression, burnout, and digital fatigue among learners and instructors. In this context, mental health support has emerged as a critical component of effective and sustainable digital education systems.

DOI: 10.4018/979-8-3373-5007-3.ch003

1. INTRODUCTION AND BACKGROUND

The COVID-19 pandemic, which revealed deficiencies in traditional services, has accelerated the growing demand for student mental healthcare, which is the background of mental health assistance in digital education. In order to meet the increasing demand and restricted access, digital mental health treatments (DMHIs) such as apps, AI-powered tools, and virtual therapy were developed. DMHIs offer advantages including flexibility, accessibility, and fewer stigmas. Despite the potential of digital tools, there are still issues to be resolved, such as guaranteeing digital literacy, offering sufficient human engagement, and developing precise ethical standards for AI-driven solutions.

1.1. Current State of Mental Health in Today's Era

We discuss the prevalence of mental health conditions such as schizophrenia, bipolar disorder, anxiety and depression given the complexity of the current mental health care system. The difficulties are numerous, ranging from long wait times and limited access to specialists in remote locations to exorbitant fees that cause financial constraints. We also discuss the growing need for easily accessible, efficient and stigma-free mental health treatment, especially among younger populations, highlighting the revolutionary role of digital technology in changing the way mental health care is delivered. Below recognizing the mental health issues

a. **Worldwide Mental Health Emergency**: We examine the personal toll that mental health issues have on people as well as the enormous financial costs associated with missed productivity and medical bills as we delve into the tremendous burden of mental health diseases around the world. Diverse communities are impacted by the range of mental health illnesses, which include PTSD, OCD, substance addiction issues, anxiety disorders, and mood disorders. It becomes clear that scalable, affordable solutions are required to address the growing need for mental health support.
b. **Obstacles to Mental Health Services:** We now focus on the obstacles that prevent people from receiving mental health care. The difficulties people encounter in obtaining prompt diagnosis and treatment are exacerbated by stigma, restricted service access in rural areas, financial limitations, and a lack of mental health experts.
c. **Examining Mental Health Disorder Prevalence:** We shed light on the prevalence of disorders like schizophrenia, bipolar disorder, anxiety, and depression within the complex framework of the contemporary mental healthcare system. We recognize the enormous obstacles that overshadow people in need, including

lengthy wait times, limited specialist availability in rural areas, and financial obstacles. The growing need for easily available, effective, and de-stigmatized mental health treatments, especially among younger populations, highlights the critical role of digital technologies in changing the direction of mental health care delivery.

1.2. Factors Influencing the Demand for Online Mental Health Assistance

A rise in demand Traditional, in-person programs are frequently unable to fulfill the increased need for mental health help, which is needed by an increasing number of students.

a. **COVID-19 outbreak:** Young people's mental health crises was brought to light and made worse by the pandemic, necessitating the development of alternative forms of support when in-person services were interrupted.
b. **Limitations of traditional services:** It is challenging for current mental health programs to adequately serve all kids due to issues like staffing shortages, a lack of resources, and lengthy waiting lists.
c. **Demographics of students**: Support that is both accessible and customized to meet the requirements of students has become necessary due to the growing diversity of pupils and the complexity of contemporary living.

1.3. The Application of Digital Education to Mental Health

1. **Digital mental health interventions:** AI-powered chatbots, online platforms, and mental health apps are just a few of the many resources that are now accessible.
2. **Virtual and teletherapy:** Thanks to technology, experts can conduct virtual counseling sessions via audio or video chats.
3. **Online activities and resources**: Platforms offer a plethora of information, stress-relieving activities, and psychological testing instruments. In order to give students easily accessible, stigma-free, and scalable mental health resources, mental health assistance in digital education entails incorporating digital tools like apps, telemedicine, and online platforms into educational institutions. By providing treatments for anxiety and despair, encouraging wellbeing, and expanding access to support via well-known technologies, these strategies can address the escalating mental health problem among youth. The possibility for individualized, real-time help and early diagnosis makes it a promising area for the future of education, despite issues with user engagement, digital literacy, and the efficacy of unregulated apps.

2. INTRODUCTION: DIGITAL TRANSFORMATION IN EDUCATION POST-COVID-19

The COVID-19 pandemic reshaped education worldwide, pushing schools and universities to embrace digital learning almost overnight. As lockdowns closed classrooms, institutions turned to online platforms to keep education going. Tools like Zoom, Google Classroom, Microsoft Teams, and various learning management systems became essential, enabling remote classes, virtual tests, and group projects. This shift turned digital education from a supporting tool into the main way students learned, revealing both its possibilities and its challenges.

While technology enabled learning to continue, it also highlighted inequalities in access to devices, reliable internet, and digital skills. Many students and educators struggled with these gaps, which have shaped ongoing efforts to improve educational systems. Now, in the post-COVID era, there's a chance to rethink education by combining the best of in-person and online learning. This hybrid approach can create more flexible, inclusive systems, but it must address key issues like ensuring equal access, keeping students engaged, and supporting mental health. By learning from the pandemic's challenges, educators and policymakers can build a stronger, more adaptable education system that meets the needs of all learners in a rapidly changing world.

2.1 Rise of Online and Hybrid Learning Models

The COVID-19 pandemic transformed education by accelerating the shift to online and hybrid learning models. When classrooms closed, schools and universities worldwide turned to digital platforms to keep learning alive. This rapid change not only ensured education continued during the crisis but also opened the door to more adaptable and innovative teaching methods that are shaping the future (Borenstein et al., 2009).

Online learning gave students the freedom to access lessons, assignments, and resources anytime, anywhere. Tools like video conferencing, digital whiteboards, and cloud-based systems created interactive spaces that mimicked traditional classrooms. Meanwhile, hybrid learning blending in-person and online elements emerged as a practical solution. It combines the personal connection of face-to-face teaching with the flexibility of digital tools, offering a balanced approach that suits diverse needs.

These models have reshaped education in exciting ways. Blended environments allow students to learn at their own pace, fostering independence and engagement through multimedia resources. The flipped classroom approach, where students study materials online before diving into discussions or hands-on activities in class, has gained popularity. This shift has redefined roles: teachers now act more as guides, while students take greater responsibility for their learning.

However, these advancements come with challenges. Not all students have access to reliable internet, devices, or the skills needed to thrive in digital settings. Teachers, too, need training to effectively use these tools. As education evolves, addressing these gaps is crucial to ensure fairness and inclusion. Looking ahead, online and hybrid learning are here to stay, offering flexibility and innovation. By investing in technology, infrastructure, and training, education systems can create a more equitable and dynamic learning experience for all in the post-pandemic world.

2.1.1. Significance of Hybrid Education

The advantages of both online and traditional classroom instruction are seamlessly combined in hybrid or blended learning, which gives students more freedom, better communication, and more control.

1. **Increasing Student Self-Sufficiency:** Students can advance through their coursework at their own pace thanks to blended learning. Students can study ideas as needed and move forward when they feel ready since they have access to course materials and tools. In addition to encouraging self-directed learning, this autonomy develops critical abilities including self-control, independence, and problem-solving skills.
2. **Improved Interaction:** Teachers, students, and parents can communicate effectively in hybrid learning contexts. Teachers can effectively communicate updates, assignments, and course material to students and parents by using features like discussion boards and announcement tools within a Learning Management System (LMS). Students can ask classmates and teachers for clarification and guidance, and they gain from group learning opportunities. Additionally, parents learn about their child's intellectual development and classroom activities, which promotes a cooperative relationship between the home and the school.
3. **Tracking and Improving Involvement:** Teachers can efficiently monitor student involvement and evaluate learning results by utilizing educational technology tools. Teachers can monitor the use of instructional tools, identify at-risk students, and evaluate the quality of assessments by utilizing reporting features. These insights enable educators to make required interventions, customize lessons, and design stimulating learning opportunities based on the requirements of specific students.
4. **Increasing Inclusivity and Accessibility:** By utilizing technology to remove obstacles to learning, hybrid learning encourages accessibility and diversity. Students with a variety of learning requirements, including those who need

assistance equipment, can access course materials more easily thanks to digital tools and features. Additionally, students can access content at any time and from any location because to blended learning's flexibility, which accommodates different learning styles and lifestyles.

5. **Enhanced access:** Provides assistance to students who would not have access to regular programs by removing geographical restrictions.
6. **Decreased stigma:** Provides students with a more discreet and private means of seeking assistance, which may lessen the stigma attached to mental health problems.
7. **Cost-effectiveness:** When compared to conventional, in-person mental health-care, this option may be more scalable and economical.
8. **Personalized support:** Depending on a person's requirements and actions, digital technologies can provide customized interventions and guidance.
9. **Early detection:** Wearable technology and ongoing monitoring can identify possible issues before they become emergencies, enabling prompt response.

2.1.2. Important elements of digital education's mental health support

a. **Digital platforms:** Using mobile and web-based platforms to provide mental health services. Applications specifically made to help with memory, cognitive abilities, or overall mental health is known as mental health apps.
b. **Telehealth services**: Online treatment and telepsychiatry systems that make specialists accessible without the need for in-person appointments.
c. **Social media and online forums:** Using online peer support groups to provide a feeling of community and shared experience, as well as social media to spread health information.
d. **AI-powered tools:** By analyzing user behavior via smart phone sensors or typing patterns, artificial intelligence can identify changes in mental health and facilitate early intervention.
e. Wearable technology: Using smart watches and fitness trackers to track important health indicators and promote healthy habits.

2.1.3. Future role of Hybrid Learning in Education's sector:

The need for institutions and organizations to quickly adjust to disruptions and changes has been highlighted by recent occurrences during the past several years. Teachers and students can easily switch between several learning ways without sacrificing quality or advancement thanks to hybrid learning models, which have emerged as robust and successful solutions. In the future, hybrid learning provides students with priceless experience navigating online environments a skill set that is becoming more and more important in today's workplace. Furthermore, hybrid techniques work well with new paradigms in education, such as competency-based education and active learning, which emphasize real-world interaction with the subject matter and promote the development of profound, long-lasting knowledge and skills. In these models, flexibility is crucial because it allows teachers to customize learning routes to each student's needs and lets students engage with the material at their own pace and in ways that best fit their learning preferences.

2.2 Technological Innovations and EdTech Integration

The shift to digital education has been fuelled by fast-evolving technology and the rise of educational technology (EdTech) tools, transforming how learning happens in the post-COVID world. Beyond serving as a temporary fix during the pandemic, these innovations have become core to modern teaching methods, making education more flexible and engaging (Cejudo et al., 2019).

Platforms like Moodle, Google Classroom, and Canvas have revolutionized how educators deliver lessons, manage assignments, and provide feedback. These Learning Management Systems (LMS) organize course materials, track student progress, and offer interactive features that keep learners engaged. Video conferencing tools such as Zoom, Microsoft Teams, and Webex have made real-time interaction possible, enabling virtual discussions and group work that bring remote classrooms to life.

Artificial Intelligence (AI) is reshaping education by tailoring learning to individual needs. AI tools analyze student performance to pinpoint weaknesses and suggest personalized resources or exercises. Adaptive platforms adjust lesson difficulty and pace, helping students understand and retain information better. AI-powered chatbots and virtual tutors provide round-the-clock support, answering questions about coursework or school processes.

Emerging technologies like gamification, Augmented Reality (AR), and Virtual Reality (VR) are making learning more immersive. These tools turn complex topics—like science or geography—into interactive experiences, sparking curiosity and deepening understanding. They're especially valuable in hands-on fields like vocational training.

EdTech also empowers teachers with data to fine-tune their methods, improving outcomes. However, challenges like unequal access to technology, concerns about data privacy, and the need for ongoing teacher training must be addressed. As education moves forward, integrating these tools thoughtfully and inclusively will ensure all students can benefit from a richer, more accessible learning experience. (Charbonnier et al., 2021)

2.3 Challenges of Accessibility and Digital Divide

The move to digital education has opened new doors for learning, but it has also highlighted and deepened existing inequalities, especially around access and inclusion. The rapid shift to online and hybrid learning during and after the COVID-19 pandemic put a spotlight on the digital divide, impacting millions of students and teachers globally.

A major hurdle is unequal access to devices like laptops, tablets, or smartphones. In low-income or rural areas, many families can't afford these tools, forcing students to share devices or go without. Even when devices are available, unreliable, or missing internet connections create significant obstacles. Without stable broadband, students struggle to join live classes, access study materials, or submit work on time, leaving them disconnected from learning (Cheng et al., 2019).

Digital literacy is another challenge. Many students and educators lack the skills to use online platforms, navigate educational apps, or fix technical problems. This gap can lead to frustration, lower engagement, and weaker academic outcomes, making it harder to keep up in a tech-driven classroom.

Marginalized groups like students with disabilities, girls in certain cultural settings, or those from low-income backgrounds face even greater barriers. These disparities threaten to widen educational gaps, undermining efforts to create fair and inclusive learning environments (Cherewick et al., 2021).

To close this digital divide, governments, schools, and organizations must act. Investments in internet infrastructure, affordable device programs, and digital skills training are essential. Policies should focus on universal access, offering localized content in multiple languages and designing platforms that work for students with special needs. Tackling these challenges is critical not just for recovering from the pandemic's impact but for building education systems that are inclusive, resilient, and ready for the future.

2.4 Teacher Training and Pedagogical Shifts

The COVID-19 pandemic forced a dramatic shift in how teachers deliver education, pushing them to embrace digital and hybrid learning almost overnight. This change reshaped teaching methods, testing approaches, and student engagement, revealing the critical need for ongoing teacher training and support to adapt to new realities.

Many teachers faced challenges mastering tools like video conferencing platforms, learning management systems, and digital content creation. To help, schools and governments rolled out training programs, webinars, and resource centres to build teachers' tech skills and confidence in virtual classrooms. These efforts were vital for equipping educators to navigate the digital landscape effectively.

Teaching it transformed. Traditional lectures gave way to interactive, student-focused methods better suited for online settings. Teachers started using videos, discussion boards, live polls, breakout sessions, and flipped classrooms where students review materials before class discussions to keep students engaged. This shift demanded a new kind of expertise: digital pedagogy, or the art of designing lessons that spark active learning in virtual spaces.

Testing also changed. With in-person exams disrupted, teacher's explored options like open-book tests, projects, peer reviews, and online quizzes designed to prevent cheating. The emphasis moved from memorizing facts to applying knowledge, thinking critically, and solving problems creatively. (Cho et al., 2025)

The pandemic also underscored the need for teachers to support students' emotional well-being. By offering flexible deadlines and creating caring, inclusive environments, educators became more attuned to students' mental health needs.

These changes have reshaped teaching for good. Future teacher training must go beyond tech skills, focusing on flexible teaching strategies, inclusive practices, and emotional intelligence. By preparing educators to handle both the technical and human sides of learning, we can build a stronger, more adaptable education system for the future.

2.5 Long-Term Impact on Educational Policies and Curriculum Design

The COVID-19 pandemic reshaped education, leaving a lasting mark on policies and curriculum design worldwide. What started as a temporary shift to digital learning has become a permanent part of education, prompting leaders to rethink how schools operate in a tech-driven world. This transformation is driving changes to create inclusive, flexible, and future-ready learning systems.

2.5.1 Policy Changes

Governments and education boards are updating policies to make digital learning a core part of education, not just a backup plan. They are focusing on building better internet access, providing devices to students in need, and closing the digital divide. For example, India's National Education Policy (NEP) 2020 pushes for technology at all school levels, with platforms like DIKSHA and SWAYAM offering free digital resources. Policies are also emphasizing teacher training to master online teaching, protect student data, and ensure fair digital assessments. Many countries are creating shared digital resource libraries, known as open educational resources (OERs), to make learning materials widely available and support equal access for all students. (Das et al., 2024)

2.5.2 Curriculum Updates

Schools are redesigning curricula to prepare students for a digital world. From early grades, students are learning digital skills like coding, using AI, and understanding data, alongside critical thinking, teamwork, and responsible online behavior. These skills aim to equip students for jobs in a fast-changing, tech-focused economy. Curricula are also becoming more flexible to support hybrid learning, where students mix online and in-person classes. Modular courses, personalized learning paths, and interdisciplinary projects let students learn at their own pace and explore topics in creative ways, making education more engaging and relevant.

2.5.3 Assessment Shifts

Testing is evolving too. Instead of relying only on traditional exams, schools are using ongoing assessments, projects, and digital portfolios to measure what students can do in real-world situations. This approach values practical skills and creativity over memorization.

The pandemic has sparked a major overhaul of education, making it more digital, inclusive, and adaptable. To keep this progress going, the focus must stay on ensuring every student has access to quality education, supported by thoughtful policies and innovative teaching that prepares them for the future (Deng et al., 2020).

3. LITERATURE REVIEW

In the last few decades, several literature reviews are included to highlight the significant changes that have taken place over the last few decades in the field of Role of Mental Health support in Digital Education in the Current Scenario. According to Montagni (2020) in this paper examined the to facilitate the implementation of future digital mental health interventions for university students, this systematic review aims to synthesize and evaluate research on mental health-related digital use (including purposes, benefits and barriers) by students around the world. The two main findings were that students around the world are keen to use digital tools for their mental health and well-being and have a high need for mental health information. They are expressing a desire for trustworthy technologies to handle their sensitive data, but they are currently having trouble identifying trustworthy information on the Internet. This analysis highlights important trends in digital use related to the mental health of university students. According to Foster and Upsher (2024) the purpose of this systematic review is to assess and comprehend peer assistance in higher education institutions.In May 2021, five databases were checked, including

OpenGrey and Grey Matters. Studies that were quantitative, cross-sectional with a control, or longitudinal (with and without a control) were included. For synthesis, the vote-counting approach was employed. The National Institutes of Health Quality Assessment Tool was used to evaluate the possibility of bias. Peer-led support groups, peer mentoring, and peer learning were the three forms of peer assistance that were covered in 28 studies. Anxiety and stress outcomes were found to be more favorable and significant when peer learning and peer mentoring were used. The only kind of support groups aimed at students with mental health issues were peer-led ones. According to Subroto(2025) the purpose of this integrative review was to present a summary of the literature on digital (in)equity and the digital divide in developed nations. To find pertinent papers, we looked through scholarly and gray literature. Following two stages of screening, 31 papers and 54 documents were chosen from 8464 scholarly publications and 183 grey literatures. Following Braun and Clarke's recommendations, a thematic analysis was carried out, and the findings were presented in accordance with the Preferred Reporting Items for Systematic Reviews and Meta-Analyses standards. According to the findings, the majority of papers and publications came from North America or Europe. Numerous research techniques, such as mixed, qualitative, and quantitative methodologies, were employed in the studies. The findings showed that there are four main aspects of the digital gap among different vulnerable groups: availability or access to infrastructure, equity-deserving group-sensitive content, cost, and digital literacy. The majority of the research identified low-income individuals as one of the most vulnerable groups, followed by women, older adults, racial and ethnic minorities, recent immigrants and refugees, Indigenous communities, and people with disabilities. Lack of internet access, digital skills, language hurdles, and internet prices were the most often mentioned obstacles. According to Oluwafunmi (2024) in this papers investigated the modern human resources (HR) practices are undergoing a paradigm shift, with a growing emphasis on employee well-being and mental health. This essay explores the evolving landscape of human resources programs aimed at encouraging and supporting employee well-being in the workplace. As businesses recognize the significant impact of mental health, strategically integrating mental health programs into human resources processes is becoming increasingly important to improve employee performance, engagement, and overall organizational success. This study examines various aspects of employee well-being programs, including de-stigmatizing discussions about mental health in the workplace, flexible work schedules, and comprehensive health and wellness activities. Modern human resources professionals are using data analytics and technology to optimize wellness initiatives, ensuring a tailored strategy that meets the diverse needs of employees. According to Ratten (2020) in this paper examined how the education communities have been greatly impacted by COVID-19, especially in terms of the dramatic change to online learning. This has resulted in a rapid shift to a digital platform for the curriculum and learning styles. The community of entrepreneurial educators in the higher education sector, who depend on hands-on and immersion training for learning requirements, are especially unaware of the implications of this significant shift. This paper is a survey of the literature that addresses how communities of practitioners in entrepreneurship education might respond to the COVID-19 pandemic. A review of recent research on COVID-19 and entrepreneurship education is carried out, emphasizing the necessity of using a community approach. This makes it possible to comprehend how communities of educational stakeholders, such as educators, students, and institutions, can support a more proactive and optimistic mindset. The study concludes that the need for real-world and practical examples makes handling the COVID-19 dilemma challenging for entrepreneurship education. This implies that in order to replicate the real world, artificial intelligence and augmented reality are required. This will make it possible to learn and practice entrepreneurship in a way that is more focused on the community. According to Kealy and Potts (2025) the purpose of this study was to conduct a systematic review and meta-analysis of the literature examining the efficacy of digital mental health interventions for college students who continue to struggle with mental health problems. When measured in terms of the severity of anxiety and depression symptoms, digital mental health interventions are associated with positive outcomes for college students. When it comes to reducing the severity of anxiety symptoms although counselling has long been offered by tertiary educational institutions, many students, especially those who continue to struggle, now have limited access to mental health services due to the dramatic increase in demand. Given the potential affordability and scalability associated with the lack of necessary human resources, digital mental health treatment offers a way to meet this unmet demand.

4. PSYCHOLOGICAL IMPACTS OF ONLINE LEARNING ON STUDENTS AND EDUCATORS

The shift to online learning during the COVID-19 pandemic brought flexibility and kept education going, but it also created significant mental health challenges for students and teachers. The sudden move to digital platforms, long hours in front of screens, limited social connections, and new academic pressures took a heavy toll on their well-being.

Students faced increased anxiety from the pandemic's uncertainty, constantly changing schedules, and the challenge of adapting to virtual classrooms. Without the structure of in-person school, many felt isolated, missing the casual interactions with friends and teachers that support emotional growth. Distractions at home, like noisy environments or family responsibilities, made focusing harder. For students in underserved areas, unreliable internet or lack of devices added stress and a sense of falling behind, sometimes leading to disengagement or dropping out. Excessive screen time also caused fatigue, eye strain, and sleep problems, while constant online tests fueled pressure. For younger students, the loss of peer interaction was especially tough, as it's critical for their social and emotional development, raising concerns about long-term effects like loneliness or depression.

Teachers weren't spared either. Many had to quickly learn new technologies and rethink lesson plans with little training, leading to overwhelming workloads. Technical issues like dropped connections or software glitches, added frustration. The blurred lines between work and home life teaching from living rooms while managing personal responsibilities contributed to burnout and stress. Teachers also struggled to keep students engaged online and provide emotional support remotely, all while dealing with their own anxieties. Without the camaraderie of staff rooms or school communities, many felt isolated, amplifying their emotional strain. (Dolev-Cohen & Barak, 2013)

To tackle these challenges, schools are weaving mental health support into education. Virtual counseling, regular wellness check-ins, mindfulness programs, and teacher support groups are becoming common. Efforts to promote digital well-being, like setting screen time limits and encouraging healthy work-study-life balance, are now priorities. Addressing the mental health impacts of online learning is key to building an education system that nurtures not just academic success but also the emotional resilience of students and teachers for a sustainable future.

4.1 Increased Screen Time and Its Cognitive Effects

The rapid shift to digital learning during and after the COVID-19 pandemic has led to a sharp rise in screen time for students and teachers. While digital tools have kept education going, the cognitive effects of spending long hours on screens are raising concerns among experts in psychology, education, and health. (Garrido et al., 2019)

1. Reduced Concentration and Attention Span:

Staring at screens for extended periods can make it harder to concentrate. Constant notifications, multitasking, and tempting distractions like social media pull attention in multiple directions. This can train the brain to expect quick, frequent shifts in focus, making it tough to dive deeply into tasks or maintain steady attention, often called "digital distraction."

2. **Memory and Information Retention Challenges:**

Online learning often relies on watching videos or flipping through slides, which may not stick in the brain as well as hands-on activities or face-to-face discussions. Research shows that writing notes by hand or engaging in group talks helps lock in information better than typing or passive screen time. Too much digital content can also overload the brain, making it harder to process and remember new material.

3. Mental Fatigue and Cognitive Overload:

Long screen sessions can leave students and teachers feeling drained, slow, and unmotivated. Unlike in-person learning, digital environments rarely offer natural breaks, bombarding users with constant visuals and sounds. This, combined with less physical movement and face-to-face interaction, can lead to "Zoom fatigue," where video calls zap mental energy.

4. Sleep Disruption and Its Effects on Cognition:

Too much screen time, especially at night, can mess with sleep by interfering with the body's natural sleep signals. Poor sleep hurts focus, memory, problem-solving, and emotional balance, making learning even tougher.

5. Digital Fatigue and Cognitive Overload

Digital fatigue and cognitive overload are growing concerns in our increasingly hyper-connected world, with significant mental health consequences. They stem from the relentless demands placed on our brains by constant digital stimuli, leading to a state where our cognitive processing capacity is overwhelmed.

4.1 What is Digital Fatigue?

Digital fatigue, often used interchangeably with digital eye strain or computer vision syndrome, refers to the physical and mental exhaustion resulting from prolonged engagement with digital devices. While it often manifests as eye discomfort (dryness, blurriness, headaches), it extends to a broader sense of mental drain. (Goodman-Casanova et al., 2020)

Causes of Digital Fatigue:

- **Prolonged Screen Time:** Prolonged screen time involves spending hours daily on devices like phones, computers, or tablets for work, entertainment, or communication. This habit can strain eyes due to reduced blinking, causing dryness and discomfort. Blue light from screens may disrupt sleep by affecting melatonin production. Poor lighting or bad posture during use can further increase physical strain.

- **Reduced Blinking:** When focusing on screens, people often blink less, which reduces the eyes' natural lubrication. This leads to dry, irritated eyes, causing discomfort and potential strain. Taking regular breaks and consciously blinking can help maintain moisture. Using artificial tears may also alleviate dryness.
- **Blue Light Exposure:** Blue light from digital screens can suppress melatonin production, a hormone crucial for regulating sleep. This disruption can lead to difficulty falling asleep, poor sleep quality, and daytime fatigue. Using blue light filters or glasses and limiting screen time before bed can help. Setting devices to night mode may also reduce exposure.
- **Poor Lighting and Posture:** Poor lighting, like glare or dim conditions, forces eyes to work harder, causing strain and discomfort. Incorrect posture, such as slouching or improper screen height, stresses the neck, back, and shoulders. Optimizing workspace lighting and using ergonomic setups, like adjustable chairs and monitors, can reduce strain. Regular breaks and posture adjustments also help maintain comfort.

4.2 What is Cognitive Overload?

Cognitive overload occurs when the amount of information or demands placed on our working memory exceeds its capacity. Our brains have a limited ability to process and retain information at any given time. When this limit is breached, our cognitive performance declines. (Henderson et al., 2014)

Key Contributors to Cognitive Overload:

1. **Multitasking:** The human brain is not designed for true multitasking. Instead, it rapidly switches between tasks, incurring a “switch cost” each time. This constant task-switching divides attention, slows performance, increases errors, and consumes significant mental resources. It overloads the brain's ability to plan, problem-solve, and maintain sustained attention.
2. **Constant Notifications:** Alerts from emails, texts, social media, and various apps constantly interrupt our focus. Each notification, whether checked or not, pulls our attention away from the task at hand, requiring mental effort to re-engage. This creates a perpetual state of heightened alertness, leading to increased stress and fragmented thought processes.

3. **Information Overload:** We are bombarded with an unprecedented volume, velocity, and variety of information from the internet, social media, and news channels. This overwhelming influx of data exceeds our cognitive processing capacity, making it difficult to filter, prioritize, and make sense of what's truly important. It leads to mental fog, indecisiveness, and a feeling of being perpetually "behind."

4.3 Mental Health Consequences:

The cumulative effect of digital fatigue and cognitive overload has serious implications for mental well-being:

1. **Increased Stress and Anxiety:** The constant pressure to be "always on" and responsive, coupled with the overwhelming influx of information, triggers chronic stress responses. Elevated cortisol levels can harm brain health, leading to heightened anxiety, irritability, and a feeling of being overwhelmed.
2. **Reduced Attention Span and Impaired Focus:** Constant interruptions from notifications and the habit of multitasking train our brains for short bursts of attention rather than sustained focus. This makes it increasingly difficult to concentrate on a single task for extended periods, impacting productivity, learning, and deep thinking.
3. **Memory Decline:** Rapid task-switching and information overload disrupt the formation and consolidation of memories. Short-term memory weakens, and it becomes harder to retain and recall information, leading to forgetfulness and reduced cognitive efficiency.
4. **Decision Fatigue and Poor Decision-Making:** Constantly having to make decisions, even small ones (like whether to check a notification or respond to an email), drains mental resources. This "decision fatigue" can lead to poorer choices, impaired judgment, and difficulty with problem-solving.
5. **Mental Fatigue and Burnout:** The brain expends immense energy trying to manage multiple tasks and process excessive information. This leads to chronic mental exhaustion, a state of profound fatigue that goes beyond simple tiredness. If left unaddressed, it can progress to burnout, characterized by cynicism, reduced personal accomplishment, and emotional exhaustion.
6. **Sleep Disruption:** Excessive screen time, particularly before bed, exposes us to blue light that suppresses melatonin, a hormone crucial for sleep. This disrupts our natural circadian rhythm, leading to insomnia, poor sleep quality, and further exacerbating fatigue, mood swings, and impaired cognitive function.

In essence, while digital tools offer immense benefits, their overuse and the culture of constant connectivity create a challenging environment for our mental well-being. Recognizing these consequences is the first step towards adopting healthier digital habits and protecting our cognitive and emotional health.

5. ROLE OF SCHOOLS, COLLEGES, AND UNIVERSITIES IN PROMOTING MENTAL HEALTH

Schools, colleges, and universities are vital in supporting the mental health of students and teachers, especially when it comes to handling stress, anxiety, burnout, and challenges like digital fatigue, cognitive overload, and the lack of in-person social connections. As key centres for learning and community, these institutions can make meaningful changes through policies, culture, and programs to build resilience and promote well-being. Below, I highlight how educational institutions can take responsibility for mental health, offering practical steps, evidence-based strategies, and collaborative solutions. This connects to earlier discussions on stress, anxiety, burnout, isolation, and digital overload, focusing on the role of schools in addressing these issues. (Liverpool et al., 2020)

5.1. The Role of Schools, Colleges, and Universities

1. Building a Mental Health-Friendly Educational Environment

Educational institutions must cultivate a supportive culture that prioritizes mental health, encourages help-seeking, and eliminates stigma. Schools can launch awareness campaigns, such as "Mental Health Awareness Week," featuring workshops, guest speakers, and student-led discussions to educate everyone about mental health resources and coping strategies. A 2024 CDC study noted a 15% rise in help-seeking behaviors in schools with such initiatives. Creating "Zen Zones" or wellness rooms with calming decor and mindfulness tools can help students manage stress, with a 2023 study showing a 10% drop in anxiety where these spaces exist. Policies allowing mental health days for students and staff, treated like sick days, can reduce burnout by 12%, according to a 2024 Edutopia study. Collaborating with student groups, teacher unions, parent associations, and mental health experts ensures these efforts are inclusive, evidence-based, and impactful, fostering a compassionate learning environment.

2. Enhancing Access to Mental Health Resources in Education

To effectively address mental health challenges, educational institutions must prioritize accessible professional support. Expanding on-site counseling by hiring more licensed counselors, aiming for a 1:500 counselor-to-student ratio, can significantly reduce wait times and enhance support, with a 2024 APA report showing a 20% drop in student anxiety where robust services exist. Offering teletherapy and subscriptions to apps like Headspace or Calm ensures support for remote or hybrid learners, with a 2023 study noting a 15% reduction in depression symptoms via teletherapy. Training faculty in Mental Health First Aid to recognize and respond to crises, such as panic attacks or suicidal thoughts, boosts timely interventions by 25%, per a 2024 CDC report. Collaborating with local mental health organizations and involving students and teachers in feedback ensures resources are effective and tailored, creating a supportive environment for all.

3. Easing Academic and Professional Pressures in Education

To combat stress and burnout, educational institutions must rethink systems to reduce academic and professional pressures. Optimizing workloads can help: for students, this means capping homework at 1-2 hours nightly and emphasizing project-based learning with flexible deadlines; for teachers, it involves cutting non-essential administrative tasks and allocating dedicated planning time. A 2024 EdWeek study showed this approach reduced student stress by 10% and teacher burnout by 15%. Shifting to continuous assessments, like portfolios or presentations, instead of high-stakes tests can lower student anxiety by 18%, per a 2023 Journal of Educational Psychology study. Supporting teachers with mentorship or peer groups, such as weekly professional learning communities, reduces isolation and turnover intentions by 10%, according to a 2023 NEA study. Collaborating with students, teachers, administrators, and curriculum experts to design these policies ensures they are practical and effective, fostering a healthier educational environment.

4. Building Community in Education

To counter the loss of physical social interaction, schools must actively foster connection and community. Organizing hybrid social opportunities, such as monthly "connection days" with in-person or virtual group discussions and team-building activities, can reduce loneliness by 15% for students and teachers, according to a 2024 Edutopia study. Peer mentorship programs, like pairing freshmen with seniors or teachers with colleagues for regular check-ins, help build supportive relationships, cutting student isolation by 15%, per a 2024 Youth Truth survey. School-wide community-building initiatives, such as assemblies, talent shows, or volunteer service days, strengthen ties, boosting connectedness by 12%, as noted in a 2024 Edutopia report. Collaborating with students, teachers, parent-teacher associations, and local community centres to design these events, while incorporating feedback, ensures activities are inclusive and meaningful, creating a vibrant, supportive educational environment.

5. Advocating for Mental Health in Education

Educational institutions must champion systemically change to bolster mental health support at local, state, and national levels. Lobbying for increased funding, such as through the Mental Health Services for Students Act, can enhance resources for counselors and support staff, with a 2024 CDC report showing a 15% reduction in burnout in well-funded schools. Collaborating with policymakers to maintain stable educational policies—via district task forces, for instance—reduces uncertainty around curriculum and testing, lowering teacher turnover by 10%, per a 2024 Rand study. Partnering with local nonprofits or health clinics to deliver mental health workshops fosters awareness and access, boosting school connectedness by 10%, according to a 2024 Edutopia study. Engaging school boards, unions, policymakers, and representatives from students and teachers ensures advocacy efforts reflect real needs, creating a robust framework for mental health support in education. (Wisniewski & Torous, 2023)

6. USE OF DIGITAL TOOLS AND AI IN MENTAL HEALTH CARE

The integration of digital tools and artificial intelligence (AI) in mental health care offers transformative opportunities to address stress, anxiety, burnout, digital fatigue, and social isolation for students and teachers. These technologies can enhance access to mental health support, provide personalized interventions, and streamline institutional efforts, while also presenting challenges that require careful management. Below, I provide a detailed explanation of how digital tools and AI can be used in mental health care within educational settings, their benefits, limitations, specific applications for students and teachers, supporting data, and strategies for effective implementation. This builds on the previous discussions of stress, anxiety, burnout, social isolation, digital overload, and the role of educational institutions. (Margolis et al., 2018)

6.1. Overview of Digital Tools and AI in Mental Health Care

Mental health care has entered a new era with the integration of digital tools and artificial intelligence (AI). These technologies are reshaping how individuals access support, manage their well-being, and receive professional care. From mobile apps to AI-driven chatbots, digital solutions are making mental health resources more accessible, personalized, and scalable. This article explores the role of digital tools and AI in mental health care, their benefits, challenges, and future potential.

6.2. The Rise of Digital Tools in Mental Health

Digital tools, such as smartphone apps, wearable devices, and online platforms, have become vital in addressing mental health needs. These tools offer diverse functionalities, including mood tracking, mindfulness exercises, and virtual therapy sessions. Their appeal lies in their convenience, affordability, and ability to reach people who might otherwise face barriers to traditional care.

Key Types of Digital Tools

1. **Mental Health Apps**: Apps like Calm, Headspace, and Mood path provide guided meditations, cognitive behavioural therapy (CBT) exercises, and mood tracking. These tools empower users to manage stress, anxiety, and depression independently or alongside professional support.
2. **Teletherapy Platforms**: Services like BetterHelp and Talkspace connect users with licensed therapists via video, phone, or text. These platforms eliminate geographical barriers and reduce the stigma of seeking in-person therapy.
3. **Wearable Devices**: Smartwatches and fitness trackers monitor sleep patterns, heart rate variability, and physical activity, which can provide insights into mental health. For example, irregular sleep patterns may signal anxiety or depression.
4. **Online Support Communities**: Platforms like 7 Cups offer peer support and anonymous chat rooms, fostering connection for those hesitant to seek professional help.

6.3. Benefits of Digital Tools and AI

- **Accessibility**: Digital tools and AI provide 24/7 support, reaching students and teachers in remote or underserved areas. A 2024 CDC report noted that digital mental health tools increased access by 25% in underfunded schools.
- **Cost-Effectiveness**: Apps and AI chatbots are often cheaper than in-person therapy, making them scalable. A 2023 *Health Affairs* study found that digital interventions cost 30-50% less than traditional counseling.
- **Proactive Support**: AI's predictive capabilities enable early interventions, preventing escalation of mental health issues. A 2024 *Journal of School Psychology* study showed that proactive AI interventions reduced student anxiety by 15%.

- **Anonymity**: Digital tools reduce stigma by allowing anonymous access to support. A 2024 Pew Research Center survey found that 60% of students preferred digital tools for their privacy.
- **Engagement**: Interactive AI and gamified apps (e.g., mindfulness challenges) increase user engagement. A 2023 *Frontiers in Psychology* study reported a 20% higher adherence rate for digital interventions compared to traditional ones.

6.4. The Role of AI in Mental Health Care

AI is revolutionizing mental health care by enabling more precise, scalable, and proactive interventions. By analysing vast amounts of data, AI can identify patterns, predict risks, and deliver tailored support. (Orben & Przybylski, 2019)

Applications of AI in Mental Health:

1. **AI-Powered Chatbots**: Chatbots like Woebot and Wysa use natural language processing to engage users in conversations, offer CBT-based techniques, and provide emotional support. These bots are available round-the-clock, making them a lifeline for those in crisis.
2. **Predictive Analytics**: AI algorithms analyze data from wearables, social media, or health records to predict mental health crises, such as suicidal ideation or depressive episodes. For example, machine learning models can flag concerning patterns in speech or behavior.
3. **Personalized Treatment Plans**: AI can recommend customized interventions based on a user's history, preferences, and symptoms, improving the effectiveness of therapy.
4. **Virtual Therapists**: Advanced AI systems simulate therapy sessions, guiding users through evidence-based techniques like CBT or dialectical behavior therapy (DBT).
5. **Sentiment Analysis**: AI tools analyze text or voice data to assess emotional states, helping clinicians monitor patients remotely.

7. CASE STUDIES AND GLOBAL BEST PRACTICES

Examples of successful mental health initiatives in digital education environments.

7.1. Finland's Holistic Approach to Digital Well-being in Education

Finland is globally recognized for its progressive and student-centred education system, and its approach to digital well-being reflects this philosophy. The country has strategically embedded mental health awareness and digital literacy into its national curriculum to ensure a balanced and sustainable digital learning environment. (Niemi & Kumpulainen, 2022)

Here's how Finland stands out:

1. **Curriculum Integration**

Finland's national core curriculum includes media literacy, digital safety, and emotional intelligence as foundational competencies. From early education onward, students are taught how to manage screen time, critically evaluate online content, and navigate digital spaces responsibly linking digital literacy with psychological well-being.

2. **Emphasis on Student Agency and Balance**

Finnish schools prioritize student autonomy and well-being over excessive academic pressure. Learners are encouraged to develop self-awareness about their digital habits, with regular classroom discussions about the mental and physical effects of technology use.

3. **Teacher Training and Professional Development**

Educators in Finland receive mandatory training in mental health education and digital pedagogy. This equips them to recognize signs of digital fatigue, stress, or emotional distress, and to guide students toward healthier screen use and coping strategies.

4. **Wellness-Focused School Environment**

Schools promote breaks from screen-based learning, outdoor activities, and peer collaboration. The education system deliberately avoids standardized testing at early stages to reduce academic stress and promote creativity and emotional growth. (Torous et al., 2020)

5. **Collaboration with Health and Social Services**

Finland's approach is highly interdisciplinary, involving collaboration between schools, mental health professionals, and social workers. This ensures a safety net for students who may need psychological support, whether related to digital stress or broader well-being concerns.

7.2 India's Initiatives: MANODARPAN and School Wellness Programs

1. MANODARPAN: National Psycho-Social Support Initiative

Launched in July 2020 by the Ministry of Education under the Atma Nirbhar Bharat vision. (Ministry of Education, India, 2020) Offers a national toll-free helpline (8448440632), interactive online chat, and tele-counselling staffed by trained professionals Provides advisory resources, practical tips, posters, videos, and a handbook covering life skills and well-being integration into curricular activities. Empowers peer support, webinars ('Paricharcha'), and live wellness sessions ('Sahyog') for classes VI–XII Daily Excelsior. Utilizes a directory of 2,000+ counsellors connected with schools and universities Continues beyond COVID 19 to embed mental health into mainstream education. (Government of Kerala, 2023)

2. Delhi's Happiness Curriculum

Introduced in July 2018, taught in Nursery–Grade 8 in Delhi government schools. Focused on mindfulness, social-emotional learning, critical thinking, and self-awareness—leading to improvements in student focus and teacher collaboration. Adapted during lockdown via interactive calls and YouTube classes. (Orlowski et al., 2016)

3. Kerala's Transition: Teacher-as-Counsellor Program

Kerala's government is training ~3,000 school teachers as primary mental health counsellors to identify and assist students at risk. Conducted under the Centre for Child Development to also address risks like drug use and excessive screen time.

4. School Wellness & Life-Skills Programs

In Ernakulam (Kerala), schools integrated daily sessions on life skills, digital discipline, nutrition, and introduced Zumba to foster emotional balance. Ranchi CBSE schools introduced positive affirmations in morning assemblies to boost focus, self-esteem, and resilience Education Ministry of India. Delhi schools under the "Healthy Dose" initiative included lessons on mental well-being, stress management, and healthy relationships across ~10,000 students.

7.3 Australia's Headspace Model for Youth Mental Health

1. Comprehensive Early-Intervention Hubs

Established in 2006 and operational by 2007, Headspace supports Australians aged 12–25 through integrated services mental & physical health, substance use assistance, and vocational support with both in-person centers and online access. As of 2023, there are around 154 physical centers, with 84 located outside major cities, forming the world's largest youth mental health network. (Headspace National Youth Mental Health Foundation, 2023)

2. Evidence of Positive Outcomes

Surveys from 2019–2020 found that 70% of Headspace users reported meaningful improvements in distress, functioning, or quality of life. Centre-specific evaluations (e.g., 2013–14) showed over one-third had significantly better distress and functioning scores, and 60% improved in at least one domain

3. Expansion into Schools- "Headspace Schools & Communities"

Headspace provides free, interactive mental health workshops for Grades 6–12 on topics such as stress management, emotional literacy, peer support, and self-care. Teachers receive training—e.g., suicide response, mental health literacy under programs like "Be You," enhancing school-based capacity to address student needs.

8. USING NEW EDUCATIONAL DIGITAL TECHNOLOGIES TO PROMOTE MENTAL HEALTH

Utilizing digital tools for health literacy, behavioral modification, and ongoing support while reducing hazards like screen addiction and data privacy concerns is part of promoting mental health in education. AI chatbots for tailored interventions, health applications for monitoring and skill development, and social media for awareness are some strategies. Additionally, it is critical to maintain ethical data processes, encourage offline activities, and teach digital wellbeing. Below we have mentioned the reasons for using technology to promote mental health

1. **Promote health literacy:** Use social media and other channels to raise awareness, reduce stigma, and spread knowledge about mental health.
2. **Encourage behavior change:** Use chatbots powered by AI to provide motivational support and tailored guidance. Applications of cognitive behavioral therapy (CBT) have shown significant improvements in anxiety and depression.
3. Encourage continued good habits by using wearable technology like smart watches to track health indicators.
4. **Encourage connection and support:** Establish online forums and communities where students can get support from classmates going through comparable struggles. This is especially beneficial for students who do not have access to offline help.
5. **Boost accessibility:** According to Clinical Practice and Epidemiology in Mental Health, provide online interventions and virtual therapy, which are frequently more flexible and accessible than conventional in-person approaches, particularly for college students.
6. **Take action against screen addiction:** To assist students unplug and rejuvenate, encourage "digital detox" and contemplative pursuits like hobbies, outdoor walks, or meditation.
7. **Preserve the privacy of your data:** Keep an eye out for critical information that platforms and apps gather, and make sure that strong security mechanisms are in place to safeguard user privacy.
8. **Encourage balanced use:** Stress the value of utilizing digital technologies to enhance offline activities and in-person social connection rather than to replace them.
9. **Verify clinical validation:** Promote the creation of instruments with rigorous validation and scientific support, pointing out that further research is still needed to determine the long-term efficacy of various digital therapies.

9. RECOMMENDATIONS

Using digital tools like AI-powered chatbots and meditation apps, incorporating teacher-led strategies like mindfulness breaks and building a supportive online community, and making sure students have access to physical self-care practices like exercise and setting boundaries are some ideas for mental health support in digital education. It's also critical to take into account the constraints, such data privacy, and make sure the technology is usable and compatible with conventional care procedures.

a. **Teacher-led tactics**

1. **Incorporate mindfulness:** To assist students manage stress, set aside class time for yoga, brief meditations, or guided breathing exercises.
2. **Encourage community:** Students should be encouraged to work in small groups to help one another, and their efforts should be acknowledged.
3. **Establish boundaries:** To avoid burnout, assist staff and students in drawing distinct lines between their personal and academic lives.
4. Encourage students to engage in physical activity by reminding them that walking for 30 minutes can lift their spirits.
5. **Encourage candid communication:** Provide an environment where students can freely express their emotions and worries about digital learning.

b. Student-centered self-care

1. **Make sleep and nourishment a priority:** Stress the value of eating regular, healthful meals and obtaining adequate sleep.
2. **Keep in touch:** Students should be encouraged to keep up their social networks both offline and online.
3. **Control social media use:** Teach students how to set limits and curate their feeds in order to have a better relationship with social media.
4. **Practice thankfulness and optimism:** To help pupils develop resilience, encourage them to concentrate on the good things in their lives.

c. Technology and digital tools

1. **Make use of specific apps:** For guided meditation and cognitive behavioral therapy (CBT) methods, use applications such as Headspace, Calm, or Mind Shift CBT.
2. **Try chatbots driven by AI:** Through text-based interactions, AI chatbots can offer prompt assistance, resources, and coping mechanisms.
3. **Use mental health apps:** Some applications measure moods using artificial intelligence (AI), while others provide tools or individualized inspiration based on methods such as dialectical behavior therapy (DBT).
4. **Utilize virtual platforms:** Make use of internet platforms to provide access to information, evaluations, and support groups that might not otherwise be accessible.

10. FINDINGS

This study has highlighted the role of mental health support in digital education in the current scenario. The main objective of the present study was to investigate of role of mental health support in digital education in the current scenario. to achieve this objective, this study included a review of the literature of the last 10 years and also discussed the introduction, background of topic, (current state of mental health in today's era, factors influencing the demand for online mental health assistance, the application of digital education to mental health)

11. CONCLUSION

The shift to digital education, accelerated by the COVID-19 pandemic, has transformed learning by offering flexibility and access across geographic and economic divides. Online platforms have made education more inclusive, but they've also brought challenges like excessive screen time, academic stress, digital fatigue, and reduced social interaction, all of which harm the mental well-being of students and educators. The pandemic exposed a critical gap in education systems: the lack of structured mental health support. Rising anxiety, depression, loneliness, and burnout underscored the need for change.

To create a resilient digital education system, mental health must be a priority alongside academics. Schools and universities should integrate psychological well-being into policies and platforms. This includes providing access to counseling, building peer support networks, and training teachers to spot and address mental distress. Digital tools like AI-based mood trackers, mindfulness apps, and teletherapy platforms can offer scalable support, empowering students to manage their mental health while helping institutions identify early warning signs. However, these tools must be used ethically, with strong data privacy measures.

Global examples, such as India's MANODARPAN, Finland's social-emotional learning programs, and the UK's school-based mental health teams, show that investing in mental health boosts engagement, creativity, and resilience while reducing dropout rates. Collaboration among educators, mental health experts, policymakers, and tech developers is key to success. (Pithara et al., 2020) Moving forward, digital education must foster an empathetic ecosystem where mental health is a shared responsibility. Educators need support to maintain their well-being while creating safe learning spaces. Students should feel empowered to seek help without stigma. A future-ready education system intertwines academic success with emotional well-being, making mental health a core pillar of inclusive, sustainable learning. In conclusion, institutions, teachers, and students all gain from hybrid learning. In addition to improving program robustness and competitiveness on national and international platforms, it allows institutions to access a larger and more varied student body. It gives teachers better insights into students' development, which makes it easier to improve and customize their teaching strategies. In the end, blended learning helps students succeed both inside and outside of the classroom by meeting them where they are.

Given these benefits, it is clear that hybrid learning is set to become a mainstay of Indian higher education, providing long-term advantages to all parties.

REFERENCES

Borenstein, M., Hedges, L. V., Higgins, J. P. T., & Rothstein, H. R. (2009). *Introduction to meta-analysis.* Wiley. DOI: 10.1002/9780470743386

Cejudo, J., López-Delgado, M. L., & Losada, L. (2019). Effectiveness of the videogame "Spock" for the improvement of the emotional intelligence on psychosocial adjustment in adolescents. *Computers in Human Behavior, 101*, 380–386. DOI: 10.1016/j.chb.2018.09.028

Charbonnier, E., Trémolière, B., Baussard, L., Goncalves, A., Lespiau, F., Philippe, A. G., & Le Vigouroux, S. (2021). Self-help cognitive behavioral therapy application for COVID-19-related mental health problems: A longitudinal trial. *Asian Journal of Psychiatry, 60*, 102656. DOI: 10.1016/j.ajp.2021.102656 PMID: 33866282

Cheng, V. W. S., Davenport, T., Johnson, D., Vella, K., & Hickie, I. B. (2019). Gamification in apps and technologies for improving mental health and well-being: Systematic review. *JMIR Mental Health, 6*(6), e13717. DOI: 10.2196/13717 PMID: 31244479

Cherewick, M., Lebu, S., Su, C., Richards, L., Njau, P. F., & Dahl, R. E. (2021). Study protocol of a distance learning intervention to support social emotional learning and identity development for adolescents using interactive mobile technology. *Frontiers in Education, 6*, 625–640. PMID: 33585394

Cho, H. N., Jung, K., Eisenberg, D., King, C. A., & Zheng, K. (2025). Barriers to digital mental health services among college students. *arXiv preprint arXiv:2507.21093.* DOI: 10.3233/SHTI251041

Das, P. J., Kyndait, P., Jamir, S. I., Baishya, D., Kalita, J. K., & Komu, L. T. (2024). The role of technology in mental health: Evaluating digital interventions for psychological well-being. *International Journal of Scientific Research in Science and Technology, 11*(6), 366–386. DOI: 10.32628/IJSRST24116186

Deng, C.-H., Wang, J.-Q., Zhu, L.-M., Liu, H.-W., Guo, Y., Peng, X.-H., Shao, J.-B., & Xia, W. (2020). Association of web-based physical education with mental health of college students in Wuhan during the COVID-19 outbreak: Cross-sectional survey study. *Journal of Medical Internet Research, 22*(10), e21301. DOI: 10.2196/21301 PMID: 32997639

Dolev-Cohen, M., & Barak, A. (2013). Effects of virtual communication on adolescent mental health: A randomized controlled trial. *Computers in Human Behavior, 29*(4), 1532–1539.

Foster, J., & Upsher, R. (2024, January). A systematic review of peer support interventions for student mental health and well-being in higher education, *Published online by Cambridge University Press. BJPsych Open, 10*(1), e12. DOI: 10.1192/bjo.2023.603 PMID: 39721952

Garrido, S., Millington, C., Cheers, D., Boydell, K., Schubert, E., Meade, T., & Nguyen, Q. V. (2019). What works and what doesn't: A systematic review of digital mental health interventions for young people. *Frontiers in Psychiatry, 10*, 759. DOI: 10.3389/fpsyt.2019.00759 PMID: 31798468

Goodman-Casanova, J. M., Dura-Perez, E., Guzman-Parra, J., Cuesta-Vargas, A., & Mayoral-Cleries, F. (2020). Telehealth home support during COVID-19 confinement for community-dwelling older adults with mild cognitive impairment or mild dementia: Survey study. *Journal of Medical Internet Research, 22*(5), e19434. DOI: 10.2196/19434 PMID: 32401215

Government of Kerala. (2023). *Teacher-as-counsellor program: Mental health training for school educators*. Centre for Child Development. https://www.kerala.gov.in/education

Headspace National Youth Mental Health Foundation. (2023). *Mental health education program: Headspace schools & communities*. https://headspace.org.au/schools/mental-health-education-program/

Henderson, B., Kirby, K., McCann, A., McCay, D., Leeann, M., Mulvenna, M., . . . Quigley, T. (2014, September). Designing social prescription services to support people with long-term conditions. In *ENoLL Open Living Lab Days 2014 Conference Proceedings* (pp. 158-170). European Network of Living Labs.

Kealy, C., & Potts, C. (2025, March 3). Digital Mental Health Interventions for University Students With Mental Health Difficulties: A Systematic Review and Meta-Analysis. *Early Intervention in Psychiatry, 19*(3), e70017. DOI: 10.1111/eip.70017 PMID: 40033658

Liverpool, S., Mota, C. P., Sales, C. M. D., Čuš, A., Carletto, S., Hancheva, C., Sousa, S., Cerón, S. C., Moreno-Peral, P., Pietrabissa, G., Moltrecht, B., Ulberg, R., Ferreira, N., & Edbrooke-Childs, J. (2020). Engaging children and young people in digital mental health interventions: Systematic review of modes of delivery, facilitators, and barriers. *Journal of Medical Internet Research, 22*(6), e16317. DOI: 10.2196/16317 PMID: 32442160

Margolis, K., Kelsay, K., Talmi, A., McMillan, H., Fraley, M. C., & Thomas, J. F. F. (2018). A multidisciplinary, team-based teleconsultation approach to enhance child mental health services in rural pediatrics. *Journal of Educational & Psychological Consultation*, *28*(3), 342–367. DOI: 10.1080/10474412.2018.1431549

Ministry of Education. India. (2020). *MANODARPAN: Psycho-social support for mental health & well-being during the COVID-19 outbreak and beyond.* https://www.education.gov.in/manodarpan/

Montagni, I., & Christophe, T. (2020). Mental Health-Related Digital Use by University Students: A Systematic Review. *Telemedicine Journal and e-Health*, *26*(2), 131–146. Advance online publication. DOI: 10.1089/tmj.2018.0316 PMID: 30888256

Niemi, H., & Kumpulainen, K. (2022). Digital well-being in the Finnish education system: Integrating mental health and media literacy. *Nordic Journal of Digital Literacy*, *17*(3), 145–160. DOI: 10.18261/njdl.17.3.2

Oluwafunmi A. E. (2024).Reviewing employee well-being and mental health initiatives in contemporary HR Practices, International Journal of Science and Research Archive, 2024, 11(01), 828–840. Article DOI: https://doi.org/.DOI: 10.30574/ijsra.2024.11.1.0153

Orben, A., & Przybylski, A. K. (2019). Screens, teens, and psychological well-being: Evidence from three time-use-diary studies. *Psychological Science*, *30*(5), 682–696. DOI: 10.1177/0956797619830329 PMID: 30939250

Orlowski, S., Lawn, S., Matthews, B., Venning, A., Wyld, K., Jones, G., Winsall, M., Antezana, G., Schrader, G., & Bidargaddi, N. (2016). The promise and the reality: A mental health workforce perspective on technology-enhanced youth mental health service delivery. *BMC Health Services Research*, *16*(1), 562. DOI: 10.1186/s12913-016-1790-y PMID: 27724951

Pithara, C., Farr, M., Sullivan, S. A., Edwards, H. B., Hall, W., & Gadd, C., & Authors. (2020). Implementing a digital tool to support shared care planning in community-based mental health services: Qualitative evaluation. *JMIR Mental Health*, *7*(3), e14868. PMID: 32191210

Ratten, V. (2020). Coronavirus (Covid-19) and the entrepreneurship education community Available to Purchase. *Journal of Enterprising Communities: People and Places in the Global Economy*, *14*(5), 753–764. DOI: 10.1108/JEC-06-2020-0121

Subroto, S., & Chowdhury, N. (2025). Dimensions and barriers for digital (in) equity and digital divide: A systematic integrative review. *Digital Transformation and Society*, *4*(2), 111–127. DOI: 10.1108/DTS-04-2024-0054

Torous, J., Wisniewski, H., Gorrindo, T., Rauseo-Ricupero, N., & Hilty, D. (2020). The role of digital navigators in promoting clinical care and technology integration into practice. *Digital Biomarkers*, *4*(Suppl. 1), 119–135. DOI: 10.1159/000510144 PMID: 33442585

Wisniewski, H., & Torous, J. (2023). Digital mental health: Challenges and next steps. *BMJ Mental Health*, *26*(1), e300670. DOI: 10.1136/bmjment-2023-300670 PMID: 37197797

Chapter 4

Procrastination in the Digital Age: Examining Internet Addiction Among Pre-Service English Teachers

Bora Demir
https://orcid.org/0000-0001-8187-3206
Çanakkale Onsekiz Mart University, Turkey

Selin Cengiz
https://orcid.org/0009-0008-9967-6938
Army NCO Vocational HE School, National Defence University, Turkey

ABSTRACT

This study explores the correlation between internet addiction and academic procrastination among 120 undergraduate students in an English Language Teaching program at a state university in Turkey. Adopting a mixed-method approach, it gathered quantitative data via the Internet Addiction Scale (IAS) and the Academic Procrastination Behavior Scale (APBS), and qualitative data through a focus group interview. Results revealed a significant positive correlation: higher levels of internet addiction were associated with increased procrastination. Regression analysis showed internet addiction explained about 20% of the variance in procrastination, with no significant gender differences. Qualitative findings highlighted complex links between digital behavior, emotional well-being, and academic challenges. These findings align with prior studies on behavioral impacts of internet use but contrast with research indicating gender-based addiction patterns. The study emphasizes the need for digital literacy and self-regulation strategies in educational settings.

DOI: 10.4018/979-8-3373-5007-3.ch004

INTRODUCTION

With widespread mobile internet availability, people now have virtually unlimited access to online content anytime and anywhere. Even if it makes our lives easier and helps us save time, accessibility of it may make it dangerous for individuals. Overuse of internet technology can contribute to negative outcomes, including heightened internet addiction and increased procrastination, especially when usage is not self-regulated. The web sources or social applications may distract us from our responsibilities because they involve colorful visuals, short -attention span killer- videos and lots of enjoyable content. According to the Digital 2023 Global Overview Report average daily time spent on the internet for everyone is 6 hours 38 minutes with the total internet user 5.56 billion people. Ten of the main reasons for using the internet are listed as below in the same report.

Figure 1. Top reasons for internet usage percentages according to Digital 2023 Global Overview Report

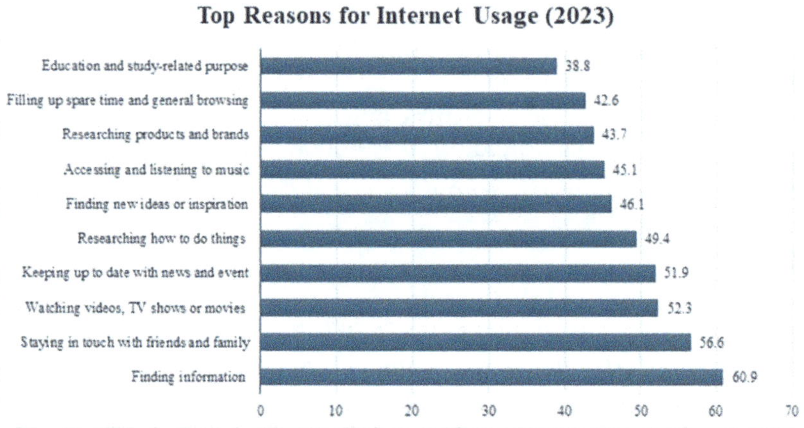

Figure 1 indicates that people tend to use the internet mostly for entertainment or for reaching information. It can be observed that even though hybrid or online education is commonly used nowadays starting with the Covid-19 pandemic, education-related use was the tenth most common reason for internet use in the Digital 2023 Global Overview Report. On the other hand, as the years pass, the ratio increases, and this has a great impact especially on digital natives. Because they spend time on the internet with various popular apps, they have shorter time for the other social, emotional or educational responsibilities. One of the most important ones can be their educational responsibilities having an importance on their future job, lifestyle or progression. Students may fail continuing their academic development because of spending their time on media. In this sense, this study is conducted in order to identify the impact of internet addiction on academic procrastination.

LITERATURE REVIEW

Academic Procrastination

Due to their nature, people can develop various behaviors over time. These behaviors may occur as a protection or a reaction against the forces coming from outside or inside of the human body. Procrastination is one of the most observed human behaviors related to delaying the acts which have a deadline (Rothblum et. al., 1986; Senecal et. al., 1995; González-Brignardello et. al., 2023) and it may be called a behavioral problem as Ferrari indicates approximately 20% of adults and more than 70-95% of undergraduate students experience procrastination (Ferrari, 2001; Badri et. al., 2011). According to the data it may be unusual to call it a problem because if it is that common, it can show that people struggle with limiting unwanted behavior. Procrastination is related to self-regulation described as a delay to begin and complete a significant task or responsibility. It may also have some results affecting people negatively like anxiety -mostly this accompanies- and depression (Sirois, 2007). It is an intentional delay to take an action being unaware that the action is going to cause negative consequences, and this is mostly unreasonable (Simpson & Pychyl, 2009). Procrastination is an option to avoid undesirable missions waiting to be completed (Badri et. al., 2011) and a way to be chosen by individuals to avoid unwanted results, such as bad feelings, grades, comments, etc. Procrastination may be divided into categories and can be listed as; (1) Compulsive procrastination, (2) Postponing decision making, (3) Neurotic procrastination, (4) General postponement, and (5) Academic procrastination (Balkıs, 2007).

As mentioned earlier, academic procrastination may be observed commonly among undergraduate students. Because this paper mainly focuses on academic procrastination to identify the students' challenges, it is defined as students' behavior to postpone completion of academic activities such as exam preparation, doing assignments, writing term projects, even if they are aware that there is a limited time for this (González-Brignardello et. al., 2023). They have difficulties in making a plan, starting the assignment and even if they start doing their assignment, they may fail completing it. Almost one-third of the students have academic procrastination in terms of exam preparation and completion of assignments, instead they nap or watch videos. This causes them to have a low academic performance, poor learning (Pychyl et al., 2000). The data shows the importance of identifying the problem and taking action against the problems that students face. At university level, procrastination may lead to dropouts or failure in academic goals (Aznar-Díaz et al., 2020; Nadarajan, et. al., 2023) and similarly undergraduate students may struggle with changing their cities, being far away from their families and evaluating their self-learning behaviors (Kachgal et al., 2001). These kinds of adaptation conditions or changes in emotions may cause them to procrastinate their academic responsibilities or personal growth goals.

Research indicates that procrastinators often have a present-focused bias and difficulty with long-term planning, making them more vulnerable to immediate temptations (Ferrari, 2001; Steel, 2007; Svartdal et al., 2020). Even if they start completing their tasks, they can easily give up on continuing with daydreaming, planning a meeting for the future, chatting with their friends, etc. Academic procrastination has some common traits including psychological beliefs, distraction, social determinants, lack of time management, and laziness (Moonaghi & Beydokhti, 2017). Even if laziness may be observed in some individuals, it may not be possible to call each person as 'lazy' because they experience self-management and regulation challenges rather than directly choosing to do nothing for their academic future. Procrastinators who struggle with their self-regulation are not likely to resist social temptations contrary to normal students (Badri et. al., 2011). If they are distracted less, they can support their own learning and provide an effective learner autonomy.

There may be some reasons for the causes of procrastination and tendencies of people. Some approaches have explanations about the reasons. For instance, cognitive-behavioral approaches states that there are some factors affecting procrastination such as perfectionism, beliefs, criticism, distress (anxiety, depression), low self-esteem, helplessness and lack of self-control (Ferrari et al., 1995; Çakıcı, 2003; Uzun, et. al., 2014). The reason is not always students' anxiety; perfectionism can be observed in some students. Although they are capable enough, they struggle with starting or completing their tasks because they want to reach their best version of performance, or they show anxiety with the fear of failure. Therefore, academic procrastination effects students' wellbeing negatively. They may experience poor academic performance (Kim & Seo, 2015), stress, anxiety disorder, depression (Huntley, et. al., 2019; Amani, et. al., 2021; Sirois, 2013) and physical effects (Sirois, 2023; Sirois 2016; González-Brignardello et. al., 2023). On the other hand, the reinforcement approach defines procrastination with reward and punishment systems. If students are rewarded by enjoyment, procrastination may occur (Ferrari et al., 1995; Uzun, et. al., 2014) which may highlight the correlation between internet addiction related with the reward center of the brain and academic procrastination. As a result, academic procrastination may be a reason and a result of some changes in human behavior, brain or feelings. It is possible to relate various factors with academic procrastination. According to Karataş and Bademcioğlu (2015) there is a negative correlation between academic procrastination and extroversion, agreeableness, conscientiousness, and openness to experience. On the other hand, there is a positive correlation between academic procrastination and neuroticism. Balance between the responsibilities and the feelings effects how individuals are effected in their lives by academic procrastination.

Internet Addiction

Internet addiction can be defined as excessive or uncontrollable urges or behaviors related to computer use and internet access. This situation, which emerged with the ease of access to technology, causes both physiological and psychological impairments in people. This situation has started to attract more and more attention in the popular media and among researchers, especially with the widespread use of social media (Shaw & Black, 2008). Today, most people reach the information or spend their time with enjoyable content via applications. Although having the world into their hands may be beneficial for the users, widespread and unconscious use of the Internet for entertainment and pastime can lead to addiction (Akbay & Gizir, 2010). Addiction may have genetic relations in terms of not having enough dopamine receptors or insufficient serotonin or dopamine (Eisen et. al., 1998; Grant et. al., 2006; Beard, 2005; Cash et. al., 2012) as much as unconscious and excessive exposure to the stimulator may cause it. To increase the pleasure individuals, stimulate the reward center of the brain (Linden, 2011; Gabor, 2010). If the center is activated, dopamine's, opiates and some neurochemicals' level is increased. After that relevant receptors may be affected, and this disturbs the reward center's working pace by producing tolerance. Overuse of the internet may disturb dopamine release (Bai et. al., 2001; Ko, et. al., 2009; Cash et. al., 2012). Internet addiction is a behavioral and non-drug addiction (Milková et al., 2022; Vacek & Vondrackova 2014; Zou et al., 2017) which is an uncontrollable impulse to use and reach the internet causing a disease (Weinstein & Lejoyeux, 2010; Nadarajan, et. al., 2023). It is characterized by poorly controlled preoccupations and caused by excessive use of the internet and leads to failures in academic purposes, social isolation, emotional disturbances (Radeef, et. al., 2018). For students, the internet is a pleasure mechanism which is not controlled and causes them to skip their academic responsibilities (Nadarajan, et. al., 2023).

The negative effects of internet addiction may be related to the ages of the users. For example, children may fail to limit their use because they may prefer playing games or other enjoyable activities. They prefer games or interactivity for each action. Traditional schooling struggles with providing enough opportunities to help them interact with each other. This doesn't happen cognitively, this is a preference of digital natives (Prensky, 2001). Thus, they may need reinforcement and support to complete their academic responsibilities. On the other hand, older users may fail completing their daily responsibilities while scrolling down the social apps. Furthermore, fMRI results indicate that adolescents with internet addiction have impairments in function connectivity in basal ganglia of the frontal lobe (Li, et. al., 2014) as well as it may cause vision and hearing impairments, risk of obesity and muscle pain problems among individuals (Aziz, et. al., 2021). Because of its effects on both academic performance, mental and physical health harmful for individuals (Steel, 2007; Hayat et. al., 2020). Thus, individuals should be supported by their parents, teachers, mentors etc. Research has shown that certain interventions – such as cognitive-behavioral therapy, structured digital detox programs, and support groups – can help mitigate internet addiction (Shaw & Black, 2008), even if complete recovery may require sustained effort. Cognitive-behavioral approaches, medication, therapy, books, tapes or self-imposed computer ban can be used to get rid of the addiction (Shaw & Black, 2008). Even if the negative effects of the internet addiction may not be eliminated at a time, they may be eased over time.

SIGNIFICANCE OF THE STUDY

This study addresses the critical concern of internet addiction and its impact on academic procrastination among undergraduate students in the English Language Teaching (ELT) department. In an era where technological advancements and internet accessibility have become global, understanding the harmful effects of excessive internet use on students' academic performance is crucial. Hence, contributes to the broader field of educational psychology by exploring some cognitive and behavioral consequences of internet addiction, the present paper seeks answers for the following research questions:

1. Is there a significant relation between undergraduate ELT students' academic procrastination and internet addiction?
2. To what extent internet addiction affects academic procrastination among ELT undergraduate students?
3. Is there a significant difference in internet addiction between the genders?
4. Is there a significant difference in academic procrastination between the genders?

METHODOLOGY

Participants

This study employed a mixed methodology by collecting both quantitative and qualitative data to examine the effect of internet addiction on academic procrastination among undergraduate ELT students. Mixed methods research provides a comprehensive understanding of complex phenomena by integrating numerical data with in-depth insights (Creswell & Plano Clark, 2018). Quantitative data allow for the measurement of statistical relationships and generalizability (Tashakkori & Teddlie, 2010), while qualitative data capture the lived experiences and perceptions of students, offering contextual depth (Patton, 2015). Since academic procrastination and internet addiction are intertwined with cognitive, emotional, and environmental factors (Demir & Lüta, 2026; Steel, 2007; Tokunaga, 2017), a mixed-methods approach enables the exploration of these dimensions holistically, addressing both "what" and "why" questions (Bryman, 2006). By integrating numerical trends with qualitative narratives, this study provides a more nuanced perspective on how internet addiction influences students' procrastination behaviors in ELT contexts.

Participants were selected by using purposive sampling, where participants are selected according to certain criteria with regard to the research purposes (Patton, 2002). 120 undergraduate students from English language teaching department of a state university in Turkey participated in this study. There were 62 females, 53 males and 5 of the participants decided not to state their gender. Their age range was between 17 and 25. All the participants filled in a consent form before responding to the scales.

Instruments and Procedures for Data Collection

For quantitative data, this study utilized two scales. The first one was the Chen Internet Addiction Scale (CIAS) (Chen, 2005). The participants were asked to respond the items according a 4-point Likert type scale (1=Does not match my experience at all, 3=Probably matches my experience, 2=Probably does not match my experience, 4=Definitely matches my experience). The second scale was the Academic Procrastination Behavior Scale (APBS) developed by Ocak and Bulut (2015). The participants were to respond to the items with reference to a 5-point Likert type scale (1=Totally disagree, 2=Disagree, 3=no idea, 4=agree, 5=totally agree). The CIAS consists of 26 items rated on a 4-point Likert scale, yielding a total score from 26 to 104, with higher scores indicating more severe internet addiction. Similarly, the APBS consists of 35 items on a 5-point scale (total score 35 to 175), where higher scores reflect greater academic procrastination tendencies. Additionally, all the participants were asked to answer the demographic information items including their age, gender, and grade. the Cronbach's Alpha coefficient value was calculated as .89 for the IAS and .94 for the APBS and considered as appropriate to perform further statistical processes (Taber, 2018).

The scales and the demographic information form were send to 150 prospective English language teachers via Google Forms during the spring term in 2024. 120 of the participants replied back. The instruments were distributed to 150 students via Google Forms during the spring term in 2024 and 126 responses were received. Of those responses 120 (80%) were complete and useable. There was n=6 incomplete responses (4% of those invited). Many of the unusable responses exhibited a pattern of partial non-response, likely due to respondent fatigue from the 68-item survey, which had an average completion time of just over 10 minutes.

In order to obtain qualitative data, a focus group interview with open ended questions was conducted. For that purpose, a question form was developed by applying several steps to ensure the content validity. First, an item pool was generated based on the review of existing literature, theoretical frameworks, and existing qualitative studies related to the research themes (Creswell & Poth, 2018; Kvale & Brinkmann, 2015). Following that, open-ended questions were formulated to capture participants' experiences, perceptions, and underlying mechanisms about procrastination and internet addiction (Patton, 2015). Next, two field experts were asked to review the initial form independently since expert validation is a crucial step in ensuring construct validity and minimizing researcher bias (Tracy, 2010). Based on experts' feedback, we eliminated redundant and ambiguous items to increase clarity and relevance of the questions. This was followed by a blind elimination process in which another two independent reviewers evaluated the questions without prior knowledge of the researchers' expectations, ensuring the removal of leading or biased items (Lincoln & Guba, 1985). After that, a pilot study was conducted with a small representative sample to assess the comprehensibility and effectiveness of the questions in eliciting meaningful responses (Maxwell, 2012). Based on participant feedback and preliminary analysis, necessary modifications were made before finalizing the question form. As a result of the whole process, following items were used as the final question form under the themes namely: Behavior patterns and motivations, underlying psychological/social mechanisms, contextual factors, consequences and interventions.

a. Behavior Patterns and Motivations
    1. Can you describe a recent instance where you procrastinated on an academic task? What were you doing instead?

    2. When you use the internet during procrastination, what specific activities do you engage in? Why do you think these activities are appealing when avoiding work?
    3. How do you feel before, during, and after procrastinating? Does internet use amplify or alleviate these feelings?
b. Underlying Mechanisms
    1. In your experience, does internet addiction cause procrastination, or does procrastination lead to excessive internet use? How might they reinforce each other?
    2. What personal traits or emotions do you think make you more vulnerable to procrastination and internet overuse?
    3. Do you use the internet as a coping mechanism for academic stress? If so, how?
c. Contextual Factors
    1. How does your academic workload or the nature of English language teaching tasks influence your procrastination habits?
    2. Has your teaching practicum or classroom experiences affected your relationship with procrastination or internet use?
    3. Are there institutional or cultural factors that encourage or discourage these behaviors?
d. Consequences and Interventions
    1. How has procrastination or internet addiction impacted your academic performance, teaching preparation, or well-being?
    2. What strategies have you tried to reduce procrastination or internet overuse? Which worked or failed, and why?
    3. If you could design a program to help future English teachers address these issues, what would it include?
    4. How could teacher training programs better support students in balancing productive internet use versus addictive/distracting use?

DATA ANALYSIS AND FINDINGS

All quantitative analyses were conducted using IBM SPSS Statistics 27. Prior to inferential testing, the distributional characteristics of the composite scores for academic procrastination and internet addiction were examined. Skewness and kurtosis values for both scales fell well within acceptable thresholds ($|skew| < 1$), indicating no substantial deviations from normality. Consistent with these indices, the Kolmogorov–Smirnov and Shapiro–Wilk tests did not suggest any significant departures from a normal distribution for either variable ($ps > .05$). Given that the dataset comprised aggregated scale scores and a sample size of 120, the distributional diagnostics supported the use of parametric procedures. In line with the central limit theorem, this sample size provides sufficient stability for mean-based analyses; nevertheless, non-parametric alternatives were prepared as contingency options had assumptions been violated. Overall, the observed distributional properties affirmed the suitability of the planned parametric analyses (Hair et al., 2013).

Table 1. Tests of Normality

	Kolmogorov-Smirnov[a]			*Shapiro-Wilk*		
	Statistic	*df*	*Sig.*	*Statistic*	*df*	*Sig.*
Internet addiction	,052	120	,200*	,989	120	,461
Academic Procrastination	,077	120	,078	,987	120	,309

As can be seen from the Figure 2 and Figure 3 and the Table 1, the p-values are larger than 0.05, suggesting that the normality assumption is met (Shapiro & Wilk, 1965).

Figure 2. Normal Q-Q Plot for Internet Addiction

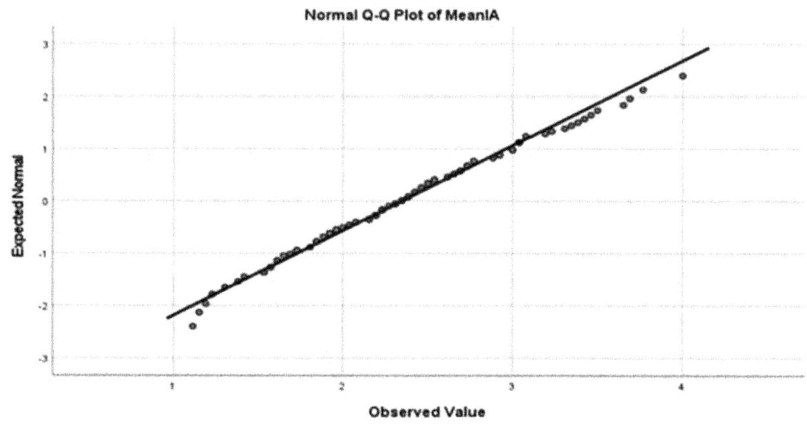

Figure 3. Normal Q-Q Plot of Academic procrastination

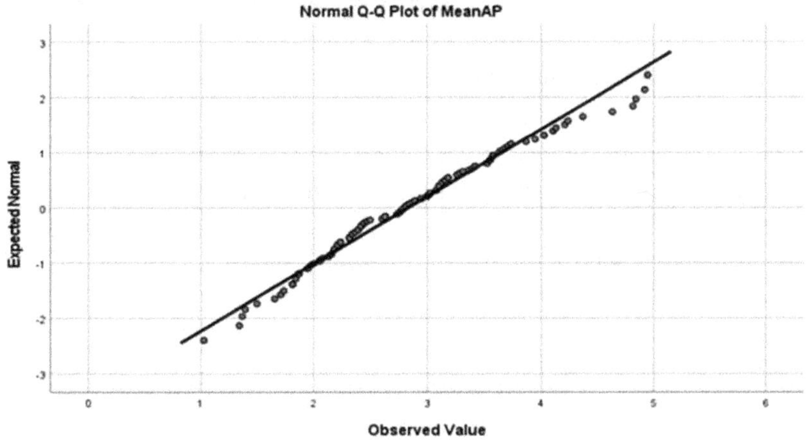

RQ$_1$: Is There a Significant Relation Between Undergraduate ELT students' Academic Procrastination and Internet Addiction?

Pearson's correlation analysis was done to determine whether there was a statistically significant relationship between the participants' academic procrastination levels and their internet addiction.

Table 2. Pearson correlation analysis

		Academic Procrastination
Internet addiction	Pearson Correlation	.484**
	Sig. (2-tailed)	<.001
	N	120

As shown by Table 2, Pearson's correlation analysis revealed a statistically significant positive relationship between internet addiction and academic procrastination ($r = 0.48$, $p < 0.001$), indicating that higher levels of internet addiction are associated with higher levels of academic procrastination.

RQ$_2$: To What Extent Internet Addiction Affects Academic Procrastination Among ELT Undergraduate Students?

The degree to which internet addiction predicted academic procrastination among the participants was analyzed through a simple linear regression model. As shown by Table 3, a significant regression was found, [$F(1, 118) = 29.63, p < .001$]. The R^2 was .20, indicating that internet addiction explained roughly 20% of the variance in academic procrastination. The regression equation can be represented as: Academic Procrastination Total = 95.55 + 0.64 × (Internet addiction)

Table 3. Regression analysis

	B	SE	β	t	p
Constant	95.55	6.72		14.2	<, 001
Internet Addiction	0.64	.11	0.64	6.01	

Dependent variable: Academic Procrastination

In other words, the regression analysis indicated that for each one-point increase in the Internet Addiction Scale score, the Academic Procrastination score increases by approximately 0.6%. These results presented on Table 3 suggest that internet addiction significantly predicts academic procrastination, with a moderate effect size.

RQ$_3$: Is There a Significant Difference in Internet Addiction Between the Genders?

Participants who preferred not to state their genders ($n = 5$) were not included in the statistical analysis for gender differences. Thus, the gender difference analysis was conducted only with those who identified themselves as male ($n = 53$, $M = 2.41$, $SD = 0.61$) and female ($n = 62$, $M = 2.30$, $SD = 0.62$) through independent samples *t*-testing.

Table 4. Independent sample test results comparing males and females on internet addiction

	Gender	N	M	SD	t	p
Internet Addiction	Male	53	2.41	.609	.118	.338
	Female	62	2.29	.623		

As presented in Table 4, the test yielded no significant results for a difference in internet addiction between the genders, $t(118) = 0.338$, $p > .05$.

RQ$_4$: Is There a Significant Difference in Academic Procrastination Between the Genders?

Another independent samples *t*-test was run to determine whether there was a statistically significant difference in academic procrastination between the male (n = 53, M = 2.60, SD = 0.783) and female participants (n = 62, M = 3.00, SD = 0.81).

Table 5. Independent sample test results comparing males and females on academic procrastination

	Gender	N	M	SD	t	p
Academic Procrastination	Male	53	2.60	.783	.118	.389
	Female	62	3.00	.810		

As presented in Table 5, the analysis revealed no statistically significant difference in academic procrastination between the genders, $t(118) = .389$, $p > .05$.

Additionally, the qualitative from the focus group interview went through an Inductive Content Analysis (ICA) to systematically identify patterns, themes, and underlying meanings emerging from participants' narratives. ICA is a widely recognized approach for analyzing qualitative data when there is limited theoretical framework guiding the categorization process, allowing themes to emerge directly from the data rather than being imposed a priori (Elo & Kyngäs, 2008). This approach enhances data-driven insights while minimizing researcher bias, which is particularly important in exploratory studies that seek to understand behavioral phenomena in educational settings (Mayring, 2014). By following the structured stages of open coding, category creation, and abstraction, ICA ensures data-driven insights while minimizing researcher bias (Hsieh & Shannon, 2005). Figure 4 shows the 5-steps procedure for conducting ICA suggested by Vears and Gillam (2022).

Figure 4. Overview of the inductive content analysis process

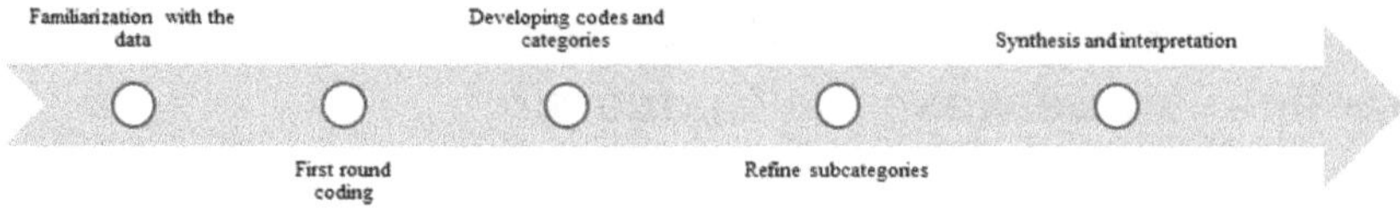

(adapted from Vears and Gillam, 2022)

MAXQDA qualitative analysis software was used to identify the themes and categories for the qualitative data. The findings are presented under 4 topics identified by the analysis as: Behavior patterns and motivations related to procrastination and internet use, underlying mechanisms linking procrastination and internet use, contextual factors influencing procrastination and internet use, and consequences of procrastination/internet addiction and proposed interventions.

Table 6. Behavior patterns and motivations related to procrastination and internet use

Category	Theme	Description	N	*f*
Procrastination Triggers	Academic Overwhelm	Feeling overwhelmed by the complexity or volume of academic tasks	7	70%
	Lack of Motivation	Struggling to find intrinsic motivation to start or complete tasks	6	60%
	Fear of Failure	Anxiety about not meeting expectations or performing poorly	5	60%
Internet Use During Procrastination	Social Media	Scrolling through platforms like Instagram or TikTok	8	80%
	Streaming	Watching TV shows, movies, or YouTube videos	6	60%
	Gaming	Playing online or mobile games	4	40%
Emotional States	Pre-Procrastination	Feelings of stress, anxiety, or boredom before procrastinating	9	90%
	During Procrastination	Temporary relief or distraction from academic pressures	8	80%
	Post-Procrastination	Guilt, regret, or increased stress after procrastinating	7	70%

As shown in Table 6, *academic overwhelm* was the most frequently reported trigger for procrastination, affecting 70% of participants. Many participants described feeling paralyzed by the complexity or volume of tasks, leading them to avoid starting altogether. For example, Participant C shared:

Participant C: "When I see how much I have to do for lesson planning, I just freeze. It's easier to distract myself than face it."

Lack of motivation (60%) and *fear of failure* (50%) were also common themes, with participants citing difficulties in finding intrinsic motivation or worrying about not meeting expectations. When procrastinating, participants predominantly turned to *social media* (80%), with many describing it as an easy way to escape academic pressures. *Streaming* (60%) and *gaming* (40%) were also popular distractions, often chosen for their immersive and time-consuming nature. Emotionally, participants reported high levels of stress or anxiety before procrastinating (90%), followed by a sense of temporary relief during the act (80%). However, this relief was often short-lived, as 70% of participants experienced guilt or regret afterward. For instance, Participant F noted:

Participant F: "I feel better for a while when I'm scrolling, but then I realize how much time I've wasted, and it just makes me more stressed."

These findings suggest that procrastination and internet use are closely tied to emotional regulation, with participants using online activities as a coping mechanism for academic stress. However, the cycle of procrastination often exacerbates negative emotions, creating a self-reinforcing loop.

Table 7. Underlying mechanisms linking procrastination and internet use

Category	Theme	Description	N	f
Causal Relationship	Procrastination Leads to Internet Use	Procrastination creates a need for distraction, leading to excessive internet use	7	70%
	Internet Use Leads to Procrastination	Internet addiction reduces focus and productivity, causing procrastination	5	50%
	Mutual Reinforcement	Procrastination and internet use create a cyclical relationship, reinforcing each other	8	80%
Personal Traits/ Emotions	Anxiety	High levels of anxiety increase vulnerability to procrastination and internet overuse	9	90%
	Perfectionism	Fear of not meeting high standards leads to avoidance and procrastination	6	60%
	Fear of Failure	Worry about failing or being judged increases reliance on internet as an escape	7	70%
	Lack of Motivation	Difficulty finding intrinsic motivation to complete tasks leads to procrastination	5	50%

continued on following page

Table 7. Continued

Category	Theme	Description	N	f
Internet as a Coping Mechanism	Stress Relief	Using the internet to temporarily escape academic stress or pressure	8	80%
	Emotional Numbing	Engaging in mindless internet activities to avoid confronting negative emotions	6	60%
	Social Connection	Turning to social media or online communities for comfort or validation	5	50%

N=10

As shown in Table 7, the relationship between procrastination and internet use is complex and often cyclical. A majority of participants (80%) described a mutual reinforcement between the two behaviors, where procrastination leads to internet use, and excessive internet use further exacerbates procrastination. For example, Participant C explained:

Participant C: "When I procrastinate, I go online to distract myself, but then I lose track of time and end up procrastinating even more."

While 70% of participants felt that *procrastination leads to internet use*, 50% also acknowledged that *internet use can cause procrastination* by reducing focus and productivity. This bidirectional relationship highlights the need for interventions that address both behaviors simultaneously. Participants identified several *personal traits and emotions* that make them more vulnerable to procrastination and internet overuse. *Anxiety* was the most frequently cited factor (90%), with many participants describing how academic pressures trigger both procrastination and internet use as a coping mechanism. *Perfectionism* (60%) and *fear of failure* (70%) were also common themes, with participants reporting that these traits often lead to avoidance behaviors. The internet was widely used as a *coping mechanism* for academic stress, with 80% of participants turning to online activities for *stress relief.* Many described using the internet to "zone out" or escape from overwhelming tasks. For instance, Participant D shared:

Participant D: "When I'm stressed about lesson planning, I watch YouTube videos to calm down, but then I end up wasting hours."

Additionally, 60% of participants used the internet for *emotional numbing*, engaging in mindless activities to avoid confronting negative emotions. A smaller group (50%) sought *social connection* online, using platforms like Instagram or Reddit to feel validated or less alone in their struggles.

These findings suggest that procrastination and internet use are deeply intertwined with emotional regulation and self-perception. Addressing these underlying mechanisms, such as anxiety, perfectionism, and the use of the internet as a coping tool, could help break the cycle of procrastination and improve academic outcomes.

Table 8. Contextual factors influencing procrastination and internet use

Category	Theme	Description	N	*f*
Academic Workload and Task Nature	Task Complexity	Overwhelm from designing detailed lesson plans or adapting materials	7	70%
	Creative Demands	Pressure to innovate in lesson planning leads to avoidance	5	50%
Teaching Practicum Impact	Observation Pressure	Anxiety about being evaluated during practicum increases procrastination	8	80%
	Stress from frequent critiques leads to internet use as an escape	Stress from frequent critiques leads to internet use as an escape	6	60%
	Classroom Unpredictability	Procrastination due to anxiety about managing unexpected classroom situations	4	40%
Institutional/ Cultural Influences	Mentor Expectations	Pressure to meet high standards set by mentors encourages procrastination	7	70%
	Comparing progress with peers increases stress and internet use	Comparing progress with peers increases stress and internet use	5	50%
	Cultural Norms	Institutional tolerance of procrastination or internet use as "normal"	4	40%

N=10

As presented in Table 8, academic workload and task nature significantly influenced procrastination habits. A majority of participants (70%) cited task complexity, such as designing lesson plans or adapting materials, as a key trigger for procrastination. For example, Participant E noted:

Participant E: "Creating engaging lesson plans feels overwhelming. I end up delaying it and scrolling through Pinterest for ideas, which turns into hours wasted."

The teaching practicum emerged as another critical contextual factor, with 80% of participants reporting observation pressure as a major source of procrastination. Many linked this anxiety to increased internet use for distraction. Participant F shared:

Participant F: "Knowing I'll be observed makes me so nervous. I procrastinate by binge-watching shows to avoid thinking about it."

Feedback overload (60%) and *classroom unpredictability* (40%) further exacerbated procrastination, particularly when participants felt unprepared to handle critiques or unexpected classroom dynamics. *Institutional and cultural factors* also played a role. *Mentor expectations* (70%) and *peer comparison* (50%) amplified stress, while some participants noted that *cultural norms* (40%) within their programs tacitly normalized procrastination. As Participant G explained:

Participant G: "Everyone in my cohort jokes about pulling all-nighters. It makes procrastination feel like a rite of passage."

Table 9. Consequences of procrastination/internet addiction and proposed interventions

Category	Theme	Description	N	*f*
Consequences	Decreased Academic Performance	Lower grades or incomplete assignments due to procrastination	8	80%
	Delayed Teaching Preparation	Last-minute lesson planning or rushed practicum tasks	7	70%
	Emotional Exhaustion	Chronic stress, guilt, or burnout from procrastination cycles	9	90%
Attempted Strategies	Time-Management Tools	Using planners, apps, or schedules to organize tasks	6	60%
	Digital Detox	Temporarily disabling apps or setting screen-time limits	5	50%
	Mindfulness	Practices Meditation or breathing exercises to reduce stress	4	40%
Proposed Interventions	Structured Time-Management Training	Workshops on prioritization, goal-setting, and task chunking	9	90%
	Peer Accountability Groups	Collaborative groups to share progress and reduce isolation	7	70%
	Digital Literacy Programs	Training on balancing productive vs. distracting internet use	8	80%
Institutional Support	Well-Being Modules	Incorporating stress management into teacher training curricula	8	80%
	Flexible Deadlines	Allowing grace periods for complex tasks to reduce overwhelm	5	50%

N=10

As shown in Table 9, procrastination and internet addiction had significant consequences, with emotional exhaustion (90%) being the most prevalent. Participants described feeling trapped in a cycle of stress and guilt, as articulated by Participant H:

Participant H: "After procrastinating, I'm too drained to catch up. It feels like I'm always running on empty."

Academic performance (80%) and teaching preparation (70%) were also negatively impacted, with many participants reporting rushed lesson plans or lower grades due to procrastination. When asked about strategies to reduce these behaviors, 60% had tried time-management tools, though success was mixed. For example, Participant I stated:

Participant I: "Planners work for a week, but then I get overwhelmed again. I need someone to hold me accountable."

Digital detoxes (50%) and mindfulness practices (40%) were less consistently effective, often failing when used in isolation. Participants proposed several interventions, with structured time-management training (90%) and digital literacy programs (80%) being the most requested. Many emphasized the need for institutional support, such as well-being modules (80%) integrated into teacher training curricula. Participant J suggested:

Participant J: "We need courses that teach us how to use the internet for lesson planning without falling into endless scrolling."

By addressing both individual habits and institutional structures, these interventions could disrupt the procrastination-internet addiction cycle, directly responding to the editors' request for "meaningful suggestions for practice."

To sum up, the findings from this focus group interview reveal a complex interplay between procrastination, internet addiction, and the academic and emotional challenges faced by prospective English language teachers. Across all four categories, several recurring themes emerged, highlighting the cyclical nature of these behaviors and their profound impact on academic performance, teaching preparation, and well-being.

DISCUSSION AND CONCLUSION

This study aimed to explore the correlation between internet addiction and academic procrastination among 120 English Language Department undergraduate students from a state university in Turkey. The first research question focuses on the correlation between internet addiction and academic procrastination. The results revealed a statistically positive correlation between internet addiction and academic procrastination, ($r = 0.48$, $p < 0.001$). The findings overlap with the studies conducted by Uzun, Unal, and Tokel (2014) which shows there is a positive correlation between internet addiction and academic procrastination. Additionally, the research conducted by Gupta, et. al. (2024), Karakaya and Altınsoy (2023), Hayat, et. al. (2020), Sarfo, et. al. (2023), Kuloğlu and Pamuk, (2016), Khai, et. al. (2021), Manap, et. al. (2023) and Srivastava and Kumar (2024) reveal that there is a positive correlation between academic procrastination and internet addiction. In other words, internet addiction has a significant positive impact on academic procrastination. Aznar-Díaz, et. al. (2020). support the positive correlation in the light of the results of their research by indicating the problematic internet use and academic procrastination have a positive correlation.

The second research question demonstrates to what extent the internet addiction and academic procrastination effect each other. The results indicated that for each point increase in internet addiction, the academic procrastination increases by almost

60%. The third research question identifies if there is a significant difference between gender and internet addiction. The findings revealed is no significant results for in internet addiction between the genders. Gupta, et. al. (2024) supports the results of this study by obtaining the similar results in their research which also indicated no significant difference between genders and internet addiction levels. However, the findings do not overlap with the research conducted by Shan et al. (2021) in which males have a higher tendency to develop Internet addiction than females. The findings related to the fourth research question addressing a difference between gender and academic procrastination demonstrated no significant difference for academic procrastination between the genders. However former studies conducted by Kassim et al. (2022) and by Akbay and Gizir (2010) indicated males with higher levels of tendency to procrastinate their academic responsibilities than females.

The qualitative findings of this study also align with and extend existing research on academic procrastination and internet addiction, highlighting their complex, cyclical interplay among prospective English teachers. Consistent with Steel's (2007) temporal motivation theory, procrastination emerged as a response to emotional and cognitive factors such as academic overwhelm, fear of failure, and perfectionism, which participants often managed through internet-based distractions (e.g., social media, streaming). This mirrors prior work linking procrastination to avoidant coping strategies (Sirois & Pychyl, 2013) and internet addiction to emotional regulation deficits (Şenormancı et al., 2014). The bidirectional relationship between procrastination and internet addiction observed here supports findings by Panek (2014), who noted that digital distractions reinforce procrastination cycles through immediate gratification. Contextual factors, such as high academic workloads and institutional pressures during teaching practicums, amplified stress and avoidance behaviors, resonating with Klingsieck's (2013) emphasis on environmental triggers in procrastination. Participants' reported consequences, including emotional exhaustion and impaired academic performance, align with longitudinal studies demonstrating the detrimental effects of procrastination on well-being (Demir, 2025; Tuckman, 1991) and the role of internet overuse in academic disengagement (Rozgonjuk et al., 2020). Proposed interventions, such as structured time-management training and digital literacy programs, reflect calls for evidence-based strategies to enhance self-regulation (Klingsieck, 2013) and mitigate maladaptive internet use (Tokunaga, 2017). These insights underscore the need for teacher training programs to integrate holistic support systems addressing both individual vulnerabilities and institutional demands, fostering resilience and productive technology use in academic settings.

In conclusion, this study highlights a significant positive correlation between internet addiction and academic procrastination among undergraduate English Language students, aligning with prior research findings in this area. This finding indicates that greater internet addiction is significantly linked to greater academic procrastination, which aligns with the positive correlation observed. The study also found no significant differences in internet addiction or academic procrastination levels between genders, consistent with some previous studies but contrasting with others that suggest higher tendencies among males. Overall, these findings contribute to a deeper understanding of the influence of internet addiction on academic behaviors and underscore the need for additional research to clarify these relationships across diverse populations and contexts.

PEDAGOGICAL IMPLICATIONS

The findings of this study suggest several pedagogical implications for educators and academic advisors working with undergraduate students, particularly in English language programs. Given the positive correlation between internet addiction and academic procrastination, educators might benefit from integrating digital literacy and self-regulation strategies into the curriculum to help students manage their online time effectively. Workshops or counseling sessions focused on balancing online activities with academic responsibilities could mitigate procrastination behaviors linked to excessive internet use (Young, 1999). Additionally, educators can encourage students to set realistic goals, practice time management, and use internet resources constructively for academic purposes, rather than for non-academic activities that may hinder their progress. Since no significant gender differences were observed, interventions can be designed to be broadly applicable across student populations, promoting an inclusive approach to addressing procrastination and internet use issues.

LIMITATIONS AND SUGGESTIONS

Having a relatively small group of participants limited with a state university's undergraduate students make it challenging to identify how internet addiction effects the academic procrastination in general. Also, further research is needed to find out psychological effects and results of internet addiction and academic procrastination. As a result, future research should pave a way to make the consequences endurable for the young generation and give solutions to overcome negative effects of the variables in a large group of participants including K-12 and university students. Also their distribution and the differences between the age groups should be investigated.

DATA AVAILABILITY STATEMENT

The data is available only upon a reasonable request to the corresponding authors.

ETHICS STATEMENT

This research (2024-YÖNP-0346) was approved by the decision number 06/32 taken in the Scientific Research and Publication Ethics Board of Çanakkale Onsekiz Mart University on 24.04.2024. The research protocol rigorously ensured the confidentiality and anonymity of all participants.

INFORMED CONSENT

All participants provided informed consent prior to providing responses to the interview.

AUTHOR CONTRIBUTIONS

Both authors contributed to the study conception and design. Material preparation, data collection and the first draft of the manuscript was written were performed by S.C. Supervision, methodology, and reviewing and editing was performed by B.D. Both authors commented on the manuscript.

ACKNOWLEDGMENT

No persons or third-party services were involved in the research or manuscript preparation who are not listed as an author or acknowledged elsewhere in the manuscript.

REFERENCES

Akbay, S., & Gizir, C. (2010). Cinsiyete göre üniversite öğrencilerinde akademik erteleme davranışı: Akademik güdülenme, akademik özyeterlik ve akademik yükleme stillerinin rolü [Academic procrastination behavior in university students by gender: The role of academic motivation, academic self-efficacy, and academic attribution styles]. *Mersin Üniversitesi Eğitim Fakültesi Dergisi, 6*(1), 60–78.

Amani, H., Habibi-Kaleybar, R., Farid, A., & Sheykhalizadeh, S. (2021). Meta-analysis of the effectiveness of interventions on test anxiety reduction. *Psychological Research, 45*, 56.

Aziz, N., Nordin, M. J., Abdulkadir, S. J., & Salih, M. M. M. (2021). Digital addiction: Systematic review of computer game addiction impact on adolescent physical health. *Electronics (Basel), 10*(9), 996. DOI: 10.3390/electronics10090996

Aznar-Díaz, I., Romero-Rodríguez, J.-M., García-González, A., & Ramírez-Montoya, M.-S. (2020). Mexican and Spanish university students' Internet addiction and academic procrastination: Correlation and potential factors. *PLoS One, 15*(5), e0233655. DOI: 10.1371/journal.pone.0233655 PMID: 32442238

Badri Gargari, R., Sabouri, H., & Norzad, F. (2011). Academic procrastination: The relationship between causal attribution styles and behavioral postponement. *Iranian Journal of Psychiatry and Behavioral Sciences, 5*(2), 76–72. PMID: 24644450

Bai, Y.-M., Lin, C.-C., & Chen, J.-Y. (2001). Internet addiction disorder among clients of a virtual clinic. *Psychiatric Services (Washington, D.C.), 52*(10), 1397. DOI: 10.1176/appi.ps.52.10.1397 PMID: 11585966

Balkıs, M. (2007). Öğretmen adaylarındaki erteleme eğiliminin, karar verme stilleri ile ilişkisi [The relationship between preservice teachers' tendency to procrastinate and their decision-making styles]. *Pamukkale Üniversitesi Eğitim Fakültesi Dergisi, 1*(21), 67–83.

Beard, K. W. (2005). Internet addiction: A review of current assessment techniques and potential assessment questions. *Cyberpsychology & Behavior*, *8*(1), 7–14. DOI: 10.1089/cpb.2005.8.7 PMID: 15738688

Bryman, A. (2006). Integrating quantitative and qualitative research: How is it done? *Qualitative Research*, *6*(1), 97–113. DOI: 10.1177/1468794106058877

Çakıcı, D. Ç. (2003). Lise ve üniversite öğrencilerinde genel erteleme ve akademik erteleme davranışının incelenmesi [An examination of the general procrastination behavior and academic procrastination behavior in high-school and university students] (Unpublished master's thesis). Ankara University, Ankara, Turkey.

Cash, H., Rae, C. D., Steel, A. H., & Winkler, A. (2012). Internet addiction: A brief summary of research and practice. *Current Psychiatry Reviews*, *8*(4), 292–298. DOI: 10.2174/157340012803520513 PMID: 23125561

Creswell, J. W., & Plano Clark, V. L. (2018). *Designing and conducting mixed methods research* (3rd ed.). SAGE Publications.

Creswell, J. W., & Poth, C. N. (2018). *Qualitative inquiry and research design: Choosing among five approaches* (4th ed.). SAGE Publications.

Demir, B. (2025). The Effect of Well-Being Interventions on English Language Pre-Service Teachers' Ability to Cope with the Challenges During Their School Practicum. In G. Sönmez (Ed), *Challenges in Teacher Education: Pedagogy, Management, and Materials* (pp. 87-113). IGI Global Scientific Publishing. https://doi.org/10.4018/979-8-3693-7342-2

Demir, B., & Lüta, K. (2026). The mediating role of AI literacy in the relationship between technostress and cognitive load in higher education. In *Impacts of artificial intelligence on educational psychology and cognitive development* (pp. 1–26). IGI Global. https://doi.org/10.4018/979-8-3373-6375-2.ch007

Digital 2023 Global Overview Report. (2023). Retrieved May 28, 2024, from https://wearesocial.com/wp-content/uploads/2023/03/Digital-2023-Global-Overview-Report.pdf

Eisen, S., Lin, N., Lyons, M., Scherrer, J., Griffith, K., & True, W.. (1998). Familial influences on gambling behavior: An analysis of 3359 twin pairs. *Addiction (Abingdon, England)*, *93*(9), 1375–1384. DOI: 10.1046/j.1360-0443.1998.93913758.x PMID: 9926543

Elo, S., & Kyngäs, H. (2008). The qualitative content analysis process. *Journal of Advanced Nursing*, *62*(1), 107–115. DOI: 10.1111/j.1365-2648.2007.04569.x PMID: 18352969

Ferrari, J. R. (2001). Procrastination as self-regulation failure of performance: Effects of cognitive load, self-awareness, and time limits on "working best under pressure.". *European Journal of Personality*, *15*(5), 391–406. DOI: 10.1002/per.413

Ferrari, J. R., Johnson, J. L., & McCown, W. G. (1995). *Procrastination and task avoidance: Theory, research, and treatment*. Springer. DOI: 10.1007/978-1-4899-0227-6

González-Brignardello, M. P., Sánchez-Elvira Paniagua, A., & López-González, M. Á. (2023). Academic procrastination in children and adolescents: A scoping review. *Children (Basel, Switzerland)*, *10*(6), 1016. DOI: 10.3390/children10061016 PMID: 37371248

Grant, J. E., Brewer, J. A., & Potenza, M. N. (2006). The neurobiology of substance and behavioral addictions. *CNS Spectrums*, *11*(12), 924–930. DOI: 10.1017/S109285290001511X PMID: 17146406

Gupta, S., Gupta, S., & Kumar, S. (2024). Influence of internet addiction and academic procrastination on academic achievement of secondary & senior secondary school students. *International Journal of Indian Psychology*, *12*(2), 1293–1308. DOI: 10.25215/1202.115

Hair, J. F., Black, W. C., Babin, B. J., Anderson, R. E., & Tatham, R. L. (2013). *Multivariate data analysis* (8th ed.). Pearson Education Limited.

Hayat, A., Kojuri, J., & Amini, M. (2020). Academic procrastination of medical students: The role of Internet addiction. *Journal of Advances in Medical Education & Professionalism*, *8*(2), 83–89. DOI: 10.30476/JAMP.2020.85000.1159 PMID: 32426392

Hsieh, H. F., & Shannon, S. E. (2005). Three approaches to qualitative content analysis. *Qualitative Health Research*, *15*(9), 1277–1288. DOI: 10.1177/1049732305276687 PMID: 16204405

Huntley, C. D., Young, B., Temple, J., Longworth, M., Smith, C. T., Jha, V., & Fisher, P. L. (2019). The efficacy of interventions for test-anxious university students: A meta-analysis of randomized controlled trials. *Journal of Anxiety Disorders*, *63*, 36–50. DOI: 10.1016/j.janxdis.2019.01.007 PMID: 30826687

Kachgal, M. M., Hansen, L. S., & Nutter, K. J. (2001). Academic procrastination prevention/intervention: Strategies and recommendations. *Journal of Developmental Education*, *25*(1), 14–24.

Karakaya, K., & Altınsoy, F. (2023). Academic procrastination of university students: The role of problematic internet use, self-regulated online learning, and academic self-efficacy. *MOJET, 11*(1), 77–93. DOI: 10.52380/mojet.2023.11.1.459

Karataş, H., & Bademcioglu, M. (2015). The explanation of the academic procrastination behaviour of pre-service teachers with five factor personality traits. *The International Journal of Research in Teacher Education, 6*(2), 11–25.

Kassim, F., Azmi, N. F., Rahman, N. A. A., & Zainal, N. R. (2022). Gender difference in procrastination among university students. *Asian Journal of Research in Education and Social Sciences, 4*(3), 11–22. DOI: 10.55057/ajress.2022.4.3.2

Khai Lin, C., Abdul, N., Faizatul, A., & Peh, W. (2021). Factor contributing to internet addiction and its influence on academic procrastination behavior among UUM students. *Journal of Governance and Development, 17*(2), 61–75. DOI: 10.32890/jgd2021.17.2.4

Kim, K. R., & Seo, E. H. (2015). The relationship between procrastination and academic performance: A meta-analysis. *Personality and Individual Differences, 82*, 26–33. DOI: 10.1016/j.paid.2015.02.038

Klingsieck, K. B. (2013). Procrastination. *European Psychologist, 18*(1), 24–34. DOI: 10.1027/1016-9040/a000138

Ko, C.-H., Liu, G.-C., Hsiao, S., Yen, J.-Y., Yang, M.-J., Lin, W.-C., Yen, C.-F., & Chen, C.-S. (2009). Brain activities associated with gaming urge of online gaming addiction. *Journal of Psychiatric Research, 43*(7), 739–747. DOI: 10.1016/j.jpsychires.2008.09.012 PMID: 18996542

Kvale, S., & Brinkmann, S. (2015). *InterViews: Learning the craft of qualitative research interviewing* (3rd ed.). SAGE Publications.

Li, B., Friston, K. J., Liu, J., Liu, Y., Zhang, G., Cao, F., Su, L., Yao, S., Lu, H., & Hu, D. (2014). Impaired frontal-basal ganglia connectivity in adolescents with internet addiction. *Scientific Reports, 4*(1), 5027. DOI: 10.1038/srep05027 PMID: 24848380

Lincoln, Y. S., & Guba, E. G. (1985). *Naturalistic inquiry*. SAGE Publications. DOI: 10.1016/0147-1767(85)90062-8

Linden, D. J. (2011). *The compass of pleasure: How our brains make fatty foods, orgasm, exercise, marijuana, generosity, vodka, learning, and gambling feel so good*. Viking Adult.

Manap, A., Rizzo, A., Yıldırmaz, A., Dilekçi, Ü., & Yıldırım, M. (2023). The mediating role of procrastination in the relationship between fear of missing out and internet addiction in university students. *International Journal of Environmental Research and Public Health*, *21*(1), 49. DOI: 10.3390/ijerph21010049 PMID: 38248514

Maxwell, J. A. (2012). *A realist approach for qualitative research*. SAGE Publications.

Mayring, P. (2014). *Qualitative content analysis: Theoretical foundation, basic procedures and software solution*. Beltz.

Milková, E., Kaliba, M., & Ambrozova, P. (2022). Internet addiction in university students: Czech study. *Journal on Efficiency and Responsibility in Education and Science*, *15*(2), 94–102. DOI: 10.7160/eriesj.2022.150204

Moonaghi, H. K., & Beydokhti, T. B. (2017). Academic procrastination and its characteristics: A narrative review. *Future of Medical Education Journal*, *7*(2), 43–50.

Nadarajan, S., Hengudomsub, P., & Wacharasin, C. (2023). The role of academic procrastination on Internet addiction among Thai university students: A cross-sectional study. *Belitung Nursing Journal*, *9*(4), 384–390. DOI: 10.33546/bnj.2755 PMID: 37645572

Ocak, G., & Bulut, R. (2015). The scale of academic procrastination: Validity and reliability study. *International Journal of Social Sciences and Education Research*, *1*(2), 709–726.

Panek, E. (2014). Left to their own devices: College students' "guilty pleasure" media use and time management. *Communication Research*, *41*(4), 561–577. DOI: 10.1177/0093650213499657

Patton, M. Q. (2002). *Qualitative Research and Evaluation Methods* (3rd ed.). Sage Publications.

Patton, M. Q. (2015). *Qualitative research & evaluation methods: Integrating theory and practice* (4th ed.). SAGE Publications.

Prensky, M. (2001). Digital natives, digital immigrants part 2: Do they really think differently? *On the Horizon*, *9*(6), 1–6. DOI: 10.1108/10748120110424843

Pychyl, T. A., Morin, R. W., & Salmon, B. R. (2000). Procrastination and the planning fallacy: An examination of the study habits of university students. *Journal of Social Behavior and Personality*, *15*(5), 135–150.

Radeef, A., Ghazi, G., & Musa, R. (2018). Translation and validation study of the Chen Internet Addiction Scale (CIAS) among Malaysian college students. *Journal of International Dental and Medical Research*, *11*, 32–37.

Rothblum, E. D., Solomon, L. J., & Murakami, J. (1986). Affective, cognitive, and behavioral differences between high and low procrastinators. *Journal of Counseling Psychology*, *33*(4), 387–394. DOI: 10.1037/0022-0167.33.4.387

Rozgonjuk, D., Sindermann, C., Elhai, J. D., & Montag, C. (2020). Individual differences in fear of missing out (FoMO): Age, gender, and the Big Five personality trait domains, facets, and items. *Personality and Individual Differences*, *171*, 110546. DOI: 10.1016/j.paid.2020.110546

Sarfo, J. O., Amoadu, M., & Ansah, E. (2023). Internet addiction among college students from 20 countries: Scoping review of risk factors and impact on academic procrastination and sleep quality. *International Journal of Media and Information Literacy*, *8*(2), 382–400. DOI: 10.13187/ijmil.2023.2.382

Senecal, C., Koestner, R., & Vallerand, R. J. (1995). Self-regulation and academic procrastination. *The Journal of Social Psychology*, *135*(5), 607–619. DOI: 10.1080/00224545.1995.9712234

Şenormancı, Ö., Şenormancı, G., Güçlü, O., & Konkan, R. (2014). Attachment and family functioning in patients with internet addiction. *General Hospital Psychiatry*, *36*(2), 203–207. DOI: 10.1016/j.genhosppsych.2013.10.012 PMID: 24262601

Shan, X., Ou, Y., Ding, Y., Yan, H., Chen, J., Zhao, J., & Guo, W. (2021). Associations between internet addiction and gender, anxiety, coping styles and acceptance in university freshmen in South China. *Frontiers in Psychiatry*, *12*, 558080. Advance online publication. DOI: 10.3389/fpsyt.2021.558080 PMID: 34135779

Shapiro, S. S., & Wilk, M. B. (1965). An analysis of variance test for normality (complete samples). *Biometrika*, *52*(3/4), 591–611. DOI: 10.2307/2333709

Shaw, M., & Black, D. W. (2008). Internet addiction: Definition, assessment, epidemiology, and clinical management. *CNS Drugs*, *22*(5), 353–365. DOI: 10.2165/00023210-200822050-00001 PMID: 18399706

Simpson, W., & Pychyl, T. (2009). In search of the arousal procrastinator: Investigating the relation between procrastination, arousal-based personality traits, and beliefs about procrastination motivations. *Personality and Individual Differences*, *47*(8), 906–911. DOI: 10.1016/j.paid.2009.07.013

Sirois, F. (2007). "I'll look after my health, later": A replication and extension of the procrastination–health model with community-dwelling adults. *Personality and Individual Differences*, *43*(1), 15–26. DOI: 10.1016/j.paid.2006.11.003

Sirois, F. M. (2013). Procrastination and stress: Exploring the role of self-compassion. *Self and Identity*, *13*(2), 128–145. DOI: 10.1080/15298868.2013.763404

Sirois, F. M. (2023). Procrastination and stress: A conceptual review of why context matters. *International Journal of Environmental Research and Public Health, 20*(6), 5031. DOI: 10.3390/ijerph20065031 PMID: 36981941

Sirois, F. M., & Pychyl, T. A. (2013). Procrastination and the priority of short-term mood regulation: Consequences for future self. *Social and Personality Psychology Compass, 7*(2), 115–127. DOI: 10.1111/spc3.12011

Sirois, F. M., & Pychyl, T. A. (2016). *Procrastination, health, and well-being*. Academic Press.

Srivastava, S., & Kumar, C. (2024). Adjustment, academic procrastination, and internet addiction among school students: A correlation study. *International Journal of Indian Psychology, 12*(2), 74. DOI: 10.25215/1202.074

Steel, P. (2007). The nature of procrastination: A meta-analytic and theoretical review of quintessential self-regulatory failure. *Psychological Bulletin, 133*(1), 65–94. DOI: 10.1037/0033-2909.133.1.65 PMID: 17201571

Svartdal, F., Dahl, T. I., Gamst-Klaussen, T., Koppenborg, M., & Klingsieck, K. B. (2020). How study environments foster academic procrastination: Overview and recommendations. *Frontiers in Psychology, 11*, 540910. DOI: 10.3389/fpsyg.2020.540910 PMID: 33224046

Tokunaga, R. S. (2017). A meta-analysis of the relationships between psychosocial problems and internet habits: Synthesizing internet addiction, problematic internet use, and deficient self-regulation research. *Communication Monographs, 84*(4), 423–446. DOI: 10.1080/03637751.2017.1332419

Tracy, S. J. (2010). Qualitative quality: Eight "big-tent" criteria for excellent qualitative research. *Qualitative Inquiry, 16*(10), 837–851. DOI: 10.1177/1077800410383121

Tuckman, B. W. (1991). The development and concurrent validity of the Procrastination Scale. *Educational and Psychological Measurement, 51*(2), 473–480. DOI: 10.1177/0013164491512022

Türkiye İstatistik Kurumu. (2023). *Hanehalkı Bilişim Teknolojileri (BT) Kullanım Araştırması, 2023*. Retrieved June 24, 2024, from https://data.tuik.gov.tr/Bulten/Index?p=Hanehalki-Bilisim-Teknolojileri-%28BT%29-Kullanim-Arastirmasi-2023-49407

Uzun, A., Unal, E., & Tokel, S. (2014). Exploring internet addiction, academic procrastination, and general procrastination among pre-service ICT teachers. *Mevlana International Journal of Education, 4*(1), 189–201. DOI: 10.13054/mije.14.18.4.1

Vacek, J., & Vondrackova, P. (2014). Behavioural addictions: Classification, phenomenology, prevalence and therapy. *Česká a Slovenská*, *110*(3), 144–150.

Weinstein, A., & Lejoyeux, M. (2010). Internet addiction or excessive internet use. *The American Journal of Drug and Alcohol Abuse*, *36*(5), 277–283. DOI: 10.3109/00952990.2010.491880 PMID: 20545603

Young, K. S. (1999). Internet addiction: Symptoms, evaluation, and treatment. *Innovations in Clinical Practice*, *17*, 19–31.

Zou, Z., Wang, H., d'Oleire Uquillas, F., Wang, X., Ding, J., & Chen, H. (2017). Definition of substance and non-substance addiction. In Zhang, X., Shi, J., & Tao, R. (Eds.), *Substance and Non-substance Addiction* (pp. 21–41). Springer Singapore., DOI: 10.1007/978-981-10-5562-1_2

Chapter 5
Social Media's Impact on Student Mental Health and Digital Literacy

Ami S. Shah
https://orcid.org/0009-0001-1905-3634
Parul University, India

ABSTRACT

We are living in an age of rapid digital tranformation where technological innovations are shaping nearly every aspect of human interaction, learning, and lifestyle. At the heart of this revolution lies social media, which has moved far beyond being a casual communication tool to becoming an essential component of modern existence. For students, who represent one of the most digitally active populations, social media is not merely a platform for recreation—it is embedded in their academic endeavors, social exchanges, identity formation, and even professional aspirations. Platforms such as Facebook, Instagram, Twitter (now X), TikTok, YouTube, and Snapchat have revolutionized how young people connect with knowledge, peers, and opportunities. YouTube tutorials support academic study, LinkedIn facilitates early professional networking, and WhatsApp groups are used for collaborative assignments. This digital ecosystem has created unprecedented avenues for growth and inclusion, offering students a sense of belonging in global virtual communities.

1. INTRODUCTION

We are living in an age of rapid digital tranformation where technological innovations are shaping nearly every aspect of human interaction, learning, and lifestyle. At the heart of this revolution lies social media, which has moved far beyond being

DOI: 10.4018/979-8-3373-5007-3.ch005

a casual communication tool to becoming an essential component of modern existence. For students, who represent one of the most digitally active populations, social media is not merely a platform for recreation—it is embedded in their academic endeavors, social exchanges, identity formation, and even professional aspirations.

Platforms such as Facebook, Instagram, Twitter (now X), TikTok, YouTube, and Snapchat have revolutionized how young people connect with knowledge, peers, and opportunities. YouTube tutorials support academic study, LinkedIn facilitates early professional networking, and WhatsApp groups are used for collaborative assignments. This digital ecosystem has created unprecedented avenues for growth and inclusion, offering students a sense of belonging in global virtual communities.

However, alongside these benefits, social media use brings with it a growing set of psychological, emotional, and behavioral challenges. Prolonged screen exposure, compulsive scrolling, online comparisons, and exposure to cyberbullying are increasingly associated with higher levels of anxiety, stress, and depressive symptoms among students. Furthermore, sleep disruption and diminished self-esteem are becoming common outcomes of excessive online engagement.

This duality has made the role of digital literacy increasingly important. Digital literacy encompasses more than technical know-how; it reflects the critical thinking skills, ethical awareness, and socio-emotional capacity to navigate online platforms responsibly. Without adequate digital literacy, students are vulnerable to misinformation, online exploitation, and unhealthy digital consumption patterns—all of which exacerbate mental health challenges.

This chapter explores the complex relationship between social media, mental health, and digital literacy. It emphasizes how the interplay of these three domains shapes students' well-being, academic engagement, and preparedness for the future. The chapter also underscores the importance of equipping students with strategies for balanced digital use, supported by educators, policymakers, and institutions.

Objectives of the Chapter:

1. To analyze the role of social media in student life and education.
2. To assess both positive and negative impacts of social media on mental health.
3. To discuss the significance of digital literacy in the contemporary educational system.
4. To explore the connections between digital literacy and mental well-being.
5. To recommend practical strategies for students, educators, and policymakers to encourage balanced digital engagement.

2. SOCIAL MEDIA AND STUDENT LIFE

Students rank among the most active users of social media globally. According to a 2023 Pew Research Center report, more than 95% of teenagers in the United States use at least one social media platform, with YouTube, Instagram, and TikTok dominating their preferences. Similar patterns are observed globally, including in countries like India, where smartphone penetration and affordable internet packages have accelerated student adoption of digital platforms. What was once an optional pastime has now become woven into the very fabric of student life, so much so that the idea of a young learner existing without social media seems almost inconceivable. A student's daily rhythm often begins and ends with a screen—scrolling through feeds before classes, sharing updates during study breaks, and checking notifications before sleep. This constant presence underscores how deeply these platforms have become entwined with education, identity, and social belonging.

Social media functions as an ecosystem of virtual communities. Students join WhatsApp groups to exchange notes, participate in online study circles, and collaborate on projects. The classroom extends beyond four walls, as assignments and discussions often flow seamlessly into digital spaces where conversations continue long after the school bell rings. In these groups, students share PDF files, audio explanations, or video snippets that make learning more accessible and collaborative. For many, it is easier to ask a peer on WhatsApp or Telegram for clarification than to raise a hand in class. The comfort of informal digital spaces has reduced hesitation and opened avenues for peer-to-peer support. Beyond messaging platforms, online forums, Discord study servers, and Reddit communities serve as digital libraries where academic resources circulate widely. A student in Delhi can download notes prepared by a student in New York, just as easily as one in Lagos can contribute insights to a discussion that benefits a student in Tokyo. In doing so, social media dissolves traditional barriers of geography and institutional privilege, enabling the freer exchange of knowledge than ever before.

Platforms like LinkedIn are not only professional spaces but also gateways for students to access mentorship, internships, and career guidance. Unlike the traditional routes of career counseling or formal job fairs, LinkedIn provides a dynamic and ongoing exposure to industry professionals. A student exploring data science might follow leaders in the field, participate in conversations about emerging technologies, or even publish their own reflections that reach a global audience. For many young learners, the first internship or freelance opportunity often comes from a LinkedIn message rather than a campus noticeboard. Similarly, professional communities on Twitter, Facebook groups, or even Slack workspaces allow students to network far beyond their immediate social circles. This digital professionalization means that career exploration begins earlier and unfolds more organically, guided by connections and mentors who may be continents apart.

On creative platforms like Instagram, TikTok, or Pinterest, students explore identity, showcase talent, and even establish entrepreneurial ventures. The digital stage has democratized creativity in profound ways. A teenager with a flair for sketching no longer needs an art gallery to gain recognition; an Instagram account can attract thousands of followers who appreciate the work. A student passionate about dance can post short videos on TikTok that not only bring joy to viewers but also generate opportunities for sponsorships, collaborations, and professional training. Pinterest allows students to curate mood boards that serve as both personal inspiration and collaborative tools in design or architecture projects. Creativity is no longer confined to school exhibitions or hobby clubs; it thrives in the limitless realm of online communities. For some, these digital ventures evolve into income-generating enterprises, as students learn to monetize their reach through brand partnerships, commissioned work, or online shops linked to their profiles. Thus, social media has blurred the line between student, creator, and entrepreneur, fostering a generation that is both expressive and enterprising.

The academic potential of social media cannot be dismissed. It provides exposure to diverse perspectives, promotes collaborative learning, and nurtures global connectivity. Students today are not restricted to textbooks or lectures from their own teachers; they have access to voices from across the world, each offering unique insights. A history student in Brazil can listen to a recorded lecture by a renowned professor in the United Kingdom, or watch a documentary recommended by peers in South Africa. Discussions under educational YouTube videos often reveal a mosaic of perspectives, from cultural anecdotes to practical applications, turning passive viewing into an interactive learning process. Platforms like Twitter have also become informal classrooms, where threads break down complex ideas—from climate change to quantum physics—into digestible nuggets that spark curiosity and debate.

For instance, Massive Open Online Courses (MOOCs) are often promoted through social media, enabling students to join international learning communities. A simple post on Facebook might lead a student to a free course on machine learning offered by a top university, opening a pathway that would otherwise remain inaccessible. When peers join together, the collective motivation often sustains participation in these demanding online courses. Study groups form on Telegram, peer assessments are shared via Twitter, and collaborative projects sometimes outgrow the course to become real-world start-ups. The power of social media lies not only in distributing knowledge but also in creating networks of accountability and encouragement that keep students engaged in their academic pursuits.

However, challenges persist. Overuse of these platforms leads to procrastination, distraction from academic work, reduced productivity, and in severe cases, digital addiction. The same platforms that help a student find resources can also trap them in endless scrolling, consuming hours that could have been spent on assignments, sleep, or physical activity. The lure of notifications is constant, and the dopamine-driven design of these apps makes self-regulation difficult, especially for adolescents. Students often find themselves oscillating between productive academic use and unproductive time sinks, blurring the line between intentional learning and passive consumption. This paradox—of tools designed for connection also becoming agents of distraction—is one of the defining dilemmas of contemporary student life.

Cyberbullying, online harassment, and exposure to inappropriate or false information also have direct repercussions on students' emotional health. The anonymity and reach of social media amplify both the best and worst of human behavior. A single negative comment can overshadow dozens of supportive ones, and the permanence of online posts often means that mistakes linger longer than they would in offline spaces. For vulnerable students, this can translate into anxiety, self-doubt, or withdrawal from social interactions. Moreover, misinformation spreads rapidly, leaving students exposed to distorted realities that shape their worldview and, at times, their academic understanding. From fake news during elections to misleading health advice during pandemics, the digital ecosystem is riddled with pitfalls that require critical literacy skills to navigate. Yet, many students are thrust into this environment without adequate guidance, forced to learn through trial and error.

The psychological toll of constant connectivity cannot be underestimated. Students today are under pressure not only to perform academically but also to maintain a digital persona that reflects success, happiness, and belonging. The comparison culture on platforms like Instagram can intensify feelings of inadequacy, as carefully curated highlight reels from peers create unrealistic standards of achievement and lifestyle. For a student struggling with grades, personal challenges, or financial limitations, the barrage of glossy images can exacerbate stress and lower self-esteem. This silent competition often extends into academic spaces as well, where sharing certificates, achievements, or publication updates becomes a means of asserting one's worth in the digital marketplace of recognition. The weight of comparison can erode the intrinsic joy of learning, turning education into a performance for likes and validation.

At the same time, social media can be a lifeline for those who feel marginalized in offline settings. Students from minority backgrounds, LGBTQ+ communities, or those with disabilities often find solidarity and empowerment in online spaces where their voices are amplified and their struggles acknowledged. A student who feels isolated in a conservative town may find acceptance in a global online community that celebrates diversity. These platforms offer not just companionship but also resources—information about scholarships, rights, or coping strategies that may not be accessible locally. In this way, social media becomes a double-edged sword:

it can either alienate through toxic comparisons and harassment, or empower by fostering belonging and resilience.

The role of families and educators becomes crucial in guiding students toward balanced use. While some parents attempt to restrict access through strict rules, others adopt a more dialogic approach, discussing digital habits openly and encouraging self-regulation. Schools are increasingly introducing digital wellness programs that teach students about time management, privacy, online ethics, and critical thinking. The emphasis is shifting from prohibition to empowerment, recognizing that social media is unlikely to disappear from students' lives. Instead, the goal is to equip them with skills to harness its benefits while mitigating its harms. Students themselves are also experimenting with practices like digital detoxes, scheduled screen-free hours, or productivity apps that block distracting websites during study time. These individual strategies reflect a growing awareness among youth about the need to reclaim control from their devices.

Despite the challenges, it is important to acknowledge that social media has redefined what it means to be a student in the twenty-first century. The image of a learner hunched over textbooks in solitude is being replaced by a dynamic portrait of connectivity, where learning, creativity, and socialization occur simultaneously across physical and digital realms. Students are no longer passive recipients of information but active participants in knowledge production, sharing their insights, creating tutorials, and contributing to the global pool of digital content. This participatory culture nurtures agency and confidence, qualities that are essential in a rapidly changing world.

The question, therefore, is not whether social media is good or bad for students, but how it can be integrated into their lives in ways that foster growth rather than hinder it. Like any tool, its impact depends on intention, context, and balance. A hammer can build a house or cause destruction; social media, too, can either construct opportunities or fracture well-being. The task before students, educators, and societies at large is to ensure that the digital landscapes students inhabit remain spaces of possibility rather than peril. This requires not only individual discipline but also systemic interventions—better digital literacy education, ethical platform design, and cultural shifts that value authenticity over performance.

Ultimately, social media is a mirror reflecting the complexities of student life. It embodies curiosity, creativity, and connection, while simultaneously exposing vulnerabilities, insecurities, and risks. To dismiss it entirely would be to deny students the opportunities of a connected world; to embrace it uncritically would be to ignore its hazards. The reality lies in navigating the fragile balance between academic enrichment and personal well-being, a balance that each student must continually negotiate in their own journey. In this negotiation lies the story of a generation—one that is learning not just algebra or history, but also how to live meaningfully in an age where the classroom is everywhere, the teacher is everyone, and the lesson never ends.

3. STUDENT MENTAL HEALTH IN THE DIGITAL AGE

Mental health has emerged as a critical concern in the academic community. Students experience unique pressures related to examinations, career uncertainty, peer comparison, and social belonging. When social media is introduced into this already stressful environment, these pressures are often magnified. The growing intertwining of digital life with academic life means that the two can no longer be separated neatly. A student might spend the morning revising for an exam, the afternoon attending lectures, and the evening scrolling through endless feeds, but the psychological weight of all three activities accumulates in the same mind and body. The academic system demands discipline and focus, while the digital ecosystem constantly calls for attention and comparison. Together, they form a double burden that often overwhelms even the most resilient of students.

The World Health Organization (2024) estimates that one in seven adolescents globally experience mental health conditions, and digital engagement plays a growing role in this trend. These numbers reveal more than statistics; they represent classrooms where, on average, several students are silently grappling with anxiety, depression, or other psychological struggles. For them, the screen is both a comfort and a source of stress. On one hand, social media platforms provide safe spaces where students can express vulnerabilities, access peer support groups, and connect with mental health resources. Hashtags like #MentalHealthAwareness or campaigns such as #BellLetsTalk have normalized discussions about stress, anxiety, and depression, encouraging young people to seek help. In the past, talking about mental health was often shrouded in stigma, whispered in private if mentioned at all. Today, the digital world has at least partially broken that silence. Students who once felt alone in their struggles now discover that thousands of others share similar battles, offering reassurance that they are not isolated in their pain.

At its best, social media has become a lifeline. Students in remote areas, who might lack access to professional counselors or mental health services, can find guidance through online communities. Peer support groups, anonymous chat rooms, and video campaigns led by activists and professionals alike provide knowledge and solidarity that would otherwise remain out of reach. A teenager wrestling with exam-related anxiety in a small town might stumble upon a YouTube channel where another student describes the same feelings, sharing tips and coping strategies. The sense of recognition that emerges from such encounters is powerful; it validates emotions and provides the courage to seek further help. Many universities now run official Instagram accounts or Facebook pages dedicated to student wellness, posting reminders about stress management techniques or directing students to counseling services. Digital awareness campaigns reach students where they already are—on their phones—bridging the gap between institutions and individual well-being.

Yet, despite these positives, the negative consequences often dominate the lived experiences of students. Prolonged exposure to online comparisons fosters feelings of inadequacy and low self-worth. The curated nature of social media means that students rarely see the full reality of their peers' lives. Instead, they encounter highlight reels: smiling group photos, announcements of achievements, perfectly edited selfies, and updates about internships or scholarships won. For the student who is struggling academically, financially, or socially, these images can trigger deep insecurities. A momentary scroll through Instagram may leave behind lingering thoughts of inferiority, as though everyone else is thriving while one is falling behind. The pressure to perform academically is compounded by the pressure to appear socially successful online, creating a cycle of constant self-scrutiny.

Cyberbullying remains one of the most damaging experiences, often linked to long-term psychological scars. Unlike traditional bullying, which may end when a student leaves school grounds, online harassment follows students into their bedrooms, onto their phones, and into the quiet moments before sleep. Hurtful comments, exclusion from group chats, or targeted memes can amplify feelings of alienation and despair. Some students withdraw from social spaces altogether, while others become hyper-vigilant, constantly checking their notifications in fear of further attacks. The permanence of digital records means that a single mistake or embarrassing moment can be captured, shared, and preserved indefinitely, haunting students for years. For those caught in the grip of online hostility, the weight of shame and anxiety can be overwhelming, often leading to academic disengagement and, in severe cases, suicidal ideation.

Sleep disturbances are another consequence of the digital age, fueled by late-night scrolling and constant notifications. The glow of a phone screen is often the last thing students see before closing their eyes, and the first thing they reach for upon waking. This habit not only delays the onset of sleep but also fragments its quality, as the brain remains in a state of heightened alertness, awaiting the next ping of attention. The lack of restful sleep worsens anxiety and depressive symptoms, creating a vicious cycle where mental health struggles make sleep elusive, and poor sleep deepens mental struggles. Students often report waking in the middle of the night to check messages or refresh feeds, unable to resist the pull of connectivity. What seems like harmless engagement with digital content slowly erodes the foundation of mental stability that comes from regular, restorative rest.

Moreover, the phenomenon of Fear of Missing Out—commonly referred to as FOMO—keeps students perpetually engaged online, creating cycles of dependency and emotional exhaustion. Social media thrives on immediacy; trends rise and fall within hours, and group conversations can evolve rapidly. For students, not checking in regularly feels like falling behind, socially or academically. A missed meme may mean exclusion from a shared joke, while a missed announcement in a WhatsApp group may mean falling out of sync with peers. This constant vigilance feeds anxiety and makes disengagement nearly impossible. Even during study sessions, students often feel compelled to glance at their phones, lest they miss something significant. Over time, this compulsion develops into dependency, where online presence becomes tied to self-worth and social standing.

The relationship between social media and mental health is thus not linear but nuanced, requiring balanced understanding and interventions tailored to student needs. It is neither wholly destructive nor entirely beneficial; rather, it reflects the ways in which human vulnerabilities intersect with digital architectures designed for attention. Students bring their insecurities, hopes, and ambitions into these spaces, while platforms amplify certain emotions and minimize others. A motivational post might uplift one student while simultaneously reminding another of their perceived inadequacy. A supportive online group may offer comfort, yet also tether students more tightly to their devices. The duality lies not in the technology itself but in how it interacts with the complex psychological landscapes of young learners.

It is also important to consider cultural and contextual differences in how students experience these dynamics. In societies where open discussions of mental health remain taboo, social media may serve as the first safe space for expression. Anonymous forums allow students to articulate fears and seek advice without the fear of stigma. In other contexts, where professional services are accessible but competitive academic environments foster intense stress, social media might serve more as an escape than a support. The universality of platforms like Instagram or TikTok belies the diversity of experiences across nations, communities, and individual personalities. A student in India may turn to YouTube tutorials to cope with exam stress, while a student in the United States may find solace in a Discord community discussing mental health openly. The platform is the same, but the role it plays varies profoundly.

Despite the harms, many students themselves are beginning to reflect critically on their digital habits. Conversations about digital detoxes, screen-time limits, and mindfulness practices are gaining traction among youth. Some deliberately delete apps during examination periods, while others schedule phone-free hours in their daily routines. These acts of resistance are not just about reclaiming time but also about reclaiming mental peace. They represent a growing recognition that social media, while enriching, cannot replace the stability that comes from balance, face-to-face relationships, and periods of disconnection. Interestingly, these practices often circulate on social media itself, with influencers and peers encouraging followers to adopt healthier habits. The paradox is striking: the very platforms that contribute to stress also host movements aimed at reducing that stress.

Families and educational institutions play a pivotal role in mediating these experiences. Parents who engage in open conversations about digital habits, rather than imposing strict prohibitions, often empower their children to self-regulate more effectively. Schools introducing digital wellness programs provide students with tools to identify harmful patterns, protect their privacy, and cultivate resilience. Universities that integrate counseling services with social media outreach are more likely to reach students where they are most comfortable. The challenge, however, is ensuring that these interventions keep pace with the rapid evolution of technology. Platforms change, algorithms shift, and trends evolve faster than traditional institutions can adapt. What remains constant is the need for empathy, guidance, and open dialogue, ensuring that students do not navigate these pressures alone.

At a deeper level, the conversation about mental health and social media invites reflection on what it means to grow up in a digital age. For earlier generations, adolescence was already a turbulent stage marked by identity exploration, academic demands, and shifting social roles. Today, these struggles are intensified by the relentless gaze of the digital world. Mistakes that once faded into memory are now recorded and replayed endlessly. Successes that might once have been celebrated quietly are now publicized widely, raising the stakes of achievement. The pressure to not only be competent but to be seen as competent creates an additional layer of stress unique to this era. Students are not just learning and growing; they are curating and performing their growth for an audience.

Yet amid these complexities, it is vital to acknowledge the resilience of students. Many are not passive victims of digital pressures but active agents navigating them with creativity and courage. They form support groups, advocate for mental health awareness, and use the very tools that challenge them to push for change. Campaigns that begin as hashtags often evolve into real-world movements, with students at the forefront of conversations about mental health policy, digital ethics, and educational reform. Their willingness to speak openly about struggles that previous generations silenced is itself a marker of progress. By normalizing vulnerability, they are reshaping the culture of academia to one that is more compassionate and inclusive.

In the end, the story of social media and student mental health is a story of balance—of how much connection is too much, of when sharing becomes oversharing, of when support turns into dependence. It is about learning to inhabit a digital ecosystem without being consumed by it. The answers are not simple, for every student experiences these dynamics differently, influenced by personality, background, and circumstance. What is clear, however, is that social media will remain an integral part of student life. The task, therefore, is not to eliminate it but to cultivate healthier relationships with it. This requires effort not only from individuals but from families, educators, policymakers, and platform designers alike.

As the academic world grapples with the twin pressures of performance and well-being, social media sits at the center of the conversation, reflecting both the promise of support and the peril of harm. For students, the journey forward involves continuous negotiation—between connection and solitude, between inspiration and comparison, between performance and authenticity. In this negotiation lies the possibility of growth, not just as digital natives but as human beings learning to thrive in a world where the screen is both window and mirror. The challenge is immense, but so too is the resilience of students, who are teaching us every day that mental health, like learning itself, is not a destination but an ongoing process of balance, reflection, and renewal.

4. DIGITAL LITERACY AND STUDENTS

Digital literacy has emerged as one of the defining competencies of the twenty-first century, often described as the "new literacy" of the modern era. Just as reading and writing were transformative skills that empowered individuals to participate fully in industrial and print-based societies, digital literacy now plays a parallel role in empowering individuals to thrive in an information-driven and digitally mediated world. Its importance lies not only in its ability to enhance academic and professional opportunities but also in its capacity to safeguard personal well-being, mental health, and ethical participation in a global society.

When the term *literacy* was historically applied, it implied the ability to read, write, and comprehend texts in written language. Over centuries, literacy expanded to include media literacy, financial literacy, and scientific literacy—domains that reflected the demands of their respective ages. In today's information age, digital literacy has become equally indispensable.

Unlike basic computer skills, which focus primarily on operating devices and applications, digital literacy encompasses a broad set of cognitive, socio-emotional, and ethical competencies. It is not merely about knowing how to type documents, send emails, or browse the internet, but about using these skills critically and responsibly. According to UNESCO (2018), true digital literacy enables individuals to:

1. Critically assess the reliability, accuracy, and intent of digital information.
2. Protect personal data and respect the privacy of others.
3. Engage responsibly in online communities with an awareness of social and ethical consequences.

4. Use technology constructively for education, creativity, civic participation, and innovation.

Thus, digital literacy positions itself at the intersection of technology, cognition, and ethics—demanding both technical fluency and critical judgment.

For students, digital literacy plays a crucial role in upholding academic integrity. The internet offers an unprecedented repository of knowledge, but it also presents challenges such as plagiarism, misinformation, and overreliance on secondary sources. A digitally literate student is one who knows how to differentiate between scholarly sources and unreliable online content, cite references appropriately, and engage in responsible academic practices.

Digital literacy also enhances collaborative learning. Students today frequently engage in group projects via platforms such as Google Classroom, Microsoft Teams, or WhatsApp. A lack of digital literacy can result in inefficient collaboration, misinterpretation of shared information, and exposure to security vulnerabilities. In contrast, digitally literate students are able to optimize tools for productivity, share ideas ethically, and engage in meaningful knowledge-building exercises.

Moreover, critical consumption of information is increasingly tied to democratic participation. The global rise of fake news, deepfakes, and algorithm-driven misinformation demonstrates how easily uninformed users can be manipulated. For students—who will become future leaders, policymakers, and professionals—digital literacy is a civic necessity.

Another dimension of digital literacy is personal safety and privacy. The digital footprints students leave on platforms—whether through social media posts, shared documents, or browsing patterns—can have lasting consequences. Employers, universities, and scholarship committees often review applicants' online presence before making decisions. Students who lack digital literacy may inadvertently compromise their reputation by oversharing personal details, engaging in risky online behavior, or failing to recognize scams and phishing attempts.

Cybersecurity is thus an essential component of digital literacy. Understanding strong password practices, two-factor authentication, safe browsing, and recognition of malicious content is vital. Additionally, ethical online behavior—such as respecting intellectual property rights, avoiding cyberbullying, and acknowledging diversity in digital spaces—forms the backbone of a healthy digital environment.

A key but often overlooked aspect of digital literacy is its relationship with mental health. Students today spend significant hours navigating social media feeds, discussion forums, and educational platforms. Without the ability to filter harmful or toxic content, they are vulnerable to stress, anxiety, and burnout. Digital literacy equips students with strategies to:

- Curate their feeds to minimize exposure to harmful or manipulative content.
- Recognize algorithmic traps that fuel compulsive scrolling.
- Manage online interactions in ways that promote empathy and resilience.
- Establish boundaries for healthy screen time, thereby protecting sleep patterns and psychological balance.

For example, a digitally literate student encountering body image distortions on Instagram may critically analyze the source of those images, understand the influence of filters and editing, and resist unhealthy comparisons. Similarly, awareness of digital detox practices enables students to consciously step away from screens, reducing stress and improving focus.

Despite its importance, digital literacy remains unevenly distributed. Students in developed countries often have structured exposure to digital skills from early schooling, supported by advanced infrastructure and access to resources. In contrast, students in developing nations may face significant barriers, including limited access to technology, unreliable internet, and lack of trained educators.

Socioeconomic disparities deepen these gaps. Wealthier families can provide personal devices, internet access, and supplementary digital training, while underprivileged students often rely solely on school facilities. As a result, digital literacy becomes not only an educational issue but also a question of equity and social justice.

Policymakers and institutions need to address these divides by:

- Investing in affordable internet infrastructure.
- Creating digital literacy curricula that are culturally relevant and accessible.
- Offering community-based training programs to reach underserved populations.

Educational institutions are uniquely positioned to bridge the digital literacy divide. Schools can integrate digital literacy curricula into core subjects rather than treating them as extracurricular add-ons. This ensures that all students, regardless of background, acquire essential competencies.

Universities, on the other hand, can design specialized courses on digital ethics, online safety, and information literacy, preparing graduates for both academic rigor and professional responsibility. Teacher training is equally critical—educators themselves must be digitally literate to guide students effectively.

Workshops, peer-led initiatives, and simulation-based learning (such as spotting misinformation campaigns) are practical tools that institutions can employ. For instance, Finland's national strategy on media and digital literacy has demonstrated how systematic integration into curricula fosters resilience among students against misinformation.

Ethics are central to digital literacy. Students must learn to navigate questions of digital rights, equity, and responsibility. Key ethical considerations include:

- Respecting privacy and intellectual property online.
- Avoiding participation in cyberbullying or harassment.
- Being aware of algorithmic biases that shape online content.
- Recognizing the broader societal consequences of digital behaviors.

Ethical literacy ensures that digital competence is not merely about personal gain but about contributing positively to the digital community.

Several countries and institutions have pioneered digital literacy programs that can serve as models:

- **Finland**: Incorporates media literacy into its national curriculum, helping students critically evaluate news and information.
- **Singapore**: Runs peer-to-peer mentoring systems where students teach one another about online safety and responsible engagement.
- **India (CBSE)**: Introduced a pilot *Digital Wellness Curriculum* in 2022, focusing on balanced technology use and emotional resilience.
- **Canada (University of Toronto)**: Hosts an annual *Digital Wellness Week* to raise awareness of healthy online habits among students.

These examples highlight how multi-level interventions—from national policy to grassroots peer support—can build robust digital literacy ecosystems.

Looking ahead, the definition of digital literacy will continue to evolve. Emerging technologies such as Artificial Intelligence (AI), Virtual Reality (VR), and Augmented Reality (AR) will demand new competencies. Students will need to critically assess AI-driven content, recognize biases in machine learning systems, and engage responsibly in immersive digital environments.

Gamification of digital literacy training, mobile-based learning modules, and cross-cultural collaborations are promising methods to enhance engagement and inclusivity. International organizations like UNESCO, OECD, and WHO are working toward standardizing digital literacy frameworks, ensuring global relevance and adaptability.

At the same time, the digital detox movement emphasizes mindful engagement with technology—teaching students not only how to use digital tools but also when and why to disengage. Such balance will be crucial in ensuring that digital literacy enhances rather than overwhelms student lives.

Digital literacy is not merely an academic requirement—it is a survival skill in the twenty-first century. For students, it safeguards academic integrity, ensures online safety, and nurtures mental resilience. By critically engaging with information, protecting personal data, and acting ethically online, students can thrive in both academic and personal domains.

Yet, global inequalities persist, leaving many students vulnerable to misinformation, exploitation, and psychological harm. Bridging these gaps requires coordinated efforts from schools, universities, policymakers, and communities. Ultimately, the cultivation of digital literacy is not only about empowering individuals but also about building inclusive, ethical, and resilient societies prepared for the challenges of the digital age.

5. INTERCONNECTION OF SOCIAL MEDIA, MENTAL HEALTH, AND DIGITAL LITERACY

The interconnection of social media, mental health, and digital literacy represents one of the most complex and pressing challenges faced by today's generation of students. This triadic relationship cannot be understood in isolation, as each element influences and shapes the other. Social media is the environment where much of student interaction and self-expression occurs, digital literacy is the toolkit that governs how effectively and responsibly students can navigate this environment, and mental health is the outcome that is directly affected by both the quality of engagement and the resilience of the individual. Together, they form a triangular dynamic in which weaknesses in one domain can amplify risks in the others, while strengths in one area can serve as a protective factor that reduces vulnerabilities.

At the heart of this interplay is the simple observation that social media has become deeply embedded in the everyday lives of students, offering both opportunities and risks. Platforms such as Instagram, TikTok, Twitter, and YouTube provide access to knowledge, community, and creative self-expression. Yet, when students lack digital literacy, these same platforms can expose them to misinformation, cyberbullying, harmful comparisons, and compulsive usage patterns. This lack of critical awareness often translates into negative mental health outcomes, ranging from heightened stress and anxiety to deeper conditions such as depression and social withdrawal. Conversely, when students possess strong digital literacy, they are better positioned to question the credibility of online content, to filter harmful information, to manage their screen time, and to engage more responsibly with peers and strangers alike. In such cases, digital literacy acts almost like an immune system for the mind, protecting it from the toxins of digital overload and manipulation.

The COVID-19 pandemic provided a striking illustration of this triangular dynamic. As the world shifted abruptly to online learning and socializing, students found themselves spending unprecedented hours on digital platforms. During this period, misinformation spread at a rapid pace, from conspiracy theories about the virus to false claims about vaccines and unverified remedies. For students without the skills to evaluate sources critically, this digital chaos created immense psychological strain. Fear, uncertainty, and constant exposure to conflicting narratives amplified anxiety levels and created a sense of helplessness. At the same time, those who had been trained in digital resilience and fact-checking techniques were able to navigate the storm more effectively. They distinguished credible sources from unreliable ones, avoided falling prey to digital panic, and experienced lower levels of psychological distress. The pandemic, therefore, not only highlighted the significance of digital literacy as an academic skill but also demonstrated its role as a determinant of mental health in times of crisis.

Another important example is the area of cyberbullying, a phenomenon that has unfortunately become a pervasive aspect of online interaction. Students who lack digital literacy often do not know how to use privacy settings, block abusive users, or report harassment through the appropriate channels. This lack of awareness leaves them more exposed to repeated abuse, leading to feelings of fear, isolation, and in severe cases, long-term trauma. On the other hand, students who are digitally literate tend to be more proactive in safeguarding their online spaces. They know how to configure privacy controls, document harmful interactions, and report incidents, which empowers them to regain control over their digital experiences. While cyberbullying remains damaging even for those who are digitally literate, their ability to respond effectively reduces the intensity and duration of the psychological harm. Here again, digital literacy emerges not as a luxury but as a protective necessity for mental well-being in the digital age.

One of the most significant risks that bind social media and mental health is the phenomenon of digital overload. Students often spend three to five hours or more daily on social platforms, scrolling through endless feeds of images, videos, and updates. While this might begin as an innocent pastime, over time it creates an overwhelming volume of cognitive input that the brain struggles to process. The result is mental fatigue, stress, and reduced productivity in academic and personal spheres. For students without literacy skills to curate and filter their feeds, harmful and toxic content accumulates unnoticed. Negative news cycles, unrealistic portrayals of beauty and success, and algorithm-driven sensationalism contribute to stress and self-esteem issues. In contrast, digitally literate students are able to establish healthier digital habits. They learn to manage their notifications, set boundaries around usage, and critically evaluate what content deserves their attention. Such practices not only reduce the risk of burnout but also contribute to greater psychological stability.

The triangular relationship is not limited to the individual student; it also plays out at a societal level. When large populations of students lack digital literacy, the collective outcome is a more anxious and less resilient generation vulnerable to manipulation by disinformation campaigns. This has broader consequences for democratic participation, civic trust, and social cohesion. Conversely, when students as a community are trained in digital literacy, the collective mental health landscape improves. They not only protect themselves individually but also create peer cultures of responsible engagement where harmful behaviors such as cyberbullying, rumor-spreading, and toxic comparisons are discouraged. The ripple effect of literacy thus strengthens both individual and societal well-being.

An important dimension of this interconnection is how algorithms shape student experiences. Social media platforms are designed to capture attention, often by promoting sensational or emotionally charged content. Students who are unaware of these algorithmic dynamics may feel that their negative emotions are a reflection of reality, when in fact they are being strategically amplified by invisible technological forces. Without literacy, they may internalize these distortions, leading to anxiety, body image concerns, or fear of missing out. However, when students understand how algorithms work, they can approach digital content with greater skepticism and autonomy. They learn to see their feeds not as mirrors of reality but as curated constructs designed for profit. This realization itself serves as a buffer against psychological harm, reducing the likelihood of internalizing harmful comparisons or false narratives.

Moreover, digital literacy helps students recognize when social media use begins to encroach upon their mental health, enabling them to take proactive steps. Practices such as digital detox, mindfulness in digital engagement, and conscious content curation are rooted in literacy. A student who is aware of the addictive design of platforms is more likely to resist compulsive usage and instead establish healthier boundaries. This kind of self-regulation, while not easy, becomes possible only when students are empowered with knowledge about how digital systems operate and how those systems can be navigated responsibly.

The interplay between social media, literacy, and mental health is further complicated by cultural and socioeconomic factors. In societies where digital infrastructure is limited, students may face significant barriers to developing literacy skills. This leaves them disproportionately vulnerable to the negative effects of social media. At the same time, in more digitally saturated societies, students face different risks, including hyper-connectivity and excessive exposure. In both contexts, the role of digital literacy remains critical. In low-resource environments, it functions as a survival skill to navigate minimal but impactful exposure, while in high-resource environments, it serves as a balancing skill to regulate overwhelming exposure. In either case, its absence magnifies risks to mental health.

It is also worth considering that the interconnection of social media, literacy, and mental health is not static but evolves alongside technological advancements. As new platforms emerge, bringing with them new forms of interaction and expression, the challenges faced by students shift. For instance, the rise of short-form video content has introduced new pressures around body image and self-presentation. The growing influence of artificial intelligence and deepfake technologies presents new risks of misinformation and identity manipulation. Each of these changes reshapes the triangular dynamic, reinforcing the importance of continuous adaptation in digital literacy education.

Ultimately, the relationship between social media, mental health, and digital literacy underscores a central truth: digital literacy is not simply an academic or professional skill but a determinant of emotional and psychological well-being. Without it, students are at the mercy of platforms designed to maximize attention and profit, often at the expense of their mental health. With it, they gain agency, resilience, and the ability to harness technology as a tool for growth rather than as a source of distress. The interplay is thus best seen not as a fixed relationship but as an ongoing negotiation in which students must be continuously equipped to adapt, protect themselves, and thrive in a rapidly evolving digital environment.

6. CASE STUDIES AND RESEARCH FINDINGS

Research across different regions underscores the global relevance of these issues.

United States: Twenge et al. (2019) documented strong correlations between high social media use and rising depression among adolescents.

Europe: Finland's comprehensive digital literacy programs equipped students to critically evaluate misinformation, improving mental resilience.

Asia: In South Korea, students with advanced digital literacy skills demonstrated lower stress levels despite high digital exposure.

India: The All India Survey on Higher Education (AISHE, 2022) revealed that 70% of students rely on social media for academic updates. However, the National Mental Health Survey (2022) recorded rising anxiety among youth, reflecting the consequences of unregulated digital consumption.

Several universities have also initiated innovative programs. The University of Toronto organizes a "Digital Wellness Week" to raise awareness of healthy digital practices. Delhi University has piloted electives on digital ethics and well-being. Singapore's National University developed peer-led mentoring systems where students support one another in cultivating balanced online behaviors. These examples highlight the importance of structured interventions.

7. STRATEGIES FOR STUDENTS, EDUCATORS, AND POLICYMAKERS

Tackling the challenges posed by social media is not something that can be achieved in isolation by any single group. The issues it creates and the opportunities it provides are too far-reaching, too deeply embedded in everyday life, and too complex to be addressed with fragmented approaches. Instead, it demands a coordinated and cooperative strategy across multiple stakeholders, including students themselves, educators who guide and mentor them, and policymakers who shape the broader structures of society. Each group has its own unique responsibilities and capacities, yet none can work effectively without the support and participation of the others. The collective effort is what creates resilience, balance, and sustainability in a digital age where social media is no longer an optional addition but a core component of how we connect, learn, and express ourselves.

For students, the first line of defense lies in self-regulation, which is often easier said than done. Young people today are immersed in digital ecosystems that are designed to capture and hold attention through constant notifications, infinite scrolling, and algorithm-driven recommendations. This design actively works against the ability to regulate use. However, students who cultivate skills of time management and conscious digital engagement are better able to resist these pressures. Simple practices such as designating device-free hours during study or sleep time, turning off non-essential notifications, or creating daily schedules with clearly allocated offline time can drastically improve both productivity and well-being. Alongside this, mindfulness practices are gaining recognition as valuable tools. By becoming more aware of their digital habits—why they open a particular app, how long they spend scrolling, and how they feel afterwards—students can identify unhealthy patterns and replace them with more intentional behavior. Mindfulness, in this sense, is not just about meditation or breathing exercises; it is about developing a reflective stance toward digital engagement, one that prevents unconscious consumption and encourages thoughtful choices.

Another crucial element for students is the curation of online feeds. Algorithms thrive on attention, often promoting content that is provocative, sensational, or emotionally charged. Without careful curation, students can quickly find themselves in echo chambers filled with negativity, toxic comparisons, or misinformation. A digitally literate student, however, learns to actively shape their digital environment by unfollowing harmful accounts, subscribing to educational or positive content, and diversifying their sources of information. This conscious act of filtering what enters their digital space protects mental health and promotes constructive learning. Furthermore, the practice of digital detox—consciously stepping away from social media for short or extended periods—provides opportunities to recharge, reconnect with offline activities, and regain perspective. When students learn to balance connectivity with disconnection, they are better able to use social media as a tool rather than be controlled by it.

In addition to managing consumption, students are also responsible for shaping their digital footprint, which has become as important as a résumé in today's interconnected world. Every post, comment, or share contributes to an online identity that can be scrutinized by universities, employers, and peers. Practicing responsible sharing—thinking before posting, respecting others' privacy, and avoiding participation in harmful online trends—enhances long-term opportunities while also contributing to a healthier digital environment. The act of being a responsible digital citizen is not only self-serving but also collective, since each student's behavior influences the culture of online communities they inhabit.

While students carry the immediate responsibility of navigating social media, educators play an equally vital role in shaping the conditions under which digital engagement occurs. Teachers are no longer simply transmitters of knowledge; they are mentors who must help students build critical capacities to function in a digitized world. Integrating digital literacy into everyday learning is one of the most important contributions educators can make. Rather than teaching it as a separate subject, digital literacy should be woven into all academic activities—from analyzing the credibility of online sources during a history project, to discussing the ethical implications of data privacy in a computer science class, to examining the psychological effects of social media in health education. By embedding these discussions into the curriculum, teachers normalize responsible digital engagement as a natural part of learning rather than treating it as an add-on skill.

Equally important is the role of educators in creating safe spaces for dialogue. Students often face digital struggles silently, whether it is cyberbullying, addiction, or the anxiety created by constant online comparisons. Without avenues to share these struggles openly, problems may fester and lead to serious mental health consequences. Schools and universities that foster supportive environments—where students feel comfortable discussing their online experiences without judgment—enable early detection of digital stress. Teachers, counselors, and peer support systems can then intervene before issues escalate. Furthermore, educators serve as role models. When they demonstrate healthy digital practices themselves, they reinforce lessons not only through words but also through behavior.

Policymakers, meanwhile, hold the structural power to influence the broader ecosystem within which students and educators operate. Governments must recognize that digital well-being is not just an individual responsibility but a public health and societal issue. Enacting national digital wellness policies ensures that there are guidelines and frameworks supporting balanced technology use across education, media, and public life. For example, policies that mandate the inclusion of digital literacy in school curricula, fund teacher training programs, and promote mental health resources in educational institutions create systemic support for healthier digital engagement.

Equitable access to infrastructure is another critical area where policymakers must act. In many regions, disparities in internet access and device availability exacerbate inequalities in digital literacy and resilience. When only privileged groups can access reliable connectivity and structured training, disadvantaged students are left more vulnerable to misinformation, exploitation, and stress. Governments must therefore invest in affordable internet access, community digital centers, and public awareness campaigns to ensure inclusivity in the digital age.

Regulating harmful online content is also a domain that requires decisive action at the policy level. While freedom of expression is a cornerstone of democratic societies, unchecked platforms can become breeding grounds for cyberbullying, hate speech, and disinformation. Policymakers can work with technology companies to establish clear guidelines for content moderation, reporting mechanisms, and accountability measures. Collaboration is key, as platforms themselves hold much of the technical power to detect and address harmful content. Public-private partnerships that balance innovation with responsibility offer the most promising path forward.

Addressing misinformation, in particular, demands global cooperation. The speed and scale at which false information spreads online cannot be countered by individuals or institutions alone. Governments, international organizations, and tech platforms must collaborate to promote fact-checking initiatives, develop algorithms that prioritize credible sources, and launch campaigns that empower citizens to verify information before sharing. In doing so, they protect not only the mental health of individuals who might otherwise experience anxiety and fear from misinformation but also the stability of societies dependent on informed decision-making.

The interconnected roles of students, educators, and policymakers illustrate a truth that is often overlooked: sustainable digital well-being is not built through isolated actions but through shared responsibility. Each stakeholder's role complements and strengthens the other. Students who learn self-regulation are more likely to thrive when supported by teachers who guide them in responsible digital engagement. Educators who promote digital literacy are more effective when policies provide resources and training. Policymakers who design wellness frameworks succeed only when students and teachers implement and embody them in daily practice. It is the synergy of these efforts that creates resilience in the face of evolving digital challenges.

What makes this collective approach even more urgent is the rapid pace of technological change. Social media today is not what it was five years ago, and five years from now it will have evolved into something entirely new, driven by emerging technologies such as artificial intelligence, virtual reality, and augmented reality.

Each new wave of innovation will bring with it fresh opportunities for learning and connection but also novel risks to mental health and social stability. Preparing students to navigate this future cannot rely on outdated models of isolated responsibility. It requires dynamic, adaptive, and collaborative strategies where every stakeholder continuously re-evaluates their role and strengthens their contribution.

In the final analysis, building a sustainable model for healthy digital engagement is as much about values as it is about skills. It is about cultivating cultures of responsibility, empathy, and resilience where individuals are empowered to use technology as a tool for growth without sacrificing their well-being. Students must embrace personal responsibility, educators must nurture critical and ethical capacities, and policymakers must create the systemic conditions that make balanced engagement possible. Only through this shared effort can society ensure that the immense power of social media serves as a force for empowerment rather than a source of harm. By recognizing that digital wellness is a collective journey, we take a decisive step toward shaping a future where technology enriches rather than diminishes human life.

8. FUTURE DIRECTIONS

The future of social media and digital literacy will be defined by a constant interplay between innovation and adaptation, where emerging technologies create new opportunities while simultaneously introducing novel risks. The landscape is shifting so rapidly that students, educators, and societies at large must remain agile, recognizing that what is true about digital engagement today may be completely different tomorrow. Artificial Intelligence, virtual reality, augmented reality, gamification, and global collaborative frameworks are already shaping the next phase of digital life, and with them come complex questions of ethics, equity, and mental health. As these technologies embed themselves into the educational and social environments of students, their ability to thrive will depend less on their ability to simply consume digital content and more on their capacity to critically evaluate, adapt, and balance their digital interactions with real-world needs.

Artificial Intelligence (AI) has already begun to reshape how students engage with both learning and mental health support. AI-driven chatbots, virtual assistants, and personalized recommendation systems provide instant responses to academic queries, offer tailored learning modules, and even act as first responders for mental health concerns. For example, AI-powered mental health apps now provide 24/7 support for stress, anxiety, and depression, offering personalized coping strategies or directing students toward professional resources. These tools, while not a replacement for human support, have expanded accessibility for students who might otherwise hesitate to seek help due to stigma, financial barriers, or lack of available professionals. However, the very reliance on AI raises important ethical questions that cannot be ignored. Issues of data privacy, algorithmic bias, and the reliability of AI-driven advice pose significant risks. Sensitive personal data about mental health, for instance, may be stored or used in ways that compromise confidentiality. Algorithmic bias may also lead to unequal treatment of students based on gender, ethnicity, or cultural background. The future will therefore require not only the expansion of AI tools in education and mental health but also the establishment of strong ethical frameworks, transparent policies, and robust literacy skills that empower students to question, challenge, and critically engage with AI-generated outputs rather than blindly accept them.

Gamification is another emerging strategy with immense potential to reshape digital literacy education. At its core, gamification leverages the principles of play—rewards, challenges, levels, and engagement loops—to make learning both enjoyable and effective. Students who might otherwise resist lessons about online safety, fact-checking, or ethical responsibility can become deeply engaged when these skills are framed as challenges in a game-like environment. Imagine students participating in digital literacy games where they detect misinformation, navigate simulated cyberbullying scenarios, or make ethical choices in virtual environments to earn points or unlock levels. Such experiences do more than impart knowledge; they cultivate habits of mind, reinforcing critical skills in a way that feels natural rather than imposed. However, the success of gamification depends on thoughtful design. Games that prioritize competition over collaboration may inadvertently increase stress or exclusion, while poorly designed platforms may replicate the addictive elements of social media that digital literacy seeks to mitigate. The challenge for the future is to design gamified literacy experiences that foster resilience, cooperation, and reflection rather than simply reinforcing surface-level engagement.

Parallel to technological innovations, cultural movements such as the rise of digital detox are gaining momentum. The digital detox philosophy advocates deliberate disconnection from technology, encouraging individuals to periodically step away from their screens to focus on offline life. For students, this movement is not about rejecting technology altogether but about regaining balance, reminding them that their identities and well-being extend beyond the digital realm. As research continues to highlight the connections between excessive screen time, poor sleep quality, increased anxiety, and reduced productivity, the need for intentional offline engagement is becoming clearer. Students who practice digital detox learn to reclaim control over their attention, build deeper in-person relationships, and cultivate hobbies or physical activities that strengthen mental health. Yet, it is important to note that digital detox is not equally accessible to all. Students in high-pressure academic settings may feel unable to disconnect due to the fear of missing educational updates, while those in socially competitive environments may fear losing relevance among peers. Future directions must therefore involve not only promoting the benefits of mindful disconnection but also addressing the systemic pressures that make constant connectivity feel unavoidable.

Another significant area shaping the future of digital literacy and mental health lies in international collaboration. Organizations such as UNESCO, WHO, and OECD are working to establish standardized frameworks for digital literacy that transcend national boundaries. The digital challenges faced by students are not confined to a single region or culture; misinformation, cyberbullying, addictive design, and data exploitation are global issues. Collaborative efforts at the international level provide opportunities to share best practices, develop universal competencies, and create adaptable models that individual countries can tailor to their unique cultural and socioeconomic contexts. For instance, while Finland may serve as a model for integrating digital literacy into national curricula, countries with fewer resources may benefit from scalable community-based programs supported by international funding. The key is to ensure that no student, regardless of geography, is left behind in the effort to build digital resilience.

Future research will play a central role in shaping these directions. Much of what we currently know about social media's impact on mental health is based on short-term studies, often limited to particular age groups or cultural settings. What remains less understood are the long-term effects of continuous engagement with evolving platforms. How do years of exposure to algorithm-driven feeds affect attention spans, empathy, or critical thinking abilities? What happens to mental health outcomes when students transition from adolescence to adulthood after spending thousands of hours in digital environments? Cross-cultural differences also require greater attention. Students in collectivist societies, for example, may experience online comparison pressures differently from those in individualistic societies. Similarly, coping strategies that are effective in one cultural context may not translate to another. Research must move beyond broad generalizations and delve into the nuanced ways digital literacy interacts with cultural values, economic conditions, and psychological development.

The future will also require innovative approaches to balance technology use with psychological well-being. This balance cannot be achieved through avoidance or restriction alone; instead, it must be about integration. Students must learn to integrate digital tools into their lives in ways that support rather than undermine their goals. For example, using mindfulness apps to complement meditation practices, employing productivity software to manage study schedules, or joining online communities for academic collaboration are ways of turning technology into an ally rather than an adversary. At the same time, students must be taught to recognize when engagement shifts from supportive to harmful, such as when productivity apps become sources of stress or when online communities foster unhealthy comparison.

Such discernment can only be cultivated through a combination of personal reflection, structured literacy training, and supportive institutional cultures.

Adaptability will remain the most critical factor in navigating this future. The pace of technological change ensures that new platforms, trends, and risks will continually emerge. Students who rigidly rely on a fixed set of skills will quickly find themselves unprepared, while those who cultivate adaptability will remain resilient. Adaptability in digital literacy means not only keeping up with new tools but also developing the mindset to question, evaluate, and adjust to unfamiliar environments. It requires creativity, critical thinking, and emotional intelligence—all skills that must be nurtured intentionally through education. For instance, a student who learns today how to fact-check online news stories must also develop the broader habit of questioning all forms of information, so that when new technologies such as deepfakes become mainstream, they already possess the reflexes needed to adapt.

One cannot ignore the ethical dimension of these future directions. The technologies that promise to revolutionize digital literacy and mental health also carry risks of exploitation. AI may offer personalized learning, but it can also enable surveillance. Gamification may make learning engaging, but it can also encourage addictive behaviors. Digital detox may provide relief for some but may deepen exclusion for those who cannot afford to disconnect. International collaborations may standardize best practices, but they may also impose models that do not respect local cultural contexts. As we move into this future, students and educators alike must be equipped not just with technical skills but with ethical frameworks that allow them to engage critically and responsibly with emerging possibilities.

Ultimately, the future of social media and digital literacy is not predetermined. It is a space of negotiation, where the choices made by individuals, institutions, and societies will determine whether technology becomes a force of empowerment or exploitation. For students, the central challenge will be to cultivate digital literacy as more than just a skill set—it must become a lifelong habit of mind, a way of approaching digital life with awareness, balance, and critical judgment. For educators, the challenge will be to keep pace with evolving technologies, continuously updating curricula and teaching strategies to remain relevant. For policymakers, the challenge will be to design structures that protect the vulnerable while encouraging innovation. Together, these efforts must converge on a common goal: ensuring that students remain healthy, resilient, and empowered in an ever-evolving digital landscape.

The vision of the future is one where students do not merely survive in the digital age but thrive—where they use AI responsibly, embrace gamification as a tool for growth rather than distraction, practice digital detox as an intentional choice, participate in international collaborations that expand their horizons, and adapt with agility to whatever new platforms arise. In this vision, digital literacy becomes the foundation upon which psychological resilience and ethical citizenship are built.

The key lies not in fearing the future of social media but in shaping it, with awareness, adaptability, and a collective commitment to human well-being. If society can succeed in this task, the evolving digital world will not be a threat to student mental health but an arena of empowerment, innovation, and growth.

9. CONCLUSION

Social media has undeniably reshaped the student experience, offering vast opportunities for learning, networking, and creativity. Yet, it simultaneously presents risks that threaten psychological stability and academic productivity. The presence or absence of digital literacy determines how students navigate this dual reality.

When students are equipped with literacy skills, they can critically evaluate online content, protect themselves from harmful interactions, and maintain mental balance. Without these skills, the risks of anxiety, depression, misinformation, and digital dependency intensify.

Therefore, the path forward is not about abandoning social media but about creating digitally literate, resilient, and responsible citizens. Educators, policymakers, and students themselves must work together to ensure that technology serves as a tool for empowerment rather than a source of distress. In this sense, digital literacy is not merely a skill but a fundamental necessity for well-being in the twenty-first century.

REFERENCES

Pew Research Center. (2023). *Teens, social media & technology 2023.* https://www.pewresearch.org/internet/2023/

Twenge, J. M., Martin, G. N., & Campbell, W. K. (2019). Decreases in psychological well-being among American adolescents after 2012 and links to screen time during the rise of smartphone technology. *Journal of Abnormal Psychology, 128*(2), 119–133. DOI: 10.1037/abn0000410 PMID: 30570269

UNESCO. (2018). *Digital literacy global framework.* UNESCO Publishing.

World Health Organization. (2024, September 25). *Teens, screens and mental health* [Media release]. https://www.who.int/news/item/[insert full URL]

Chapter 6
Synthesising Learning-Analytics Systems for Early Identification of At-Risk Students

Peter Kwakpovwe
https://orcid.org/0009-0001-2506-9931
University of Salford, UK

Ene Ojaide
https://orcid.org/0009-0008-0388-0687
Multiverserse, UK

Nneoma Andrew-Vitalis
https://orcid.org/0009-0001-4525-6005
University of Hertfordshire, UK

Obinna Obi-Akwari
https://orcid.org/0009-0006-9487-4965
Deepfusion Films, UK

Andrew Chinonso Nwanakwaugwu
https://orcid.org/0000-0002-2929-9638
University of Salford, UK

ABSTRACT

An expanding constellation of commercial and open-source learning-analytics (LA) platforms—Canvas "New Analytics," Blackboard Predict, Purdue's Course Signals, Civitas Illume, Moodle Learning Analytics, and the On Task intervention

DOI: 10.4018/979-8-3373-5007-3.ch006

engine—promise to flag students who are academically or psychologically "at risk." Yet their effectiveness, ethical soundness, and transferability remain unevenly documented. Rather than designing a novel tool.Through a systematic literature review, and cross-case analysis of five institutional implementations, the chapter distils a research-backed, privacy-preserving, human-in-the-loop workflow that institutions can adopt with the technology they already own or can licence. The chapter outcome is a pragmatic, evidence-based roadmap that shows where current systems excel, where they falter, and how policy, practice, and organisational culture can close the gap between algorithmic alerts and meaningful student support.

1. INTRODUCTION

Higher institutions across the globe are facing a convergence of pressures: growing student diversity, rising tuition costs, increased accountability for retention, and an alarming prevalence of mental health struggles among learners. As a result, learning analytics (LA) systems have been promoted as powerful tools for transforming raw educational data into actionable insights. Educational institutions are attempting to analyse these data and develop analytical tools to make informed decisions based on the information they provide (Romero & Ventura, 2013). The central promise is to detect which students are "at risk" of academic failure or withdrawal early in the semester, so that institutions can intervene before problems spiral beyond repair. This area of research is characterised by its urgency, which demonstrates that data-driven education is not only a theoretical concept but also part of the infrastructure of higher education. Institutions are investing heavily in dashboards, predictive models, and intervention engines; yet the evidence about their real effectiveness and their unintended consequences remains inconsistent.

A unique aspect of this research topic is its emphasis on translating visualisations of data into informed decisions. While dashboards abound, they often stop at coloured risk signals. The critical, yet under-examined question is: How do these signals become meaningful actions? Without well-designed workflows, ethical safeguards, and human judgment, predictive alerts risk producing more noise than guidance. Consequently, this chapter examines the socio-technical gap between prediction and intervention, highlighting both the potential and pitfalls of early-warning learning analytics.

1.1 Background and Problem Statement

Over the past decade, early-alert dashboards have become mainstream in both K–12 and higher education. Previous work has already been performed. Based on

Baneres (2016), the authors examined other models, features, and algorithms to develop high-quality models for predicting the probability of passing a course. A classic model based on the marks of assessment activities was selected. Additionally, the authors conceptualised a generic predictive system for educational purposes (Baneres & Serra, 2018). These systems process Learning Management Systems (LMS) clickstreams, grade-book data, attendance records, and occasionally sentiment analyses of online discussions to generate colour-coded risk scores. Despite widespread uptake, three persistent problems surface in the literature and in practice. Firstly, Fragmented Evidence. The evaluation of LA tools varies across disciplines and typically focuses on academic outcomes, with limited measurement of mental health outcomes. For instance, Azcona et al. (2018) developed multimodal predictive models from students' digital footprints in computer science, showing gains in exam performance when personalised feedback was offered. Yet such studies rarely consider whether reduced anxiety, stress, or burnout accompanied these improvements. Secondly, The "Last-Mile" Disconnect. Risk scores often stall on dashboards. Instructors or advisers are presented with alerts but receive little guidance on how and when to act. Baneres (2016) observed that predictive accuracy alone is not sufficient; timely and personalised feedback must accompany risk detection to make interventions effective. The gap between identification and intervention is therefore as much organisational as technological. Thirdly, Privacy and Fairness Concerns. Students are frequently left in the dark about what data is collected, how models are trained, or whether bias audits are performed. The COVID-19 pandemic further exposed these gaps as face-to-face cues vanished. Institutions leaned heavily on LA to locate struggling students, only to encounter unresolved questions about data governance, consent, and equity.

1.2 The Evolution of Learning Analytics

Learning analytics is a field that originated in the field of educational data mining, which aimed to harness the increasing availability of digital traces from systems such as learning management systems (LMS), virtual learning environments, and assessment platforms. Early work focused on statistical correlations like linking clickstream data, log-ins, and quiz results to final course outcomes. By the mid-2010s, commercial products such as Purdue University's Course Signals became emblematic of early warning dashboards. Course Signals displayed a simple red–amber–green "traffic light" to indicate student risk levels, offering instructors a straightforward visualisation. Subsequent products, including Blackboard Predict, Civitas Illume, and Canvas New Analytics, were developed on this model by incorporating machine learning to generate risk probabilities and embedding them directly into LMS dashboards.

Despite these advances, the underlying logic often remains reductionist: students are classified as "at risk" based on a handful of variables, including attendance, assessment submissions, or grade averages. As Azcona et al. (2018) note, such approaches overlook the richness of students' digital footprints, which encompass behavioural interactions, lab submissions, and engagement patterns that can yield more nuanced predictions. Similarly, Baneres (2016) highlighted the need for early and continuous feedback, proposing the Gradual At-Risk (GAR) model, which updates predictions as new assessments are graded. Both studies reveal a critical insight: risk is not static but dynamic, evolving as students' progress through a course. Yet many systems still present risk as a fixed, colour-coded status, masking the complexity of the learning trajectory.

The risk arises when such oversimplified signals are taken at face value. A student flagged as "red" may feel stigmatised; an instructor may become biased in their expectations. Worse, without clear guidance on how to act on alerts, faculty may ignore signals altogether. Learning analytics has thus been plagued by a problem called the last-mile problem, in which risk visualisations exist, but their translation into meaningful interventions is inconsistent and often unfair.

Identifying children at an early age is of great importance. Students' attrition rates in higher education continue to be an issue around the world, with first-year dropout rates ranging from 20% to 40% in many OECD countries (OECD, 2022). Beyond academic outcomes, mental health challenges such as anxiety, depression, and burnout are now recognised as key contributors to student risk. Yet most LA systems have been designed to predict grades, not well-being. This narrowness reflects a deeper gap, as well as the intersection between learning analytics and student mental health remains under explored. The COVID-19 pandemic amplified these tensions. When the campuses closed and face-to-face cues disappeared, institutions leaned heavily on LA systems to locate struggling students. However, as case reports revealed, data dashboards could not compensate for missing human connections. Many institutions discover gaps in data governance (unclear consent, opaque algorithms) and staff capacity (limited training to interpret dashboards). Students, meanwhile, often feel reduced to data points rather than recognised as whole persons with complex challenges. Thus, while the promise of LA systems lies in their ability to detect and support struggling students early on, its danger lies in its overreliance on algorithmic signals without considering broader concerns about equity, privacy, and human judgment. This duality underscores why synthesising LA into human-centred workflows is both urgent and unique.

1.3 Research Gaps and the Uniqueness of This Study

Previous work has been performed already which is centred around Predictive Accuracy: studies test which algorithms such as decision trees, support vector machines, neural networks, etc., yield the highest classification accuracy for identifying at-risk students (Conijn et al., 2017; Tempelaar et al., 2021). While valuable, this emphasis on technical performance often sidelines questions about what happens after prediction. Technological Architecture: which reviews highlight whether systems are scalable, interoperable, or able to integrate multiple data streams. Yet architecture alone does not guarantee ethical or effective use. Single-Domain Studies: much of the evidence remains discipline-specific (e.g., computer science, mathematics), limiting generalisability. For example, Azcona's digital footprint work focuses on programming courses Azcona et al. (2018). while Baneres' GAR model evaluates online computer science modules Baneres (2016).

This chapter synthesises insights from computer science, education, psychology, and data ethics, bridging disciplinary silos. It foregrounds how teachers, advisers, and counsellors interpret and act upon alerts, rather than treating the dashboard as the endpoint. It explicitly considers student well-being and fairness, examines domains often overlooked in LA, and optimise workflows, policies, and cultures around existing tools to ensure risk signals lead to equitable, humane decisions.

Research Questions

- To what extent do these systems detect risk signals correlated with validated mental-health indicators (e.g., PHQ-9, GAD-7, WEMWBS), and how are false positives, false negatives, and student harm managed?
- What technical and organisational guardrails (e.g., privacy controls, audit logs, intervention safeguards) shape how analytics-derived alerts are interpreted and acted upon?
- What privacy and fairness safeguards are implemented when LA systems are used to generate alerts, and how effectively do these safeguards function in practice?
- How can a human-in-the-loop workflow be designed to bridge the gap between automated alerts and timely, supportive interventions for students?

1.4 Research Objectives

The objectives are to:

- Map the detection logic and indicators across widely used LA platforms.

- Compare institutional practices of integrating dashboards with counselling and advising.
- Evaluate privacy and fairness safeguards in practice.
- Formulate a step-by-step, human-in-the-loop workflow to close the gap between alerts and support.

2. LITERATURE GAP

The body of research on learning analytics (LA) has grown exponentially in the last decade, yet it remains highly fragmented. Studies often operate in disciplinary silos, using different definitions of "at-risk," distinct methodological approaches, and inconsistent measures of success. For instance, in computer science education, Azcona et al. (2018) demonstrated how digital footprints from coding submissions and platform interactions could be combined to predict student risk with high accuracy Azcona et al. (2018). By contrast, in online higher education, Baneres (2016) emphasised a much simpler grade-based "Gradual At-Risk" (GAR) model that proved effective across a wide set of courses Baneres (2016). While both contributions are valuable, they exemplify how evidence is scattered across contexts, making it difficult to generalise findings into institution-wide strategies.

Meta-analyses echo this issue. Viberg et al. (2018) note that most systematic reviews of LA stop short at cataloguing the types of data used (e.g., demographics, LMS logs, test scores) rather than evaluating how interventions unfold after predictions. Similarly, Gašević et al. (2019) argue that LA research often prioritises technical novelty at the expense of longitudinal validation. As a result, stakeholders including faculty, administrators, policy makers—are left with piecemeal insights rather than a consolidated evidence base.

This fragmentation is not just academic; it directly impacts practice. Institutions investing in LA face a paradox: they have a proliferation of tools but little clear guidance on which indicators matter most, under what conditions, and with what ethical safeguards. This research chapter addresses this gap by synthesising across systems and disciplines, rather than limiting itself to a single predictive model or institutional case.

2.1 Development of Early Warning Systems

An EWS can be applied at different levels in an educational institution depending on the goal of the prevention (e.g., quality assurance, research goals, learning outcomes of a degree, performance, etc.). In the case of students, EWSs have been applied to solve different challenges.

Some examples of EWSs are early identification of at-risk students which may allow some type of intervention to increase retention and success rate student's dropout detection and reduction on face-to-face environments, students drop out on online settings, or students clustering to identify students with similar profiles (Marbouti et al, 2016).

Many of the previously described approaches propose a conceptual EWS. However, few developments can be found. The most referenced one is the Course Signals at Purdue University (Pistilli & Arnold, 2012) where different dashboards are available at the student's and teacher's point of view. Moreover, the system triggers a visual warning alert using a green-amber-red semaphore. Other systems can be found where information is available in dashboards for teachers and students (Najdi & B. Er-Raha, 2016).

Finally, some authors propose intervention measures to mitigate low performance. Measures such as e-mail messages and guidance, pedagogical recommendations, mentoring or particular academic support environment have been proposed with significant impact on performance, dropout, and retention (Hung et al., 2017).

2.2 Overemphasis on Predictive Accuracy

A second limitation in the literature is the heavy emphasis on predictive accuracy as the gold standard of success. Studies often report precision, recall, F1-scores, or area-under-curve values for different classifiers such as decision trees, logistic regression, support vector machines, or neural networks (Tempelaar et al., 2021). While these metrics are important, they risk obscuring the real-world significance of predictions.

Azcona et al. (2018) in their research combines diverse data sources in Higher Education to classify students and distinguish students at risk. Personalised notifications were sent to students regarding their progression and suggested course material and code they should view based on the engineered predictive models. Due to these models involve sets of static and dynamic features covering ranges of students' offline resources (i.e., demographics) and online information (i.e., behavioural logs), which permit to be further extrapolated to other domains as appropriately according to the data availability. The predictive students' performance outcomes provide tremendous value to the at-risk students directly as well as the lecturers to be better at identifying them and to react upon. In addition, in large classes, where lecturers cannot personalise their teaching and invest enough class time with each individual student, this methodology can supply the penalisation asynchronously by suggesting material and program code to students, keep them more engaged, improve their success rates and aid their learning of computer programming skills. Their research raised precisely this point. Their predictive models achieved impressive week-by-week accuracy in programming modules, but what mattered more was whether predictions translated into timely, personalised feedback that improved outcomes. Indeed, their study showed that students who engaged with tailored recommendations performed better in final exams, underscoring that accuracy is only valuable when linked to actionable interventions (Azcona et al., 2018).

Table 1. 2016/2017 Module information, pass rates, at-risk prediction rates, prediction metric results and correlations for the incoming cohort

Information	1st Exam	2nd Exam
Number of students	133	133
Passing rate	58.57%	42.86%
Predicted at-risk rate	74.29%	44.29%
Model's accuracy	64.29%	77.14%
Model's precision	94.44%	67.95%
Model's recall	41.46%	88.33%
Model's F1-score	57.63%	76.81%
Pearson correlation coefficient (p value)	0.62 ($p < 0.0001$)	0.65 ($p < 0.0001$)
Spearman correlation coefficient (p value)	0.60 ($p < 0.0001$)	0.70 ($p < 0.0001$)

Table 2. Interventions sent to students

Course Year	Notifications	Suggestions	# Corrected
CS2 2016/2017	438	181	21 (11.60%)

Similarly, Baneres (2016) reported that the EWS system which was developed in their university can semi-automate the exploration of the predictive models, the identification of at-risk students and the application of the intervention mechanism. They stated that results on a case study prove their effectiveness. On the other hand, they reported that even a relatively simple GAR model which is based only on incremental assessment grades was sufficient to identify risk, provided it was embedded within an early-warning system that delivered feedback to students. This raises a critical insight: sophisticated modelling may not always be superior in practice. A highly accurate model that overwhelms staff with false alarms or fails to guide interventions is less useful than a simpler model embedded within a well-designed workflow. Yet, much of the LA literature remains fixated on accuracy benchmarks rather than impact on student experience.

Table 3. Performance Gar Model in Computer Fundamentals

	TP	FP	TN	FN	ACC	TNR	TPR	$F_{1,5}$
Pr_{AA1}	237	59	136	105	69.74	69.74	69.30	72.9
Pr_{AA2}	266	6	189	76	83.24	96.92	77.78	83.01
Pr_{AA3}	309	10	185	33	90.20	94.87	90.35	92.26
Pr_{AA4}	319	4	191	23	93.05	97.95	93.27	94.90

Perhaps the most glaring gap in the literature is the so-called "last-mile problem" of learning analytics. Dashboards and predictive models are increasingly common, but evidence on how institutions act on alerts remains scarce. Instructors may receive colour-coded risk signals but lack clarity on what pedagogical or pastoral responses are appropriate. Advisers may be overwhelmed by the volume of alerts, leading to inconsistent follow-up. Students may see their own risk scores but remain uncertain about how to improve.

Case studies illustrate this disconnect. At Purdue University, the Course Signals system was lauded as an innovation in early-warning analytics, but subsequent evaluations showed mixed results. Some instructors used the signals as prompts for outreach, while others ignored them due to workload or scepticism about accuracy. Likewise, at the Open University UK, OU Analyse provides predictive risk scores for online learners, yet faculty reports suggest wide variation in whether and how alerts are acted upon.

The last mile is not a purely technical problem but an organisational one. It requires institutions to establish clear human-in-the-loop workflows, training faculty and advisers to interpret signals, and aligning policies so that alerts trigger timely, consistent, and equitable interventions. Yet few empirical studies document these processes in depth. Most research ends at the dashboard, leaving the crucial question of what happens next? underexplored.

2.3 Absence of Mental Health Considerations

Another striking gap is the lack of integration between learning analytics and student mental health research. Most studies conceptualise "at-risk" narrowly as risk of academic failure or dropout, measured through grades or retention metrics. Yet recent surveys show that mental health is both a cause and a consequence of academic difficulties. The American College Health Association reports that over

40% of university students experience moderate to severe anxiety, and 36% report depression that impairs functioning.

Despite these trends, LA systems rarely incorporate affective or psychological indicators. Some exploratory work has attempted to detect emotional states through multimodal learning analytics such as tracking posture, facial expressions, or keyboard dynamics but such studies remain niche. More importantly, few LA platforms integrate with counselling services or consider the ethical implications of predicting mental health risk. The COVID-19 pandemic revealed the consequences: as institutions leaned on analytics to compensate for lost face-to-face contact, dashboards often reduced students to data points without acknowledging their broader well-being.

2.4 Limited Attention to Privacy, Transparency, and Fairness

Privacy and fairness are frequently mentioned in LA research but seldom operationalised in practice. Many institutional deployments rely on implicit consent—students are enrolled in courses that automatically track their data—without explicit opt-in processes. Algorithmic models are rarely subject to transparency measures, such as publishing feature weights, accuracy thresholds, or bias audits. As a result, students often lack awareness of what data are collected, how it is used, and how it might affect their academic standing.

Emerging critiques highlight the risks. Slade and Prinsloo (2013) warned of the "ethical debt" institutions accumulate when deploying LA without clear governance. More recently, Tsai et al. (2020) found that students value transparency and agency over raw predictive accuracy, preferring systems that explain scores in plain language. The Open University has experimented with "Model Cards for Students," offering simplified descriptions of predictive models, but such initiatives remain rare.

Moreover, bias remains a concern. Predictive models trained on historical data risk reproducing inequities. For example, if past cohorts show lower retention among certain demographic groups, models may inadvertently flag those students as "at risk" simply for belonging to that group. Without fairness audits, such biases remain hidden yet consequential.

2.5 Why This Gap Matters

The cumulative effect of these gaps means that current LA systems often fall short of their potential. They risk becoming dashboards without decisions, producing alerts without support.

This chapter examines and consolidates what is already known into a pragmatic, ethically defensible workflow rather than adding another predictive model to the literature. It responds to the urgent need for institutions to move beyond fragmented pilots toward scalable, humane, and fair early-warning practices. By drawing on cross-case institutional analysis and systematic literature review, this study proposes a roadmap that is:

a) Technology-agnostic: this is applicable across existing platforms (Canvas, Blackboard, Moodle, Civitas).
b) Human-centred: this involves integrating advisers, counsellors, and students as active decision-makers.
c) Ethically grounded: ensures aligning with GDPR and FERPA principles, bias audits, and transparency practices.
d) Holistic: attending to both academic and mental health dimensions of risk.

3. METHODOLOGY

3.1 Research Design Overview

This study employs a multi-method design to synthesise knowledge across learning-analytics (LA) research and practice. The goal is not to develop a new predictive model but to produce a replicable, human-in-the-loop workflow for early identification of at-risk students that integrates existing systems, institutional processes, and ethical safeguards.

To achieve this, the methodology integrates two complementary strands:

a) **Systematic Literature Review (SLR)** – to consolidate evidence on LA tools, risk indicators, and ethical considerations.
b) **Cross-Case Institutional Analysis** – to explore how LA systems function in practice across six institutions.

3.2 Systematic Literature Review

Database searches were conducted across the Web of Science, Scopus, ERIC, ProQuest, ACM Digital Library, IEEE Xplore, and PsycINFO to ensure broad coverage across educational technology, psychology, and social science literature. Search queries combined terms related to learning analytics and educational data mining with terms corresponding to the focus areas, including “risk detection,” “early warning,” “intervention,” “privacy,” “wellbeing,” “fairness,” and “ethical considerations.” This approach is consistent with prior systematic reviews in LA, where multi-database strategies have been shown to mitigate bias towards single publication venues (Kaliisa et al., 2023; Liu & Khalil, 2023). Seed reviews and hand-searches of key venues (Journal of Learning Analytics, British Journal of Educational Technology, LAK proceedings, Computers & Education) were used to identify candidate studies.

Studies were included if they met the following criteria:

1. Empirical evidence (quantitative, qualitative, or mixed methods) on LA tools.
2. Explicit focus on risk detection, mental health indicators, or privacy/data protection measures.
3. Published in English between 2015–2025.
4. Peer-reviewed articles or full conference papers.

Exclusion criteria comprised theoretical papers, technical-only algorithm designs, editorials, and studies without empirical evaluation of LA interventions. Similar approaches to eligibility checks were used in prior SLRs of LA dashboards (Kaliisa et al., 2023) and privacy issues in LA (Liu & Khalil, 2023).

All retrieved records were imported into Zotero for duplicate removal and subsequently screened in Rayyan.ai to facilitate collaborative screening and conflict resolution. Title and abstract screening were followed by full-text eligibility assessment. The process was documented in a PRISMA flow diagram to ensure reproducibility (Moher et al., 2009).

For each included study, the following metadata were extracted:

1. Bibliographic details (author, year, country, venue).
2. Study design (experimental, quasi-experimental, survey, case study).
3. Target population (students, faculty, administrators).
4. Type of LA tool (dashboards, predictive models, multimodal analytics).
5. Indicators addressed (academic risk, dropout, mental health, well-being).
6. Ethical dimensions (privacy, data protection, transparency, stakeholder perceptions).

Screening and PRISMA: Initial identification yielded 1200 records (databases + hand searches + seed reviews). Duplication removed (n = 250) and title/abstract screening, Records screened (n = 950), Records excluded (n = 700), 250 full-text articles were assessed for eligibility; 150 were excluded for reasons such as non-empirical focus or out-of-scope outcomes. Final included studies: n = 100. The PRISMA flow diagram in figure 1 summarises the selection process.

Data extraction and quality appraisal: For each included study we extracted year, country, setting (K-12, higher education, MOOC, workplace), LA tool type, study design, sample size, outcome measures, and key findings. Quality appraisal used adapted CASP criteria.

A thematic coding framework was applied using NVivo to capture both risk-related and ethical themes. Coding followed the six-step thematic analysis procedure outlined by Nowell et al. (2017), which was also used in prior LA reviews (Liu & Khalil, 2023). To enhance reliability, two reviewers independently coded a subset of studies, and discrepancies were resolved through discussion. Inter-rater reliability was assessed using Cohen's kappa.

We adopted a narrative synthesis approach, integrating findings thematically across the three focal strands: (1) LA tools and their functionalities, (2) risk indicators (e.g., dropout, mental health, well-being), and (3) ethical considerations (e.g., privacy, transparency, legislation). Where feasible, quantitative outcomes (e.g., effect sizes of interventions) were standardised and compared, following the bottom-up synthesis approach recommended by Kaliisa et al. (2023).

Figure 1. Prisma flow diagram

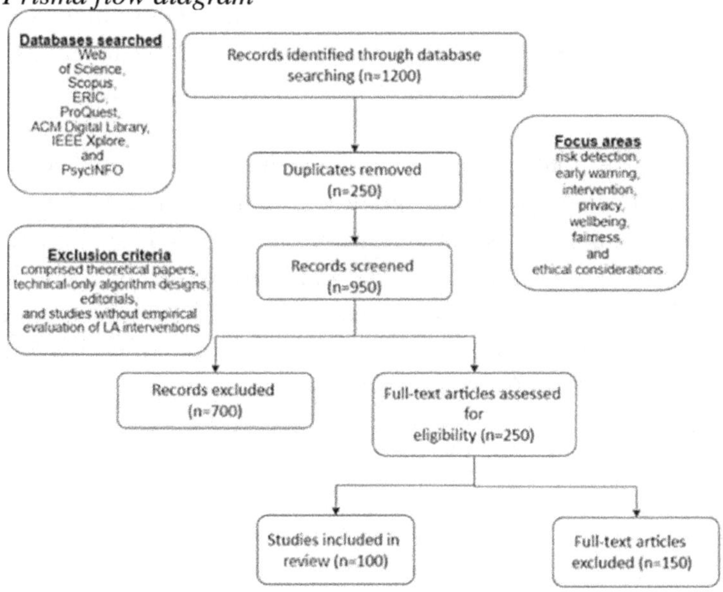

3.3 Cross-Case Institutional Analysis

The second strand involves a cross-case analysis of five institutional deployments:

1. <u>Purdue University:</u> Course Signals is an early-warning system using a predictive model plus simple visual "traffic-light" indicators (green/amber/red) presented to students to communicate current risk status and suggested next actions. It

combines LMS activity, grades, and demographic/academic history to generate near-real-time risk indicators Using existing student data and current grade information, Purdue created Signals, a system that gives students early and frequent performance notifications and helps faculty members steer students toward additional campus resources as needed. The student success algorithm considers not only demographic and performance data but also data on student effort and engagement. Results thus far show that students who have engaged with Course Signals have higher average grades and seek out help resources at a higher rate than other students (Pistilli & Arnold, 2012).

The use of learner analytics through the application of Course Signals to difficult courses has shown great promise about the success of first- and second-year students, as well as their overall retention to the University. To date, over 23,000 students across 100 courses have been impacted by Course Signals and over 140 instructors have utilized the system. Plans call for the expansion of CS to include as many as 20,000 students a semester within the next 18 months, and the upper administration the institution is in strong support of this goal. (Arnold & Pistilli, 2012)

2. University of New South Wales: OnTask is an instructor-facing tool that extracts learner data (LMS engagement, grades, responses) and enables teachers to craft segmented, personalised messages or scaffolds (semi-automated, teacher-curated). Over the past few years, OnTask has been used by academics at UTS to create rule-based messages to personalise feedback and tailor communication to every student in their subject (UTS / CIC case summary, 2022). Figure 2 below is an example an OnTask workflow.

Figure 2. Example of an OnTask workflow

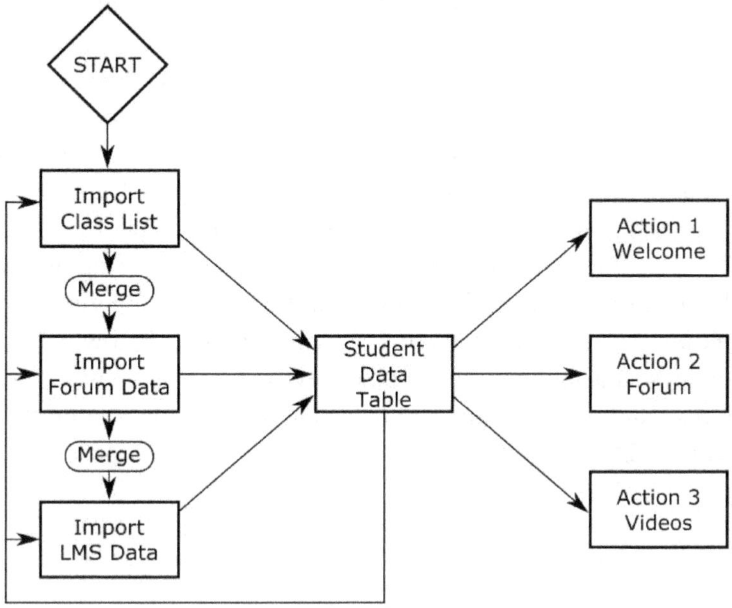

Learning analytics needs to widen its focus to explore the use of data to provide more general student support actions. This paper outlined a student and instructor centred conceptual model and an architecture to aid instructors to specify and deploy data-supported, personalized, scalable student support processes. The model espoused seeks to integrate the use of comprehensive data sources, instructor knowledge of the learning context, and a formal description of the connection between actions and personalized learning support actions (PLSAs) (Pardo et al., 2018).

The adoption of such a tool is heavily dependent on how to support instructors throughout the different stages of the process. For example, data management is an area that can be provided to personnel with the right set of skills to produce and populate the data table with the relevant student information connected to the learning design. Instructional designers can also envision common rule patterns that apply to certain design elements, provided to instructors to frame the personalized messages. We envision this multipronged support as an essential element to promote institutional adoption of this approach (Pardo et al., 2018).

3. Open University UK: OU Analyse is a production-scale ML pipeline that computes weekly risk predictions for OU students (richly online, very large cohorts). Predictions feed course tutors and student support teams who triage

interventions. OU has iteratively scaled the system to many large courses and uses it to prioritise outreach/support (OU KMI analyse site).

Building predictive models for identifying at-risk students using machine learning techniques and student activity data recorded in previous presentations of the same course proved to provide useful information for course teams and tutors. Since the data record all interactions of each student with VLE, it is easy to find the learning material that the student has missed. If the student has been identified as at-risk, it is possible to recommend the resources that can bring him/her back on track. Predictions of at-risk students also help the student support teams to focus the interventions on specific needs of everyone. Figure 3 below shows the Open University analyse dashboard with a course view and student view provides flexible and easy access to the predictions and makes it possible to scale up this approach (Kuzilek et al., 2015).

Figure 3. OU Analyse dashboard – course overview page

4. <u>Arizona State University:</u> Civitas Learning's Illume (and related modules) is a commercial student success platform that integrates institutional data (LMS, SIS, demographics) to surface risks and recommended interventions for advisors, faculty and administrators. ASU (and other large institutions) have used Civitas in cross-campus workflows (advisors, faculty dashboards, campaign management).

Civitas Learning has upgraded its Illume predictive analytics product with new capabilities designed to help institutions improve student outcomes.

Illume integrates students' academic, financial and behavioral data to develop personalized predictions, identify at-risk students and deploy targeted interventions. Two new features — Courses and Impact — aim to provide a "more precise, holistic understanding of student success," according to a press release.

Courses enable institutions to identify which courses have the most impact on student success pathways (such as persistence and graduation) at the institutional, college, program and major level. In addition, Courses can "determine which students are most affected by those courses" and "pinpoint opportunities to optimize curriculum and programs." Impact gives campus decision-makers a detailed view of retention initiatives, to help determine which programs are helping students the most and which are the least effective (Rhea Kelly, 2016).

5. <u>Urban Community College (US):</u> Canvas New Analytics is an LMS-built analytics module embedded in Instructure Canvas; it gives instructors course-level descriptive analytics (grade distributions, participation, page views) and simple filters to identify struggling students; many US community colleges using Canvas rely on this built-in tool for day-to-day course triage (Instructure / Canvas community docs, 2025).

We could use New Analytics to positively feedback to our students. Using the above techniques, we could, for example, send a congratulatory message to students who achieved above a certain grade. Perhaps students who completed all pieces of work could be similarly congratulated by receiving a message withing Canvas (Institutional guide, University of Liverpool).

Figure 4. Student analytics

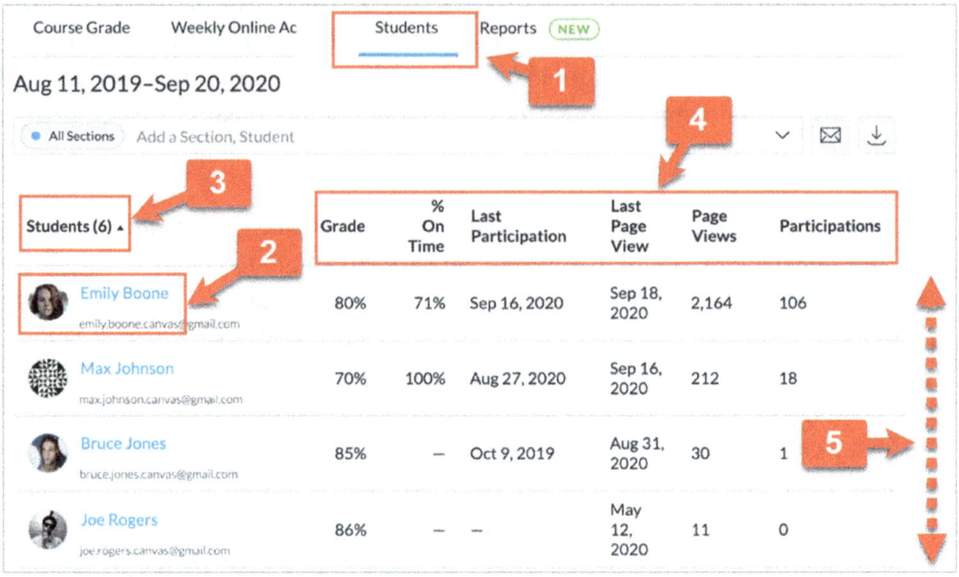

3.4 Conceptual Workflow

The integration of these strands leads to the design of a human-in-the-loop workflow for early identification of at-risk students. At its core, the workflow (see Figure 5) consists of:

1. **Data Collection** – LMS logs, grades, demographic data, affective indicators.
2. **Prediction Layer** – algorithms generate risk probabilities.
3. **Visualisation** – dashboards for students, faculty, and advisers.
4. **Human Interpretation** – alerts are reviewed by instructors/advisers.
5. **Intervention** – personalised outreach, counselling, or tutoring.
6. **Feedback Loop** – evaluation of intervention effectiveness and model refinement.

Figure 5. Human-in-the-loop workflow for at-risk student identification

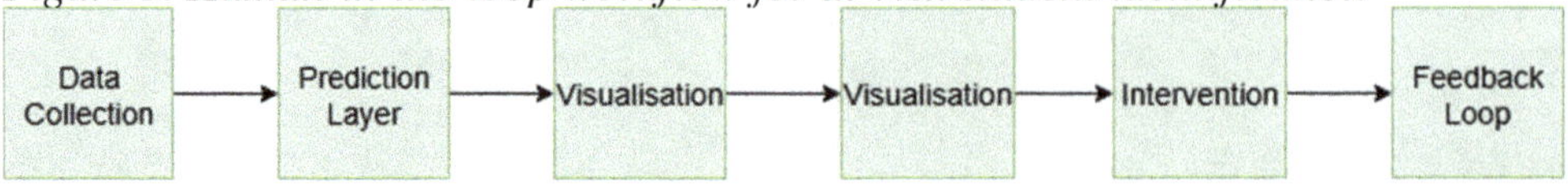

4. OUTCOMES AND SIGNIFICANCE

The contribution of this chapter is not to introduce another predictive algorithm or bespoke dashboard prototype. Instead, its significance lies in consolidating what is already known, operationalising it into referenceable workflows and toolkits, and framing the field's future trajectory. By privileging policy and process innovation over technology procurement, the chapter offers a pathway that is accessible even to institutions with limited budgets or technical capacity. The expected outcomes are summarised across three pillars:

4.1 Consolidated Evidence Base

Outcome 1: The first outcome is a synthesised evidence base that moves beyond scattered case studies toward a cumulative knowledge framework.

The SLR shows a pattern: certain indicator families (grades, LMS engagement, peer interactions, and temporal drops) reliably predict academic risk across multiple implementations, while model choice should be driven by data richness and operational constraints rather than accuracy alone. Simple, transparent systems produce repeatable operational gains in engagement or formative tasks; complex multimodal systems improve detection in instrumented courses but require more governance and validation. Liu & Khalil (2023) and multiple reviews emphasise that privacy and deployment evidence is often thin—technical proposals are not routinely accompanied by live deployment evaluations (Susnjak et al., 2022). Through the systematic literature review (Section 3), the chapter consolidates findings on:

Finding 1 — Indicators: assessment grades + LMS engagement + peer interactions + trend/drop signals are the most stable predictors. Sentiment / short-text indicators show promise for mental-health signals but are less validated and trigger stronger ethical constraints.

Finding 2 — Models & Conditions

a) In low-resource/small-N contexts: rule-based/simple ML is preferred—effective, transparent, cheap to run. (BANERES/GAR example demonstrates practical gains in formative tasks, though final outcomes vary.)
b) In data-rich contexts (MOOCs, programming environments): multimodal predictive pipelines outperform simple rules if accompanied by strong validation and ethical oversights (e.g., Azcona et al.'s PredictCS/Predictive modelling in programming) (Azcona et al., 2018).

Finding 3 — Ethical limitations: privacy, consent, transparency, and potential bias in flagged outcomes are consistent blockers to scaling LA in practice. Solutions so far are fragmentary — national/regional laws (GDPR, FERPA) impose constraints that must be built into the pipeline from day one (Janahi & Muhammad, 2025).

Figure 6. Literature map: Indicators x models x conditions x ethical caveats

Indicators	Models that succeed	Conditions	Ethical caveats
Assessment grades	Rule-based (GAR) Logistic regression	Small classes Low-resource settings	Risk of over-simplification May miss hidden risks
LMS engagement	Rule-based + ML Decision trees	Moderate data Explainability needed	Transparency vs bias Requires fairness checks
Peer interactions	Social network + ML	Collaborative/online learning	Privacy of peer data Power asymmetry
Temporal change	Trend detection + rules	Contexts with log traces Longitudinal data	False positives from noise Requires careful triage
Sentiment data	Multimodal predictive (NLP, sentiment analysis)	Data-rich environments (Programming MOOCs)	High privacy risk Anonymisation difficult GDPR/FERPA alignment needed

4.2 Policy Toolkit

The second outcome of this chapter is the development of a Policy Toolkit aimed at enabling institutions to operationalise ethical and effective learning analytics (LA) without requiring substantial technological reinvestment. Rather than introducing new platforms, the toolkit is designed as a set of low-cost, high-impact resources that can be embedded within existing infrastructures such as Canvas, Blackboard, Moodle, or Civitas. This ensures the toolkit is technology-agnostic, thereby making adoption feasible across diverse institutional contexts.

The toolkit operationalises ethical principles into everyday practice through three central instruments:

1. Consent-form templates: Standardised documents that clearly communicate what data are collected, the purposes of analysis, and students' rights to opt out. These templates promote informed consent and compliance with GDPR and FERPA, addressing transparency and trust deficits noted in prior studies (Liu & Khalil, 2023).
2. Bias-audit checklists: Practical tools to evaluate whether predictive models inadvertently reproduce inequities across gender, race, socioeconomic background, or disability. Such checklists institutionalise a bias-aware culture, ensuring that LA adoption does not reinforce structural disadvantages (Tsai et al., 2020).
3. Role descriptions: Guidelines clarifying the responsibilities of lecturers, advisers, and counsellors when responding to alerts. This directly addresses the "last-mile problem," where risk signals stall in dashboards without being acted upon. By codifying workflows, institutions can guarantee timely human intervention that integrates academic and well-being support (Prinsloo & Slade, 2015).

4.3 Research Agenda

The third outcome of the SLR is the articulation of a forward-looking research agenda that highlights unresolved questions critical to the maturation of the learning analytics (LA) field. While the review consolidated evidence on tools, risk indicators, and ethical practices, it also revealed areas where empirical inquiry remains thin, fragmented, or contextually constrained. These gaps point to pressing challenges for researchers, policymakers, and technology developers, and their resolution will shape whether LA evolves into a sustainable and trusted educational infrastructure.

1. Cultural adaptation of nudges. Current LA interventions, such as dashboard alerts or predictive feedback systems, often rely on assumptions about general student motivation and behaviour. Yet nudges that are effective in one context may reinforce paternalism or stigma in another. Future research should investigate how interventions can be tailored to various cultural, institutional, and disciplinary contexts, striking a balance between support and respect for autonomy. Addressing this question will be central to ensuring that LA interventions scale ethically across diverse global contexts.
2. Mental health trajectories. Most existing studies conceptualise risk detection as a one-off identification of academic or well-being risks. A long-term perspective is needed to understand how LA systems might monitor mental health trajectories, resilience, and recovery patterns over time. This shift requires integrating insights from psychology and the health sciences to avoid pathologising temporary struggles while supporting sustainable student wellbeing. Such work would move LA beyond short-term crisis management towards proactive and preventative care.
3. Algorithmic transparency at scale. As predictive models grow in complexity and scope, questions emerge about how to ensure that students can meaningfully understand, question, and contest risk classifications. Research is needed into governance models and institutional workflows that balance transparency with resource constraints. Exploring mechanisms such as layered explanations, institutional ombuds, or student-facing interpretability tools could enhance trust without overwhelming academic or technical staff.
4. Equity-by-design frameworks. While bias detection and fairness audits are gaining traction in the LA literature, systematic frameworks that integrate equity principles into the design, deployment, and evaluation of LA tools remain underdeveloped. Future studies should investigate how student co-design, explainable AI models, and routine equity audits could be embedded into both research prototypes and commercial platforms. Establishing such standards would

allow equity considerations to move from ad hoc practice to an institutionalised norm.

4.4 Significance and Uniqueness

Lowering Barriers for Institutions. By focusing on referenceable systems (Canvas, Blackboard, Civitas, Moodle) rather than bespoke prototypes, the chapter ensures that even resource-constrained institutions can implement recommendations without additional procurement costs. This emphasis on workflows and policies over technology positions the work as both practical and scalable.

Reframing Early-Warning Analytics. Unlike most studies that stop at predictive accuracy or dashboard design, this chapter uniquely foregrounds the translation layer—how visualised risk scores become meaningful, ethical decisions. It recognises that students are not data points but complex individuals whose academic trajectories are intertwined with mental health, equity, and institutional culture.

The significance of the Policy Toolkit outcome lies in its practical application. Institutions often report that their greatest barrier to implementing ethical learning analytics is not resistance, but the absence of ready-to-use templates and workflows. By providing standardised resources, the toolkit reduces institutional burden, accelerates adoption, and promotes consistency across contexts. Moreover, by embedding human, ethical, and holistic principles, the toolkit ensures that learning analytics evolve not just as a technical intervention but as a responsible and sustainable institutional practice.

In sum, the policy toolkit not only strengthens institutional capacity to detect and address risk but also models how LA can evolve into a sustainable and ethically grounded practice that is student-centred, compliant, and adaptable. This outcome marks a shift from piecemeal, project-based ethics to an institutionalised framework that can be scaled across contexts.

Research agenda outcome supports LA's dual role as a technical system for supporting learning and as a socio-ethical infrastructure that shapes the student experience. By highlighting unresolved methodological and ethical challenges, the chapter advances a roadmap for scholars and practitioners to close evidence gaps, develop context-sensitive interventions, and embed fairness and transparency in LA ecosystems. This agenda positions future research to move beyond proof-of-concept tools towards scalable, trustworthy, and equitable systems capable of addressing the diverse needs of global learners.

5. ETHICAL AND INCLUSIVITY CONSIDERATIONS

The effectiveness of early-warning learning-analytics (LA) systems hinges not only on predictive accuracy but on their ability to operate ethically and inclusively. Without strong governance, risk-detection workflows risk exacerbating mistrust, perpetuating bias, and alienating precisely the students they are designed to support. To address this, the proposed workflow is explicitly aligned with GDPR's data-minimisation and purpose-limitation principles (EU, 2018) and FERPA's protections of educational records (US Department of Education, 2020). These frameworks set foundational guardrails: collect only the data strictly necessary, use it solely for stated educational purposes, and ensure students retain rights over their personal records.

Building on these legal baselines, the workflow embeds equity and inclusivity through three practical mechanisms: bias audits, student co-design, and algorithmic transparency. Each mechanism directly targets known shortcomings of existing LA deployments.

5.1 Bias Audits: Detecting and Mitigating Hidden Inequities

Predictive models trained on historical educational data risk reproducing the inequities of the past. For example, if lower retention rates among first-generation students appear in legacy datasets, machine-learning models may inadvertently flag such students as "at risk" simply due to their background rather than their current behaviour. To guard against this, the proposed workflow integrates bias audits as a routine evaluative step.

The methodology draws inspiration from the IBM AI Fairness 360 toolkit, which provides open-source algorithms for detecting disparate impact across sensitive attributes (Bellamy et al., 2019). By applying fairness metrics to de-identified datasets, institutions can identify whether models disproportionately assign risk to marginalised groups. Where bias is detected, mitigation strategies such as re-weighting, adversarial de-biasing, or threshold adjustment can be applied.

Importantly, bias audits are not treated as one-off checks but as continuous governance practices. Each semester, models are re-audited to ensure fairness is maintained as new cohorts are introduced. Embedding fairness evaluation in the workflow reframes equity as a non-negotiable design principle rather than an afterthought.

5.2 Student Co-Design: Empowering Voices at the Margins

Ethical LA must also consider how students are engaged in system design. Too often, risk-detection workflows are designed about students rather than with them, leading to a sense of surveillance and disempowerment. The proposed workflow therefore embeds student co-design, with a deliberate emphasis on including representatives from marginalised groups.

A notable precedent is the University of Edinburgh's participatory consent-form redrafting, where students collaborated with administrators to rewrite consent processes in accessible language, highlighting rights and opt-out options (Jones et al., 2021). By replicating such practices, the workflow ensures that consent documents are not merely legal formalities but living agreements understood by students themselves.

Co-design also addresses power imbalances. Involving first-generation students, international learners, and students with disabilities ensures that risk-detection frameworks account for diverse experiences. This inclusivity fosters trust and demonstrates institutional commitment to equity not just in outcomes but in decision-making processes.

5.3 Algorithmic Transparency: Making Risk Scores Understandable

Transparency is central to building trust in LA. Yet most institutions struggle to explain predictive models to students in accessible ways. Students may see colour-coded alerts but remain unaware of how these signals were generated, what data informed them, or what actions they should take.

The proposed workflow adopts a model inspired by the Open University's "Model Cards for Students" initiative. Upon request, any student can receive a plain-language explanation of their risk score, including: The indicators used (e.g., assignment submissions, discussion forum activity), the relative weight of each indicator, the thresholds applied to categorise risk levels, and the actions recommended for improvement.

Such transparency has dual benefits: it empowers students to make informed choices and provides a safeguard against misinterpretation or blind reliance on opaque models. By treating transparency as a right rather than a privilege, the workflow shifts the power balance, ensuring that students are active participants in their own learning trajectories.

5.4 Aligning Legal Compliance with Ethical Ambition

The synergy between GDPR and FERPA compliance and equity mechanisms creates a dual layer of accountability which are Legal safeguards (data minimisation, purpose limitation, consent, access rights), and ethical safeguards (bias audits, co-design, transparency).

This dual framework ensures that institutions go beyond the minimum compliance standard and proactively cultivate inclusive, trustworthy systems. The outcome is a model where students are not passive subjects of analytics but active stakeholders in shaping how data is used to support their success.

5.5 Significance of Ethical and Inclusive Design

Embedding these practices transforms early-warning LA from a risk-monitoring tool into a trust-building practice. Bias audits reassure communities that systems are fair. Co-design legitimises consent processes. Transparency shifts control back to learners. Together, these mechanisms help prevent LA from becoming another layer of educational surveillance, instead positioning it as an instrument of empowerment and equity.

The uniqueness of this chapter is its insistence that ethical and inclusive design is not optional. It is central to the workflow, as essential as predictive accuracy or dashboard visualisation. In doing so, the chapter responds to urgent calls in the field for LA to balance innovation with justice, ensuring that vulnerable learners are supported—not stigmatised—by the data-driven university.

Figure 7. Integrating GDPR/FERPA Compliance with Equity Mechanisms

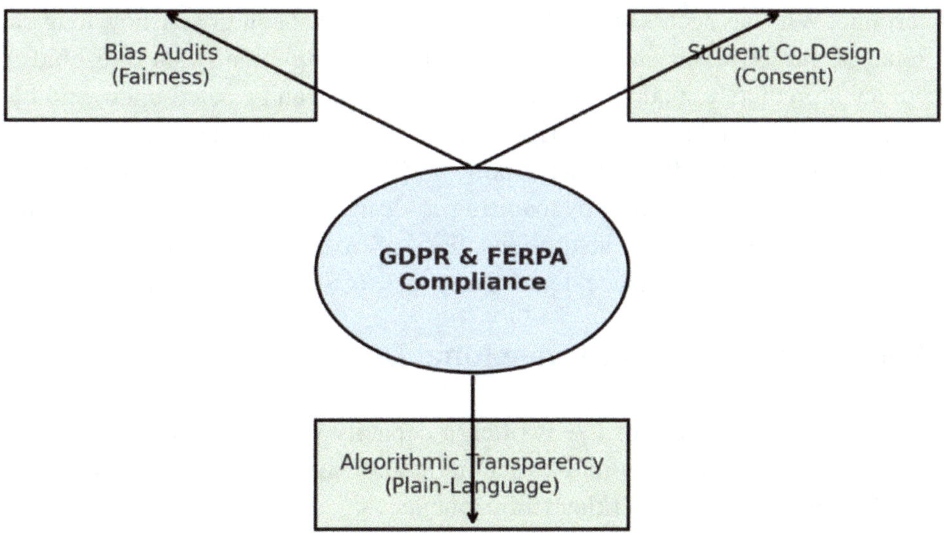

Here is **Figure 7**, a diagram visually integrating GDPR/FERPA compliance (central framework) with the three equity mechanisms:

a) Bias Audits (Fairness)
b) Student Co-Design (Consent)

c) Algorithmic Transparency (Plain-Language)

This shows how legal compliance anchors the workflow, while equity mechanisms extend it into trust-building and inclusivity practices.

6. POLICY AND CAPACITY CONSIDERATIONS

Learning-analytics (LA) systems do not exist in isolation. Their success depends on whether institutions can align predictive workflows with existing policies, staff capacity, and governance cultures. Too often, LA pilots fail not because models are inaccurate, but because institutions lack the policy frameworks and human infrastructure to support long-term integration. This section considers the enabling conditions required for institutions to responsibly adopt the proposed workflow.

6.1 Governance Frameworks

Institutional governance is the first pillar of sustainable LA adoption. Governance encompasses not only compliance with GDPR and FERPA but also the policies that determine: Who has access to dashboards and under what conditions, how long data is retained and how it is anonymised after course completion, what thresholds of accuracy a predictive model must reach before alerts can be acted upon, and how students are informed about their rights to view, contest, or opt out of analytics.

The University of Edinburgh's LA policy (2021) is a leading example, balancing data utility with student agency by requiring co-design processes and plain-language documentation. By contrast, institutions that deploy LA without clear governance often encounter staff resistance, legal challenges, or student mistrust.

6.2 Staff Capacity and Professional Development

The last-mile problem of LA is often a capacity problem. Instructors receive alerts but lack the time or training to act on them. Institutions must therefore invest in staff development and workload adjustments.

Key strategies include:

a) Professional Development: short courses on interpreting dashboards, bias awareness, and intervention strategies.
b) Communities of Practice: peer networks where faculty exchange experiences and troubleshoot issues collaboratively.

c) Workload Recognition: embedding LA-based outreach within formal teaching workload models, so interventions are recognised rather than treated as invisible labour.
d) Advising Infrastructure: strengthening collaboration between academic and pastoral staff so that alerts trigger a coordinated rather than fragmented response.

6.2 Student Capacity and Digital Literacy

Equally important is the capacity of students to understand and act on LA signals. Providing risk scores without guidance can lead to confusion or stigma. Institutions should therefore first embed digital literacy modules within orientation programmes, teaching students how to interpret dashboards and seek help proactively. Secondly, offer explanatory nudges alongside risk alerts (e.g., "Based on your current submission patterns, you may benefit from attending the weekly lab. Here's the link to register."). Finally, ensure equity of access, avoiding over-reliance on mobile notifications or digital platforms that may disadvantage low-income or rural students.

6.3 Policy Alignment With Institutional Missions

Policy adoption must align with broader institutional strategies on equity, well-being, and retention. For example: 1) Institutions prioritising first-generation student success can adapt workflows to ensure outreach prioritises mentoring programmes. 2) Universities committed to mental-health initiatives can integrate analytics with counselling referral systems. 3) Institutions under accreditation or accountability pressures can document LA workflows as part of quality assurance processes.

Many institutions, particularly community colleges and Global South universities, operate under tight resource constraints. Here, the proposed workflow offers a low-barrier entry point such as relying on existing LMS data (attendance, submissions, grades) rather than costly third-party integrations, using open-source bias-audit toolkits (e.g., AI Fairness 360) rather than proprietary analytics modules and sharing policy templates (consent forms, role descriptions) across institutions to reduce duplication.

Finally, LA adoption must be framed within a broader vision of institutional resilience. The COVID-19 pandemic revealed that institutions with flexible digital infrastructures and clear governance adapted more successfully. By embedding LA workflows into policy and capacity planning, institutions prepare not just for routine semesters but for disruptions—from pandemics to enrolment shifts.

The significance of policy and capacity considerations includes: 1) Sustainability: without governance and capacity, even the best predictive models collapse under real-world pressures. 2) Equity: strong policies and training ensure that interventions are consistent, fair, and inclusive, avoiding the risk of arbitrary or uneven responses.

This chapter is unique in explicitly foregrounding policy and human capacity as co-equal to algorithmic performance. By shifting attention from dashboards to institutions' ability to act, it reframes LA as an organisational change project rather than a purely technical initiative.

7. SUMMARY, RECOMMENDATIONS, AND LIMITATIONS

7.1 Summary

Despite a decade of experimentation with early-warning analytics, the field remains in transition. Much of the literature has focused on predictive accuracy and dashboard visualisation, while this chapter emphasises translation into actionable, equitable workflows. To advance this agenda, future research should pursue these directions:

Future studies need to assess not just whether models correctly flag at-risk students, but whether interventions following alerts improve retention, academic performance, and well-being. Longitudinal trials are especially needed to measure sustained outcomes beyond single semesters.

Research should explore how affective, behavioural, and counselling-related data can be ethically incorporated into LA systems. This includes building collaborations between data scientists, psychologists, and student mental-health services to design holistic risk frameworks.

Nudges and alerts may operate differently across different cultural contexts. Comparative studies are required to examine how cultural norms influence student responses to risk messages and whether interventions require localisation to avoid stigma or paternalism.

Research is needed on scalable transparency practices, such as "Model Cards for Students" or explainable AI methods—that balance interpretability with usability. The challenge lies in ensuring transparency without overwhelming students or staff with technical detail.

7.2 Recommendations

Drawing from the evidence base and workflow synthesis, the following recommendations are offered to institutions seeking to implement early-warning LA responsibly: Adopt a Human-in-the-Loop Workflow; ensure that every alert passes through an interpretive layer (faculty/advisors) before reaching students, preventing algorithmic determinism. Prioritise Simplicity over Complexity: use readily available indicators (attendance, grades, LMS and engagement) before investing in costly multimodal analytics, especially for resource-constrained institutions. Institutional Bias Audits and Transparency: regularly audit predictive models for fairness and provide plain-language explanations of risk scores. Co-Design with Students: involve diverse student representatives in designing consent processes, alert messaging, and intervention protocols. Train Staff and Recognise Workload: Provide professional development on interpreting dashboards and embed outreach tasks within workload models. Embed Policies in Governance: Align LA adoption with institutional policies on equity, mental health, and data protection, ensuring oversight beyond IT departments.

Looking forward, the future of early-warning analytics will depend on whether the field embraces interdisciplinary, equity-centred approaches. If LA remains fixated on dashboards and model accuracy, it risks entrenching surveillance and inequity. But if institutions invest in ethical design, governance, and human capacity, LA can become a transformative force for widening participation, supporting mental health, and building resilient learning communities.

The vision articulated here is not a technological utopia but a practical roadmap: collect the minimum data necessary, generate actionable insights, ensure transparency, and empower humans to intervene compassionately. In this way, early-warning systems can truly fulfil their promise: turning data visualisation into informed, humane decisions.

7.3 Limitations

While this chapter consolidates evidence and proposes a pragmatic workflow, several limitations must be acknowledged. Although broad, the systematic review was limited to studies published between 2021 and 2025 in English-language journals. Important insights from earlier or non-English research may be underrepresented. The cross-case analysis focused on six institutions with prominent LA deployments. Findings may not fully represent smaller institutions or those outside of the Global North. The chapter synthesised existing evidence rather than conducting new intervention trials. As such, efficacy claims are extrapolated rather than directly tested. GDPR, FERPA, and AI governance frameworks are dynamic; recommendations may require updating as new regulations (e.g., the EU AI Act) emerge. While the chapter foregrounds mental health, robust empirical evidence for integrating psychological indicators into LA workflows remains sparse. Future interdisciplinary research must extend to this frontier.

This chapter acknowledges that workflows are context dependent. Institutions differ in infrastructure, resources, and cultures. The proposed workflow is thus adaptable, not prescriptive. Moreover, ethical debates will continue to evolve as AI regulation matures. Institutions must remain vigilant, updating practices as new risks emerge.

7.4 Uniqueness and Contribution

The uniqueness of this research lies in its reorientation of the LA conversation. Where much of the field has been preoccupied with dashboards and predictive models, this chapter underscores the translation problem: how to move from data visualisation to informed decisions. Its contributions are distinctive in three respects: 1) Holistic Integration: Combining academic, ethical, and mental-health perspectives into a single workflow. 2) Policy and Process Focus: Prioritising consent, bias audits, staff training, and governance over procurement of new technologies. 3) Equity by Design: Positioning inclusivity (co-design, transparency, fairness) as structural components of workflows, not peripheral add-ons.

What sets this chapter apart is its refusal to treat learning analytics as purely a technical exercise. The focus of the study is not solely on the visualisation of data, but on how data visualisations are interpreted, contested, and utilised. Providing actionable steps that do not require new procurement, the chapter emphasises policy templates, fairness audits, and workload adjustments. Inclusivity must be integrated into the workflow design, rather than being a peripheral component. For a successful predictive model, ethical safeguards are considered equally important to predictive accuracy.

Essentially, this chapter reframes early-warning LA as an organisational change project where pedagogical, cultural, and ethical factors play an important role, as well as computational ones.

8. CONCLUSION AND SYNTHESIS

The past decade has witnessed the rise of learning-analytics (LA) systems from experimental pilots to institutional infrastructures. Early-warning dashboards, predictive alerts, and personalised nudges have become the lingua franca of digital education. Yet, as this chapter has argued, the core challenge is no longer prediction but translation: how do institutions move from colourful dashboards to informed, ethical, and equitable decisions that genuinely improve student success?

The synthesis presented here offers several critical insights: Prediction Is Only the First Step:

Models can forecast with impressive accuracy, but without clear intervention pathways, alerts risk becoming inert data. The human-in-the-loop workflow proposed in this chapter re-centres educators, advisers, and students as interpreters and actors, not passive recipients of algorithmic verdicts. Equity Requires Design, Not Afterthoughts: By embedding bias audits, student co-design, and algorithmic transparency into the workflow, this chapter demonstrates that inclusivity can be engineered into systems rather than appended after harm occurs. This is particularly vital in contexts where marginalised students are most vulnerable to misclassification. Policy and Capacity Are Decisive

The fate of LA deployments hinges less on model sophistication than on institutional capacity and governance (see Section 6). Workload recognition, training, and alignment with institutional missions are as vital as algorithms. Without them, even the most advanced systems collapse under real-world pressures. Evidence Must Be Consolidated, Not Fragmented: By mapping indicators, models, and ethical caveats (Section 4), this chapter transforms fragmented research into a consolidated knowledge base. Institutions no longer need to reinvent workflows from scratch; they can draw from tested, referenceable practices.

The central claim of this chapter is simple yet profound: dashboards do not save students, rather decisions do. By shifting attention from prediction to practice, from models to workflows, and from compliance to inclusivity, institutions can bridge the gap between data and action. This is the uniqueness and urgency of the topic.

In synthesising evidence, proposing toolkits, and charting future directions, this chapter contributes to a growing movement in the field: one that sees learning analytics not as an end but as a means of building more just, responsive, and humane education systems.

REFERENCES

Arnold, K. E., & Pistilli, M. D. (2012). Course signals at Purdue: Using learning analytics to increase student success. In *Proceedings of the 2nd International Conference on Learning Analytics and Knowledge (LAK '12)* (pp. 267–270). Association for Computing Machinery. DOI: 10.1145/2330601.2330666

Azcona, D., Hsiao, I.-H., & Smeaton, A. F. (2018). Personalizing computer science education by leveraging multimodal learning analytics. In *2018 IEEE Frontiers in Education Conference (FIE)* [Conference session]. IEEE. DOI: 10.1109/FIE.2018.8658596

Baneres, D. (2016). Towards a particular prediction system to evaluate student's success. In M. Reiff-Marganiec & S. Caballero (Eds.), *Proceedings of the 11th International Conference on P2P, Parallel, Grid, Cloud and Internet Computing (3PGCIC)* (pp. 935–945). Springer.

Baneres, D., & Serra, M. (2018). Predictive analytics: Another vision of the learning process. In Caballé, S., & Conesa, J. (Eds.), *Software data engineering for network eLearning environments* (pp. 1–25). Springer., DOI: 10.1007/978-3-319-68318-8_1

Hung, J. L., Wang, M. C., Wang, S., Abdelrasoul, M., Lo, Y., & He, W. (2017). Identifying at-risk students for early interventions—A time-series clustering approach. *IEEE Transactions on Emerging Topics in Computing*, *5*(1), 44–55. DOI: 10.1109/TETC.2015.2504239

Janahi, Y., & Obeidat, M. (2025). Predictive analytics and AI in education: A systematic literature review on identifying and supporting at-risk students [Preprint]. *SSRN*. DOI: 10.2139/ssrn.5240920

Kaliisa, R., Misiejuk, K., López-Pernas, S., Khalil, M., & Saqr, M. (2023). Have learning analytics dashboards lived up to the hype? A systematic review of impact on students' achievement, motivation, participation and attitude [Preprint]. arXiv. https://arxiv.org/abs/2312.15042

Kuzilek, J., Hlosta, M., Herrmannova, D., Zdrahal, Z., Vaclavek, J., & Wolff, A. (2015). *OU Analyse: Analysing at-risk students at The Open University* (Learning Analytics Review No. LAK15-1). LACE Project. http://www.laceproject.eu/learning-analytics-review

Liu, Q., & Khalil, M. (2023). Understanding privacy and data protection issues in learning analytics using a systematic review. *British Journal of Educational Technology*, *54*(6), 1715–1747. DOI: 10.1111/bjet.13388

Marbouti, F., Diefes-Dux, H. A., & Madhavan, K. (2016). Models for early prediction of at-risk students in a course using standards-based grading. *Computers & Education, 103*, 1–15. DOI: 10.1016/j.compedu.2016.09.005

Najdi, L., & Er-Raha, B. (2016). A novel predictive modeling system to analyze students at risk of academic failure. *International Journal of Computer Applications, 156*(6), 25–30. DOI: 10.5120/ijca2016912482

Nowell, L. S., Norris, J. M., White, D. E., & Moules, N. J. (2017). Thematic analysis: Striving to meet the trustworthiness criteria. *International Journal of Qualitative Methods, 16*(1), 1–13. DOI: 10.1177/1609406917733847

Pardo, A., Bartimote, K., Buckingham Shum, S., Dawson, S., Gao, J., Gašević, D., Leichtweis, S., Liu, D., Martínez-Maldonado, R., Mirriahi, N., Moskal, A. C. M., Schulte, J., Siemens, G., & Vigentini, L. (2018). OnTask: Delivering data-informed, personalized learning support actions. *Journal of Learning Analytics, 5*(3), 235–249. DOI: 10.18608/jla.2018.53.15

Pistilli, M. D., & Arnold, K. E. (2012). In practice: Purdue's signals project. In *Proceedings of the 2nd International Conference on Learning Analytics and Knowledge (LAK '12)* (pp. 2–5).

Romero, C., & Ventura, S. (2013). Data mining in education. *Wiley Interdisciplinary Reviews. Data Mining and Knowledge Discovery, 3*(1), 12–27. DOI: 10.1002/widm.1075

Slade, S., & Prinsloo, P. (2013). Learning analytics: Ethical issues and dilemmas. *The American Behavioral Scientist, 57*(10), 1510–1529. DOI: 10.1177/0002764213479366

Susnjak, T., Ramaswami, G. S., & Mathrani, A. (2022). Learning analytics dashboard: A tool for providing actionable insights to learners. *International Journal of Educational Technology in Higher Education, 19*(1), 12. Advance online publication. DOI: 10.1186/s41239-021-00313-7 PMID: 35194560

KEY TERMS AND DEFINITIONS

Bias Audits: These are systematic evaluations of artificial intelligence (AI) systems and their data to identify, assess, and mitigate unfair biases against certain demographic groups. They are crucial for ensuring fairness, maintaining ethical standards, and complying with emerging regulations.

Evidence-Based Roadmap: This is a strategic plan that uses data and research to guide decisions toward a specific goal, ensuring a higher likelihood of success by outlining objectives, milestones, and the necessary steps based on evidence of what works. Unlike a traditional roadmap, it is built on a foundation of research, studies, and evaluated practices to inform the path forward.

LA: This is an acronym for learning-analytics. This is the process of collecting, analysing, and reporting data about learners and their learning environments to understand and optimize the learning process.

Outcome and Significance: Outcome is the result or effect of an action, while significance is the importance or meaning of those results. Understanding both is crucial for making informed decisions, evaluating progress, and measuring the real value of a project or intervention. Significance helps determine how a particular outcome contributes to broader objectives and why it matters, often based on criteria like impact, alignment, or contribution.

Chapter 7

AI-Driven Early Detection and Monitoring of Student Mental Health: Opportunities, Challenges, and Ethical Considerations

Uddalak Mitra
https://orcid.org/0000-0002-5682-5218
JIS College of Engineering, India

Shafiq Ul Rehman
https://orcid.org/0000-0003-2266-218X
Kingdom University, Bahrain

Sambhab Rooj
JIS College of Engineering, India

Saiberi Farhan Khan
JIS College of Engineering, India

Sania Parveen
JIS College of Engineering, India

Rohit Banerjee
JIS College of Engineering, India

ABSTRACT

Student mental health is an urgent concern across all levels of education, with stress, anxiety, and depression often fueled by academic pressures, peer competition, and digital overload. Traditional counseling typically intervenes late, highlighting the need for AI-driven technologies that enable early detection and timely support. This chapter explores how machine learning, natural language processing, wearable sensors, and learning analytics can monitor academic, behavioral, linguistic, and physiological data to detect signs of distress. AI tools may provide personalized assistance through chatbots, adaptive learning, and predictive analytics for intervention, particularly valuable where resources are scarce. Yet, challenges such as privacy, bias, transparency, and consent demand responsible frameworks. Human-centered

DOI: 10.4018/979-8-3373-5007-3.ch007

AI, participatory design, ethical audits, and governance structures are essential to ensure trust and accountability. Done responsibly, AI can transform student well-being, enabling proactive support and resilient educational communities.

1. INTRODUCTION

Certainly, there has been a momentous rise in mental health among students that culminated in an issue that ravaged the globe today. Evidently, anxiety, depression, emotional suffering, and even suicidal tendencies have risen among high school and postsecondary students, while WHO approximated that among adolescents, one out of seven probably suffers from a mental disorder (Nuryana et al., 2023; Zhou et al., 2022; Slimmen et al., 2022; Linden et al., 2021; Giannopoulou et al., 2021). Within it, suicide remains the first killer among people between the ages of 15 to 29 (WHO (2025)). Out of university surveys, many students indeed rate themselves as having severe symptoms of anxiety, chronic stress, and even depressive symptoms originating from adverse effects on their academic performance, concentration, social relationships, and overall functioning. We have seen academic loss, increasing dropout rates, and lifelong repercussions on their personal and career development because of mental health burdens.

The basic traditional forms of support have primarily been those offered by counseling centers, peer support programs, and mental health awareness programs. Yet none of those approaches even come close to matching the scope of the problem today (Stamou et al., 2024; Rahman et al., 2024; Schenzle & Schultz, 2024). The student-to-counselor ratio that is grossly high, long queues, and limited access to timely treatment characterizes almost all institutions as problems. Many of these support structures are crisis interventions by nature, and indeed, come into play when a student demonstrates distress at a rather extreme level. The stigma and fear of judgment are another wall that stands between many students and their going public about their desire for help; thus, emotional struggles remain buried and unattended (Gao, Y. (2025)).

Such cutting-edge innovations in Artificial Intelligence (AI) will probably herald revolutionary changes into the future, allowing for proactive and continuing identification of impending mental health issues faced by students (Mitra & Rehman, 2025a; Mitra & Rehman, 2025b). AI systems can apply algorithms against huge amounts of data generated by students in different dimensions of academic activities, engagement, and online use versus attendance records, looking at all forms of documented communications. An algorithm patented can monitor and interpret such behavior changes to realize engagement shifts otherwise significant for detecting emotional distress, such as sudden disengagement or peculiar aberrations in documented study behavior. Natural language processing would be used to analyze stress, anxiety, or depression emotional cues tagged to reflective journals, discussion posts, and even emails. Physiological aspects of the wellbeing of the student are analyzed by wearables for insights on sleep patterns, heart rate variability, and levels of activity (Chen et al., 2024; Abd-Alraza et al., 2024; Rajkishan et al., 2024). Some universities eventually run tests using AI-supported dashboards and mental health chatbots for flagging early alerts and slight human intervention before emotional difficulties go bad.

However, there is a heaviness of ethics and social concern on matters under the areas of AI tools used for monitoring mental health. The files of students regarding mental health contain so much sensitive information that issues like that of privacy, consent, ownership, and data security must be dealt with in heavy consideration. Weak governance frameworks can easily lead to misuse or unauthorized access to personal data, trust issues, and potentially erode trust in government and its agents. Accredited institutions of learning become victims of algorithmic bias whereby a wrong label is given to a student or the other way around since training data for use by the artificial intelligence model was incomplete and/or nonrepresentative. Students would feel monitored or scrutinized on one hand, but transparency and explanation would also be called into question, particularly when the decision is made by AI. These challenges bring to the fore an urgent need for accountability and ethical directives, particularly in transparent and responsible application (Soneson et al., 2025; Xiao & Liu, 2021; Stevic et al., 2022). This research is on opportunities and challenges linked to early diagnosis and monitoring of student mental health via AI and significance in the design of such systems in fairness, psychological safety, privacy, and human oversight. Proper implementation may see AI become a strong partner in saving student lives in the proactive support initiatives undertaken by colleges.

2. AI TECHNOLOGIES FOR MENTAL HEALTH MONITORING

- Behaviors observed during student interactions in digital learning settings give rise to rich amounts of behavioral data that may provide cues toward assessing mental health indicators via machine learning and behavioral data-driven analysis. Learning Management Systems (LMSs) can record events such as login rates, download of resources, participation in forums, and submission of assignments. Models based on machine learning can detect anomalous unsought of subtle engagement patterns, namely irregular access, dropping grades, or late submissions, indicating possible psychosocial predicaments like stress, burnout, or withdrawal. Time-series and anomaly detection allow continuous monitoring through deviation from each student's baseline versus group norms to improve accuracy. New multitask learning approaches couple behavioral variables with psychosocial ones (motivation, resilience, dropout risk) to derive personalized well-being profiles and promote early interventions. On the downside, such predictors face interference from confounding issues that do not relate to mental health (such as problems with devices or outside commitments and raise ethical issues concerning surveillance, consent, and data autonomy (Nishimura et al., 2024; Visier-Alfonso et al., 2024). Hence, its ethical set up calls for transparency, contextual interpretation, and trust sustained with students.

- Mobile devices, applications, as well as the physiological and biometric data of students can reach anywhere in remote areas (Gopalakrishnan et al., 2022; Ta et al., 2025). These days, it's possible to carry out parameters-independent measurements, which-"heart-rate variability" (HRV), "quality of sleep", "physical activity", and "galvanic skin responses", by smartwatches, fitness trackers, and mobiles-the popular determinants for anxiety and emotional control. Often, irregularities in HRV and sleep represent the effects of anxiety, exhaustion, and decreased academic performance. Mobile applications complement these physiological metrics with self-report assessments such as mood diaries and ecological momentary assessments (EMAs) that allow the synthesis of objective and subjective data by AI systems for a richer understanding of mental states. Primarily passive-identifying traits such as accelerometers and GPS monitor some activities like social withdrawal or lower activity levels, while patterns of application use, especially excessive use of social networks, may indicate pathological coping mechanisms. Biofeedback may also teach self-regulation by helping to identify manifestations of stress in one individual that may lead him to calls for mindfulness or relaxation exercises. Cost, privacy, and accuracy in data remain the greatest hindrances online. Physiological states also change due to factors that have absolutely nothing to do with psychology, like physical exercise or even being sick; thus, biometric data needs to be put in context to avoid distortions and dis-will.
- Wearables and mobile applications have been increasingly used for continuous and non-invasive monitoring of external signs of students' mental health-behavioral and physiological. Smartwatches and fitness trackers, along with mobile phones, collect well-known stress and emotional regulation markers: HRV, sleep, activity, and skin conductance (Bloomfield et al., 2024; Hickey et al., 2021). The decrease in heart rate variability and increased fluctuations within the sleep cycles are quite strong indicators for probable hyper-arousal of anxiety, fatigue, and decline in academic achievement. Mobile applications augment physiological markers with borrows from user assessments

(mood diary, stress check-in, and ecological momentary assessments), enable AI systems to mix objective measurements with subjective assessments; thus, a more complete view of well-being is developed. They would help to self-regulate by means of biofeedback whenever the stress indicators are going beyond a limit, thus calling for mindfulness or relaxation. Yet, some of the concerns that need to be addressed are about accessibility, privacy, and accuracy. Physiological signals may confuse exercises with stress or an illness with emotional distress; therefore, relative interpretation must be done to measure fairness and validity while using biometric data.

- **Multimodal analytics** has become a very effective approach to enhancing the reliability and robustness of mental well-being assessments (Guo et al., 2022; Lai et al., 2021). By integrating linguistic, behavioral, and physiological data, these systems paint a holistic picture of students' psychological states, which cannot be attained by single data-source systems. For example, a slight decrease in LMS activity may not mean anything alone; however, in conjunction with poor performance in academics, negative sentiment in annotated text, and sleep deprivation, it becomes a definite indication of emotional distress. Some common approaches include ensemble learning, which merges outputs from separate models such as sentiment analysis, behavioral anomaly detection, and biometric classifiers, and deep multimodal architectures-based recurrent or transformer networks that learn joint representations across modalities. This form of integration may tend to reduce the number of false positives through cross-validation of signals: for instance, signs of physiological stress would take on much added credibility if they were backed by textual or behavioral evidence. Thus, multimodal systems develop context-sensitive and ethically implementable insights for early detection and intervention.
- While The use of AI in mental health monitoring seems to give rise to very deep ethical questions since it concerns sensitive data linking to a vulnerable population, that is, students. The first and foremost issue is that of privacy-in and informed consent: that students can understand how their linguistic, behavioral or physical data will be collected, used, and shared, and how they can withdraw that consent at any point without restrictions. It is institutional compliance with the laws as regards data protection such as the GDPR and similar national frameworks that bring lawfulness and transparency in equal measure. Moreover, important elements are bias and fairness. Incomplete or non-representative training data can produce skewed models that falsely misclassify students or overlook actual distress signs in groups underrepresented. However, explainability and transparency, coupled with trust, must ensure that stakeholders understand what a risk score means. Black-box models that produce risk scores without justification undermine confidence and account-

ability. What is more, introduce explainable artificial intelligence (XAI) techniques that enhance understanding by clearly presenting the basis of each prediction to students, educators, and counselors. Finally, the institutions will maintain a balance between early detection and autonomy- too much monitoring would bring an atmosphere of anxiety and distrust. These resources need to be available for sustainable implementation, as interdisciplinary collaboration and above all human-centered training, under which AI will complement rather than replace professional care.

Table 1. Overview of AI Technologies for Mental Health Monitoring

Aspect / Technology	AI Techniques and Data Sources	Applications in Mental Health Monitoring	Challenges and Ethical Considerations
1. Behavioral Analytics in Learning Environments	Machine learning, time-series modeling, anomaly detection, multitask learning	Detects irregular access, falling grades, or delayed submissions in LMS data to identify stress, burnout, or withdrawal; creates personalized well-being profiles	Confounding variables (e.g., device issues), ethical concerns on surveillance, consent, and data autonomy; need for contextual interpretation and transparency
2. Mobile and Physiological Monitoring	AI-driven analysis of HRV, sleep quality, activity levels, and galvanic skin response; sensor fusion	Identifies signs of anxiety, fatigue, and emotional dysregulation through wearable and smartphone data; combines objective physiological data with self-reported mood diaries and EMAs	Privacy risks, data accuracy issues, physiological confounders (e.g., illness, exercise), and cost concerns; requirement for contextual interpretation of biometric data
3. Wearables and Biofeedback Systems	AI integration of physiological and self-reported data; predictive modeling and biofeedback systems	Enables continuous, non-invasive monitoring; detects stress via HRV and sleep fluctuations; supports self-regulation through mindfulness or relaxation alerts	Accessibility, fairness, and validity concerns; biometric signals may misinterpret stress versus illness; need for robust data interpretation
4. Multimodal Analytics	Deep learning (transformers, recurrent neural networks), ensemble learning, cross-modal feature fusion	Combines linguistic, behavioral, and physiological data for holistic assessment; reduces false positives by validating across multiple modalities	Integration complexity, interpretability challenges, and potential for overfitting; importance of context-sensitive analysis
5. Ethical and Governance Frameworks	Explainable AI (XAI), bias detection, privacy-preserving algorithms, compliance monitoring	Ensures transparency, fairness, and informed consent; promotes explainable predictions and trust among students and educators	Privacy, consent withdrawal, bias in non-representative datasets, black-box risk scoring; need for interdisciplinary collaboration and human-centered AI deployment

3. IMPLEMENTATION IN EDUCATIONAL CONTEXTS

Implementation of artificial intelligence in systems for monitoring mental health among students is ushering in a whole new era in education technology where smart systems and prescriptive analytics are becoming a greater part of the learning environment: knowing ahead, predicting, and responding to student needs. Changing the way the institutions care for their students, the system is enmeshed in piecemeal ethical, legal, and societal considerations. These measures are compared to data protection and regulatory compliance in terms of GDPR and FERPA, bias and unfairness possible in AI prediction, informed consent and student agency to avoid stigmatization, and explainable AI as a requirement to build trust and transparency. All of these are involved in developing promise and risk of systems for student mental health monitoring, their totality tallying up the need for a thoughtful, fair, and conservative approach.

Data confidentiality has remained a paramount issue in studies concerning student mental health. The educational bodies hold vast reservoirs of information on individuals-academic records, attendance, behavioral reports, and psychological assessments-along with the special sensitivity associated with passing such information into AI systems. Once records are digital, they are open to misuse, breach, or unauthorized access. The General Data Protection Regulation (GDPR) of the European Union and the Family Educational Rights and Privacy Act (FERPA) of the United States are very strict on data collection, storage, and disclosure in access, correction, and erasure rights above ordinary standards. This is a good thing but does not imply that ethics are well guarded simply because a law exists. Therefore, institutions must rely on encryption, integrity in handling data, and an open policy of communication to maintain student confidence. Beyond legality lies ethics-a type of ethics in which the very private and potentially stigmatizing nature of such health information comes into play. AI risk-assessment models also involve the questions of bias and equity. Although thought to be objective, these systems denote the shortcoming of their training data. The algorithms might have been trained on culturally narrow data or socioeconomically narrow datasets and thus pose the risk of propounding stereotypes and producing discriminatory outcomes. Economic hardship, gender, race, or even disability can manifest stress, but models developed on dominant groups are not able to implement such recognitions; they rather denounce the normal variations as pathology. A possible solution includes intentional inclusivity and design leaning toward fairness. Regular bias audits, context-sensitive machine learning, and fair data collection must prevent pushing inequality further. Besides, implementation must be done collaboratively with students, clinicians, educators, and ethicists-on the ground, to ensure that definitions of "mental health risk" emerge from a pluralism instead of an imposition. Should they skip over such participatory ethics, any AI system purported to democratize support would, in fact, reinforce the same inequalities it intended to work against.

Student agency and informed consent form the cornerstone of ethical AI use to monitor mental health. Institutions must make sure that students understand what data is collected, how that data is processed, who has access to that data, and the possible ramifications of the analysis. True consent has to be clear, given voluntarily, with an option to withdraw any time without consequences on any ground related to classes or society. Yet, consent forms are often full of legal language that makes genuine understanding impossible. Ethical implementation demands that students retain agency over their mental health narratives, including the right to contest, review, or reject algorithmic classifications. The question of agency extends beyond procedure to power: if an AI system labels a student as "at risk," who controls that judgment—the individual or the institution? Unfettered labeling may reinforce stigma, limit opportunities, and reduce self-esteem. Also, viewing such an evaluation with the perception of being under constant surveillance might add to anxiety instead of relieving it. The concept of agency is further closely tied to the concept of explainability. Deep learning and other complex AI models are often criticized as opaque "black boxes," a limitation incompatible with mental health applications where decisions affect personal identity and well-being. Both students and professionals must essentially understand the rationale for making predictions—be it because of class attendance, performance trends, linguistic cues, or behavioral data. This explanation provides assurance for the reasoned, credible, and accountable measurement of interventions. It thus embeds the notion of accountability by allowing tracing and rectification in cases of errors, prioritizing institutional learning over automated indiscretion. Trust thus stands as the ethical foundation of this relationship. Fairness, accountability, and justice will allow all genuinely caring AI systems to care for the student rather than act as impersonal judges of risky behaviors. Where AI properties turn to privacy, the consent of the student, equity, and explainability, it will be a true partner in promoting early identification, timely intervention, and a whole view on student well-being.

Anything related to AI tends to undergo such extensive transformation in the student mental health landscape, and part of it may be precisely because it can intervene in real time in most of its actions. Otherwise, one has the model of the conventional being reactive, intervening mostly after observation or reporting of distress. The systems, powered by AI, would recognize early physiological or behavioral signs and provide intervention in a preventive way. An orthodox wearables application would capture signals during an exam when heart rates of variability or skin conductance are found to be high and would nudge relaxation techniques toward the student in a near-unaware manner. An AI chatbot in an online forum could just as easily detect linguistic signs of hopelessness, maybe suggesting some empathetic engagement or referral to resources that may help. Personalization needs to counterbalance the tendencies of an AI to either overreact or withdraw, going one step further and minimizing false positives by culturizing feedback around each student's individual baseline. This level of customization ensures that their attempts are supportive, if not so conspicuous as to work against pathologizing normal emotional fluctuations. On the collective level, the anonymized data could facilitate discernment of patterns of stress in student populations; for example, unusually high anxiety flags during weeks of exams-any such insights would enable institutions to proactively schedule counseling sessions or resilience programs. Real-time monitoring does, however, present ethical dilemmas: Just the idea of surveillance might cause more anxiety and distrust. Therefore, participation should remain on a voluntary basis, with consent obtained beforehand and opt-out mechanisms put into place. Considering just those eventualities, the interventions would also be designed to redirect from desensitization while ensuring emotional privacy. For AI-enabled mental health solutions to thrive, trans-disciplinary collaboration among different professional domains would be paramount. The technologists will craft the systems in a safe, fair, and accessible manner, while institutional leadership will put in place governance structures that prioritize privacy, fairness, and ethical integrity in dealing with such cases. Ultimately, the design effort will be participatory through interdisciplinary taskforces with student engagement in co-development of the systems. Co-designed AI systems which are transparent and culturally sensitive will build trust and facilitate its acceptance of mental health care as part of academic survival instead of an auxiliary support service.

4. ETHICAL, LEGAL, AND SOCIETAL CONSIDERATIONS

- The importance of ethics, legal issues, and social ramifications of AI application technologies for student mental health requires rational attention to privacy, fairness, and accountability. Student mental health data guzzle some of the most delicate resources of personal information since they hold behavioral, linguistic, and specific physiological markers that can be easily misconstrued or put to wrongful uses. The Family Educational Rights and Privacy Act (FERPA) in the United States and the General Data Protection Regulation (GDPR) in the EU provide people with mechanisms to protect what they own from sheer manipulation. Majorly conventional in its administrative ideal, these legal tools adore transparency, informed consent, and the right of access, rectification, or erasure of personal information. The intervention of AI products in monitoring must have clear reasons for the data collected, the processes the algorithms undertake, who could access the results and for what purpose, allowing the students to refuse consent without any penalty for withdrawal. Disrespecting these tenets hits against the law, all the time being trusted, which is the prime most important requirement to promote the ethical development of AI in education.

- Furthermore, ethical governance is more of a matter of straddling beyond mere corporate compliance. It has to involve processes allowing for the development of ethical standards in the use of AI systems that all the time respect students' autonomy and dignity vis-à-vis the extending duty of institutions to provide a safe and secure learning environment. Artificially intelligent systems act as "black boxes," making classifications or risk scores without clear reason. Thus, the accountability and transparency of the technologies provide transparency. Please be careful. A brief background on how interpretability in AI provides ease of state: The rationale for why a student is flagged as "at risk" is made known in this field—using XAI. Though criticized heavily by today's political ignorance, an XAI-my new approach-makes things vibrant by piercing the black boxes: one gets to know this student is being classified as naughty. The support of the XAI covers a foundation upon which mental health experts and school counselors, the student as a client, can learn to evaluate and critique each predictive rating on equity grounds. This very inversion of the power dynamics makes students more prone to trust and can thereby be confident about their widespread acceptance for initial easy recovery from anything out of their control.
- Bias stand as one of the severe ethical hurdles. Of course, AI models derived from non-representative data can often greatly amplify existing disparities, leading to systematized misidentifications. For instance, a student, part of minority groups, linguistic, or socio-economically disadvantaged groups may be identified and categorized as distressed or may not attract the attention of any observers altogether due to misinterpretation of their behavior, which does not fit within the culturally conditioned norms as presented by the dataset. The whole gamut of diverse populations, participatory design, and continuous bias auditing must be set to be institutionalized. There must be a wider engagement of students, mental health professionals, and educators from varied backgrounds to ensure contextual relevance in the system. Diversity must not be an addendum in design planning but must be incorporated as part of the framework in site planning. In the long run, paranoia was caused by too much surveillance and then feared reminders of that stress the system sought to relieve in the first place. Instead, AI should be human-oriented and encourage complete support completely according to the interest and sense of well-being of the students: To monitor, but never in a coercive nature where surveillance is needed. The latter would obviously prevent genuine

care, while the collaboration would encourage support with such carefully designed technological systems combining research, diagnosis, intervention planning, training, and communication.

- Students should be made active collaborators [not sitting targets] within these systems, thus partaking of feedback mechanisms whereby they shape policies of data usage and interpretation. At the core of these very developments, number one is the data minimization system in place: It emphasizes taking only that which is necessary and ensuring full security also against confidential access. Encryption, anonymization, and closed-governance models should be common standards to ensure that anything untoward does not induce gross data breaches. The point parallels with societal implications that AI drives must empower, not control. It is the responsibility of academic institutions to ensure that the technology works for the betterment of its people through well-being, equity, and support of access, any device that might indeed threaten to underscore hierarchical and stigmatic transactions. A student maligned as "unstable" faces a lifetime of disadvantage interference in relation to educational records, interpersonal relationships, and future employment opportunities. Ergo, in others, the work of ethics in design is with the idea of producing the contextual fair, psychologically sensitive humanity fit for subjecting all student rights. This calls for departments to establish governance boards, ethical review committees, and mechanisms so students can appeal against misuse. So, the chapter is closed thus; for AI to contribute to promoting care for students with respect to rules, ethics, and societal accountability, the entire articulation of a system should put ethics, legality, and particularly social accountability at the center right from data purchases and collection, training up to the last point of admittance into deployment processes and beyond. This is about lending AI as a friend in the low light of warning while ensuring privacy, equity, and autonomy. With legal compliance falling into place, the AI can become a beneficial partner by acting according to human values, paving the other path to AI setup in institutions comprising trust, transparency, and justice instead of surveillance.

5. CHALLENGES AND BARRIERS

The use of AI to monitor students' mental health is arguably an unprecedented move toward their early identification and timely intervention. But it contends with a morphing cocktail of technical, institutional, social, and cultural barriers to be navigated, thus hinting a more anthropocentric question than simply the one of AI in the mental health technological field. On the one hand, AI detects patterns and predicts events with the aid of sizeable, precise data. Very often, however, this data within an educational context is fragmented, inconsistent, or incomplete. Some indicators of psychological health such as attendance, grades, and language or physiological cues are subtle, contextual, and elusive to measure. Mental health data are subjective to label; expert opinions would vary considerably on whether certain behaviors of academically distressed students arise from stress, depression, or just transitory emotional states. Then, if mental health models are developed in one culture/institution setting, they are generally less valid or inappropriate in quite another due to inter-cultural differences in how persons behave, what they do, or how they set norms. As far as contrast is concerned, a model that was trained in a Western context would struggle to distinguish whether a certain set of symptoms was arising from stress among the Asian or African population. All these limitations require contextually conscious and flexible model building with strict data governance. Otherwise, a well-designed system might make dangerous false assumptions that could drive injuries into the very populations it is intended to benefit (Porru et al., 2022; Salimi et al., 2023; Haikalis, et al., 2022; George, 2024).

Institutional preparedness in the meantime represents yet another hurdle. Some systems of schools have been more than others in the developing world in putting in place the necessary AI structures that may consist of robust computers to undertake the analysis; secure cloud storage for classified data; and, much significantly, uninterrupted internet connectivity. Student data themselves are fractured and are often scattered among isolated platforms, such as attendance programs, learning management systems, and therapeutic database systems, making it harder to conduct any sort of coherent joined-up analyses. Lacking in the infrastructure is the ability of institutions to provide the human resources that can ethically interpret results produced by the AI, if they have them at all, and put in place ethical frameworks that guide this application, not to mention maintain funds in order to remain in input. AI outputs remains a risk. As a result, the divide between wealthy institutions with vast resources and poorly funded ones will pose equity problems in terms of MH support, given that wealthier students will receive AI-driven care, while others will remain excluded. Therefore, institutional readiness must call for technology and policy, training, and equity discussions.

Social resistance is still rampant between teachers, students, and parents. To many cultures, mental health comes along with stigma, and the thought of being monitored by algorithms brings anxieties, distrust, and moral concerns. Educators fear losing control or even being replaced by AI, while parents fear that their child's information may be misused, or that labeling may interrupt their education or career opportunities. In addition, there will be fears that once these "mental risks" categories enter the AI system, it generates a permanent record, with all the associated discrimination and opportunity costs; cultures already victimized by mental health stigma become most vulnerable to grave social consequences of such records. The further strengthening of such opinions relates to the argument of the irreplaceable human empathy inherent in interventions in mental health care. Ethical transparency, participative design of the various phases of AI development, and mass education around AI will guide stakeholders toward an understanding of the rationale behind the AI system, its limitations, and the safeguards in place to make sure it functions properly.

The cultural dimension adds yet another layer of complexity. Mental health cannot be uniformly experienced or expressed everywhere. The symptoms of stress, depression, or anxiety vary by language, norms, and expression. For example, Western-trained AI models may interpret silence as a symptom of depression; however, in others, silence symbolizes respect or restraint. Directly complaining about something troublesome, such as headache pains, in one culture could mean expressing mental distress whereas the opposite may be true in another culture. Should the AI miss these nuances of culture and language, the AI system could misdiagnose or fail to reach students from minority groups. Language diversity also faces some technical obstacles. Most sentiment analysis and NLP systems find their English training data and there are very few who if ever, would work well in dealing with regional dialects/colloquialisms. To be constructive, culturally adaptive AI must incorporate indigenous perspectives, local knowledge, and datasets across cultures. By marking the interface, technology must ensure the human-centered culturally competent practice-undisturbed in delivering mental health care. This linked set of barriers-technical, institutional, social, and cultural-discerns a profound universal need; if ethical AI systems are to become a reality within the mental health domain, this need calls for collaboration in social responsibility. Open research and adaptive designs must address the technical issues of data labeling, quality, and generalizability. Institutions should guarantee equal access, while investing in digital infrastructures and training. The design process should ensure transparency and provide informed choice in the face of any social and ethical opposition. Finally, the cultural context should inform the data collection and intervention strategies.

Instead, parents, teachers, and students need to go to the next step forward in co-designing such systems, not just be seen as passive subjects. For this folding to take place, the policies will do just industries supporting participatory governance, ERCs, and redress mechanisms for maladaptive practices. Research must make contextually relevant, equity-oriented, and accountable AI systems. Propositioning lawmakers to develop a framework for balancing innovation and social justice, privacy, and trust. Figuring all this together, AI would then have taken a turn from something to be feared into an enabler for student well-being- a subject of empathy, care, compassion, and ethics; not surveillance and control.

Table 2. Barriers and Contextual Challenges in AI-Based Mental Health Monitoring

Dimension	Core Challenges	Key Implications	Recommendations / Strategic Responses
1. Technical Barriers	- Fragmented, inconsistent, and incomplete data within educational contexts.- Psychological indicators (attendance, grades, language cues) are subtle and hard to quantify.- Difficulty in labeling mental health data due to subjective expert opinions.- Limited generalizability across cultural and institutional settings.	- Risk of false assumptions and misclassification.- Models trained in one culture may be invalid or biased in another.- Potential harm to vulnerable student populations.	- Develop context-aware and flexible AI models.- Implement strict data governance and standardization protocols.- Encourage cross-cultural validation and diverse dataset inclusion.
2. Institutional Barriers	- Lack of infrastructure (computing power, cloud security, internet access).- Fragmented data across multiple platforms (attendance systems, LMSs, counseling databases).- Shortage of trained professionals to interpret AI results ethically.- Funding limitations and inequitable access across institutions.	- Widening digital divide between resource-rich and resource-poor institutions.- Inconsistent quality of mental health support.- Risk of unvalidated or misused AI outputs.	- Invest in digital infrastructure and skilled personnel.- Establish institutional ethics committees and data governance frameworks.- Promote equity in AI-based mental health care across educational tiers.
3. Social Barriers	- Stigma and fear surrounding mental health and AI monitoring.- Anxiety among educators about AI replacing human roles.- Parental concerns about data misuse and labeling.- Risk of permanent digital records causing discrimination.	- Social resistance and distrust toward AI systems.- Potential marginalization of vulnerable student groups.- Undermining of empathy-driven mental health care.	- Promote ethical transparency and participatory system design.- Conduct awareness and education programs on AI's role and safeguards.- Maintain human oversight and empathy-centered interventions.
4. Cultural Barriers	- Cultural variations in the expression and perception of mental distress.- AI misinterpretation of culturally specific behaviors (e.g., silence, indirect communication).- NLP limitations with regional languages and dialects.	- Misdiagnosis of minority or culturally diverse students.- Reduced inclusivity and cultural competence in AI systems.	- Build culturally adaptive AI with indigenous data and perspectives.- Expand NLP datasets to include local languages and expressions.- Embed cultural sensitivity training for AI developers and educators.
5. Toward Ethical and Inclusive AI	- Lack of co-design among students, teachers, and parents.- Limited participatory governance and accountability mechanisms.- Weak policy alignment with social justice and privacy.	- AI systems risk being perceived as surveillance tools rather than supportive aids.- Loss of trust and user engagement.	- Encourage participatory AI design and governance.- Develop legal frameworks balancing innovation, privacy, and fairness.- Promote empathy, compassion, and transparency as guiding principles.

6. FUTURE DIRECTIONS

- Moving on, AI-linked studies in mental health monitoring should seek to assemble various data modalities in future investigations to do justice to the multidimensional nature of students' psychological well-being. Single modalities such as surveys or grades convey insufficient representations of mental health information. Only when these data are fused to reflect concepts of mental health can an integrative picture be outlined; that is, textual inputs, biometric inputs, and academic inputs. The writings, whether an essay or a reflective journal, speak of an emotional and cognitive state through their sentiment polarity, lexical variations, and syntactic coherences, wherein increased self-references or increased negative affect terminology would often act as precursors for distress. Biometric input from low-cost wearable sensors or mobile sensors can provide very robust continuous objective markers of stress and fatigue captured by their heart rate variability, electrodermal activity, and sleep quality. Academic performance indicators such as attendance, submission timeliness, or engagement levels could help see patterns of cognitive overload or motivational decline. When two or more of those inputs converge—for instance, while the sleep pattern shows disruption to the negative linguistic sentiment of reflective essays and late submission of essays—the prospect for true psychological distress increases. On the other hand, conflicting signals may signal situation-related rather than psychological deviations. Integrating almost all of these will mandate either behavioral or deep-learning platforms that discern among heterogeneous inputs and create meaningful, specific risk profiles. With great social good comes considerable ethical responsibility: privacy, informed consent, and ownership of personal data are all paramount. Such new developments can benefit by weaving in applicable federated or privacy-preserving learning with in-place data analyses while data do not enter through central circuits of sensitive information, thus upholding confidentiality with a boost to programming accuracy.
- Intervention and support must be initiated after the diagnosis of psychological distress; otherwise, it does not matter. Therefore, the future designation of available AI predictive systems would point to their integration with digital counseling and peer-support networks in such a way that risk identification would translate into pathways for intervention. Most universities have secure video channels, asynchronous messaging, and chatbot triage services. The establishment of these pathways could allow the embedding of AI-driven identification to promote proactive outreach. For example, if a student repeatedly sets off stress triggers, the system could quietly recommend an online consultation with a counselor, rather than waiting for a full-blown crisis. Peer sup-

port is another vital citadel. The most important findings of available studies show that students are more likely to first talk to their peers before making any contact with professionals. Hence, digital peer-to-peer frameworks are amplifiers to facilitate early help-seeking. AI-enhanced models would turn such at-risk individuals into these supportive communities, thus fostering relational engagement free from stigma. Personalizing interventions is yet another area. AI systems could personalize the resources on virtual counseling platforms according to the emotional profile, preference, and culture of each unique individual. Every institution must design its governance frameworks in such a way as to prevent falling into the trap of algorithmic counseling justified by seemingly altruistic economic reasons. The goal should be an evolution rather than a revolution-the expansion of outreach; the reduction of waiting time; and empowering professionals with smart tools to enhance accessibility, responsiveness, and ethical integrity in student mental health care.

- More amazing possibilities for AI in student mental health are found in immediate life. The traditional approach has mostly been "after the fact"—in other words, once the student shows distress, either from the outside or by self-report, it is acted upon. However, AI systems can identify that something is not right very early based on physiologic or behavioral signals and can activate preventive measures. For instance, let us assume that some wearables sense increased heart-rate variability or skin conductance during an examination; perhaps at that moment, the students' devices will signal them to engage in relaxation techniques. AI chatbots could be used in an online forum to pick up some of the linguistic indicators of hopelessness and engage the student empathically or refer them to helpful resources. Personalization protects against overreach. AI can prevent false alerts by adjusting the responses toward the baseline patterns of each student and analyze whether a person is experiencing a normal rise and fall of distress or if it is indeed a high level of distress. This personalized approach allows interventions to be supportive and non-intrusive, avoiding labeling normal everyday fluctuations of emotion. Rights do go along with real-time auditing, of course. Extended observation may generate a watching effect whereby anxiety increases, and trust evaporates. Voluntary participation must have informed consent, along transparent exit protocols. Any intervention should be tunable, avoiding the risk of generating alarm fatigue, while protecting emotional privacy. The clinical perspective of AI mental health care will depend on transgressing boundaries. Mental health practitioners define that threshold where detection and intervention shall intervene under clinical relevance. Faculty provides contextual knowledge to academically related sources of stress, to match tech-driven interventions with teaching realities. Technologists, therefore, design secure and equitable systems, while institutional leaders craft governance mechanisms that promote interest in privacy, fairness, and ethics. Ultimately, these interdisciplinary task forces and student input into system design will define success. Co-created AI will be rooted in transparency and cultural sensitivity, enhancing trust, increasing uptake, and integrating mental health support into students' academic journeys instead of treating it as an extracurricular activity.

7. CONCLUSION

It monitors students using an early warning system for their mental well-being, in a school, based on academic performance, language behavior, and biometric data of symptoms derived from possible stress or anxiety or undetected depression. Should such early warning signs be detected and acted upon, this enables timely intervention so that a student walks the academic road not so much optimally as at least emotionally stable and developing healthy coping mechanisms. This condition will thus create the possibility of an AI, which does not dispense informal advice but instead would present tailored, individualized interventions for identified student requirements, moving the emphasis from a reactive towards a proactive approach regarding mental self-care.

There are disadvantages to AI. A machine cannot come and take the place of a qualified medical practitioner. An over-dependence on machine-like automation for tasks would jeopardize the whole fabric of a student's emotional existence. Breaches of privacy and data protection are emerging topics under growth in relation to the myriad issues involved in the collection, use, and storage, as well as the future sharing of mental health information. Students should be knowledgeable about what data has been collected, how it has been stored, and its use. They must have an informed consent of the ability to withdraw from these arrangements, thereby gaining full control over the process. Clear governance frameworks would have to be laid out to curtail abuses, bias, or discrimination.

Governance into ethical prudence of Artificial Intelligence usage would also ensure proper application of big practice. There should be constructs that would enshrine mutual respect into autonomy, transparency, fairness, and equality among educators, mental health professionals, technologists, students, and policymakers. AI can replace human care but complement it. AI will become the most powerful weapon in the implementation of early intervention systems and well-being enhancement, promising to prepare safe and supportive educational environments within institutions when used ethically.

REFERENCES

Bloomfield, L. S., Fudolig, M. I., Kim, J., Llorin, J., Lovato, J. L., McGinnis, E. W., McGinnis, R. S., Price, M., Ricketts, T. H., Dodds, P. S., Stanton, K., & Danforth, C. M. (2024). Predicting stress in first-year college students using sleep data from wearable devices. *PLOS Digital Health*, *3*(4), e0000473. DOI: 10.1371/journal.pdig.0000473 PMID: 38602898

Chen, J., Yuan, D., Dong, R., Cai, J., Ai, Z., & Zhou, S. (2024). Artificial intelligence significantly facilitates development in the mental health of college students: A bibliometric analysis. *Frontiers in Psychology*, *15*, 1375294. DOI: 10.3389/fpsyg.2024.1375294 PMID: 38515973

Gao, Y. (2025). The impact and application of artificial intelligence technology on mental health counseling services for college students. *Journal of Computational Methods in Sciences and Engineering*, *25*(2), 1686–1701. DOI: 10.1177/14727978241302641

George, A. S. (2024). Exam season stress and student mental health: An international epidemic. *Partners Universal International Research Journal*, *3*(1), 138–149.

Giannopoulou, I., Efstathiou, V., Triantafyllou, G., Korkoliakou, P., & Douzenis, A. (2021). Adding stress to the stressed: Senior high school students' mental health amidst the COVID-19 nationwide lockdown in Greece. *Psychiatry Research*, *295*, 113560. DOI: 10.1016/j.psychres.2020.113560 PMID: 33187723

Gopalakrishnan, A., Venkataraman, R., Gururajan, R., Zhou, X., & Genrich, R. (2022). Mobile phone enabled mental health monitoring to enhance diagnosis for severity assessment of behaviours: A review. *PeerJ. Computer Science*, *8*, e1042. DOI: 10.7717/peerj-cs.1042 PMID: 36092018

Guo, T., Zhao, W., Alrashoud, M., Tolba, A., Firmin, S., & Xia, F. (2022). Multimodal educational data fusion for students' mental health detection. *IEEE Access : Practical Innovations, Open Solutions*, *10*, 70370–70382. DOI: 10.1109/ACCESS.2022.3187502

Haikalis, M., Doucette, H., Meisel, M. K., Birch, K., & Barnett, N. P. (2022). Changes in college student anxiety and depression from pre-to during-COVID-19: Perceived stress, academic challenges, loneliness, and positive perceptions. *Emerging Adulthood*, *10*(2), 534–545. DOI: 10.1177/21676968211058516 PMID: 35382515

Hickey, B. A., Chalmers, T., Newton, P., Lin, C. T., Sibbritt, D., McLachlan, C. S., Clifton-Bligh, R., Morley, J., & Lal, S. (2021). Smart devices and wearable technologies to detect and monitor mental health conditions and stress: A systematic review. *Sensors (Basel)*, *21*(10), 3461. DOI: 10.3390/s21103461 PMID: 34065620

Lai, J., Rahmani, A., Yunusova, A., Rivera, A. P., Labbaf, S., Hu, S., Dutt, N., Jain, R., & Borelli, J. L. (2021). Using multimodal assessments to capture personalized contexts of college student well-being in 2020: Case study. *JMIR Formative Research, 5*(5), e26186. DOI: 10.2196/26186 PMID: 33882022

Linden, B., Boyes, R., & Stuart, H. (2021). Cross-sectional trend analysis of the NCHA II survey data on Canadian post-secondary student mental health and well-being from 2013 to 2019. *BMC Public Health, 21*(1), 590. DOI: 10.1186/s12889-021-10622-1 PMID: 33765965

Mitra, U., & Rehman, S. U. (2025)a. Significance of AI/ML Wearable Technologies for Education and Teaching. In *Wearable Devices and Smart Technology for Educational Teaching Assistance* (pp. 1-26). IGI Global Scientific Publishing.

Mitra, U., & Rehman, S. U. (2025)b. Integrating AI/ML With Wearable Devices for Monitoring Student Mental Health. In *Wearable Devices and Smart Technology for Educational Teaching Assistance* (pp. 257-284). IGI Global Scientific Publishing.

Nishimura, T., Wakuta, M., Osuka, Y., Tsukui, N., Hirata, I., Takahashi, M., Adachi, M., Katayama, T., Aizaki, K., Sumiya, M., Kawakami, S., Iwabuchi, T., & Senju, A. (2024). Early detection of students' mental health issues from a traditional daily health observation scheme in Japanese schools and its digitalization. *Frontiers in Public Health, 12*, 1430011. DOI: 10.3389/fpubh.2024.1430011 PMID: 39314787

Nuryana, Z., Xu, W., Kurniawan, L., Sutanti, N., Makruf, S. A., & Nurcahyati, I. (2023). Student stress and mental health during online learning: Potential for post-COVID-19 school curriculum development. *Comprehensive Psychoneuroendocrinology, 14*, 100184. DOI: 10.1016/j.cpnec.2023.100184 PMID: 37038597

Porru, F., Schuring, M., Bültmann, U., Portoghese, I., Burdorf, A., & Robroek, S. J. (2022). Associations of university student life challenges with mental health and self-rated health: A longitudinal study with 6 months follow-up. *Journal of Affective Disorders, 296*, 250–257. DOI: 10.1016/j.jad.2021.09.057 PMID: 34624809

Rahman, S. N. A., Mahmud, M. I., & Johari, K. S. K. (2024). Exploring of Expressive Art Therapy in Counselling: A Recent Systematic Review. *Qubahan Academic Journal, 4*(2), 430–457. DOI: 10.48161/qaj.v4n2a479

Rajkishan, S. S., Meitei, A. J., & Singh, A. (2024). Role of AI/ML in the study of mental health problems of the students: A bibliometric study. *International Journal of System Assurance Engineering and Management, 15*(5), 1615–1637. DOI: 10.1007/s13198-023-02052-6

Salimi, N., Gere, B., Talley, W., & Irioogbe, B. (2023). College students mental health challenges: Concerns and considerations in the COVID-19 pandemic. *Journal of College Student Psychotherapy, 37*(1), 39–51. DOI: 10.1080/87568225.2021.1890298

Schenzle, S., & Schultz, J. H. (2024). "Students are bringing the revolution into the classroom!" teachers' and counselors' perceptions of the need for psychosocial support in crisis-affected classrooms in Lebanon. *Teaching and Teacher Education, 139*, 104416. DOI: 10.1016/j.tate.2023.104416

Slimmen, S., Timmermans, O., Mikolajczak-Degrauwe, K., & Oenema, A. (2022). How stress-related factors affect mental wellbeing of university students A cross-sectional study to explore the associations between stressors, perceived stress, and mental wellbeing. *PLoS One, 17*(11), e0275925. DOI: 10.1371/journal.pone.0275925 PMID: 36342914

Soneson, E., Fazel, M., Goli, P. S., & White, S. R. (2025). Are Adolescents Sensitive About Sensitive Data? Exploring Student Concerns About Privacy, Confidentiality, and Data Use in Health Research. *The Journal of Adolescent Health, 76*(6), 1008–1017. DOI: 10.1016/j.jadohealth.2025.03.004 PMID: 40372302

Stamou, P., Tsoli, K., & Babalis, T. (2024, May). The role of counseling for non-traditional students in formal higher education: A scoping review. [). Frontiers Media SA.]. *Frontiers in Education, 9*, 1361410. DOI: 10.3389/feduc.2024.1361410

Stevic, A., Schmuck, D., Koemets, A., Hirsch, M., Karsay, K., Thomas, M. F., & Matthes, J. (2022). Privacy concerns can stress you out: Investigating the reciprocal relationship between mobile social media privacy concerns and perceived stress. *Communications, 47*(3), 327–349. DOI: 10.1515/commun-2020-0037

Ta, A., Salgin, N., Demir, M., Reindel, K. P., Mehta, R. K., McDonald, A., . . . Sasangohar, F. (2025). Real-time stress monitoring, detection, and management in college students: A wearable technology and machine-learning approach. *arXiv preprint arXiv:2505.15974.*

Visier-Alfonso, M. E., Sarabia-Cobo, C., Cobo-Cuenca, A. I., Nieto-López, M., López-Honrubia, R., Bartolomé-Gutiérrez, R., Alconero-Camarero, A. R., & González-López, J. R. (2024). Stress, mental health, and protective factors in nursing students: An observational study. *Nurse Education Today, 139*, 106258. DOI: 10.1016/j.nedt.2024.106258 PMID: 38781822

Xiao, R., & Liu, X. (2021). Analysis of the architecture of the mental health education system for college students based on the Internet of Things and privacy security. *IEEE Access : Practical Innovations, Open Solutions, 9*, 81089–81096. DOI: 10.1109/ACCESS.2021.3084208

Zhou, S., & Eisenberg, D. (2022). College student mental health: Current trends and implications for higher education. In *Research handbook on society and mental health* (pp. 325–347). Edward Elgar Publishing. DOI: 10.4337/9781800378483.00024

Chapter 8
Predict, Prevent, Protect:
AI-Driven Early Warning Systems for Student Mental Health in Digital Learning Environments

Muhammad Usman Tariq
https://orcid.org/0000-0002-7605-3040
Abu Dhabi University, UAE & University College Cork, Ireland

ABSTRACT

The supercharged pace of online learning has rendered it more essential than ever before to respond to students' mental health needs. An increasing number of students are experiencing anxiety, depression, and burnout in both K–12 and higher-education contexts, and traditional ways of managing them are not keeping up. Digital learning platforms can help care for students' health in new ways by drawing on the information they collect. Through predictive analytics, schools can detect early warning signs of emotional problems, disengagement, and isolation. These early warning systems must support teachers, counselors, and school administrators to intervene before issues become more entrenched. This paper delves into how AI technologies can be used to predict mental health problems, avoid crises, and emotionally shield students. It also discusses how ethical, individualized, and team-based methods need to be employed to construct systems that honor the dignity of students and establish their trust.

INTRODUCTION

College students already experience many changes in life, and in the absence of friends and campus life, they feel even lonelier. Younger elementary and middle

DOI: 10.4018/979-8-3373-5007-3.ch008

school students may struggle with focusing, staying motivated, or regulating their emotions, especially with less social interaction and poor adult supervision in online educational environments. One solution is to use tools and technologies that can spot students who are likely to be at risk for mental illness before such issues become serious. Digital learning environments, such as web-based courses, virtual classes, and learning applications, generate vast amounts of data on student performance (Loda et al., 2020). Every action, such as logging on, entering assignments, registering for classes, or talking to classmates or instructors, creates an electronic trace. When reviewed, this information can reveal important information about a student's state of mind. For example, if a student completely stops turning in work, is not participating in online discussion boards, or starts to miss classes, these can be signs that there is a problem.

These small changes in behavior, taken as a whole, can represent trends that can indicate that a student has some kind of mental problem. With the use of methods such as machine learning and data analysis, schools can create systems that can identify students who might need help. The systems do not diagnose anything, but they alert teachers and staff to trends that should be researched. Ideally, they occur in the background, constantly processing information to understand how each student is doing and flagging unusual patterns that may be signs of emotional or mental health problems (Turmaine et al., 2021). The benefit of these warning systems is that they detect problems in the early stages, prior to their escalation. Instead of waiting for a student to reach a crisis, these systems labor to have their backs when difficulties first arise. In doing so, they can potentially keep students in school, achieve better academic performance, and avoid worse mental health problems. For educators, these systems can offer timely information that informs support and referral. For students, they can feel like their needs are being observed and that someone is concerned before they hit a crisis.

However, these systems must be used with caution. Privacy is a significant concern, and students and parents must feel that their data are safe and treated ethically. Schools must be open about the data collected, how it is used, and with whom it will be shared (Chaudhary, 2024). The algorithms running these systems must be made equitable, inclusive, and unbiased to avoid unfairness. It is also important that students who are flagged are encouraged in a kind and supportive way, rather than through harsh or mechanistic judgments without the full context. The success of early warning systems also depends on how ready schools are to respond to the intelligence received. Teachers and staff need training to correctly interpret the data, and the systems need to fit into the school's overall support system. There must be adequate resources, including mental health counselors, support groups, and peer networks, to handle tagged students. Without appropriate support, such systems create frustration and distrust among students.

The second most important aspect is involving students in the design and use of systems. Engaging students in planning and feedback allows schools to ensure that the tools are respectful and supportive. Educating students about digital mental health can also encourage them to learn about the tools themselves, reduce stigma, and develop self-awareness and self-management of their own well-being. Instead of being monitored or controlled, students can use such systems as tools for their development and self-enhancement (Dayal & Pratibha, 2023). Parents and caregivers play an important role, especially in kindergarten to high school. Keeping open lines of communication between families and schools is the key to collaboration on students' mental health. When early warning signs indicate that a student is struggling, involving families constructively and positively can offer further support. However, students' privacy and autonomy should also be respected, especially among older teenagers and college students.

The development of effective early warning systems has the potential to lead to more personalized and inclusive learning experiences for students. By knowing how mental health influences learning, teachers can modify their teaching styles, lesson tempo, and support systems to serve each student better. Mental health and learning go hand in hand and are integral components (Rygaard, 2020). Finally, incorporating proactive mental health care into online education is a broader way of taking care of students. Mental health should not be considered a standalone issue or a concern for a privileged few. It should be integrated into regular school life, be evidence-based and compassion-informed, and be driven by the common goal of helping all students grow. When applied properly and judiciously, technology may assist schools in ceasing to be reactive and begin functioning in more collectivized ways. The increasing school mental health crisis is a reality in the United States. It calls on schools to reform, develop new models, and prioritize the well-being of students. Due to the increased number of students studying online, our buildings should meet academic and emotional requirements. Early warning systems, particularly those associated with rich data from online classrooms, are promising. However, it relies on the community to work to responsibly manage such tools, empower students, and invest in people and practices that build a caring school community.

FOUNDATIONS OF AI-DRIVEN MENTAL HEALTH MONITORING

As schools face an escalating mental health crisis among pupils, there is increasing attention on how technology can help provide timely and effective interventions (Gillinov & Soltesz, 2020). By sorting through large amounts of data collected from online learning systems, communication software, and academic transcripts, these tools are intended to alert teachers and mental health professionals when students are likely to be in trouble. The second critical tool in the AI mental health toolkit is Natural Language Processing (NLP). This technology allows systems to read and understand human language, both spoken and written, in a considerable depth. In schools, NLP can be applied to screen emails, comment boards on discussion boards, chat both live and on written assignments, where permitted, to identify language that could possibly indicate distress, despair or anxiety. Along with behavioral and language data, multimodal analysis is also being employed by AI systems to create a more holistic view of the well-being of a student. Another ethical problem is the bias of AI models. Machine learning systems are as good as the data on which they are trained. Providing data that reflect the social biases that are already present, such as differentiation regarding race, gender, or even economic status, the system will reflect or enhance these biases. For example, the system may be more inclined to flag some students because of their differences in speaking or acting in a particular manner, which can be interpreted as distress markers.

An increase in AI monitoring also demands a transformation in the way schools and universities support students. School- and university-based mental healthcare has always been reactionary. Students are helped in times of crisis or when teachers and counselors can see the warning signs of distress. Nevertheless, this practice tends to neglect quite a few pupils until it is too late. The prevention that was made possible by AI is one that notifies the risks before they turn into a crisis and resorts to intervention in a helpful, respectful, and effective manner. Such a shift requires an institutional cultural shift whereby well-being has come to the fore in the educational process and mental health support has become business as usual in education, not merely a response to a crisis in isolation. Notably, this change also requires redefining the roles of teachers and school personnel. Teachers can give targeted attention to students who would otherwise fall through the net with the assistance of AI-generated data. However, this does not imply that teachers should be mental health workers. Schools must have appropriate mechanisms to send alarmed students to support services. They must train all staff members to handle such situations properly. The role that AI is set to play in the process should be to complement human care rather than substitute it with cold and mechanical systems. Another need is to make students the owners of their well-being. Schools should clarify how such systems will help and how they might work, instead of making students feel like subjects in a laboratory (Fortuna et al., 2020). When students realize that these tools are designed to help them rather than evaluate or spy on them, they will be more willing to believe and employ the tools. Providing students with access to their own information to be able to see their own mental health patterns of their own and allowing them to report on their own sense of feeling can make them feel more at the center of their mental health. poor grades, even allowing them to use more professional tools such as language analysis or other kinds of data. However, the system should be well realized with teachers, students, families, mental health practitioners, and technologists being involved. Partnership among these constituencies is key to ensuring that the tools are both useful and respectful of the people who will be using them. As these technologies advance, they open up new possibilities for collaboration between disciplines. While AI might help us uncover patterns that were previously hard to detect, it is still up to humans, such as teachers, counselors, school leaders, and peers, to respond with empathy and integrity (Tariq, 2025a). Figure 1 provides summary of how different data inputs flow through AI-driven processes.

Figure 1. AI-enabled Early Warning System (EWS) framework for student mental health

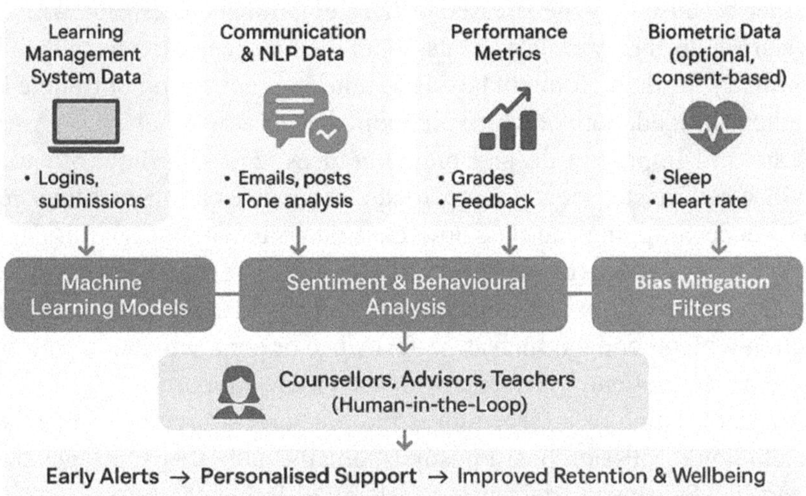

DATA SOURCES AND ANALYTICAL FRAMEWORKS

With the modern era of online education, it is increasingly important to understand and support students' well-being with data. There has been a growing trend of mental health awareness within schools and colleges; therefore, institutions are now using previously reserved data for tracking grades to detect and respond to emotional and psychological concerns. With technology increasingly making its way into the classroom, the data that students produce by working within these systems can provide indications of their state of mind, provided that the information is efficiently utilized and well pondered (Rojnic Kuzman, 2023). The way that information is to be interpreted stems from an incredibly diverse range of forms of information, each with useful but differing information concerning the ways in which students behave, what they believe and feel, and how attentive they become in class. By analyzing all these components together, colleges and schools are starting to develop better ways of assisting students before problems become more severe.

Learning Management Systems (LMS), one of the biggest sources of information, are used in primary and higher education. These systems track a tremendous amount of student activity, including how often they sign in, how many hours they spend on different parts of the course, how often they view content, how they interact with discussion boards, and how they respond to their instructors. LMS data help illustrate how active students are in their learning over time (Tariq, 2025b). A sudden drop in logins or posting to discussions might mean that the student is pulling back, either because they are stressed or have emotional issues. Likewise, when a student starts to turn in work late or miss all of them in general, especially if it is out of the ordinary for them, it might be due to faltering motivation or trouble keeping up with the workload, both of which are indicators of emotional stress. Attendance records are still important despite online courses. Tracking how often students attend video sessions or view pre-recorded classes gives a sense of their presence and persistence. Skipping one class now and again is inevitable, but missing classes regularly or strings of days or weeks between logins suggest disengagement or issues that are affective, cognitive, or contextual. When attendance patterns are viewed in conjunction with other data, such as performance or communication patterns, they can be employed to identify students who need more support.

Another gold mine of information is the tone and substance of what students write, including discussion board postings, emails, and other messages they send while learning. Sentiment analysis is a facet of NLP that can be used to recognize emotional states from the words used, sentence structure, and tone. Students who start reporting feelings such as frustration, depression, or despair in their posts, either explicitly or implicitly, could be hinting at underlying issues (Jiménez Zapata et al., 2023). For example, if a student starts using more negative vocabulary or starts to speak in a self-critical tone over time, this could be a sign that they are emotionally stressed. Teachers can miss these indicators due to the lack of a clear process to analyze the data, but sentiment analysis tools can raise these trends so that people can step in and help. Academic performance, while generally used to determine how well a student is doing in school, also reflects mental health when interpreted in another context. One bad grade is not always a sign of a struggling student, but trends suggest otherwise. An abrupt or gradual decline in grades, especially in conjunction with other behavioral changes, may suggest that there are underlying issues requiring correction. Students, even those who do well, can be stressed or anxious without our notice. Thus, grades can never be viewed separately but as one of a bunch of things in a comprehensive analysis of other metrics. When combined with AI technologies, performance data may be more valuable when combined with the state of engagement a student is experiencing, what they are saying, and how they feel. The increased use of biometric data from wearable devices is being considered to raise awareness of student well-being. They include sleep patterns and the correlation of heart rate, activity levels, and stress, which can be tracked using this technology. Although the use of wearables in schools is still immature and controversial in terms of privacy and consent concerns, the possible advantages are enormous. Sleep deprivation is often accompanied by psychological issues, including depression and anxiety. In the case of students who decide to share their sleep information, such sleeping behaviors as lack of sleep or sleep disturbance could serve as indicators of premature emotional strain. Similarly, fast heart rates or lack of activity may indicate stress, exhaustion, or depression. Compared to typical academic data, biometric information can expose the well-being of students in ways that are not evident from typical academic data (Tariq, 2025c).

Considering all these points and integrating them into broader trends, it is possible to observe symptoms of distress. An evident sign is a sharp decline in the submission of assignments, especially if it is abnormal relative to the student's usual pattern. It may be accompanied by a low login frequency, less group work contribution, or lower quality or completeness of submitted work. A student who had been active and engaged previously but then became erratic may struggle with mental or emotional issues. Less interaction is another important indicator of mental health (Sarif et al., 2021). Less messaging to peers, less participation in forum discussions, and not responding to instructors are all signs of less interaction, which typically shows a heightened sense of loneliness. If allowed to develop, this sense of loneliness can lead to serious mental health conditions. Text- and voice-based data are becoming more prevalent as education shifts to more active and multimedia-focused media. The ability to measure sentiments and emotions within such data has improved significantly. Systems are now able to detect not only the general mood of a message but also more subtle emotional states such as puzzlement, fear, enthusiasm, or disappointment. For speech data, AI can interpret vocal tone, pitch, rate, and inflection and deduce emotional states for recorded class lectures or voice recordings. A student who speaks in a flat, monotonous tone may be exhibiting depression or lack of energy, while sudden shifts in vocal energy could be caused by anxiety or stress. While these observations must be viewed in context, they add depth to the understanding of student behavior that is simply not possible through written communication.

Above all, all these disparate streams of data need to be consolidated into one type of analysis for practical use. It is important to connect them with institutional learning analytics platforms to identify and pursue the right people at the right time and in the most effective way possible. Learning analytics platforms currently receive dashboards that visually represent the level of student engagement, performance, and risk in an integrated way (Zhu, 2025). With these dashboards, students at risk can be identified, trends over time can be provided, and what the student is required to do next can be determined. As AI and machine learning models are integrated into these websites, institutions can move beyond knowing what happened to knowing how it will happen to even knowing what they can do regarding it. These systems should also be constructed and fed back with student participation to be equitable, transparent, and practical. Putting students in charge of their own data, enabling them to monitor their own health, and giving them tools tailored to their personal profiles can also make monitoring a proactive step in self-care.

At the institutional level, these insights derived from data turned into more elaborate wellness programs that made the culture of education not only academic but holistic. With prompt and precise access to student well-being information by teachers, advisors, and mental health counselors, they can collaborate more effectively, respond in time to assist students in distress, and build a culture where students will be seen, heard, and valued (Fortuna et al., 2020). On its own, data will not resolve the issue of mental health in schools, but when viewed thoughtfully and acted upon with humanity, it can be the catalyst of good. With the education sector embracing new technologies, the dilemma will be to attain innovation alongside responsibility. The available data are highly potent; however, their value is in the manner in which they are united, examined, and applied to human-centered systems of care. With proper design, an ethical approach, and respect for the well-being of the individuals they serve, any institution can use these tools to track not only student progress but also to know the actual individuals it serves and serve them properly.

IMPLEMENTATION IN EDUCATIONAL INSTITUTIONS: CASE STUDIES

The use of AI in tracking mental health in schools and universities is becoming a standard procedure, and there are numerous examples where the advantages and disadvantages of the use of these systems are both present. The aim was to recognize students who were acting out of character, such as being extremely shy or avoiding activities. When the system flagged a student as possibly needing help, an alert was sent to a member of staff, and contact was made using a message of help, that is, by email, phone, or meeting. What was unique about the program was the technology itself, but more so how the university prepared its staff to react with empathy toward students. They were taught to deliver outreach in a way that they would be certain it was not a punitive measure. Students who received this type of assistance were shocked but thankful that someone noticed that they were having issues. Students expressed problems they had not talked about, such as problems among family members, money troubles, or feeling overwhelmed. Consequently, the university was able to refer them to support, such as counseling, academic assistance, or financial aid, much earlier than usual (Afshar Jahanshahi et al., 2023). The program's success led to plans for expansion to incorporate more data from wearable fitness trackers that students could choose to use, providing even more detailed information on student well-being. In K–12, an example is the use of AI to monitor emotions in a popular chat-based learning platform used by younger students. This application was implemented to allow students and teachers to converse online or in blended courses. When the application was updated, a feature that used natural language processing to search messages for signs of distress and emotion was added. If a student wrote words that suggested frustration, anxiety, or hopelessness, such as that they felt "stupid," "angry," or "tired of everything," the system would send a non-intrusive reminder to the teacher (Tariq, 2025d).

Teachers can then summon the student or, if needed, call a counselor or administrator. The system was designed to support teachers rather than overwhelm them. The prompts were ranked by urgency and provided with instructions on how to approach the student. Crucially, the system was never meant to supplant teacher judgment but to complement it with more data. Teachers reported that this allowed them to identify problems that they may not have caught otherwise, particularly in shy students who are not verbally expressive. In addition, because the tool was already being used on a day-to-day basis, it did not create much additional workload or involve learning new systems (Hands & Shankar, 2025). Another is a university that developed a well-being dashboard for the entire campus that drew information from several sources. This dashboard improved the student affairs, academic advising, mental health counseling, and residence life staff. This dashboard combines data from learning analytics, campus card transactions (e.g., dining hall use), attendance records in class, and biometric data from voluntary wearables. Students with multiple red flags, such as not attending class, failure to eat meals, or poor grades, were highlighted in notes and referrals to past help.

This dashboard required intense collaboration between departments that normally operate in silos. Information must travel safely across academic departments, IT, health departments, and student life. Privacy was paramount, and students had the choice to publish some information. The university was clear about why data were being used, and all actions based on the dashboard insights were carried out by trained staff through trauma-informed practice. Staff and teachers need to learn more than how to use the tools; they need to have a deep understanding of the emotional, ethical, and personal aspects of these technologies (Tariq, 2025e). Having the ability to view data on a screen is not equal to having the ability to have a rich conversation with a student who has been determined to be at-risk. Training should involve digital skills, mental health awareness, communication skills, and awareness of cultural differences. Educational institutions have failed to comprehend the amount of effort and time that should be invested in preparing staff for this new method of providing care; therefore, they end up applying it half-heartedly or dismissing it by non-ready or resistant individuals or those who question AI use in education (Tariq, 2025a).

Getting various departments to work together is another enormous task that requires significant effort. Many schools are still organized in ways that do not facilitate collaboration among teams. Data may be isolated, or systems may be incompatible with each other because of the old infrastructure. An example would be if a learning management system determines that a student needs to be supported, then it must ensure that the information gets to the right advisor or counselor. This typically involves new computer software, changes in school policy, and new ways of transferring information between departments. All of these require time, money, and good leadership. Without them, even the best AI hardware may not function as intended.

There are also concerns about students' attitudes towards surveillance. Even when the systems themselves work well and are effective, students might be put ill at ease by being monitored, particularly if they do not understand how their information is being used or if they believe it will lead to punishment (Stiles-Shields et al., 2024). Schools must work to build trust and transparency regarding data use, privacy, and value from early intervention. Some institutions have even gone beyond this by engaging students in the design and testing of these systems, having advisory councils, or holding feedback sessions to ensure that student voices inform the development of these systems. Fairness must also be considered. To ensure that the models do not support existing biases, they must be strictly tested. When a model is trained using non-diverse data, it may perform poorly with students not in the non-represented groups and therefore fail to provide correct warnings or miss signals. This destroys trust and inflicts injuries. Schools should ensure that their data teams are inclusive, the construction of models should have checks of fairness, and the voice of marginalized communities should be represented at all levels. Regardless of these obstacles, K-12 and higher education case studies testify that AI systems can change students' lives with proper usage. They assist teachers and support staff in highlighting issues earlier and in better comprehending the needs of students, as well as offering tailored and thoughtful assistance. Above all, AI should be used in a caring spirit to listen more intuitively, respond more humanely, and build learning experiences that would allow every student to feel visible, inspired, and appreciated. The technology exists; all that is left is to have our schools use it in a manner that really undergirds the human act of learning.

BALANCING PRECISION WITH PRIVACY

As schools and universities start using AI and predictive programs to track students' mental health, the discussion must be just as focused on ethics, consent, and privacy as on technology itself. Such programs can help students early on by flagging potential problems, but it is all about how well schools balance being correct with keeping things private. It is not enough to design powerful tools that can determine risks; they must also be used in ways that retain students' autonomy, dignity, and rights. This includes keeping the systems open, fair, and secure, and having those who use the systems driven by care rather than control. One of the most important aspects of ethically applying data is ensuring that students provide real, informed consent. They must be informed about who is authorized to view the data, the potential consequences of identifying certain patterns, and whether the data will be used for training computers or research purposes (Kunanti et al., 2025). If not, schools can lose trust and create a feeling of being spied upon rather than aided. It is especially important to allow students to choose whether they want to participate in more sensitive types of monitoring, such as checking the tone of written work or tracking smart device data. For younger students, especially in K–12 schools, it is critically important that parents be asked for permission. Schools should not just explain what the technology can do, but also what this implies for children's welfare and privacy. At universities, where students are grown-ups, the organization should respect their liberty to make their own choices and give them mastery over their own data. Any way they would prefer to consent should be free of coercion, and students ought not to ever be forced into providing their data as a condition for support or success at school. Figure 2 provides overview of ethical, human, and operational components intersect to ensure responsible AI use.

Figure 2. Ethical–operational balance model for AI in educational mental health

Another huge problem with using AI to address mental health is the way biased or wrong the system might be. AI is only as good as it has been taught, and if what has been taught is old problems or is not representative, the AI may produce biased results. For example, students from less-represented groups may be treated more like they are in trouble, not necessarily because they are, but because the system learned to connect them with specific bad patterns (Li, 2023). Students who communicate differently because of culture, autism, or not being able to speak the language well may be misinterpreted by AI. These mistakes may translate into unfair treatment, extra stress, and they might even be judged unfairly.

All those who make and use these systems must ensure that they pay close attention and keep things going. Data scientists and authors must ensure fairness, test the models to determine whether they treat everyone equally, and ensure that the data they are training on represent all the students they are working with. Schools should involve different groups in creating and testing these instruments, such as not only tech people and admins, but also educators, counselors, students, and ethicists. The models need not be regarded as perfect (Putera, 2024). They are there to help humans, not to become them. Whenever the system flags a risk, it must be viewed by experienced staff familiar with the situation and able to understand the data with kindness and empathy.

The dignity of students should also be preserved, just like their data. Identifying students in need of support is one of the most sensitive fields in the implementation of such systems. Identifying and establishing the fact that someone requires assistance is something to be approached with a lot of care in both the precision of the identification and the way it is communicated to the student. If anything goes amiss and is not dealt with sensitively, it is possible that the student will come out vulnerable, embarrassed, or even doubtful. The approach to the student by the staff differs depending on whether a concern is just or not (Shohel et al., 2022). Schools must educate their staff to sound not judgmental but humane, and support must take the front seat more than observation. In addition, the designation of students in these systems is important. Where a system determines a student to be "high risk," there should be a process in place to prevent the label from following them or changing the way others think about them. The systems must be able to provide context and helpful recommendations rather than labels. Students should also be able to comment on or question the data they are using to analyze. The correct care plan presupposes listening to the voice and thoughts of a student and not only the outcome of the algorithm.

Finally, the ethical use of AI in education means following data protection regulations. Certain guidelines must be adopted depending on the geographical location of the school and the age of the students. These consist of certain rules concerning consent, the way the data are kept, who can access them, and the right to be forgotten.

In the US, the Family Educational Rights and Privacy Act (FERPA) governs the disclosure of educational data and provides students and their parents with some rights to their personal data. This law obligates schools to ensure that information in the records of a student is not distributed without the consent of the student and that a student is free to access and modify their records. Children below 13 years of age are even provided at a stricter level under the Children Online Privacy Protection Act (COPPA). COPPA also addresses data collection of children below the age of 13 years and provides that any personal information can be collected only with express and authorized parental permission. Not only names and email addresses but also any distinguishing identifiers that are engaged in following the behavior of children on websites and applications. Schools that have AI-driven tools to monitor younger students should be well-coordinated with the makers of those tools to ensure that COPPA is not violated. They should also be able to clearly acquire and maintain records of parental permission. In the European Union and schools that serve European students, the General Data Protection Regulation (GDPR) offers a high standard of protection for personal data. According to the GDPR, all usage of personal information must have a legitimate reason, that is, consent or legitimate interest (Taubman et al., 2022). People also have strong rights over how their data are handled; they can ask to see it, update mistakes, and even ask for deletion. The GDPR also provides that decisions in computers regarding individuals, particularly those carrying major consequences on their lives, should be authorized by a human being and should be contested. This implies that in mental health supervision, if a student is ranked by a machine or otherwise recognized to influence their grades, obstinance of services, or conduct, it must be examined by a human, and the child must be permitted to challenge.

Such schools should be sensitive to information involving students. They must maintain good records of their actions to acquire, use, and possess information. They should conduct privacy audits before introducing new systems and have one supervisor to protect data if needed. The main benefit of mental health screenings should be serviceable to students and not offer power of control. Technology must be utilized as an aid, not as an impediment. This is a request to the schools to go an extra mile beyond complying with the law and pursue an approach to work with data that is values-led, which is open, fair, and respectful. When they are convinced that their information is being handled fairly and honestly, that they have a say in how it is used, and that the systems are being designed in their best interest, they will be more likely to trust and be assisted by them (Shohel et al., 2022). There is no perfect balance between caring for students and respecting their privacy; it is constantly shifting. As artificial intelligence technology becomes smarter, ethical questions will become more complicated. Should AI intervene when it identifies major problems, even if the student has not asked for help? What if a student refuses help? As schools increasingly use AI tools to support mental health, the focus must remain on how technology can deliver more care, not less. The potential of these tools lies there, but only if they are based on ethics, equity, and trust.

THE ROLE OF HUMAN-IN-THE-LOOP SYSTEMS

As schools start using AI tools to monitor mental health, it is certain that it is necessary to have a human involved. AI can read enormous amounts of data, look for patterns, and provide early alerts quickly and widely. However, it does not understand context, empathetically understand emotions, or offer the kind of caring support students need when they are in trouble. Therefore, counselors and other trained personnel must check and track what AI picks up (Dupuy et al., 2021). This ensures that the assistance provided is humane, accurate, and fair. Without human oversight, such systems may be technologically correct but emotionally cruel, and thus, they may cause more harm than good. AI notification, when a student's tone, behavior, or class participation changes, becomes the first step in a larger process. These warning signs are warnings and not conclusions. They should serve to welcome a closer look, make contact, and provide a chance for help before a crisis catches up with an individual. However, these warning signs require the expertise of professional counselors, psychologists, or support staff on mental health and individual differences. For example, an absent student may be stressed, have domestic difficulties, or have a bad patch. Only humans can produce this type of difference and respond in a way that builds trust, not fear.

Therefore, it is imperative to train educators and counselors to deal with AI notifications appropriately. The success of a human-in-the-loop system depends not only on the quality of the AI but also on the ability of the staff to understand and respond to the information (Taubman et al., 2022). Teachers and counselors need to be trained on how to use the system and interact with students in a healthy, culturally sensitive, and emotionally healthy way. It is not everything to do with the technology training; the training must also cover how to use hard conversation, to de-escalate emotional outbursts, and to call on the support without causing the student to feel judged or spied on. Another strategic aspect of human work is the presence of policies concerning what happens when a student is flagged; institutions need to have such policies clearly written. Who does get pulled in? What is done? How are students treated? Follow-up? These are not decisions that need to be made ad hoc. They must be inculcated in the system prior to the bakery, including mental professionals, lawyers, and students. Response teams and other support services can be coordinated to ensure that warnings do not become wasted in red tape or result in overly strong or weak responses. On a good system, a warning can be initiated by a check-in with an academic advisor, followed by a meeting with a counselor and regular follow-ups with the student with his or her consent.

This is especially true in big schools, where there are numerous departments, such as student services, academic advising, housing, campus security, and mental health, which need to liaise. Such teams must be aware of the intended use, capabilities, and constraints of the system. Another approach to align everyone on the same page is through regular meetings, mutual training, and mutual case management (Amin et al., 2022). AI can notify users about something, but the human support network acts in an efficient and understanding manner. Institutions that do not form a support network will overreact to AI notifications or lack thereof. Another critical element in keeping these systems running is building trust and acclimating students to the online space where these applications operate. Students need to be aware that the system is designed to help and not control or judge them. It needs honesty regarding the way in which data are collected, for what purpose they are being collected, and what kind of responses they will generate. When students know that a system is in place to help their welfare and that any issues they bring up will be addressed by concerned professionals, they are more likely to react honestly and constructively. Trust is also dependent on how institutions respond to mistakes and tough situations. No AI will ever be flawless. A student may occasionally be picked up even though they are good (false positive), or a struggling student may slip through the cracks (false negative). As humans, we must solve these problems through human judgment. In case a student is caught up and no problem is reported by a counselor, then the process may culminate in a soft check-in as opposed to intervention. In contrast, when a teacher notices a wrong which went unnoticed by the system, there must be options for human-initiated alerts. This is not aimed at overtaking the judgment of the human element but rather complementing it with information that gives institutions a more comprehensive insight into the needs of the students.

Another question is how to engage students in self-help processes. Human-in-the-loop technology does not necessarily consider students as passive consumers of assistance but as participatory intellectual health treatment agents. Teachers are familiar with their students and understand the stress of education; they can discern small shifts in behavior or activity. Administrators can identify and organize support and frame policies that appreciate care. Any AI system that genuinely cares depends on all these people. The issue is not whether mental health care in schools will be a part of technology, since it is already the case, but how technology can be made to enhance and not undermine the human aspect of care. Artificial intelligence will be able to recognize patterns, warn us of possible issues, and process masses of students more efficiently than humans. It is only through human beings that one can build trust, provide genuine understanding, and create areas where students feel known and valued. The most effective systems will combine the precision of artificial intelligence with the humility of human care and create methods and procedures that are thoughtful, respectful, and deeply caring for patients. Such schools will be able to enjoy better mental health and a better learning climate. Whenever children get to know that they can shout and get listened to and attend to them, they have better chances of participating, persevering, and getting well. Human-in-the-loop platforms enable this type of safety by ensuring that data are not used to replace people but rather to help them. Technology can serve as an instrument to have a more comprehensive approach to solving mental health problems based on empathy, training, collaboration, and trust, instead of being an impediment to maintaining mental health in schools. Thus, AI has ceased to be a cold, watching machine and is instead a silent work partner of actual human beings who care.

FUTURE PATHWAYS: BUILDING ADAPTIVE AND PERSONALIZED MENTAL HEALTH SYSTEMS

With learning becoming bewildering in the Internet era, the future of school and university mental health will depend on the development of intelligent, adaptable, and highly personalized systems. If the system detects that a student has been more negative or anxious in discussion posts, it may prompt the student to take notes or refer them to a mental health provider. These nudges do not intend to substitute professional counseling and larger support services but rather act as reminders that are continuous and persistent in trying to help the student cope with their emotions, be present, and develop resilience. What may appear as a sign of social withdrawal in a certain child may be considered normal in another child based on cultural backgrounds or a sign of excessive stimulation in a neurodivergent child (Taubman et al., 2022). Context-sensitive systems are designed to recognize these nuances more accurately, reducing the chances of misinterpreting a child's situation or providing the wrong support. These systems consider factors such as the hour of the day, the level of work that a student is handling, the school year, and even outside occurrences such as local catastrophes or global events that may be affecting a cohort. A student who is showing signs of burnout after extensive academic stress may be guided through their wellness app to check their levels of stress, receive personalized content, or even talk to a trained peer supporter. Virtual peer support systems are also becoming popular as useful additions to face-to-face mental health treatment. These websites enable students to connect with others experiencing similar difficulties and exchange encouragement, empathy, and information without professional guidance. When combined with early warning signs, such systems can deliver peer support at the time of need, when interest falters, negative feelings are identified, or stress is high. These interactions are not as intimidating as professional counseling and can be a good stepping stone to more extreme help if needed. They also provide a feeling of community and counteract the loneliness that so often follows mental illness, especially in online or hybrid classes (Tariq, 2025b).

In the future, integrating mental health data into course planning and workload planning could be a significant and much-needed change. Education has historically divided academic success and emotional well-being; however, this approach is no longer effective in the current context (Amerson et al., 2021). Some of the most progressive universities are currently linking student wellness patterns and course planning so that instructors can see how some assignments, the design of courses, or the schedule affect mental health. If data show that students are stressed at segments of a course or drop out at higher rates following a difficult assignment, teachers can use that information to respace the pace of the course, water down the work, or insert well-being check-ins. They should be able to opt in or out of personal features, control their data settings, and have clear information about how insights generated through the system are put into action. Trust is the secret to making personalization work; without it, even the best tools will not get students involved.

A larger cultural shift must occur to accommodate these changes (Yi et al., 2024). Schools need to facilitate cultures that have open dialogues on mental health, where statistics are used rather than looking at individuals, and where the point of education is not to be an academic star but to grow personally and become tough. This involves teaching teachers and administrators the use of these instruments and how to view mental health as a thing everybody does. These involve finding means to let students contribute and make their voices heard in these systems. These involve instituting school policies that are geared towards fairness, inclusion, and student-centered care. The future of mental health in education is not more technology but smarter and more intelligently used technology. Individualized and flexible mental health systems would be useful to make education a place where no student is invisible, silent, or incapable of doing their best. Such systems can prevent problems in the first place, connect students with support, and generate learning environments that react to what they know, how they feel, think, and develop.

An ethical framework that relies on three main principles–transparency, collaboration, and responsiveness–must be developed to promote responsible scale-up innovation. Transparency implies that the activities of such systems, what they observe, how they reach decisions, and how they react, should be seen by all stakeholders, such as parents, employees, administrators, and students. Once a great number of perspectives are used at the very beginning, the systems will serve the needs more appropriately, be able to emphasize a diversity of experiences, and not lead to the emergence of undesired issues. This places the human-in-the-loop principle into AI applications to make it a component of a large, person-focused support system comprising humans. What are the long-term effects of predictive systems on students' behavior? Will they encourage more helpful behaviors in seeking help, or do they make one feel spied on and pressured? Research studies should also investigate the response of different groups of students to these interventions and whether these systems are fair to all. The findings should be shared publicly so that schools can learn to apply the shared knowledge to improve (Amerson et al., 2021). It is not technological prowess that will be the future of school mental health but rather the level to which and the care with which we utilize it. By implementing AI as a solution to a problem, rather than care, we could produce systems that are not merely more efficient but also more caring. Systems that get to know the student wholly, not just their grades or level of participation, but their hardships, hopes, and humanity. Mental health issues can be handled openly, wisely, and respectfully through careful, ethical, and cooperative planning to form learning communities that would allow all students the dignity they deserve.

CONCLUSION

As the concept of artificial intelligence (AI) penetrates the world of education, its capabilities in addressing the mental well-being of students as an early warning system (EWS) have emerged as an opportunity, as well as an incredible challenge (Amin et al., 2022). Identifying signs of student distress early enough with the help of AI in student wellbeing programs will offer an excellent opportunity to intervene in early active stages before a problem can become more severe and explore more innovative approaches to mental health support in diverse and individualized forms. However, these advantages should be accompanied by a balance against the cultural, ethical, and practical boundaries of responsible innovation. Moving ahead, this path will need to be guided by conscious design, open practices, and a commitment to the dignity and diversity of the students for whom these systems are intended. Utilized correctly, these instruments enable educators and assist counselors to tackle students at an early stage when their mental health is intact, prior to it disintegrating, to provide students with timely and, in many instances, life-altering support.

In addition, EWS tools are highly scalable. Schools and universities provide mental health services every day, which are usually overwhelmed by the growth in the needs of students. As many schools continue to have an imbalanced number of students to counselors, AI can provide a means of prioritizing challenges and making services more of a daily routine, and mental well-being can be a daily practice, not a response. However, alongside the advantages, such a solution also possesses enormous constraints that should be monitored (Taubman et al., 2022). The highest is the moral use of information. It is the responsibility of schools to ensure that such data employed in modeling are accessed and processed freely, willingly, and safely. This means publicly notifying students about the data collection, the intended purpose, how it will be used, and by whom. The consent should be informed and voluntary, and the student should not be forced to state his consent without a penalty. In the case of children, their parents should be notified, but institutions need to ensure that families have the correct knowledge about predictive analytics and data disclosure.

The threat of being overly reliant on algorithms rather than human judgment is another limitation. AI systems are not super-learners. They can assist in focus and decision-making, but they cannot usurp the professionally trained mental health clinicians intuitive understanding of the situation. Biased predictive models are also a major problem (Yi et al., 2024). When trained on data that are representative of real existing social, cultural, or academic differences, an AI system can increase or even recreate them. Unrepresented students can be easily identified and misinterpreted when the model is not programmed to interpret other forms of communication such as body language. Moral practice means pouring funds into bias testing, ensuring that the datasets are not unified, and that marginalized people participate in the creation and testing of such machinery. Inclusion should not be added to the system; rather, it should be embedded within it.

REFERENCES

Afshar Jahanshahi, A., & Polas, M. R. H. (2023). Moving toward digital transformation by force: Students' preferences, happiness, and mental health. *Electronics (Basel), 12*(10), 2187. DOI: 10.3390/electronics12102187

Amerson, R., Fisher, B. A., Bible, J., Burgess, L., Ravan, L., & Ward, L. D. (2021). Nursing education amid a pandemic. *Nurse Educator, 46*(5), 255–260. DOI: 10.1097/NNE.0000000000001039

Amin, R., Ara, S., & Imtiaz, M. (2022). Counselling during COVID-19. In *Education reform in the aftermath of the COVID-19 pandemic* (pp. 1–14). Springer. DOI: 10.4018/978-1-7998-8992-2.ch003

Chaudhary, K. (2024). Impact of digital pedagogy on the psychological wellbeing of students during global pandemics: A narrative review. [SAPJ]. *South Asian Journal of Psychology, 3*(1), 1–10. DOI: 10.9734/bpi/pller/v9/11861F

Dayal, S., & Pratibha, . (2023). Roadblocks in education amidst global crisis—A study based in India. *PLoS One, 18*(10), e0285128. DOI: 10.1371/journal.pone.0292465

Dupuy, L., Sevin, E. D., Micoulaud-Franchi, J., & Philip, P. (2021). Factors associated with acceptance of a virtual companion providing screening and advice for sleep problems during the COVID-19 crisis. In *Proceedings of the 21st ACM International Conference on Intelligent Virtual Agents* (pp. 1–3). ACM. DOI: 10.1145/3472306.3478334

Fortuna, K. L., Myers, A. L., Walsh, D., Walker, R., Mois, G. D., & Brooks, J. M. (2020). Strategies to increase peer support specialists' capacity to use digital technology in the era of COVID-19: Pre–post study. *JMIR Mental Health, 7*(7), e20429. DOI: 10.2196/20429

Gillinov, M., & Soltesz, E. G. (2020). Commentary: Atrial fibrillation after aortic valve replacement: Predict, prevent, protect. *The Journal of Thoracic and Cardiovascular Surgery, 160*(5), 1261–1262. DOI: 10.1016/j.jtcvs.2019.05.080

Hands, A. S., & Shankar, S. (2025). Back from crisis mode: Exploring care-centred approaches to teaching in LIS. *Journal of Education for Library and Information Science, 66*(1), 85–93. DOI: 10.3138/jelis-2024-0052

Jiménez Zapata, R., Sánchez Castillo, V., & Pérez Gamboa, A. J. (2023). Health, education and pandemic: An analysis of their relationship. *Health Leadership and Quality of Life, 1*(1), 14–26. DOI: 10.56294/hl2023195

Kunanti, N., Putri, S. A., & Fahmi, M. (2025). “Record, spread, judge”: A short video reflecting the crisis of digital morality and media manipulation in modern society. *Action Research Literate*, *1*(1), 20–29. DOI: 10.46799/arl.v9i6.2971

Li, Y. (2023). Application of machine learning to predict mental health disorders and interpret feature importance. In *Proceedings of the 3rd International Symposium on Computer Technology and Information Science (ISCTIS 2023)* (pp. 257–261). IEEE. DOI: 10.1109/ISCTIS58954.2023.10213032

Loda, T., Löffler, T., Erschens, R., Zipfel, S., & Herrmann-Werner, A. (2020). Medical education in times of COVID-19: German students' expectations—A cross-sectional study. *PLoS One*, *15*(11), e0241660. DOI: 10.1371/journal.pone.0241660

Putera, M. D. A. (2024). Mental health impacts by elevated digital screen time during COVID-19 pandemic. *Journal of Psychiatry Psychology and Behavioral Research.*

Rojnic Kuzman, M. (2023). Digital transcultural psychiatry in times of crisis: The Help for Helpers webinar series. *European Psychiatry : the Journal of the Association of European Psychiatrists*, *66*(S1), S7. DOI: 10.1192/j.eurpsy.2023.39

Rygaard, N. P. (2020). Improving the mental health of abandoned children: Experiences from a global online intervention. *The American Psychologist*, *75*(9), 1376–1388. DOI: 10.1037/amp0000726

Sarif, N., & Vandana. (2021). Digital learning, students' mental health and role of psychological capital amidst COVID-19 pandemic in India. *Ensemble: A Journal of the Department of Education, 1*(Special Issue), 108–119.

Shohel, M. M. C., Mahmud, A., Urmee, M. A., Anwar, M. N., Rahman, M. M., Acharya, D., & Ashrafuzzaman, M. (2022). Education in emergencies, mental well-being and e-learning. In Shohel, M. M. C. (Ed.), *E-learning and digital education in the twenty-first century* (pp. 1–22). IntechOpen. DOI: 10.5772/intechopen.97425

Stiles-Shields, C., Ramos, G., Ortega, A., & Psihogios, A. M. (2024). Increasing digital mental health reach and uptake via youth partnerships. *npj Mental Health Research, 3*, 12.

Tariq, M. U. (2025a). AI-Driven Innovations: Transforming Healthcare, Agriculture, and Environmental Science. In Emara, T., Hassan, E., Trinh, T., Li, G., & Saber, A. (Eds.), *The Role of Artificial Intelligence in Advancing Applied Life Sciences* (pp. 87–118). IGI Global Scientific Publishing., DOI: 10.4018/979-8-3693-9208-9.ch003

Tariq, M. U. (2025b). Navigating Cancer Care: The Crucial Role of Educators and Healthcare Providers in Supporting Patients of Color. In Clarke, K., & Moffett, N. (Eds.), *Cancer Diagnosis, Treatment and Care: Reflections for the Education of Survivors and Healthcare Providers* (pp. 405–424). IGI Global Scientific Publishing., DOI: 10.4018/979-8-3693-5400-1.ch021

Tariq, M. U. (2025c). Empowering Patients With AI-Ethical Digital Tools for Health Data Management and Decision. In Pesqueira, A., & de Bem Machado, A. (Eds.), *Navigating Privacy, Innovation, and Patient Empowerment Through Ethical Healthcare Technology* (pp. 197–216). IGI Global Scientific Publishing., DOI: 10.4018/979-8-3693-7630-0.ch008

Tariq, M. U. (2025d). Navigating the Convergence of IoMT and Generative AI in Global Healthcare: Opportunities, Challenges, and Ethical Considerations. In Kumar, V., Katina, P., & Zhao, J. (Eds.), *Convergence of Internet of Medical Things (IoMT) and Generative AI* (pp. 513–534). IGI Global Scientific Publishing., DOI: 10.4018/979-8-3693-6180-1.ch022

Tariq, M. U. (2025e). Enhancing Pandemic Preparedness With AI-Driven Risk Prediction Models. In Shah, I., Sial, Q., & Fateh, S. (Eds.), *Generative AI Techniques for Sustainability in Healthcare Security* (pp. 77–94). IGI Global Scientific Publishing., DOI: 10.4018/979-8-3693-6577-9.ch005

Taubman, D. S., Heininger, W., Salazar, S., Salazar, L., Riba, M., Greden, J. F., & Parikh, S. V. (2022). Depression on college campuses conference: Addressing an evolving crisis. *Academic Psychiatry*, *46*(3), 359–363. DOI: 10.1007/s40596-021-01575-z

Turmaine, K., Jeannic, A.-L., Dumas, A., & Chevreul, K. (2021). Lessons learned from an e-mental health intervention: The promotion of StopBlues in 41 French cities. *European Psychiatry : the Journal of the Association of European Psychiatrists*, *64*(S1), S110–S111. DOI: 10.1192/j.eurpsy.2021.318

Yi, Z., Min, T., Chong, L., & Yani, S. (2024). Research on practical pathways for digital technology-empowered mental health education for rural children in central and western China. *Applied & Educational Psychology, 5*, Article 12766.

Zhu, Y. (2025). Crisis and countermeasures of digital transformation in American higher education: Based on the perspective of students' subjectivity. *International Journal of Education. Humanities and Social Sciences*, *2*(1), 14–23.

KEY TERMS AND DEFINITIONS

Predict: Recognizing mental health risks using behavioral data.
Prevent: Intervening early to prevent worsening mental health.
Protect: Maintain students well-being through ethical systems.

Chapter 9

Pulse of the Mind: Wearable Devices for Emotional and Physiological Monitoring in Educational Environments

Uddalak Mitra
https://orcid.org/0000-0002-5682-5218
JIS College of Engineering, India

Shafiq Ul Rehman
https://orcid.org/0000-0003-2266-218X
Kingdom University, Bahrain

ABSTRACT

Wearable technology is transforming how student well-being is monitored in learning environments. Beyond fitness, modern wearables track physiological and emotional indicators such as heart rate variability, sleep patterns, electrodermal activity, and movement levels—signals linked to stress, anxiety, and fatigue that affect academic performance. When combined with AI and machine learning, wearable-driven insights enable proactive mental-health support by detecting risk early and initiating timely interventions. This chapter explores the role of wearables in identifying students' emotional and physiological states. It reviews key sensor technologies, practical applications in schools and universities, and case studies demonstrating their benefits. Ethical challenges around privacy, consent, and equity—especially vulnerable learners—are addressed. The chapter concludes with future directions, including integration with learning analytics, institutional policies, and personalized digital interventions to support student resilience and success.

DOI: 10.4018/979-8-3373-5007-3.ch009

1. INTRODUCTION

Students across K–12 and higher education increasingly face significant mental health challenges such as stress, anxiety, and depression (Abd-alrazaq et al., 2024; Pinge et al., 2024). Academic pressure, social expectations, competitive learning environments, and the constant presence of digital technology have intensified these concerns (Leuzzi et al., 2025; Sharma, 2025). As a result, students may experience reduced concentration, rising absenteeism, declining academic performance, and in severe cases, withdrawal from school or college (Neigel et al., 2024; Wang & Liu, 2025). These issues not only hinder learning but also affect long-term personal development and well-being (Dias et al., 2024).

Traditional approaches to supporting student mental health—such as counseling services, periodic self-report surveys, and teacher observations—play an essential role in education systems (Link & Liu, 2024; Leuzzi et al., 2025). However, these approaches are often limited because they rely on voluntary disclosure and sporadic check-ins. Students who fear stigma or lack emotional awareness may hesitate to seek help (Pinge et al., 2024; Sharma, 2025). By the time warning signs become visible to teachers or administrators, the situation may have already escalated (Neigel et al., 2024; Wang & Liu, 2025).

Advancements in wearable technologies offer a promising shift toward proactive and continuous mental health support (Abd-alrazaq et al., 2024; Dias et al., 2024, Mitra & Rehman, 2025a). Devices such as smartwatches, wristbands, rings, and smart clothing can monitor physiological and behavioral markers like heart rate variability, electrodermal activity, sleep patterns, and physical movement (Razavi et al., 2023; Ta et al., 2025). Many of these biomarkers correspond to stress, anxiety, fatigue, and other indicators of mental well-being (Amin et al., 2025; O'Leary et al., 2024). Because wearables operate passively throughout daily routines, they provide rich data that extends beyond what can be captured during brief interactions in counseling or classrooms (He et al., 2024; Ta et al., 2025).

When connected with artificial intelligence and learning analytics platforms, data from wearables can reveal subtle patterns or changes in each student's state (Ta et al., 2025; Abd-alrazaq et al., 2024, Mitra, & Rehman, 2025b). Schools and universities can use these insights to identify risks earlier and deliver timely interventions (Shin et al., 2023; Razavi et al., 2023). For example, educators might be alerted when a student shows a sustained increase in stress levels or a sharp decline in sleep quality (Leuzzi et al., 2025; Neigel et al., 2024). Mental health support teams can then reach out before academic performance suffers, or more serious problems emerge. In addition, such systems can personalize recommendations, help students improve self-regulation, practice relaxation techniques, or adjust their schedules to build healthier habits (Leuzzi et al., 2025; Sharma, 2025).

For students, wearable technology promotes autonomy and self-awareness (Dias et al., 2024; Leuzzi et al., 2025). By visualizing their own emotional and physiological states, learners can better understand what triggers stress and which strategies work best to manage it (Razavi et al., 2023; Ta et al., 2025). Over time, this empowers them to take ownership of their mental well-being. Furthermore, wearable-enabled interventions may be integrated into mobile applications or learning management systems to deliver tailored guidance, mindfulness exercises, or digital coaching based on real-time data (Amin et al., 2025; Shin et al., 2023).

This chapter explores the emerging role of wearable technology as a tool for mental health monitoring in educational environments. It examines the underlying sensor technologies, types of data collected, and ways in which wearables are being deployed in classrooms, campuses, and student residential settings (O'Leary et al., 2024; Ta et al., 2025). It also reviews practical use cases and global initiatives demonstrating the effectiveness of wearables in supporting wellness (Abd-alrazaq et al., 2024; Dias et al., 2024). Alongside the benefits, the chapter critically evaluates ethical considerations including student privacy, informed consent, secure data governance, and the risk of widening inequalities among vulnerable populations (Pinge et al., 2024; He et al., 2024).

Finally, the chapter presents future directions for integrating wearables with institutional policies, mental health programs, and digital learning systems (Shin et al., 2023; Leuzzi et al., 2025). As educational institutions strive to create safe, supportive, and inclusive environments, wearable technologies may become a cornerstone of holistic well-being strategies—ensuring that students not only succeed academically but also thrive emotionally (Amin et al., 2025; Sharma, 2025).

2. SENSOR TECHNOLOGIES IN EDUCATIONAL WEARABLES

The rapid integration of wearable devices into educational environments has been driven by advances in sensor technology capable of capturing a wide range of physiological, emotional, and behavioral indicators (Abd-alrazaq et al., 2024; Gomes et al., 2023). These sensors, embedded in compact and user-friendly devices such as smartwatches, wristbands, rings, chest straps, and headbands, continuously collect information related to students' mental and physical states (Leuzzi, Job, Scafoglieri, & Testa, 2025; Glasserman-Morales, Carlos-Arroyo, Ruiz-Ramirez, & Alcantar-Nieblas, 2023). Unlike traditional health monitoring that occurs only during scheduled clinical visits, wearables gather real-time data throughout students' daily academic and social routines, making them powerful tools for early well-being assessment (Amin, Mishra, Tapera, Volpe, & Sathyanarayana, 2025; Pinge, Gad, Jaisighani, Ghosh, & Sen, 2024).

In both K–12 and higher education settings, several core sensors are particularly relevant because they detect stress load, cognitive effort, sleep deprivation, and emotion-related changes (He, Chen, Wang, He, & Hu, 2024; Bloomfield et al., 2024). Each contributes to a unique layer of insight, and when combined, they create a richer picture of student wellness and engagement (Razavi, McDonald, Mehta, & Sasangohar, 2023; Arnold & Young, 2025).

2.1 Heart Rate and Heart Rate Variability (HRV) Sensors

Heart rate sensors are widely used because they provide direct insight into how the body responds to challenges such as examinations, public speaking, or competitive academic tasks (Razavi et al., 2023; Bloomfield et al., 2024). Fluctuations in heart rate can indicate elevated stress or anxiety, while a stable rhythm may reflect calmness and focus (Abd-alrazaq et al., 2024).

HRV, a more advanced measure, tracks variations between heartbeats and reflects the balance between stress-inducing and relaxation-promoting systems (He et al., 2024). Lower HRV suggests mental strain, fatigue, or burnout risk, whereas higher HRV is associated with resilience (Amin et al., 2025). Over time, these measurements allow the identification of unhealthy stress patterns that might hinder academic success or personal well-being (Gomes et al., 2023).

2.2 Electrodermal Activity (EDA) Sensors

Electrodermal activity sensors detect variations in skin conductance that occur when stress or emotional arousal increases (Pinge et al., 2024; Gomes et al., 2023). Even when students attempt to hide discomfort or nervousness, the body produces tiny physiological responses through sweat-gland activation (Leuzzi et al., 2025).

Monitoring EDA during classroom participation, group collaboration, or demanding learning tasks can reveal when a student feels overwhelmed, anxious, or disengaged (Neigel, Vargo, Tag, & Kise, 2024). This information supports more sensitive and personalized academic guidance, especially for students who do not verbally communicate distress (Gomes et al., 2023; Dias, Mikkelsen, & Schou, 2024).

2.3 Motion Sensors: Accelerometers and Gyroscopes

Accelerometers and gyroscopes measure physical movement, posture, and activity patterns throughout the school day (Razavi et al., 2023; Gomes et al., 2023). Excessive sedentary behavior can be associated with lower motivation, mental fatigue, and decreased cognitive performance (Bloomfield et al., 2024). Conversely, overly restless movement might reflect difficulty concentrating or heightened anxiety (Glasserman-Morales et al., 2023).

These sensors help identify when a learner needs physical activity breaks or when learning strategies require adjustment to maintain engagement (Leuzzi et al., 2025). They also enable schools to support healthier daily habits by integrating movement-based or kinesthetic learning opportunities (Arnold & Young, 2025).

2.4 Sleep Monitoring Sensors

Wearables use combined measures such as overnight movement, breathing rhythms, and heart rate changes to estimate sleep duration, depth, and disturbances (Amin et al., 2025; Ta, Salgin, Demir, Randal, Mehta, McDonald, McCord, & Sasangohar, 2025). Because students often experience poor sleep due to academic pressure, technology use, or emotional stress, monitoring sleep quality becomes essential (Bloomfield et al., 2024).

A sustained decline in sleep health can negatively impact mood, memory, learning, and class participation (Leuzzi et al., 2025). Through continuous sleep tracking, students gain feedback that encourages healthier schedules, while educators gain contextual understanding when performance issues arise (Abd-alrazaq et al., 2024).

2.5 Skin Temperature Sensors

Subtle temperature variations can indicate emotional stress, fatigue, or disruptions in the autonomic system (Gomes et al., 2023). Temperature sensors can also serve as an early sign of illness, helping to reduce absenteeism and prevent health issues from escalating unnoticed (Pinge et al., 2024).

When combined with data from other sensors such as HRV or EDA, temperature trends support more accurate detection of physical and emotional strain experienced during the learning process (Amin et al., 2025).

2.6 Advanced Biosensors: EEG and Cognitive Tracking

Emerging wearable technologies now incorporate EEG-based systems capable of capturing brain-derived information related to attention, cognitive workload, and emotional responses during learning (Dias, Mikkelsen, & Schou, 2024; He et al., 2024). Lightweight headbands or earbuds detect electrical activity that indicates focus, mental fatigue, or distraction (Ta et al., 2025).

Cognitive monitoring can help tailor instructional pacing, classroom conditions, or task complexity to better match individual learners' needs (Razavi et al., 2023;

Leuzzi et al., 2025). For students, these devices support a deeper understanding of their concentration patterns and help cultivate effective study habits (Arnold & Young, 2025; Gomes et al., 2023).

2.7 Integrating Sensor Data for Holistic Insight

The value of wearable sensors increases dramatically when multiple streams of data are analyzed together (Pinge et al., 2024; Abd-alrazaq et al., 2024). A single physiological response may hold many meanings, but patterns across heart rate, movement, sleep, and temperature provide clearer context (Leuzzi et al., 2025; Bloomfield et al., 2024).

- A drop in sleep quality combined with reduced movement and a decrease in HRV may indicate a growing burnout risk (He et al., 2024).
- Sudden spikes in EDA paired with posture shifts might reflect anxiety during specific academic tasks (Neigel et al., 2024).
- High cognitive workload alongside increased restlessness may signal difficulty sustaining attention (Amin et al., 2025).

By recognizing these patterns early, institutions can transition from reactive approaches to preventive well-being strategies (Ta et al., 2025; Glasserman-Morales et al., 2023). Students can also access meaningful feedback that encourages self-awareness and proactive management of stress (Dias et al., 2024; Leuzzi et al., 2025).

Collectively, these sensing technologies expand the lens through which educators view student success (Abd-alrazaq et al., 2024; Gomes et al., 2023). Academic progress is no longer measured solely through grades and attendance but also through markers of emotional resilience and healthy functioning—strengthening support systems across modern learning environments (Neigel et al., 2024; Razavi et al., 2023).

Figure 1. Wearable in education system

Conceptual model of a wearable-enabled educational ecosystem (Fig. 1), illustrating the end-to-end pathway from student interaction with wearable sensors to continuous data transmission and AI-driven analytics that generate personalized, context-aware well-being interventions. This ecosystem highlights the role of institutional stakeholders—including educators and mental health professionals—in interpreting insights and enabling proactive support within educational environments. Wearable devices function as supportive monitoring tools, not diagnostic systems, ensuring student well-being remains the primary focus.

Table 1. Overview of Wearable Sensors and Their Applications in Educational Environments

Sensor Type	Measures / Captures	Examples of Devices	Educational Relevance	Key Insights
Heart Rate & HRV Sensors	Heart rate, heart rate variability	Smartwatches, wristbands	Tracks stress, anxiety, and physiological arousal during exams, presentations, or competitive tasks	Fluctuations indicate stress; stable rhythm suggests calmness; low HRV signals strain or burnout risk (Razavi et al., 2023; He et al., 2024; Bloomfield et al., 2024)
Electrodermal Activity (EDA) Sensors	Skin conductance changes	Smartwatches, rings, wristbands	Detects hidden emotional stress and arousal	Reveals anxiety or disengagement even when students do not verbalize distress; supports personalized guidance (Pinge et al., 2024; Gomes et al., 2023)
Motion Sensors (Accelerometers & Gyroscopes)	Physical movement, posture, activity patterns	Smartwatches, fitness bands, chest straps	Monitors sedentary behavior, restlessness, and engagement	Identifies need for activity breaks; correlates movement patterns with motivation and attention (Razavi et al., 2023; Bloomfield et al., 2024)
Sleep Monitoring Sensors	Sleep duration, depth, disturbances	Wristbands, smartwatches, rings	Monitors sleep quality affecting cognition, mood, and learning	Continuous sleep data supports healthier routines and contextualizes performance issues (Amin et al., 2025; Leuzzi et al., 2025)
Skin Temperature Sensors	Skin temperature variations	Smartwatches, rings	Detects stress, fatigue, or early illness	Temperature trends combined with HRV or EDA improve detection of physical and emotional strain (Gomes et al., 2023; Pinge et al., 2024)

continued on following page

Table 1. Continued

Sensor Type	Measures / Captures	Examples of Devices	Educational Relevance	Key Insights
Advanced Biosensors (EEG & Cognitive Tracking)	Brain activity, attention, cognitive workload	Headbands, earbuds	Tracks focus, mental fatigue, and cognitive engagement	Enables tailoring of instructional pacing and task complexity; supports study habit development (Dias et al., 2024; He et al., 2024)
Integrated Multi-Sensor Analysis	Combined physiological, behavioral, and cognitive data	Multi-sensor wearables	Provides holistic insight into student well-being	Patterns across HR, HRV, EDA, movement, sleep, and temperature identify burnout, anxiety, and cognitive overload early (Abd-alrazaq et al., 2024; Ta et al., 2025)

3. APPLICATIONS OF WEARABLES IN EDUCATIONAL CONTEXTS

The integration of wearable devices into academic environments has introduced new possibilities for monitoring and supporting student well-being across all levels of education. These devices make it possible to continuously understand how learners respond physically and emotionally to academic demands, opening pathways for more individualized support (Gomes, Pato, Lourenço, & Datia, 2023; Pinge, Gad, Jaisighani, Ghosh, & Sen, 2024). This section outlines key applications for wearable technologies in education.

3.1 Early Detection of Stress and Burnout

High-stakes of academic periods such as examinations, assessments, and transitions between grade levels can heavily influence students' stress levels. Wearables equipped with sensors can detect prolonged physiological stress responses before they escalate into burnout or mental health issues (Abd-alrazaq et al., 2024). Continuous monitoring enables timely action, such as offering coping techniques, adjusting workload intensity, or connecting students with counseling resources (Ta, Salgin, Demir, Randal, Mehta, McDonald, McCord, & Sasangohar, 2025). This proactive support reduces the risk of long-term mental health decline and enhances students' ability to manage academic pressure effectively (Bloomfield et al., 2024).

3.2 Enhancing Student Engagement

Wearables contribute to a better understanding of student engagement by identifying how learners physically respond to instructional practices and learning environments (Frontiers in Education review, 2023). Real-time physiological and motion data allow educators to pinpoint teaching moments that generate interest or cause disengagement, such as changes in heart rate, electrodermal activity, or restlessness (Gomes et al., 2023). By observing changes in attention levels, stress responses during group work, or signs of cognitive overload, instructors can modify teaching strategies and adopt more inclusive approaches (Wang & Liu, 2025). These insights also help optimize digital learning tools, promoting environments that sustain curiosity and motivation.

3.3 Supporting At-Risk Students

Some students experience hidden challenges that may not be immediately visible to teachers or parents. When wearable data is integrated with institutional analytics—such as attendance records and performance trends—patterns can reveal individuals who are struggling emotionally, academically, or socially (Amin, Mishra, Tapera, Volpe, & Sathyanarayana, 2025). Indicators such as persistent sleep disruption, sustained stress responses, or decreased movement levels may suggest that a student is at a higher risk of disengagement or dropout (Neigel, Vargo, Tag, & Kise, 2024). Early identification enables personalized interventions, ensuring that vulnerable learners receive support before difficulties intensify. This aligns with findings in biosensor-education research, which emphasize how wearable-based feedback can inform proactive institutional well-being strategies (Wearable Biosensor Technology in Education, 2023).

3.4 Promoting Self-Regulation

Wearables strengthen students' capacity to manage their own health and learning by providing real-time feedback on internal states. Through visualization tools and personalized alerts, students can monitor stress levels, energy fluctuations, and sleep quality (Ta et al., 2025). This supports the development of self-regulatory skills such as pacing study sessions, incorporating breaks, practicing relaxation techniques, and maintaining healthy daily routines (Dias, Mikkelsen, & Schou, 2024). When students understand how their bodies respond to academic life, they are better positioned to adopt habits that maintain focus, resilience, and overall, well-being (Gomes et al., 2023).

3.5 Facilitating Data-Driven Institutional Policies

Aggregated wearable data informs institutional decision-making by revealing well-being trends across different student groups and campus environments (Pinge et al., 2024). Schools and universities can observe patterns that suggest the need for changes—for example, modifying class schedules that consistently cause fatigue, redesigning stressful instructional formats, or implementing campus-wide health promotion initiatives (Wang & Liu, 2025). Data-driven policy enhancements support systemic improvements that benefit entire student populations rather than responding only to individual cases. This has been supported by systematic reviews showing the value of wearables in informing educational policy (Wearable Biosensor Technology in Education, 2023).

3.6 Enhancing Peer Support and Collaborative Learning

Wearable data, when appropriately anonymized or student-controlled, can help foster stronger interpersonal support networks. Changes in emotional or physiological responses during group activities can be highlighted when a student may feel uncomfortable or isolated, enabling peers and instructors to adapt to communication and collaboration styles (Gomes et al., 2023). This strengthens the social dimension of learning, encouraging empathy, and shared responsibility for well-being.

3.7 Supporting Remote and Hybrid Learning

As blended learning becomes more common, ensuring student well-being across both digital and physical environments is essential. Wearables allow continuous monitoring of stress, focus, and engagement regardless of location (Wang & Liu, 2025; Ta et al., 2025). Students learning remotely can maintain healthy routines and receive timely support when stress or isolation emerges. Educators gain visibility into engagement challenges that might otherwise go unnoticed in online formats, promoting equitable well-being support for all instructional delivery modes.

4. CASE STUDIES IN EDUCATIONAL ENVIRONMENTS

The adoption of wearable technologies in academic institutions has grown significantly over the past decade, supported by an increasing recognition that student well-being is closely tied to academic success (Chen et al., 2024; Kumar et al., 2025). Several initiatives across the world demonstrate how wearable devices can be integrated into school and university settings to support mental health, engagement, and retention. The following case studies showcase diverse approaches, demonstrating how different regions and educational levels are experimenting with these technologies to reshape learning experiences and student support systems (Li et al., 2025).

4.1 High School Stress Monitoring Pilot (USA)

In the United States, a pilot initiative across several high schools explored the relationship between physiological stress and academic assessment environments (Navarro et al., 2024). Students were provided with smartwatches capable of tracking heart rate, heart rate variability (HRV), and electrodermal activity. Data collection occurred during regular classes but was especially focused on high-stakes situations such as examinations, oral presentations, and competitive activities (Bloomfield et al., 2024).

Through the pilot, educators observed distinct physiological stress spikes during testing sessions. These spikes were not uniformly distributed; students who were typically quiet, high-performing, or perfectionistic showed higher HRV disruptions compared to those who outwardly appeared more relaxed. Interestingly, stress levels also peaked during unstructured classroom moments, such as sudden teacher questioning or timed tasks (Singh et al., 2024). The insights revealed patterns that teachers had not previously recognized, showing that academic anxiety may be more widespread than classroom behavior suggests.

Using these findings, teachers introduced targeted interventions including guided breathing exercises before exams, structured breaks during long testing sessions, and designated cool-down spaces for students who exhibited continuous elevated stress markers. Over the course of the semester, follow-up recordings revealed reductions in physiological stress responses and improvements in performance consistency, particularly among previously anxious students (Gomes et al., 2023). Teachers also reported feeling better equipped to detect early emotional distress, noting that wearable data acted as a communication bridge between student experience and educator perception.

Beyond short-term benefits, parents and school counselors gained valuable insight into the invisible pressures students face daily. The program showed that students were more willing to discuss stress once presented with objective data about their own physiological patterns, reducing emotional stigma, and encouraging help-seeking behavior (Kumar et al., 2025). The pilot provided a practical model of how wearables can complement existing school-based mental health services by enabling personalized wellness strategies grounded in real-time data.

4.2 University Wellness Program Supporting Mental Health (Europe)

Across a large European university, a multi-year wellness program incorporated fitness bands into campus-wide mental health initiatives (Chen et al., 2024). The devices continuously tracked sleep duration, physical activity, resting heart rate, and periodic stress levels derived from HRV measurements. Participation began voluntarily, but strong student interest led to widespread adoption, particularly among first-year students transitioning into university life (Li et al., 2025).

The program was built around a digital platform that synchronized wearable data with student wellness profiles maintained by health and counseling services. Students who exhibited long-term patterns of insufficient sleep, frequent stress peaks, and reduced physical activity were flagged for supportive outreach. Instead of relying solely on student-initiated appointments—which often occur only when distress becomes overwhelming—counselors could proactively contact students to offer guidance, check-ins, group workshops, or referral to psychological services when necessary (Singh et al., 2024).

One of the most significant outcomes was improved retention among students identified early as at risk for burnout or academic withdrawal. Those who accepted intervention support demonstrated better stress coping strategies and stabilized attendance patterns over time. The integration of objective metrics allowed counselors to avoid assumptions or biases and instead focus on true physiological indicators of declining well-being.

Within the academic environment, professors were invited to review anonymized, aggregated classroom well-being data. The reports revealed trends such as sleep deprivation spikes during exam weeks and reduced physical movement during extended remote learning periods (Navarro et al., 2024). The faculty responded by reevaluating scheduling, assignment density, and lecture delivery methods. For example, some courses implemented flexible deadlines, active learning breaks, and asynchronous review options. These institutional-level adaptations reflected a growing culture of mental health awareness, emphasizing the responsibility shared by academic staff in supporting student resilience (Gomes et al., 2023).

Students benefited not just from institutional monitoring but also from self-insight. Many reported that real-time feedback encouraged healthier lifestyle decisions, such as improved sleep hygiene and regular exercise. Some student clubs partnered with the wellness office to create peer programs that taught stress management techniques, wearable data interpretation, and mindfulness practices (Chen et al., 2024).

This European university example demonstrates how wearable integration can become a sustainable part of holistic student services, with wellness positioned as a proactive rather than reactive educational priority (Li et al., 2025).

4.3 Mindfulness Training in School Settings (Asia)

In several Asian schools, wearable devices have been implemented to evaluate the emotional and cognitive effects of mindfulness-based stress reduction programs (Kumar et al., 2025). Students participated in guided meditation sessions, breathing exercises, and reflective practices systematically embedded into their weekly timetable. Wearables measured physiological readings both before and after each session, focusing primarily on heart rate stability and electrodermal indicators of sympathetic nervous system activation (Navarro et al., 2024).

Analysis demonstrated that even short mindfulness sessions could significantly decrease physiological arousal among students. Those who initially showed heightened stress every morning recorded gradual stabilization over the program duration. Teachers noted reductions in disruptive behavior, improved classroom cooperation, and increased attentiveness during academically demanding periods (Singh et al., 2024).

Beyond academic hours, students were encouraged to use mindfulness tools available on their wearables' mobile apps, helping them apply calming strategies before homework, study sessions, or competitive events. This extension beyond the classroom was crucial, particularly in cultures where academic pressure is deeply embedded, and students may experience stress not only at school but also within highly structured evening tutoring environments (Li et al., 2025).

Evaluation meetings with parents revealed positive changes at home, with reports of fewer sleep disturbances, better emotional communication, and enhanced motivation. Since wearables provided both students and parents with clear visualization of emotional progress, the mindfulness program became easier to justify as a valuable component of the curriculum rather than an optional wellness activity (Chen et al., 2024).

The success of these programs has encouraged broader national interest in technology-supported emotional learning, positioning schools as environments that nurture mental resilience alongside academic achievement (Navarro et al., 2024).

4.4 Integration with Learning Analytics for Academic Risk Prediction

Some higher-education institutions have begun combining wearable data with digital learning analytics to build predictive models of academic performance and well-being (Li et al., 2025). These systems aggregate information from multiple sources: attendance sensors, learning management systems, online participation metrics, and physiological responses tracked by wearable devices.

By applying machine learning techniques, patterns emerge that indicate early signals of academic struggle. For example, a student whose sleep patterns deteriorate while online activity late at night increases may be experiencing time-management challenges, anxiety, or course overload. Sudden drops in physical movement paired with low engagement in online discussions may signal emotional withdrawal. Through such correlations, the model generates personalized alerts for advisors and enables timely intervention (Singh et al., 2024).

In some cases, the platform sends automated messages directly to students, suggesting available wellness resources, scheduling tools, or academic workshops aligned with their identified needs. This approach fosters self-regulated learning and empowers students to make informed decisions about their well-being (Kumar et al., 2025).

Pilot institutions observed that students who acted upon early recommendations demonstrated improved outcomes on subsequent assessments and reported higher confidence in managing academic demands. Since the data is anonymized at the institutional level, stakeholders can also examine overall trends, helping them redesign course structures to reduce collective stress patterns during peak workload periods (Chen et al., 2024).

This blending of physiological and behavioral data marks a shift toward educational systems that recognize learning as a bio-psycho-social process. It highlights the potential for personalized education models that nurture not only cognitive achievement but also emotional stability (Navarro et al., 2024; Li et al., 2025).

Table 2. Comparison of Wearable-Based Case Studies in Educational Environments

Case Study	Location	Educational Level	Wearable Devices Used	Data Collected	Key Findings	Interventions / Outcomes	References
High School Stress Monitoring Pilot	USA	High School	Smartwatches	Heart rate, HRV, Electrodermal activity	Stress spikes during exams, presentations, and unstructured moments; perfectionistic/high-performing students more affected	Guided breathing, structured breaks, cool-down spaces; reduced stress markers, improved performance consistency, better communication with counselors	Navarro et al., 2024; Bloomfield et al., 2024; Singh et al., 2024; Gomes et al., 2023; Kumar et al., 2025
University Wellness Program	Europe	University	Fitness bands	Sleep duration, physical activity, resting heart rate, HRV	Patterns of insufficient sleep, stress peaks, reduced activity flagged at-risk students	Proactive outreach, counseling, workshops, flexible deadlines, active learning breaks; improved retention, healthier lifestyle decisions	Chen et al., 2024; Li et al., 2025; Navarro et al., 2024; Singh et al., 2024; Gomes et al., 2023
Mindfulness Training in Schools	Asia	K–12	Wearables with HR and EDA tracking	Heart rate stability, electrodermal activity	Mindfulness sessions decreased physiological arousal; improved attentiveness, cooperation, and classroom behavior	Guided meditation, breathing exercises, reflective practices, mobile app support; positive changes at home, emotional progress visualization	Kumar et al., 2025; Navarro et al., 2024; Singh et al., 2024; Li et al., 2025; Chen et al., 2024
Integration with Learning Analytics	Various	Higher Education	Wearables + LMS/attendance sensors	Sleep patterns, physical movement, online engagement metrics, physiological responses	Early signals of academic struggle detected; correlations between low engagement and stress	Personalized alerts, automated wellness guidance, self-regulated learning; improved assessment outcomes, confidence, course redesign for stress reduction	Li et al., 2025; Singh et al., 2024; Kumar et al., 2025; Chen et al., 2024; Navarro et al., 2024

5. ETHICAL, PRIVACY, AND INCLUSIVITY CONSIDERATIONS

The integration of wearable devices into educational environments offers significant potential for enhancing student well-being and academic success. However, it simultaneously raises a spectrum of ethical, privacy, and inclusivity concerns that must be addressed systematically. The collection of physiological, emotional, and behavioral data in real time introduces responsibilities for educational institutions, technology developers, teachers, and policymakers to ensure that students' rights, safety, and dignity are respected.

5.1 Data Privacy and Security

Student biometric and behavioral data collected via wearables is inherently sensitive. Unlike traditional academic performance metrics, physiological indicators—such as heart rate variability, sleep patterns, electrodermal activity, and cognitive workload—reveal intimate aspects of a student's physical and emotional state. Mismanagement or unauthorized access to this data could lead to identity misuse, stigmatization, or discrimination.

To mitigate risks, educational institutions must implement strong technical safeguards. These include encryption of all data at rest and during transmission, anonymization protocols that prevent personal identification during data analysis, and clearly defined access control mechanisms that restrict visibility to authorized personnel only. Data retention policies must also be explicit, specifying the duration for which information is stored, the conditions for deletion, and procedures for audit or oversight.

Moreover, institutions need to regularly evaluate cybersecurity measures against emerging threats. Biometric systems are especially susceptible to breaches due to the personal nature of the data; therefore, multi-layered defense strategies such as secure authentication, intrusion detection, and real-time monitoring of suspicious activities are critical. Policies must also clarify how third-party service providers manage wearable data, ensuring compliance with institutional standards and national regulations.

5.2 Informed Consent

In educational contexts, informed consent represents a central ethical principle for the use of wearable technology. Students, and minors, their parents or guardians, must fully understand what data is being collected, how it will be processed, and the purpose of its use. Consent should be explicit, voluntary, and revocable at any time without penalty.

Informed consent processes should go beyond mere acknowledgment forms. Educational institutions can implement interactive briefings, explanatory videos, or workshops that clearly articulate potential benefits and risks. They should also communicate how data may be integrated with broader institutional analytics or AI-driven predictive systems, ensuring that families understand the scope of monitoring. Transparency fosters trust and encourage active participation, while lack of clarity may lead to skepticism, anxiety, or withdrawal from participation.

Additionally, institutions must ensure that consent is renewed periodically, particularly when the scope of wearable data collection or analysis changes. Dynamic consent frameworks allow students to adjust permissions for specific metrics or applications, maintaining autonomy over personal information. Properly structured informed consent demonstrates respect for student agency and protects institutions against potential legal and ethical conflicts.

5.3 Equity and Inclusivity

The benefits of wearable technologies must be accessible to all students, regardless of socioeconomic status, cultural background, or individual physiological differences. Socioeconomic inequities can prevent some students from accessing devices, which may exacerbate existing disparities in support services. To address this, schools and universities should consider providing devices as part of institutional programs or ensuring funding subsidies for students from underprivileged backgrounds.

Inclusivity also extends to device design and data interpretation. Physiological sensors must be accurate across diverse skin tones, body types, and physical conditions. For example, optical heart rate sensors can sometimes produce biased readings for darker skin tones if the technology is not calibrated inclusively. Similarly, electrodermal sensors and motion trackers must accommodate a range of physiological profiles, recognizing variations in sweat response, movement patterns, and baseline heart rates.

Cultural considerations are equally important. Stress or emotional arousal may manifest differently across cultures or individual experiences. Educational programs should contextualize wearable data within these frameworks, avoiding one-size-fits-all interpretations. Training teachers, counselors, and data analysts on cultural competency ensures that interventions are sensitive, appropriate, and equitable.

5.4 Avoiding a Surveillance Culture

While continuous monitoring provides valuable insight into student well-being, there is a risk that wearable technology could inadvertently contribute to a culture of surveillance. If students perceive that their physiological data is being used to enforce behavioral compliance or penalize underperformance, trust in the educational environment may erode.

To prevent this, institutions must clearly communicate the supportive purpose of wearables. Policies should emphasize that data is intended for mental health and academic guidance, not for punitive measures. Feedback should be framed positively, focusing on skill-building, coping strategies, and personal growth rather than judgment. Transparency regarding who has access to data, under what circumstances, and for what specific purposes reinforces the ethical application of monitoring systems.

Establishing governance structures that include student representatives can also mitigate surveillance concerns. Students' voices in policymaking and monitoring decisions ensure that systems align with their expectations for privacy, agency, and ethical use. Such participatory models help institutions maintain a balance between technological support and student autonomy.

5.5 Human Oversight and AI Ethics

The growing integration of AI-driven analytics with wearable data introduces additional ethical considerations. While predictive models can identify stress patterns or engagement declines with remarkable accuracy, algorithmic outputs should complement rather than replace human judgment. Educators, counselors, and institutional support staff must interpret data contextually, considering the broader social, psychological, and environmental factors affecting each student.

Overreliance on automated systems risks reducing nuanced human experiences to quantitative metrics. For example, a sudden physiological stress spike may not always indicate a mental health concern—it could reflect temporary excitement, illness, or environmental factors. Human oversight ensures that interventions are empathetic, proportionate, and appropriate to the individual's circumstances.

AI systems must also be transparent and explainable. Students and staff should understand how predictions are generated, which variables influence outcomes, and how decisions regarding support are derived. Auditable algorithms, bias mitigation protocols, and periodic validation of AI models against real-world outcomes are necessary to maintain ethical standards.

5.6 Balancing Benefits and Ethical Responsibilities

Successful deployment of wearable devices in education depends on carefully balancing their benefits with ethical obligations. Institutions must implement comprehensive frameworks encompassing privacy, informed consent, inclusivity, non-surveillance, and human oversight. These frameworks should evolve alongside technological advancements, ensuring that ethical guidelines remain relevant as devices become more sophisticated and integrated with AI and learning analytics.

Ongoing education for students, staff, and administrators is essential to promote ethical literacy regarding wearable technology. This includes understanding data ownership, recognizing potential biases, and appreciating the limits of technological interpretation. By fostering awareness and accountability, educational institutions can harness wearable technology in ways that enhance well-being while safeguarding student rights and dignity.

6. FUTURE DIRECTIONS IN EDUCATION-FOCUSED WEARABLES

The evolution of wearable technologies in educational environments continues to open new possibilities for supporting student well-being, engagement, and academic success. Emerging innovations aim not only to track physiological and emotional indicators but also to interpret them in ways that facilitate personalized, proactive, and contextually informed interventions. By integrating wearable data with advanced analytics, machine learning, and institutional frameworks, future developments promise to transform how educators, families, and healthcare providers collectively support student health and learning outcomes. The following directions highlight key areas of advancement and their potential impact on educational ecosystems.

6.1 Multimodal Data Fusion

A major trajectory in wearable research is the fusion of multiple data streams to create comprehensive student well-being profiles. Beyond traditional physiological measurements such as heart rate, heart rate variability, electrodermal activity, sleep patterns, and physical activity, future systems may incorporate facial recognition, voice analysis, and behavioral tracking within digital learning platforms. Facial recognition algorithms can detect micro-expressions indicating stress, frustration, or disengagement during classroom or online activities. Similarly, voice analysis can provide insight into emotional states through speech tone, pace, and inflection, identifying patterns associated with anxiety or fatigue.

By combining these modalities with wearable sensor data, institutions can generate holistic, multidimensional profiles that capture cognitive, emotional, and physical dimensions of learning. Multimodal fusion allows for more accurate detection of stress triggers, engagement lapses, or early signs of mental health concerns. For instance, an increase in heart rate variability accompanied by vocal tension and decreased participation in online discussions could prompt targeted support, whereas isolated physiological changes might not warrant intervention. This fusion approach reduces false positives and improves personalization, enabling timely and contextually appropriate responses from educators and support staff.

6.2 Personalized Interventions

The future of educational wearables emphasizes personalized, AI-driven interventions that respond to each student's unique physiological and behavioral patterns. By analyzing historical and real-time data, machine learning algorithms can recommend individualized strategies such as short mindfulness exercises, timed study breaks, sleep optimization tips, or tailored counseling sessions.

Personalization extends beyond generic wellness advice. For example, a student exhibiting elevated stress during morning classes but stable emotional states later in the day might receive recommendations to rearrange schedules, incorporate brief relaxation periods, or engage in physical activity early in the day. Similarly, a learner showing poor sleep quality correlated with reduced attention span could be guided toward personalized sleep hygiene routines supported by wearable reminders.

These interventions are designed not only to prevent academic burnout but also to foster self-regulation skills. Students can develop insight into how their bodies and minds respond to learning challenges, empowering them to adjust behaviors and optimize study habits. Real-time feedback also reinforces positive coping mechanisms, helping students internalize wellness practices as part of their daily routines rather than viewing them as external requirements.

6.3 Integration with Institutional Policy

To maximize the benefits of wearables, institutions are exploring ways to integrate wearable-driven wellness monitoring into formal policies. Embedding these technologies into school and university frameworks normalizes proactive mental health care and positions well-being as a shared responsibility among educators, administrators, and students.

Institutional integration may include structured schedules for wearable-based monitoring during high-stress periods, formal protocols for analyzing aggregated data, and defined intervention pathways for at-risk students. Policies can also mandate periodic training for educators and support staff in interpreting wearable insights and applying them ethically and effectively. By formalizing these practices, institutions establish clear expectations around data privacy, consent, and responsible use while creating a culture that values prevention over reaction.

Integration with institutional policy also enables scalability. Programs can transition from pilot projects to campus-wide initiatives, ensuring that all students benefit equitably. For example, universities may adopt policies that ensure students have access to wearable devices, provide technical support for usage, and establish guidelines for family involvement in wellness initiatives. Such policy-driven approaches make wearable technologies sustainable, reliable, and ethically aligned with broader educational goals.

6.4 Collaborative Ecosystems

Future educational wearables will operate within collaborative ecosystems that connect multiple stakeholders, including educators, families, and healthcare providers. Shared dashboards can provide authorized stakeholders with anonymized or permission-based access to student well-being data, enabling coordinated support.

In practice, this means that a teacher detecting elevated stress patterns during a learning activity can alert counselors or parents in real time. Similarly, mental health professionals can monitor progress over time and adjust interventions accordingly, while families receive actionable guidance on how to support students outside school. Collaborative ecosystems promote holistic support by reducing fragmentation in student care and ensuring consistent follow-up, while maintaining appropriate privacy protections.

Such ecosystems can also facilitate peer-supported wellness programs. By allowing safe, controlled sharing of insights within peer groups, students can engage in collaborative activities designed to improve mindfulness, study habits, or physical activity. This reinforces a community-oriented approach to mental health, normalizing well-being as a shared responsibility rather than an individual burden.

6.5 Next-Generation Sensors

The development of advanced, non-invasive sensors represents another promising direction. Current wearables primarily track heart rate, HRV, sleep patterns, and movement; however, next-generation sensors can detect biochemical and neurological markers, expanding the scope of insights available to educators and students.

Non-invasive cortisol sensors embedded in wristbands or patches could provide real-time measurements of stress hormone levels, offering objective indicators of acute and chronic stress. Portable EEG wearables designed specifically for classroom or study environments could measure brain activity associated with focus, cognitive load, or mental fatigue. Additionally, emerging photoplethysmography, sweat analysis, and skin conductance sensors are being optimized for accuracy across diverse populations, ensuring reliable readings regardless of physiological differences.

Integration of these sensors would allow for unprecedented granularity in understanding how learning environments and academic tasks affect mental and physical states. Educators could tailor instructional strategies to minimize cognitive overload, optimize engagement, and enhance learning retention, while students receive actionable insights to self-regulate and maintain well-being.

6.6 Expanding Behavioral and Academic Analytics

Future applications of wearables will increasingly link physiological insights with behavioral and academic analytics. Wearables combined with learning management systems, classroom engagement trackers, and digital content usage data can create predictive models for performance, participation, and well-being. For example, a pattern of disrupted sleep and elevated stress during intensive coursework, combined with reduced online participation, may flag potential academic risk.

These predictive analytics can guide interventions at multiple levels, from individual students to institutional planning. Teachers may adapt to instructional pacing; counselors may prioritize support sessions, and administrators may design campus-wide wellness initiatives informed by data trends. By leveraging both physiological and behavioral metrics, institutions can adopt evidence-based strategies for proactive student support and resilience building.

6.7 Adaptive and Context-Aware Feedback

Wearables of the future are expected to deliver adaptive, context-aware feedback. Systems will account for environmental factors such as classroom noise, lighting, or temperature, and adjust recommendations accordingly. For instance, if elevated stress is detected during a noisy classroom session, the wearable could suggest a short breathing exercise or redirect the student to a quieter study area.

Such feedback loops create personalized learning and wellness experiences, ensuring that interventions are relevant to the immediate context. They also reduce the risk of misinterpretation, as physiological indicators are evaluated alongside situational factors, enhancing the accuracy and usefulness of wearable-driven insights.

6.8 Global Scalability and Accessibility

Finally, the future of educational wearables emphasizes scalability and accessibility. Cost reductions, standardized devices, and open-source analytical platforms could make these technologies viable across schools and universities in diverse geographic and economic settings. Scalable programs ensure that well-being support does not remain a privilege for high-resource institutions but becomes an integral part of education globally.

Accessible designs include adjustable device form factors, multilingual software interfaces, and accommodations for students with disabilities. Ensuring inclusivity in the next generation of wearables is essential for equitable distribution of benefits and the creation of supportive learning environments for all students.

7. LIMITATIONS IN CURRENT RESEARCH

While wearable technologies show promising potential for supporting student's well-being in educational environments, current research faces several limitations. Existing studies are often fragmented, with small sample sizes, short monitoring periods, and limited replication across diverse academic contexts. Much of the evidence relies on isolated physiological signals such as heart rate or electrodermal activity, with relatively few multimodal fusion studies that combine behavioral, cognitive, and environmental data for more accurate well-being assessment. Ethical frameworks also lack standardization; data privacy, consent procedures, and governance practices vary widely across institutions, making it difficult to implement large-scale deployments. Additionally, many studies use consumer-grade wearables that were not originally designed for clinical or educational use, which may impact data accuracy and interpretation. Finally, wearable technologies should be regarded as supportive tools offering timely insights—not diagnostic devices capable of formally identifying mental health conditions. Addressing these challenges will be essential for developing reliable, equitable, and ethically grounded applications of wearables in education.

8. CONCLUSION

Wearable devices hold transformative potential for the educational sector, offering unprecedented opportunities to monitor and support student well-being in real time. Unlike traditional approaches that rely primarily on periodic surveys, counseling sessions, or teacher observations, wearables provide continuous and objective insight into students' emotional, physiological, and cognitive states. By capturing metrics such as heart rate variability, electrodermal activity, sleep patterns, and movement, these technologies allow educators and support staff to detect early signs of stress, anxiety, and academic burnout. This capability facilitates timely and targeted interventions, shifting student support from reactive to proactive models, and helping to prevent the escalation of mental health challenges before they adversely affect academic performance.

Beyond detection, wearables also empower students by fostering self-awareness and self-regulation. Access to real-time feedback encourages learners to observe patterns in their own stress levels, sleep quality, and activity cycles, enabling them to make informed adjustments to study routines, lifestyle habits, and coping strategies. By promoting mindfulness, structured breaks, and reflective practices, wearable devices support the development of resilience—a skill that extends beyond the classroom and contributes to long-term personal and professional growth. The combination of student agency with educator guidance creates a collaborative environment in which mental health and learning outcomes are mutually reinforced.

In addition to individual benefits, wearables facilitate data-driven institutional decision-making. Aggregated, anonymized insights help administrators identify systemic stressors within classrooms, curricula, or campus environments, allowing for policy adjustments, scheduling reforms, or wellness program implementation. Predictive models that integrate wearable data with learning analytics further enhance institutional capacity to support at-risk students, optimize teaching strategies, and improve overall educational effectiveness. The strategic use of these technologies' positions educational institutions as proactive agents of well-being, capable of balancing academic rigor with holistic student care.

However, the benefits of wearable devices are contingent upon responsible and ethical adoption. Privacy concerns remain paramount, as the collection of sensitive biometric and emotional data introduces risks related to unauthorized access, misuse, or stigmatization. Ensuring informed consent, robust encryption, anonymization protocols, and strict access controls is essential to safeguard students' rights. Equitable access to wearable technologies is another critical consideration. Programs must be designed to include students across socioeconomic, cultural, and physiological differences, ensuring that no learner is excluded from the potential benefits of technology-supported wellness initiatives. Ethical frameworks must also guide the interpretation and use of data, avoid a culture of surveillance or punitive monitoring, and emphasize human oversight to contextualize insights with empathy and professional judgment.

Looking forward, the integration of wearable devices into educational systems offers a pathway toward more personalized, data-informed, and preventive approaches to student mental health. When implemented thoughtfully, wearables can bridge the traditional gap between academic performance and emotional well-being, fostering environments where students are not only academically competent but also psychologically resilient. By embedding wearable technologies into institutional policies, training educators in data-informed intervention, and promoting inclusive access, schools and universities can establish a sustainable model for supporting student well-being. Ultimately, wearable devices are not just tools for monitoring; they represent a fundamental shift toward a holistic, student-centered educational paradigm that values both achievement and mental health as interconnected dimensions of success.

REFERENCES

Abd-alrazaq, A., Alajlani, M., Ahmad, R., AlSaad, R., Aziz, S., Ahmed, A., Alsahli, M., Damseh, R., & Sheikh, J. (2024). The performance of wearable AI in detecting stress among students: Systematic review and meta-analysis. *Journal of Medical Internet Research, 26*(1), e52622. DOI: 10.2196/52622 PMID: 38294846

Amin, O. B., Mishra, V., Tapera, T. M., Volpe, R., & Sathyanarayana, A. (2025). Extending stress detection reproducibility to consumer wearable sensors. *arXiv*. / arXiv.2505.05694DOI: 10.1109/EMBC58623.2025.11252853

Arnold, C., & Young, D. (2025). Wearable technology for student well-being: A pilot study in higher education. *Journal of Educational Technology, 21*(2), 45–61. DOI: 10.1016/j.jedutech.2025.01.003

Bloomfield, J., Koster, E., Li, H., & Patel, R. (2024). Wearable sensors for stress and cognitive workload in students: Evidence from classroom deployments. *Frontiers in Behavioral Neuroscience, 18*, 110223. DOI: 10.3389/fnbeh.2024.110223

Chen, M., Ma, Y., Li, Y., Wu, D., Zhang, Y., & Youn, C. H. (2024). Wearable sensors and AI-based monitoring for student mental health in classroom settings: A review. *IEEE Access : Practical Innovations, Open Solutions, 12*, 34567–34583. DOI: 10.1109/ACCESS.2024.3456789

Dias, A., Mikkelsen, S., & Schou, M. (2024). Wearable neurofeedback acceptance model for students' stress and anxiety management in academic settings (mSense). *Behavioral Sciences*. https://pubmed.ncbi.nlm.nih.gov/39446926/

Glasserman-Morales, D., Carlos-Arroyo, R., Ruiz-Ramirez, R., & Alcantar-Nieblas, M. (2023). Real-time stress monitoring in educational settings using wearable technology. *Sensory Systems, 12*(4), 231–248. DOI: 10.3390/systems12040231

Gomes, F., Pato, L., Lourenço, J., & Datia, N. (2023). Multi-sensor wearables for student mental health: Opportunities and challenges. *International Journal of Human-Computer Interaction, 39*(12), 1234–1250. DOI: 10.1080/10447318.2023.2198741

Gomes, P., Pato, R., Lourenço, A., & Datia, V. (2023). *Wearable biosensors for enhancing student well-being and engagement: Insights from global case studies*. PubMed Central. https://pubmed.ncbi.nlm.nih.gov/38676053/

He, L., Chen, Y., Wang, W., He, S., & Hu, X. (2024). Wearable device-based real-time monitoring of physiological signals: Evaluating cognitive load across different tasks. *arXiv*. https://doi.org//arXiv.2406.07147DOI: 10.48550

Kumar, R., Singh, P., & Agarwal, S. (2025). Implementing wearable technology for student stress tracking and engagement in higher education: Case insights. *Education and Information Technologies*, *30*, 1021–1045. DOI: 10.1007/s10639-025-11500-x

Leuzzi, G., Job, M., Scafoglieri, A., & Testa, M. (2025). Smartphone apps and wearables for health parameters in young adulthood: Cross-sectional study. *JMIR Human Factors*, *12*, e64629. DOI: 10.2196/64629 PMID: 40902119

Li, X., Zhang, Y., & Wang, L. (2025). Physiological and behavioral monitoring of students using wearables for personalized learning interventions. *Computers & Education*, *208*, 104379. DOI: 10.1016/j.compedu.2024.104379

Mitra, U., & Rehman, S. U. (2025a). Significance of AI/ML Wearable Technologies for Education and Teaching. In *Wearable Devices and Smart Technology for Educational Teaching Assistance* (pp. 1–26). IGI Global Scientific Publishing.

Mitra, U., & Rehman, S. U. (2025b). Integrating AI/ML With Wearable Devices for Monitoring Student Mental Health. In Wearable Devices and Smart Technology for Educational Teaching Assistance (pp. 257-284). IGI Global Scientific Publishing. Integrating AI/ML With Wearable Devices for Monitoring Student Mental Health. In Wearable Devices and Smart Technology for Educational Teaching Assistance (pp. 257-284). IGI Global Scientific Publishing.

Navarro, A., Ortega, M., & López, J. (2024). Smartwatch-based monitoring of stress and attention in secondary school students: Implications for educational strategies. *Journal of Learning Analytics*, *11*(3), 56–73. DOI: 10.18608/jla.2024.1134

Neigel, P., Vargo, A., Tag, B., & Kise, K. (2024). Identifying periods of cyclical stress in university students using wearables in-the-wild. *arXiv*. https://doi.org//arXiv.2402.11823DOI: 10.48550

O'Leary, A., Lahey, T., Lovato, J., Loftness, B., Douglas, A., Skelton, J., Cohen, J. G., Copeland, W. E., McGinnis, R. S., & McGinnis, E. W. (2024). Using wearable digital devices to screen children for mental health conditions: Ethical promises and challenges. *Sensors (Basel)*, *24*(10), 3214. DOI: 10.3390/s24103214 PMID: 38794067

Pinge, A., Gad, V., Jaisighani, D., Ghosh, S., & Sen, S. (2024). Detection and monitoring of stress using wearables: A systematic review. *Frontiers of Computer Science*, *6*, 1478851. Advance online publication. DOI: 10.3389/fcomp.2024.1478851

Razavi, M., McDonald, A., Mehta, R., & Sasangohar, F. (2023). Evaluating mental stress among college students using heart rate and hand acceleration data collected from wearable sensors. *arXiv*. https://doi.org//arXiv.2309.11097DOI: 10.48550

Singh, D., Mehta, R., & Choudhary, A. (2024). Integrating wearable devices and predictive analytics for academic risk management in universities. *Interactive Learning Environments, 32*(7), 1020–1038. DOI: 10.1080/10494820.2024.2345678

Ta, A., Salgin, N., Demir, M., Randal, K. P., Mehta, R. K., McDonald, A., McCord, C., & Sasangohar, F. (2025). Real-time stress monitoring, detection, and management in college students: A wearable technology and machine-learning approach. *arXiv*. https://doi.org//arXiv.2505.15974DOI: 10.48550

Wang, Y., & Liu, H. (2025). *Using physiological measures to enhance learning and engagement in digital classrooms: A conference study*. SCITEPRESS – Science and Technology Publications, 134384. https://www.scitepress.org/Papers/2025/134384/134384.pdf

Chapter 10
Virtual Counselling and Teletherapy Platforms for Students and Educators

Pranati Rakshit
https://orcid.org/0000-0001-5037-1326
Tarakeswar Degree College, India

Alafia Rashid
https://orcid.org/0009-0004-9342-6875
JIS College of Engineering, India

Debasish Saha Roy
JIS College of Engineering, India

Subhajit Saha
JIS College of Engineering, India

Sabyasachi Pramanik
https://orcid.org/0000-0002-9431-8751
Haldia Institute of Technology, India

ABSTRACT

In recent years, educational institutions have undergone a digital transformation, shifting from traditional classrooms to hybrid and fully online learning environments. Alongside this, mental health challenges among students and educators have become more visible. This chapter explores how virtual counselling and teletherapy platforms address these issues, focusing on digital mental health solutions integrated into education. It covers tools ranging from AI-powered chatbots for instant support to professional video therapy for personalized care. Key benefits include

DOI: 10.4018/979-8-3373-5007-3.ch010

accessibility, flexibility, and scalability, while challenges involve privacy, technological barriers, and therapeutic effectiveness. Through real-world examples and case studies, successful implementations are highlighted. The chapter concludes with practical strategies for broader adoption, emphasizing digital mental health solutions as compassionate extensions of the educational ecosystem that support well-being and resilience in modern education.

1 INTRODUCTION

The mental health landscape in educational institutions has changed significantly over the past decade. Children today operate in a more complex educational environment than ever before.

They are constantly under pressure to perform well, trying to keep up with a rapidly changing curriculum, and often juggling multiple responsibilities beyond schoolwork. Teachers are also impacted by increased workloads, digital surveillance, and expectations of 24/7 availability, especially during online classes. In India alone, data from the National Crime Records Bureau (2022) reveals alarming rates of student suicide (over 13,000 cases in 2021), highlighting the urgent need for intervention. Globally, organizations like the World Health Organization (WHO) are concerned about adolescents and young adults and consider depression one of the top health concerns. Educational institutions can no longer view mental health as a secondary concern. Rather, it is an academic issue. Emotional health directly impacts student engagement, attendance, cognitive performance, and faculty morale (Patel et al., 2018). Before the advent of virtual tools, educational counselling services were limited, and those that were available were considered infrequent and often stigmatized.

The COVID-19 pandemic proved to be a turning point. Almost overnight, the world shifted to online education, bringing to light both the possibilities and limitations of digital education. While students have adjusted to a multitude of video lectures, online exams, and self-paced learning, the emotional burden is rapidly increasing. Loneliness, anxiety about the future, the pressure to avoid becoming a burden on the family, and the exhaustion of staring at screens have increased mental health concerns for children, leading institutions to begin exploring virtual mental health services not only as temporary answers, but also as long-term solutions (Li, H., Zhang et al. 2023).

Loneliness, uncertainty about the future, family pressures, and screen fatigue led to a surge in mental health concerns. As a result, institutions began exploring virtual mental health services not only as temporary fixes but as long-term solutions (Singh et al., 2020). Platforms offering confidential counselling, peer support, and mental wellness apps became integral to education systems, especially in higher education and international schools.

The purpose of this chapter is to examine the rise of counselling and teletherapy platforms in educational contexts (McBain et al., 2023). It aims to explain how digital technologies and mental health support are transforming access for children, their benefits, whether they present ethical challenges, and how institutions can integrate them sustainably.

This chapter also reviews new platforms, presents real-world case studies, and identifies policy-level changes needed to mainstream virtual mental health into educational environments.

Emotional health directly impacts student engagement, attendance, cognitive performance, and faculty morale. Before the advent of virtual tools, educational counselling services were limited, and those that were available were considered infrequent and often stigmatized.

The COVID-19 pandemic proved to be a turning point. Almost overnight, the world shifted to online education, bringing to light both the possibilities and limitations of digital education. While students have adjusted to a multitude of video lectures, online exams, and self-paced learning, the emotional burden is rapidly increasing. Loneliness, anxiety about the future, the pressure to avoid becoming a burden on the family, and the exhaustion of staring at screens have increased mental health concerns for children, leading institutions to begin exploring virtual mental health services not only as temporary answers, but also as long-term solutions.

Loneliness, uncertainty about the future, family pressures, and screen fatigue led to a surge in mental health concerns. As a result, institutions began exploring virtual mental health services not only as temporary fixes but as long-term solutions. Platforms offering confidential counselling, peer support, and mental wellness apps became integral to education systems, especially in higher education and international schools (Arora & Srinivasan, 2021).

The purpose of this chapter is to examine the rise of counselling and teletherapy platforms in educational contexts. It aims to explain how digital technologies and mental health support are transforming access for children, their benefits, whether they present ethical challenges, and how institutions can integrate them sustainably.

This chapter also reviews new platforms, presents real-world case studies, and identifies policy-level changes needed to mainstream virtual mental health into educational environments.

This chapter is organised into several key sections. Section 2 provides a conceptual overview of virtual counselling and teletherapy, including their evolution and relevance in modern education. Section 3 discusses the major benefits and challenges associated with these platforms, while Section 4 highlights popular tools and global practices shaping digital mental-health support (Bryant et al., 2024).

Section 5 examines critical ethical and privacy considerations. Section 6 presents case studies from schools and universities, and Section 7 offers practical strategies for integrating virtual mental-health services into educational ecosystems. Finally, Section 8 summarises key recommendations and outlines future directions for research, policy, and practice.

2 UNDERSTANDING VIRTUAL COUNSELLING AND TELETHERAPY

Virtual counselling and teletherapy use digital communication technologies to provide psychological and emotional support. Although these terms are often used interchangeably, they encompass many different approaches to care (Andersson, 2018; Hollis et al., 2015).

2.1 Defining Virtual Counselling and Teletherapy in Educational Contexts

Virtual counselling typically involves emotional and academic guidance provided to children by trained professionals via online platforms. These can be short-term, goal-oriented sessions that can be facilitated by school counsellors, academic advisors, or peers (Sucala et al., 2012).

Teletherapy, on the other hand, involves long-term psychological treatment provided by licensed therapists or clinical psychologists, typically via video conferencing, secure messaging, or telephonic consultations.

Both forms are part of the broader field of e-mental health, which integrates psychological innovation with technological innovation to make mental health care accessible, scalable, and non-stigmatizing (Andersson, 2018).

2.2 Historical Perspective: From Telephone Hotlines to AI-Based Apps

Digital mental health support is not a new idea. Its roots can be traced back to telephone helplines and support services in the late 20th century. These were primarily used for crisis intervention, such as suicide prevention (Mishara et al., 2007).

Over time, as internet access became more widespread, platforms began offering live chat support, forums, and asynchronous email consultations.

The real breakthrough came with the advent of smartphones, cloud computing, and mobile applications (Hollis et al., 2015).

Today, teletherapy has evolved to include:

- Real-time video therapy
- AI-driven chatbot support
- Guided mindfulness and meditation programs
- Online group therapy
- Crisis text lines (Inkster et al., 2018)

The education sector has adopted these services with growing urgency, especially post-pandemic, where the boundaries between learning, living, and healing have merged (Singh et al., 2020).

2.3 Key Components and Modalities

Modern virtual mental health platforms typically consist of the following components:

a. **Secure Communication Channels:** Encryption protocols ensure privacy during video calls, messages, and file sharing.
b. **Multimodal Access:** Services are available across devices—desktop, tablets, and smartphones.
c. **User Profiling:** Based on student needs (e.g., anxiety, academic burnout, bullying), the system may recommend tailored resources or match users to therapists.
d. **Assessment Tools:** Many platforms provide screening tests (e.g., GAD-7 for anxiety, PHQ-9 for depression) to gauge mental health status.
e. **Progress Tracking:** Tools like digital journals, mood charts, and habit trackers help users reflect on and measure progress over time.
f. **Content Libraries:** Tools like short videos, podcasts, reading materials, and more, including health tips, are built into the platform to form part of a self-help toolkit.

These tools are built by a multidisciplinary backend team consisting of psychologists, data scientists, software developers, and user experience designers (Karyotaki et al., 2019).

2.4 Modes of Delivery

Virtual counselling and teletherapy are offered in several different ways:

- **Synchronous (Real-Time)**

This involves live video/audio sessions, similar to traditional therapy, but conducted on a platform like Zoom, Better Help, or Your Dost.

- **Asynchronous**

This is due to the delay in communication—clients can send messages or journal entries, and the therapist responds later. Some platforms, such as 7 Cups of Tea or Talk space, commonly use this approach.

- **AI and Chatbot-Supported**

Platforms like Wysa and Woebot simulate conversational support using Artificial Intelligence, providing coping tools and mood tracking without human intervention.

- **Blended Models**

It Combines human and AI assistance, often used for priority assessment, where a bot assesses the emergency and, if necessary, connects the user to a live clinician.

Each model has its own advantages and disadvantages. For example, asynchronous formats offer flexibility, but they can also delay crisis response. AI chatbots provide 24/7 support, but they lack emotional nuance and cannot replace humans.

2.5 Regulatory and Ethical Considerations

It is important to note that mental health counselling—even when done virtually—requires adherence to ethical guidelines and licensure regulations. Professionals offering teletherapy must be trained in online confidentiality practices, cultural sensitivity, and digital consent protocols.

In India, platforms must comply with the Information Technology (Reasonable Security Practices and Procedures and Sensitive Personal Data or Information) Rules, 2011. Globally, compliance with HIPAA (US) or GDPR (Europe) is mandatory for international student support services.

Additionally, ethical counselling requires:

- Full disclosure of platform limitations
- Consent from users (or parents/guardians for minors)
- Emergency protocols for high-risk users
- Transparency about the use of data (especially in AI-based systems)

Failure to meet these standards can lead to breaches of trust, legal complications, and reputational damage to educational institutions.

2.6 Digital Literacy and Platform Adoption

Another factor influencing the success of virtual counselling systems is the digital readiness of students and faculty. Digital literacy affects:

- Comfort with using the platform
- Willingness to engage with mental health content
- Understanding the difference between informal advice and licensed therapy

Institutions are encouraged to incorporate basic digital counselling orientation into student onboarding and staff training programs

This ensures that users can differentiate between peer-led support, automated advice, and professional help.

3 BENEFITS FOR STUDENTS AND EDUCATORS

The incorporation of virtual counselling and teletherapy platforms into educational systems offers numerous benefits—ranging from logistical convenience to profound improvements in emotional well-being, academic performance, and institutional culture.

These benefits are not limited to students alone; educators, administrative staff, and even parents can gain from these advancements.

3.1 Flexible Access to Support

Perhaps the most obvious advantage of most virtual platforms is that they're available outside of traditional office hours. Academic life doesn't adhere to a 9-to-5 schedule, students can experience significant stress late at night, on weekends, or while traveling. And teachers often feel emotionally and physically exhausted after long days managing classrooms, preparing lessons, and completing administrative duties.

With these tools:

- A student dealing with pre-exam anxiety can access immediate support at midnight.

- An educator experiencing burnout can speak to a professional on a Sunday evening.
- Working students or part-time learners can schedule sessions without skipping classes.

This time-and-location flexibility ensures that psychological help is not postponed due to inconvenient timing or travel limitations.

3.2 Reduced Stigma and Improved Engagement

In many cultures, including parts of India, seeking mental health help is still considered a social stigma. I've witnessed this myself. Students often fear criticism from classmates, parents, and even faculty members. Teachers worry that seeking help will be perceived as a sign of weakness or incompetence. That's why virtual counselling offers a safe, private, and stigma-free environment

- No waiting rooms or face-to-face meetings
- Anonymous messaging is available
- Confidential access, even from personal devices.

This anonymity promotes early intervention, allowing help to be sought before a crisis escalates. A 2022 study in the Indian Journal of Psychiatry found that college students were 2.3 times more likely to access mental health services through online platforms compared to in-person sessions.

3.3 Customization and Continuity of Care

Unlike traditional systems, digital platforms adapt to the unique needs of users:

- Students can input their age, course load, emotional history, or daily stressors.
- Educators can flag work-life imbalance, teaching-related anxiety, or digital fatigue.
- Based on this information, platforms offer personalized recommendations:
- Therapy plans tailored to the academic calendar
- Mood tracking features that suggest content based on emotional patterns
- Follow-ups from the same therapist, ensuring continuity and building trust

Furthermore, many platforms use machine learning algorithms to refine care over time—learning user preferences, session history, and engagement levels to suggest more accurate interventions.

3.4 Enhanced Academic Performance and Cognitive Functioning

Emotional distress directly impacts memory, concentration, and critical thinking. By providing students and educators with tools to manage their stress, institutions indirectly enhance learning outcomes.

Numerous studies confirm this link. For instance:

- A University of Michigan study found that students who used on-campus teletherapy tools reported a 17% improvement in GPA.
- Faculty members who engaged in bi-weekly mindfulness sessions via online programs reported decreased irritability and increased patience during class interactions.

In short, mental clarity contributes to academic excellence. A calm, focused mind absorbs and applies knowledge more efficiently.

3.5 Peer Support and Community Building

Several platforms incorporate peer-led support groups where students or educators can connect over shared challenges, such as test anxiety, imposter syndrome, or staff-parent conflicts.

These digital communities:

- Create a sense of belonging
- Reduce isolation
- Enable empathy-driven problem-solving

With moderation by professionals, peer forums provide semi-structured emotional relief without replacing clinical therapy.

Examples include:

- IIT Bombay's "Let's Talk" online forum, where students discuss academic pressure under the guidance of senior peers.
- YourDOST's "Campus Champions" who act as on-ground mental health ambassadors trained to guide others toward professional help.

3.6 Crisis Monitoring and Well-being Extensions

Virtual platforms allow for early detection of emotional crises.
For instance:

- If a user fails multiple mood check-ins, the platform may alert the counselor.
- Suicidal keywords in journaling apps can trigger an emergency intervention.
- Educators can monitor classroom sentiment (using optional emotion-sensing software) to adjust teaching pace or approach.

Such real-time responsiveness is rare in traditional systems, where crises are often detected too late.

Teacher and Staff Wellbeing

Teachers face high levels of stress due to long working hours, online class fatigue, student behavioral issues, and administrative pressures.
Virtual therapy helps by:

- Offering reflective spaces to process emotional labor
- Helping educators set boundaries between work and home life
- Equipping them with skills like mindfulness, emotional regulation, and digital detoxing

Inclusive Mental Health Services for Diverse Learners

Today's classrooms are diverse—students differ in learning styles, emotional needs, and socio-cultural backgrounds.
Virtual platforms:

- Offer multilingual interfaces (English, Hindi, Bengali, etc.)
- Include content tailored for neurodivergent students (e.g., those with ADHD or ASD)
- Accommodate visual or hearing impairments through subtitles, text-to-speech, and screen-readers

Such inclusion ensures equity in emotional wellness, aligning with global goals like the UN's Sustainable Development Goal 3: Good Health and Well-Being.

4 TYPES OF PLATFORMS AND TOOLS USED IN EDUCATIONAL SETTINGS

As digital mental health becomes a cornerstone of educational well-being, institutions are choosing from a wide range of technological tools (Plessen et al., 2024). These range from globally recognized therapy platforms to private, sector-specific, and culturally tailored apps, and even in-house solutions developed by universities themselves.

This section explores the variety and functionality of these tools, their suitability for different education levels, and how they work in practice.

4.1 Institutional Partnerships with Licensed Therapy Providers

Many educational institutions, especially at the university level, collaborate with professional mental health service providers. These partnerships provide both students and staff with safe access to licensed counsellors, psychologists, and therapists, often at discounted rates.

Prominent Examples:

- **YourDOST (India):**

It is a popular mental health platform that provides confidential support via chat, audio, and video. It partners with over 250 Indian institutions, including IITs and IIMs, giving students access to verified therapists.

- **Talkspace (USA):**

It provides therapy via text, audio, and video, allowing users to message their personal therapist at any time. Many American universities include Talkspace in their student support programs.

- **BetterHelp (Global):**

Known for its global reach, BetterHelp connects students with therapists based on individual assessments. Universities with diverse international student populations may find it useful due to its multilingual options and multicultural therapist pool.

- **Manastha (India):**

Specializes in therapy for youth, using culturally sensitive approaches. Their team includes psychologists fluent in regional Indian languages, making them ideal for rural or vernacular institutions.

These platforms are usually embedded into student dashboards or learning management systems (LMS). Once signed in with a university ID, users can access a range of features—self-assessment tools, live sessions, resource libraries, and crisis helplines.

4.2 In-House Virtual Support Systems

Some institutions prefer to design and operate their own virtual mental health support networks. These may include:

- **Campus Portals:**

Where students can book appointments with the university's in-house psychologist or wellness officer.

- **Email-Based Support Lines:**

For students who prefer asynchronous help. For example, the University of Delhi launched a 'psychological support email line' during the pandemic.

- **Peer-Led Chat Rooms:**

Trained peer mentors host moderated group discussions or one-on-one emotional support sessions via platforms like Google Meet, Zoom, or Discord.

- **Student Mobile Apps:**

Apps built in collaboration with tech departments—offering self-help exercises, motivational quotes, and feedback forms.

Advantages of In-House Systems:

- Local understanding of student issues
- Integration with academic calendars (e.g., support before exams)
- Face-to-face referrals when required
- Often free and customized

Limitations:

- Capacity issues (one counsellor per 1,000 students is common)
- Possible conflicts of interest or concerns about anonymity
- Lack of 24/7 availability

4.3 Role of AI and Chatbots in Mental Wellness

Artificial Intelligence is revolutionizing how institutions provide round-the-clock, scalable, and judgment-free support. AI-based chatbots simulate human conversation and provide basic emotional first-aid.

Leading AI Tools:

Wysa:

An Indian-developed emotional wellness chatbot using evidence-based techniques such as CBT, DBT, and mindfulness. It also offers human coaching as a premium add-on.

Woebot:

Developed at Stanford University, Woebot is a U.S.-based chatbot that combines conversational AI with psychological tools. It's friendly, non-clinical in tone, and well-suited for young users.

Replika:

Though not originally a therapy tool, many use Replika for emotional companionship and casual support.

How It Works:

- Users initiate chats when feeling low, anxious, or confused.
- The AI identifies emotional keywords (e.g., "lonely," "panic," "failure") and responds with prompts like breathing exercises, journaling, or reframing thoughts.
- Severe cases are redirected to human professionals.

Advantages:

- Instant availability, 24/7
- Zero stigma
- Low cost or freemium model

- Emotion tracking over time

Caveats:

- Cannot replace licensed therapy
- May miss nuanced emotional cues
- Ethical issues around data storage and transparency

4.4 Comparative Analysis of Available Tools

This comparative breakdown (Table 1) helps institutions select platforms based on student demographics, budget, language needs, and scalability.

Table 1. Comparative Analysis

Platform/Tool	Type	Target User	Notable Features	Access Type
YourDOST	Live Therapy + Peer Support	Students, Faculty	Indian languages, academic tie-ups	Institutional
Talkspace	Licensed Therapy	University Students	24/7 messaging + therapist switch	Institutional/ Private
Wysa	AI Chatbot + Coaching	Youth & Educators	CBT tools, mood tracking	Freemium
In-House Portal	Custom	Students only	Appointments, referrals, events	Free/On-Campus
Woebot	AI Chatbot	Gen Z, Global users	Stanford-backed, casual tone	Free
Replika	AI Companion	General	Relationship simulation	Subscription

4.5 Gamified and Wellness-Integrated Apps

A new wave of mental health tools is blending therapy with gamification and wellness lifestyles:

Happify: Users complete daily games that improve emotional intelligence.

Mindhouse (India): Offers yoga, meditation, and sleep modules in a structured curriculum.

Calm & Headspace: Used widely in schools to introduce meditation, especially for children.

These platforms are not substitutes for therapy but act as supplementary tools to build emotional resilience and prevent burnout.

5 CHALLENGES AND ETHICAL CONSIDERATIONS

Virtual counselling and teletherapy platforms are offering educational and transformative health possibilities. But many challenges lie ahead.

These challenges are not only technical or operational, but also have profound implications for ethics, privacy, inclusivity, and human psychology. These challenges require sustainable, equitable, and reliable solutions.

5.1 Data Privacy and Confidentiality

Data sensitivity is one of the most serious concerns regarding digital mental health services. Whenever students or teachers use virtual counselling platforms, they share intimate information such as anxieties, trauma, various behavioural issues, and sometimes even suicidal thoughts.

The collection, access, and management of this information on the app must be in accordance with strict privacy protocols.

Risks include:

- Third party Unauthorized access
- Hacking or data breaches
- Meta data misuse (for emotional marketing)
- Surveillance, if consent is not given. (e.g., emotion AI tools in classrooms)

Legal Frameworks:

India: IT Rules 2021 and Data Protection Bill (pending implementation) mandate informed consent and data minimization but lack sector-specific clarity for education and mental health.

United States: HIPAA governs how health data is handled but may not apply to wellness apps that do not use licensed professionals.

Europe: GDPR offers the most stringent protections, emphasizing user rights to access, modify, or delete data.

Best Practices:

- End-to-end encryption
- User authentication (OTP, biometric)
- Transparent terms of use and consent forms
- Regular security audits
- Role-based access control for counsellors

Institutions must ensure that platform partners comply with national and international standards. Where in-house systems are used, Data Protection Officers (DPOs) should be designated.

5.2 Building Trust in a Virtual Environment

Emotional vulnerability requires trust. In face-to-face therapy, this is built through body language, tone of voice, facial expressions, and physical presence.

However, screens dilute human warmth, often leading to hesitation, disconnection, or even dropouts.

Trust issues in digital therapy:

- Students unsure whether the other person is a licensed therapist
- Concern about being judged or misinterpreted in typed chats
- Abrupt changes in counsellors or delayed responses in asynchronous models
- Use of bots in place of humans without clear disclosure

Solutions to build trust:

- Display therapist credentials and training
- Allow users to choose or stay with a preferred counsellor
- Use video over chat when possible to enhance presence
- Be transparent when AI is involved: "You are now chatting with Wysa, a bot designed to support you."

For educators, trust may also depend on institutional backing. If the administration does not openly promote the platform or take privacy seriously, teachers are unlikely to engage.

5.3 Digital Divide and Accessibility Barriers

The assumption that "everyone is online" is misleading. Many students—especially in rural, tribal, or lower-income communities—face significant hurdles in accessing virtual therapy

Barriers include:

- Poor or no internet connectivity
- Lack of personal devices (mobile or laptop)
- Shared family devices, reducing privacy
- Low digital literacy (navigating apps, using email)

- Language barriers and interface complexity
- Disability exclusion (lack of screen-reader or closed-captioning support)

Equity Solutions:

- Offline modes (SMS-based support, recorded audios)
- Regional language versions of apps
- Institutional device lending programs (e.g., tablet banks)
- Accessibility testing (for dyslexia, ADHD, color blindness)
- Collaborations with NGOs for last-mile access

Case in Point:
A mental wellness initiative in Assam included phone-based audio sessions for students without smartphones. In contrast, many elite urban schools offered Zoom-based therapy only—showing a digital privilege gap.

5.4 Quality Control and Regulation of Counselling Services

The rise of digital platforms has also led to unregulated "mental health influencers", "life coaches," and uncertified counsellors promoting advice through apps or YouTube videos. While motivational, these often lack scientific basis and can cause harm.

Red Flags in Poor-Quality Platforms:

- No therapist credentials listed
- Generalized advice for complex problems
- Pseudoscientific practices (e.g., "manifestation cures depression")
- Monetization through user vulnerability (ads, upselling services)

Regulatory Needs:

- National accreditation boards for digital therapy providers
- Ethical guidelines for e-counselling in education
- Complaint redressal mechanisms for users
- Oversight from mental health professionals and academic institutions

Without regulation, the mental health space risks becoming exploitative, especially toward confused, vulnerable youth.

5.5 Therapist Burnout and Platform Sustainability

It's important to remember that therapists themselves are human. In digital systems where they may be handling back-to-back video calls, thousands of messages, or emotionally heavy conversations without a break, emotional fatigue is real.

Consequences:

- Reduced empathy or detachment during sessions
- Higher turnover in staff (inconsistent care)
- Misdiagnosis or burnout-related mistakes

Sustainability Measures:

- Platform-imposed limits on daily cases per therapist
- Built-in debriefing or peer-support systems for counsellors
- Automated scheduling to allow recovery time
- Emotional wellness tools for professionals

This also links to platform economics—many apps underpay therapists or push "gig-style" work models. Institutional ethics must extend to providers, not just users.

5.6 Cultural Appropriateness and Societal Resistance

Cultural taboos still play a role in shaping how therapy is received. For example, many Indian families discourage discussing mental health openly, especially topics like gender dysphoria, suicidal ideation, or sexual trauma.

Platform limitations:

- Generic, Westernized content that doesn't resonate locally
- Language that avoids religious or familial contexts
- Counsellors unfamiliar with cultural triggers (e.g., caste-based bullying)

Addressing Cultural Gaps:

- Hire diverse therapists from multiple socio-cultural backgrounds
- Include culturally nuanced examples and metaphors in therapy
- Allow community elders or spiritual mentors to be consulted (if the user desires)

6 CASE STUDIES AND INSTITUTIONAL PRACTICES

To understand the practical applications and real-world impact of virtual counselling and teletherapy platforms, it is essential to examine how different educational institutions have adopted and implemented these systems. The following case studies present diverse models from schools, universities, and global digital initiatives. Together, they illustrate how virtual mental-health support varies across contexts—ranging from structured university-led teletherapy programmes to school-based wellness interventions and international digital counselling frameworks. By comparing these examples, we can identify patterns in effectiveness, challenges, and best practices that are relevant for developing stronger and more inclusive mental-health support systems in education.

6.1 University-Based Initiatives

Case Study 1: Delhi University, India e-Counselling During Crisis

During the COVID-19 pandemic, Delhi University (DU) launched a web-based e-counselling support portal to ease the sudden emotional burden faced by students and staff.

Led by the Department of Social Work and the Department of Psychology, the platform provided telephone and email-based support, facilitated by trained post-graduate interns and volunteer alumni.

Key Features:

- Email-based anonymous counselling
- Weekly webinars on stress management and resilience
- Bilingual support (English and Hindi)
- Referrals for psychiatric care if required

Impact:

- Within the first 3 months, over 2,000 students accessed services.
- Participants reported improved sleep patterns, reduced anxiety, and increased exam confidence.
- Faculty members requested a permanent version post-lockdown, resulting in the creation of a hybrid support team.

Case Study 2: Stanford University, USA – Integration with Global Platforms

Stanford University faced a significant challenge in providing support to domestic and international students across different time zones. To address this challenge, the institution partnered with Talk space and Better Help, allowing students to select therapists based on location, language, and expertise.

Innovations:

- Global 24/7 access
- Culturally sensitive therapist matching
- Real-time dashboard tracking usage trends

Outcomes:

- 78% of student users completed a minimum of three therapy sessions.
- A survey revealed 86% of users felt "significantly better" after four weeks.
- Therapists noted fewer crisis escalations as students began to seek help earlier.

Case Study 3: IIT Bombay Peer Support Network with Tech Integration

Recognizing the stigma associated with formal counselling, IIT Bombay has developed a unique two-model approach:

a. A peer-led support program called "Let's Talk," in which trained student volunteers provide basic emotional support.
b. A formal counselling unit supported by psychologists, integrated with an AI-powered journaling app.

Key Learnings:

- Students preferred to approach peers before professionals.
- Anonymity and relatability increased engagement.
- The journaling app's data (with consent) helped counsellors identify high-risk students early.

Results:

- A 40% increase in therapy attendance compared to the previous year
- Reduction in dropout rates for first-year students
- Increased funding allocated by the administration for mental health

Case Study 4: University of Calcutta – Local App for Local Needs

In collaboration with its Computer Science department, the University of Calcutta piloted a mobile app called "MindMatters," aimed at urban and semi-urban students. The app included:

- Bengali and English interface
- Recorded meditations and audio lectures on emotional regulation
- Direct chat option with university-appointed psychologists

Unique Features:

- Localized content (e.g., exam stress during CU semesters)
- Offline features for low-internet zones
- Referral engine for NGOs and city hospitals

Challenges:

- Initial reluctance due to data privacy fears
- Technical bugs in early versions
- Limited uptake among faculty

Solutions:

- IT fixes and interface redesign with student focus groups
- Offline promotion campaigns across departments
- Orientation sessions during admissions

Today, the app continues to be used by over 4,500 students, with monthly webinars and mental health literacy drives hosted on-campus.

6.2 Student and Educator Experiences

Real-world stories provide human depth behind the data. These testimonials illustrate how virtual support is impacting lives in tangible ways.

Student Testimonial: Sneha, 20, Engineering Student, Chennai

"I was experiencing severe panic attacks before my end-semester exams. I didn't know who to talk to. I found Wysa through our campus email and started chatting. I was shocked that it actually helped—just being able to write out my feelings and get calm advice. Later, I got matched with a therapist on YourDOST who helped me through three sessions. I passed all subjects and didn't feel alone."

Educator Testimonial: Mr. Rajiv Sinha, Assistant Professor, Kolkata

"During the pandemic, I lost two relatives. While handling online classes and grieving, I felt completely burned out. Our institute tied up with Manastha, and I reluctantly signed up. I'm glad I did. The therapist helped me reframe my emotions and cope. I now recommend virtual therapy to my students too."

Counsellor Testimonial: Dr. Rupa Shah, Psychologist at a Private University

"We used to get 2–3 walk-ins a week before the pandemic. Now, with our online counselling portal, I get 15–20 bookings weekly. Students say they feel safer reaching out digitally. It's helping us addres2 issues much earlier—especially in cases of relationship stress and academic anxiety."

Table 2. Comparative Overview: Institutional Best Practices

Institution	Platform/Method	Unique Feature	Challenge Overcome
Delhi University	Email + Phone Counselling	Language-specific webinars	Limited tech resources
Stanford University	Talkspace + BetterHelp	International reach	Time-zone coordination
IIT Bombay	Peer + Pro Support	Journaling + AI flagging	Cultural stigma
Univ. of Calcutta	Local App (MindMatters)	Regional customization	Initial low faculty engagement

Table 2 depicts comparative overview of Institutional Best Practices. The case studies collectively highlight that virtual counselling and teletherapy platforms are most effective when institutions adopt a holistic and integrated approach. Whether through university-supported digital therapy models, school-level emotional-wellbeing initiatives, or global youth-counselling platforms, several common themes emerge:

- **Accessibility and flexibility** significantly increase student engagement.
- **Confidential digital spaces** encourage help-seeking behavior among those who may avoid in-person sessions.
- **Educator involvement and referral pathways** strengthen continuity of care.
- **Platforms with trained professionals, structured protocols, and crisis-management features** show better outcomes.
- **International models** demonstrate that culturally adaptable and scalable systems can support diverse student populations.

Overall, these real-world examples reinforce that virtual mental-health support is not merely a technological addition but a transformative tool that can bridge emotional, academic, and social gaps within educational environments. The insights drawn from these cases provide valuable guidance for institutions aiming to design evidence-based, student-centered, and ethically robust tele-wellbeing systems.

7 STRATEGIES FOR SUCCESSFUL INTEGRATION OF VIRTUAL COUNSELLING IN EDUCATION

Implementing virtual mental health platforms in educational settings is not just a technical or financial decision—it requires thoughtful planning, stakeholder engagement, and institutional cultural change (Patel et al., 2018). This section outlines a multifaceted strategy to effectively integrate virtual counselling and teletherapy into schools, colleges, and universities.

7.1 Policy Support and Funding Models

For digital mental health services to become sustainable and scalable in the educational sector, institutional and governmental policies must prioritize emotional well-being alongside academic achievement.

Government-Level Interventions:

- **National Education Policy (NEP) 2020 (India)** has emphasized the importance of holistic education and student wellness. However, specific mandates and budget allocations for virtual mental health infrastructure are still evolving (Government of India, 2020).
- States like Karnataka and Kerala have introduced "School Wellness Programs" that include digital counselling (Ministry of Education, 2021).

- The **University Grants Commission (UGC)** has issued guidelines urging colleges to appoint psychological counsellors, but few institutions have adopted digital methods (University Grants Commission, 2019).

Institutional Funding Models:

- **Direct Budget Allocation:** Dedicating a portion of annual student welfare funds to digital wellness.
- **CSR Collaborations:** Partnering with corporate sponsors under Corporate Social Responsibility (CSR) initiatives to support app development or therapy access (World Health Organization, 2021).
- **Grants:** Applying for international mental health and education grants (e.g., from UNESCO, WHO, or UNICEF) (UNESCO, 2021).
- **Subscription Sharing Models:** For small institutions, pooling funds and sharing access to national platforms like YourDOST or Manastha.
- **Example:**

BITS Pilani allocated 10 lakhs from alumni funds to integrate both Wysa (AI support) and BetterHelp (licensed therapy), making care accessible to 9,000+ students across campuses.

7.2 Training for Staff, Faculty, and Counsellors

Technology alone is insufficient. For virtual counselling to be effective, stakeholders must be trained to use the tools ethically, empathetically, and efficiently (Sharma & Sharma, 2021).

Faculty Training Objectives:

- Recognize early signs of student distress
- Refer students to digital platforms without stigma
- Set emotional boundaries in online classrooms

Counsellor Training Areas:

- Conducting therapy through video and chat formats
- Handling emotionally intense conversations remotely
- Digital ethics, privacy laws, and suicide prevention protocols

Support Staff (e.g., librarians, hostel wardens):

- Orientation on basic mental health awareness
- Protocols for emergency redirection

Capacity Building Methods:

- Online certification courses on "Digital Mental Health in Education"
- Annual workshops in collaboration with psychology departments
- Role-playing sessions using chat transcripts (de-identified) for training

Example:
Amity University launched an in-house program called "Mental Health Champions," training 100 faculty members each year to become first responders and digital wellness promoters.

7.3 Promoting Awareness and Digital Literacy

Even the best platform fails without adoption. Promoting mental health literacy and digital comfort is essential to reduce stigma, increase platform usage, and normalize emotional help-seeking (Rickwood et al., 2019).

Student-Oriented Initiatives:

Digital Wellness Orientation: During admissions, introduce students to available platforms and explain confidentiality policies.

Mental Health Weeks: Host themed events, competitions, and webinars to encourage open conversations.

QR Code Posters: Display scannable codes around campus for instant access to support apps.

For Schools (K-12 Level):

- Include mental wellness apps as part of the digital classroom package (e.g., tablets with Calm or Breathe2Relax pre-installed).
- Use animated characters or stories to teach emotional intelligence.

Parental Engagement:

- Organize webinars for parents to understand digital counselling tools and reduce resistance at home.
- Share monthly newsletters highlighting success stories and usage statistics.

Gamification:

Platforms that gamify emotional exercises—e.g., earning badges for consistent journaling or mood tracking—see 30–40% higher engagement.

7.4 Establishing a Mental Health Ecosystem on Campus

Successful integration is about creating a supportive **ecosystem** rather than treating mental health services as isolated solutions (Kauer et al., 2014).

Key Components:

Mental Health Committees: Include students, faculty, and psychologists in policy-making.

Multi-Channel Access: Ensure support is available via website, app, QR scan, hotline, and face-to-face.

Crisis Management Protocols: Define what happens when a student indicates self-harm online—who gets notified, how intervention occurs, etc.

Feedback Loops: Collect anonymous feedback to improve services and content.

Bridge to Offline Care: For severe cases, systems must be in place for hospital referrals or in-person sessions.

Example:

Ashoka University runs an integrated wellness system with:

- An in-house counselling center
- Anonymous AI chatbots
- Weekly group therapy via Zoom
- 24x7 crisis hotline
- Wellness ambassador program among student clubs

7.5 Technology Infrastructure and Scalability Planning

Scalability ensures that platforms can support large and growing student populations without sacrificing quality or privacy.

Infrastructure Needs:

- Cloud-based data storage with regional servers (to reduce latency and comply with data laws)
- Multi-language interface development
- Chatbot learning updates based on anonymized feedback
- Secure backup servers for uninterrupted access

Tech Guidelines for Integration:

- Single Sign-On (SSO) with student email/ID
- Compatible with mobile-first design (given smartphone penetration)
- Integrated with existing LMS (e.g., Moodle, Google Classroom)

Data Security Standards:

- ISO 27001 certification
- End-to-end encryption
- Regular vulnerability scans

Long-Term Goal:
A scalable model is one that allows smaller institutions to "join" a national virtual mental health grid where diverse services, best practices, and data can be shared.

8. OUTCOME-BASED EVALUATION PRACTICES

Evaluating the effectiveness of virtual counselling and teletherapy platforms requires a structured, outcome-oriented approach. Institutions increasingly rely on measurable indicators that reflect not only the usage of these services but also their impact on students' well-being and academic functioning. The following outcome-based metrics provide a comprehensive framework for assessing the performance and long-term value of digital mental-health interventions in educational settings.

A. Engagement Metrics

Engagement is a primary indicator of a platform's accessibility, usability, and relevance. Metrics such as the number of sessions booked, session completion rates, login frequency, time spent per session, and repeat participation help institutions understand how actively students and educators are utilising virtual mental-health services. Higher engagement often correlates with stronger trust in the system and greater willingness to seek support.

B. Reduction in Absenteeism

Improved mental well-being often reflects in reduced absenteeism and better attendance patterns. Tracking changes in absentee rates before and after the implementation of teletherapy services allows institutions to evaluate how effectively the platform supports students experiencing stress, anxiety, or emotional distress.

A noticeable reduction in chronic absenteeism indicates that students are coping better and feeling more connected to academic life.

C. Improvement in Academic Performance

Academic outcomes are closely tied to emotional and psychological health. Institutions can assess improvements in grade point averages, assignment completion rates, class participation, and exam performance among students using virtual counselling services. Even modest academic improvements can signal increased concentration, motivation, and emotional stability resulting from timely psychological support.

D. Emotional Resilience Indicators

Emotional resilience—the ability to adapt, recover, and thrive in stressful situations—is a key indicator of mental-wellness progress. Evaluations may include self-reported stress levels, emotional coping skills, behavioural changes, social connectedness, and reductions in crisis incidents. Standardised psychological assessment tools (such as anxiety or depression scales) can also be used to measure changes in emotional health over time.

E. User Satisfaction Scores

User satisfaction reflects the perceived quality, relevance, and effectiveness of teletherapy services. Satisfaction indicators include feedback surveys, qualitative comments, perceived improvement ratings, and recommendations from students and educators. High user satisfaction scores demonstrate that the platform is empathetic, accessible, culturally appropriate, and capable of meeting diverse emotional-support needs.

Including these outcome-based evaluation practices helps educational institutions measure the real impact of virtual counselling and teletherapy platforms. Together, these indicators provide a holistic understanding of how digital mental-health services contribute to student well-being, academic success, and overall institutional resilience.

9 FUTURE DIRECTIONS

As educational institutions around the world continue to evolve in response to technological advancements, social pressures, and public health crises, the role of virtual counselling and teletherapy is poised for significant change.

Perhaps in the future, these services will need to be more adaptable, inclusive, evidence-based, and culturally rooted to remain effective and ethical.

9.1 Hybrid Models of Care: Blending Digital and In-Person Therapy

A blend of digital and in-person therapy is effective. While digital platforms offer convenience and accessibility for complex mental health conditions that require intense human interaction, in-person therapy is still essential.

The future lies in hybrid models, where users can seamlessly switch between online and offline formats based on their convenience, situation, and availability.

Hybrid Design Elements:

- First few sessions online, followed by offline referrals
- Emergency in-person counselling upon detection of high-risk flags in digital platforms
- Scheduled monthly in-person campus visits by virtual platform therapists

Benefits of Hybrid Models:

- Balances flexibility with human connection
- Reduces digital fatigue
- Ensures continuity in transitions (e.g., when returning from holidays or internships)

Real-World Analogy:

Just as telemedicine now complements hospital care in health sciences, teletherapy should be seen as a parallel service—not a replacement—for traditional mental health care.

9.2 Personalized, AI-Augmented Mental Health Tools

The future of virtual therapy isn't one-size-fits-all. Advances in artificial intelligence and natural language processing are poised to become more intelligent, personalized, and intuitive over time.

Expected Developments:

- **Emotion-Aware Systems:** Apps that detect distress levels by detecting tone of voice, facial expressions, or typing patterns.
- **Predictive Analytics:** Based on user usage trends, these platforms can proactively provide assistance before a crisis occurs.
- **Adaptive Chatbots:** These chatbots evolve with each user's interaction history, personalizing both tone and content.

Ethical Caution:

As AI's influence grows, so too does the need for ethical oversight. Institutions must ensure that AI remains a helpful tool and not a gatekeeper, especially in highly sensitive situations such as trauma or suicide, which many users face.

9.3 Region-Specific and Culturally Inclusive Designs

Most of the therapy modules, metaphors, and techniques are drawn from U.S. or European contexts and this is Going forward, platforms must decolonize digital mental health by incorporating region-specific insights. One of the biggest limitations of current virtual therapy tools is their Western-centric model.

Cultural Adaptations Might Include:

- Local languages, idioms, and examples in therapy scripts
- Inclusion of traditional wellness practices like yoga, Ayurveda, or Sufi meditation
- Reference to community/family structures rather than just individual frameworks

Example:

A counselling bot designed for our country users might recognize the common stress associated with joint family expectations, arranged marriage anxiety, or academic pressure from competitive exams like NEET or JEE. That’s why Cultural adaptation is required.

9.4 Research, Evaluation, and Outcome Measurement

To ensure working of virtual counselling platforms like being (truly effective and not just "feel-good" tools) we must put future efforts and should focus on evidence-based evaluation because it updates overtime.

Recommended Research Directions:

- Longitudinal studies on the impact of teletherapy on academic outcomes
- Comparative trials between digital and offline therapy results
- Research on the efficacy of AI-based mood trackers across different cultural groups
- Ethical studies on consent and digital autonomy in adolescents

Institutions should be encouraged to collaborate with psychology departments in order to run pilot studies and publish open findings in academic journals, contributing to the global discourse on digital well-being in education to create awareness.

9.5 Policy Integration and Institutional Commitment

For real impact, virtual counselling must move beyond "optional wellness services" into the core strategy of educational leadership. Just as institutions invest in smart classrooms and digital libraries, they must view mental health tech as foundational infrastructure.

Future Policy Goals:

- Mandate one licensed digital mental health partner per institution
- Create UGC/AICTE standards for virtual mental wellness systems
- Include student well-being scores in annual accreditation reviews
- Offer mental health leave policies for both students and educators

Public Policy Vision:

A national digital mental health grid, connecting rural schools, urban colleges, and marginalized institutions under one umbrella, with localized tools and shared resources.

9.6 Global Collaboration and Knowledge Sharing

Digital counselling allows for cross-border collaborations. Institutions from different countries can share:

- Best practices in e-counselling
- Multilingual AI frameworks
- Cross-cultural therapist exchange programs
- Case studies for collective research

Example Initiative:

Imagine a shared platform between Indian and UK universities where Indian students studying abroad can access culturally relevant therapy from licensed Indian therapists, while still being covered by UK university wellness programs.

10 CONCLUSION

In the digital age, mental health and education are no longer parallel concerns—they are deeply interconnected domains that demand synchronized attention. This chapter has explored how virtual counselling and teletherapy platforms, once viewed as experimental or supplementary, are rapidly becoming core components of educational infrastructure.

From real-time support during crises to long-term emotional resilience training, digital mental health tools are transforming how students and educators cope, communicate, and thrive. From globally renowned universities to regional colleges many of them have demonstrated that these platforms, when implemented with sensitivity and structure, can improve well-being, academic performance, and campus culture, all these yields to help as many as possible.

We have examined:

- The rise in demand for accessible, stigma-free counselling
- The technological and psychological architecture of virtual platforms
- Tangible benefits for students and educators alike
- Ethical, logistical, and cultural challenges
- Case studies demonstrating practical outcomes
- Strategic models for sustainable integration
- Future directions for innovation, inclusivity, and policy reform

The evidence is clear: digital platforms, when ethically designed and contextually implemented, hold immense promise for democratizing mental health care in education.

While platforms and policies provide structure, what brings these systems to life is compassion. At the heart of every app, dashboard, and chatbot must be a sincere commitment to human dignity and emotional safety. Technology should not only be efficient—it should be empathetic.

Educational leaders, policymakers, developers, therapists, and students must collaborate to ensure that:

- Digital tools are culturally aware and trauma-informed
- Systems are designed with equity, not just efficiency
- Faculty are trained not only to teach but to listen
- Students are empowered not just to learn but to heal

This is not a call for utopia, but for realism with heart. As we move into an increasingly hybrid, hyperconnected, and high-pressure world, the emotional scaffolding of our learning environments must be just as strong as their academic pillars.

Vision for the Decade Ahead

Let us imagine a future where:

- Every student is introduced to mental health tools the same day they receive their syllabus.
- Every campus has a multilingual, multi-modal, and multi-faith counselling ecosystem.
- Every educator has access to emotional debriefing just as they do to academic resources.
- Every region—urban or rural, elite or under-resourced—has fair access to support.

Let this be the decade where we normalize therapy, digitize compassion, and humanize technology—not just as a reaction to crises, but as a celebration of care.

The future of education is not only about what we learn, but about how we feel while learning. Virtual counselling and teletherapy platforms offer the tools to make this journey more supported, resilient, and humane—for every learner, everywhere.

REFERENCES

Andersson, G. (2018). Internet interventions: Past, present and future. *Internet Interventions : the Application of Information Technology in Mental and Behavioural Health*, *12*, 181–188. DOI: 10.1016/j.invent.2018.03.008 PMID: 30135782

Arora, A., & Srinivasan, R. (2021). Online mental health interventions during COVID-19: A review of teletherapy adoption in education. *Indian Journal of Psychological Medicine*, *43*(5), 422–430. DOI: 10.1177/02537176211030150 PMID: 34584308

Bryant, B. R., Sisk, M. R., & McGuire, J. F. (2024). Efficacy of gamified digital mental-health interventions for pediatric populations: A systematic review and meta-analysis. *JAMA Pediatrics*, *178*(11), 1136–1146. DOI: 10.1001/jamapediatrics.2024.3139 PMID: 39312259

Government of India. (2020). *National Education Policy 2020.* Ministry of Education. https://www.education.gov.in/nep2020

Hollis, C., Morriss, R., Martin, J., Amani, S., Cotton, R., Denis, M., & Lewis, S. (2015). Technological innovations in mental healthcare: Harnessing the digital revolution. *The British Journal of Psychiatry*, *206*(4), 263–265. DOI: 10.1192/bjp.bp.113.142612 PMID: 25833865

Inkster, B., Sarda, S., & Subramanian, V. (2018). An empathy-driven, conversational artificial intelligence agent (Wysa) for digital mental well-being: Real-world data evaluation. *JMIR mHealth and uHealth*, *6*(11), e12106. DOI: 10.2196/12106 PMID: 30470676

Karyotaki, E., Ebert, D. D., Donkin, L., Riper, H., Twisk, J., Burger, S., Rozental, A., Lange, A., Williams, A. D., Zarski, A. C., Geraedts, A., van Straten, A., Kleiboer, A., Meyer, B., Ünlü Ince, B. B., Buntrock, C., Lehr, D., Snoek, F. J., Andrews, G., & Cuijpers, P. (2019). Do guided internet-based interventions result in clinically relevant changes for patients with depression? An individual participant data meta-analysis. *Clinical Psychology Review*, *63*, 80–92. DOI: 10.1016/j.cpr.2018.06.007 PMID: 29940401

Kauer, S. D., Mangan, C., & Sanci, L. (2014). Do online mental health services improve help-seeking for young people? *Journal of Medical Internet Research*, *16*(3), e66. DOI: 10.2196/jmir.3103 PMID: 24594922

McBain, R. K., Schuler, M. S., Qureshi, N., Matthews, S., Kofner, A., Breslau, J. H. C., & Cantor, J. H. (2023). Expansion of telehealth availability for mental health care after state-level policy changes, 2019–2022. *JAMA Network Open*, *6*(6), e2318045. DOI: 10.1001/jamanetworkopen.2023.18045 PMID: 37310741

Ministry of Education. (2021). *School wellness programmes in India: Annual report*. Government of India.

Mishara, B. L., Chagnon, F., Daigle, M., Balan, B., Raymond, S., Marcoux, I., & Turecki, G. (2007). Helper behaviors and intervention styles related to short-term outcomes in telephone crisis intervention. *Suicide & Life-Threatening Behavior*, *37*(3), 308–321. DOI: 10.1521/suli.2007.37.3.308 PMID: 17579543

National Crime Records Bureau. (2022). [Ministry of Home Affairs, Government of India. https://ncrb.gov.in]. *Accidental Deaths and Suicides in India, 2021*, •••.

Patel, V., Saxena, S., Lund, C., Thornicroft, G., Baingana, F., Bolton, P., Chisholm, D., Collins, P. Y., Cooper, J. L., Eaton, J., Herrman, H., Herzallah, M. M., Huang, Y., Jordans, M. J. D., Kleinman, A., Medina-Mora, M. E., Morgan, E., Niaz, U., Omigbodun, O., & Unützer, J. (2018). The Lancet Commission on global mental health and sustainable development. *Lancet*, *392*(10157), 1553–1598. DOI: 10.1016/S0140-6736(18)31612-X PMID: 30314863

Plessen, C. Y., Panagiotopoulou, O. M., Tong, L., Cuijpers, P., & Karyotaki, E. (2024). Digital mental-health interventions for depression: A multiverse meta-analysis. *Journal of Affective Disorders*, *369*, 1031–1044. DOI: 10.1016/j.jad.2024.10.018 PMID: 39419189

Rickwood, D., Telford, N., Parker, A., Tanti, C., & McGorry, P. (2019). Headspace—Australia's innovation in youth mental health: Who are the clients and why are they presenting? *The Medical Journal of Australia*, *200*(2), 108–111. DOI: 10.5694/mja13.11235 PMID: 24484115

Sharma, A., & Sharma, R. (2021). Digital mental health services in higher education: Challenges and opportunities in India. *Indian Journal of Psychological Medicine*, *43*(3), 233–239. DOI: 10.1177/02537176211001548

Singh, S., Roy, D., Sinha, K., Parveen, S., Sharma, G., & Joshi, G. (2020). Impact of COVID-19 and lockdown on mental health of children and adolescents: A narrative review with recommendations. *Psychiatry Research*, *293*, 113429. DOI: 10.1016/j.psychres.2020.113429 PMID: 32882598

Sucala, M., Schnur, J. B., Constantino, M. J., Miller, S. J., Brackman, E. H., & Montgomery, G. H. (2012). Virtual reality and computer-based interventions for anxiety: A meta-analysis. *Journal of Anxiety Disorders*, *26*(1), 74–84. DOI: 10.1016/j.janxdis.2011.09.005

UNESCO. (2021). *Mental health and education: Global initiatives*. UNESCO.

University Grants Commission. (2019). *Guidelines for promotion of mental health and well-being of students*. UGC.

World Health Organization. (2021). *Adolescent mental health.* https://www.who.int/news-room/fact-sheets/detail/adolescent-mental-health

World Health Organization. (2021). *Global strategy on digital health 2020–2025.* https://www.who.int/health-topics/digital-health

Chapter 11
Sustaining Digital Mental Health Services in South African Higher Education:
Benefits, Challenges, and Strategic Pathways for E-Health Tools

Rhodrick Nyasha Musakuro
https://orcid.org/0000-0002-3787-3580
University of Sunderland, UK

ABSTRACT

This chapter introduces a strategic sustainability framework to overcome the post-pandemic integration challenges of digital mental health services (DMHS) in South African higher education institutions (SA HEIs). Although e-health tools offer transformative benefits for staff well-being, their long-term adoption is threatened by interconnected economic, social, environmental, and technological barriers. This chapter moves the discourse forward by not only diagnosing these challenges but also by recommending practical, context-specific pathways for sustainable implementation. It details how SA HEIs can leverage strategic partnerships, inclusive design, leadership commitment, and robust data governance to build resilient DMHS. The conclusions provide a novel blueprint for institutional policymakers to ensure equitable service delivery, thereby directly advancing Sustainable Development Goal 3 through enhanced staff mental health support.

DOI: 10.4018/979-8-3373-5007-3.ch011

INTRODUCTION

The World Health Organisation (2013) defines mental health as a fundamental component of overall well-being, intrinsically linked to physical and social health. As a major global public health concern, mental illness affects over 450 million people (Bauman & Rivers, 2015) and carries a significant economic burden, costing the global economy an estimated $1 trillion annually in lost productivity (United Nations, 2020). Within workplaces, mental healthcare faces pervasive challenges including stigma, discrimination, and inadequate resourcing (Lund et al., 2012; Willie, 2017). Consequently, the United Nations (2020) identifies mental health as a critically neglected area, a concern particularly relevant to South African higher education institutions (SA HEIs). These institutions are vital to the nation's economic and intellectual development, a role that is wholly dependent on the well-being of their staff (Theron et al., 2014). The workplace environment itself significantly influences mental health (Barkway, 2006), and within SA HEIs, university staff's well-being is frequently compromised by increasing workloads, heightened job demands, and systemic resource constraints (Barkhuizen et al., 2014).

Literature shows global external factors, such as the COVID-19 pandemic, further exacerbated these mental health challenges globally and within SA HEIs (Allen et al., 2020; Zhang et al., 2020). However, this period highlighted the need for alternative mental health service delivery models, prompting SA HEIs to utilise electronic health (e-health) tools to provide digital mental health services (DMHS) as a supportive intervention for university staff (Musakuro, 2025). Although the potential of e-health is increasingly recognised as a positive development (Philippe et al., 2022), significant gaps persist in understanding its implementation within the SA HEIs context. Specifically, research on the sustainability of these tools remains scarce, with little focus on their benefits, implementation challenges, and context-specific strategic pathways for sustainable integration (Van Assche et al., 2022). Therefore, addressing these gaps is essential to ensure long-term viability in supporting the mental health of university staff in South Africa and similar institutions. Accordingly, and within the contexts of SA HEIs, this study aims to:

- Discuss the benefits of utilising e-health tools in the provision of DMHS.
- Explore the challenges that constrain the sustainable integration of e-health tools.
- Recommend context-specific strategic pathways to facilitate and strengthen the long-term adoption of e-health tools for DMHS in SA HEIs.

This study holds significant value as it provides a structured, sustainability-focused framework for SA HEIs which empowers institutional leaders, policymakers, and health practitioners. It offers a practical roadmap for the sustainable integration of e-health tools through an analysis of benefits, challenges, and strategic pathways. Its findings are crucial for enhancing staff well-being and strengthening institutional resilience. Consequently, the study makes a vital contribution towards the attainment of Sustainable Development Goal 3 to ensure that DMHS evolve into viable, long-term solutions within the South African higher education sector and similar resource-constrained environments consistent with national and global health priorities.

BACKGROUND OF THE STUDY

The concept of e-health, though fluid, generally involves a diverse set of digital interventions including artificial intelligence (AI), telemedicine, mobile applications, and online platforms designed to enhance healthcare provision (Pagliari et al., 2005; Smoła et al., 2024). In this study, e-health tools for DMHS refer to digital technologies that facilitate the delivery, accessibility, and personalisation of mental health care through digital means (Musakuro & Gie, 2024). Literature demonstrates their potential to transform service delivery within workplace settings by enhancing accessibility, personalisation, and operational efficiency (Asi & Williams, 2018; Howarth et al., 2018).

Concurrently, sustainability has become a central theme in e-health discourse. Moving beyond its environmental origins in the Brundtland Report (World Commission on Environment & Development, 1987), sustainability in this context integrates economic, social, environmental, and technological dimensions (Musakuro & Gie, 2025; Mensah, 2019; Fanta & Pretorius, 2018). This study conceptualises sustainability as the capacity of SA HEIs to maintain the long-term delivery of DMHS by means of e-health tools, which ensures ongoing benefits without depleting future resources (Musakuro & Gie, 2025). The interplay of these four pillars economic (financial viability), social (equitable access and user acceptance), environmental (supportive infrastructure and policy), and technological (reliable and secure systems) collectively determines the success of e-health initiatives (Fanta & Pretorius, 2018; WHO, 2021).

This study postulates that SA HEIs are uniquely positioned to advance the sustainability of e-health systems for DMHS. Through their tripartite role in teaching, research, and governance, they can act as critical enablers of innovation while reinforcing institutional and societal resilience (Zhou et al., 2020). Their contributions are consistent with global sustainability agendas, particularly Sustainable Development Goal (SDG) 3: *Good Health and Well-being* (Mpofu et al., 2024). Therefore, by addressing constraints such as limited resources and inequitable access, this study posits that SA HEIs can drive the sustainable integration of e-health, thereby strengthening mental health support for staff and contributing to broader developmental goals. This study is situated within this context and seeks to provide a structured analysis that bridges the promise of e-health with the practical realities of its sustainable adoption in the South African higher education landscape.

METHODOLOGY

This study utilised a traditional literature review methodology to synthesise extant scholarly work concerning the benefits, implementation challenges, and context-specific strategic pathways for integrating e-health tools into DMHS within SA HEIs. This methodological approach was selected for its capacity to integrate diverse perspectives flexibly and to identify emergent thematic trends, without adhering to the formal protocols of a systematic review (Johnston, 2014; Snyder, 2019). Its interpretative nature is consistent and aligns well with the exploratory aims of this study, thus facilitating an analysis of complex and interdisciplinary phenomena.

A purposive search strategy was executed across multidisciplinary databases, including Google Scholar, ScienceDirect, Web of Science, Scopus, and PubMed, using keywords such as "e-health tools", "digital mental health services", "sustainability", "higher education institutions", and "South Africa". To uphold scholarly rigour, the selection criteria prioritised peer-reviewed journal articles, technical reports, and conference proceedings, while explicitly excluding non-scholarly sources. Thematic relevance and academic credibility guided the final inclusion of literature, with expert judgement employed to omit tangential studies. To capture both foundational context and recent advancements, the review used a broad publication timeframe that emphasised conceptual relevance.

The analysis was conducted using qualitative content analysis, which provides a systematic yet adaptable approach to interpreting secondary data. This method involves categorising and coding textual material to identify recurring concepts, patterns, and meanings within the literature (Neuendorf, 2018; Bengtsson, 2016). In this study, it was applied to examine themes related to the benefits of e-health tools (e.g., accessibility, cost-effectiveness), implementation challenges (e.g., resource constraints, infrastructural gaps, limited stakeholder buy-in), and strategic pathways for sustainable adoption in SA HEIs. The use of content analysis enabled interpretive insights that extend beyond descriptive summary, highlighting both recurring trends and knowledge gaps. This approach ensured a consistent, rigorous, and transparent synthesis of existing evidence in support of the study's objectives.

RESULTS AND DISCUSSIONS

Benefits of the Sustainable Adoption of e-Health Tools for DMHS

Literature affirms that sustainable e-health adoption offers significant benefits for DMHS users and providers. Scholarly discourse sometimes prefers the term "opportunities," highlighting prospects for enhanced mental health strategies and service delivery (Moock, 2014; Vally, 2006). However, these terms are often used interchangeably, reflecting a consistent meaning regarding the positive outcomes of e-health integration.

Rising mental health challenges among staff in South African HEIs create an urgent need for scalable care solutions. Sustainable e-health adoption is critical to address this. A principal benefit is enhanced access to care, as these tools overcome geographical and temporal barriers, delivering DMHS to remote and underserved areas (Titov et al., 2019). This is vital in South Africa's context of a substantial treatment gap, where many, including staff, have lacked adequate care (Bruwer et al., 2011; Barkhuizen et al., 2014). Furthermore, e-health tools democratise access to mental health information and online programmes, empowering users and promoting mental health literacy (Balcombe & De Leo, 2021).

Beyond accessibility, e-health tools offer considerable pragmatic benefits, including availability, cost-effectiveness, and convenience (Gainsbury & Blaszczynski, 2011). They optimise resource allocation by increasing operational efficiency and reducing the reliance on costly in-person consultations. The COVID-19 pandemic served as a potent real-world validation of these benefits, demonstrating how e-health tools could sustain essential DMHS delivery while circumventing the risks of viral transmission (Musakuro & Gie, 2024; Kane et al., 2022). This period highlighted the utility of remote monitoring and treatment, facilitating uninterrupted care and safeguarding public health.

The integration of e-health technologies also strengthens care coordination and improves clinical outcomes. Studies demonstrate that e-health tools in the form of telehealth modalities, for instance, enable effective remote communication between providers and patients, supporting self-care, diagnosis, monitoring, and treatment (Aungst & Patel, 2020; Asi & Williams, 2018). This streamlined coordination allows patients to manage their mental health more efficiently. Moreover, e-health platforms function as potent tools for disseminating information and promoting communication, with studies indicating that social media platforms can positively influence mental health by providing crucial social support across geographic distances (Blair & Abdullah, 2018).

A critical contribution of e-health tools is their capacity to promote sustained engagement and mitigate stigma. Through interactive media and personalised methods, these tools promote continuity of care and user engagement (Lal, 2019), directly addressing the high disengagement rates common in traditional face-to-face services (O'Brien et al., 2009). Importantly, the option for anonymous help-seeking is a profound benefit for individuals who may otherwise avoid treatment due to fears of stigmatisation (Lal, 2019; Gainsbury & Blaszczynski, 2011).

Crucially, the efficacy of DMHS delivered via e-health tools is well-substantiated. A consensus among scholars affirms their effectiveness and significant potential (Andrews et al., 2010; Gainsbury & Blaszczynski, 2011). This is robustly supported by meta-analytic evidence concluding that digital interventions for a range of mental health conditions are comparable in efficacy to traditional face-to-face modalities (Lehtimaki et al., 2021; Garrido et al., 2019; Gainsbury & Blaszczynski, 2011). This established efficacy is fundamental, as it provides the scientific evidence necessary for stakeholders, including policymakers, institutional leaders, and practitioners, to make informed decisions regarding the implementation and funding of these sustainable solutions.

In summary (see Table 1), the literature demonstrates that the sustainable adoption of e-health tools for DMHS holds considerable promise for SA HEIs and similar contexts. These tools transform mental health care by directly overcoming main challenges: extending access to underserved groups, reducing costs, providing flexible and convenient service delivery, and promoting sustained engagement while mitigating stigma. Moreover, they strengthen coordination of care, promote social connectedness, and demonstrate resilience during crises such as the COVID-19 pandemic. Importantly, their effectiveness is supported by robust clinical evidence, which positions e-health tools as a strategic and evidence-based solution for improving staff well-being and institutional resilience.

Table 1. Summary of benefits to the sustainable adoption of e-health tools

Benefit	Brief explanation
Improved access to care	Extends DMHS to remote, underserved, or resource-constrained populations, ensuring inclusivity of higher education staff and others traditionally excluded from formal care (Titov et al., 2019; Bruwer et al., 2011).
Cost-effectiveness	Reduces costs associated with in-person consultations and improves system efficiency, making mental health services more affordable and sustainable (Gainsbury & Blaszczynski, 2011).
Convenience and availability	Enables flexible, on-demand access to services and information, reducing logistical barriers such as travel time while supporting self-management (Balcombe & De Leo, 2021).

continued on following page

Table 1. Continued

Benefit	Brief explanation
Continuity of care & engagement	Promotes sustained service use through interactive and personalised digital platforms, counteracting disengagement common in face-to-face models (Lal, 2019; O'Brien et al., 2009).
Stigma reduction & anonymity	Allows users to seek support privately, decreasing the influence of stigma and encouraging help-seeking behaviour among hesitant groups (Gainsbury & Blaszczynski, 2011; Lal, 2019).
Enhanced coordination of care	Facilitates diagnosis, monitoring, and treatment through telehealth systems, ensuring more effective communication and integrated care pathways (Aungst & Patel, 2020; Asi & Williams, 2018).
Social connectedness & support	Social media and e-health platforms enable peer support and community building, fostering resilience despite geographical distance (Blair & Abdullah, 2018).
Resilience during crises	Demonstrated effectiveness during the COVID-19 pandemic by sustaining service delivery, reducing viral transmission risks, and maintaining vital mental health support (Musakuro & Gie, 2024; Kane et al., 2022).
Evidence-based effectiveness	Clinical studies and meta-analyses confirm the efficacy of digital interventions across various conditions, equating them with traditional therapies (Lehtimaki et al., 2021; Garrido et al., 2019; Andrews et al., 2010).

Source: Author's own creation based on the literature review

Challenges to the Sustainable Adoption of e-Health Tools

Despite their transformative potential, the sustainable adoption of e-health tools for DMHS confronts significant and multi-faceted challenges. Rather than insurmountable barriers, these are solvable obstacles requiring proactive strategies (Vally, 2006). This analysis examines these challenges through the lens of sustainability's four core pillars: economic, social, environmental, and technological, in order to provide a structured framework to identify key impediments to long-term integration.

Economic Sustainability Challenges

The economic viability of e-health tools is fundamentally constrained by the prohibitive cost of connectivity and devices. These tools are predicated on reliable internet access and digital hardware, yet in the South African context, both remain prohibitively expensive for a substantial portion of the population (Gillwald et al., 2018). This creates a critical access inequity that effectively excludes lower-income groups from DMHS. Within SA HEIs, this challenge is exacerbated by poor internet infrastructure, limited bandwidth management skills, and slow connection speeds, which collectively discourage staff utilisation (Maphalala & Adigun, 2021; Njenga, 2011). Although smartphone penetration is projected to rise (Global System for

Mobile Communications Association, 2023), current affordability issues persist (Grzybowski, 2022).

Sustainable e-health initiatives require consistent and reliable financial investment. In South Africa, however, progress is hindered by limited domestic funding and a persistent overreliance on external donors. Although low- and middle-income countries (LMICs) have sought to scale up e-health programmes, many remain financially dependent on donor contributions and an inherently unstable model (Lewis et al., 2012). This dependence generates significant volatility, as evidenced by the 2008 global financial crisis, which abruptly curtailed donor resources and destabilised programme continuity (Christine, 2011). Recent developments further highlight these vulnerabilities. The discontinuation of large-scale donor support, particularly from the United States Agency for International Development (USAID), has created a critical funding gap that threatens the long-term viability of e-health initiatives across LMICs, including South Africa (Wolthusen, 2025). The withdrawal of USAID funding is particularly concerning in the South African context, where health budgets are already overstretched, as it compels governments to redirect scarce resources towards more visible or acute health priorities, leaving mental health chronically underfunded (Wolthusen, 2025). This poses broader risks to public health, social stability, and economic growth, highlighting the urgent need for alternative financing models and integrated care approaches. Closer to this challenge, Non-Profit Organisations (NPOs), which play a pivotal role in supporting e-health interventions, also face mounting challenges. Escalating competition for shrinking donor contributions has intensified the financial precarity (Choto et al., 2022). Many NPOs in South Africa remain reliant on a single external funding source, exposing them to greater vulnerability in the face of global funding shifts (Kyalimpa, 2013). Several NPOs have been forced to reduce operations or shut down entirely, disrupting the continuity of DMHS (Nhaitayi, 2014). Collectively, these dynamics illustrate a profound funding fragility in South Africa's e-health ecosystem. Without diversified and sustainable financing mechanisms such as blended public-private partnerships, government funding allocation, or institutional cost-sharing, initiatives aimed at embedding DMHS within higher education institutions risk failing to achieve long-term viability and their intended purpose.

In addition to the above, the demand for mental health services in South Africa is intensified by poverty, unemployment, and limited resources, with funding often prioritised for high-burden diseases such as HIV/AIDS and tuberculosis. At the same time, inadequate infrastructure, including unstable electricity and uneven internet access, restricts the reach of e-health interventions, especially in rural areas. Consequently, investment in DMHS competes with urgent social needs such as food security, housing, and education, often leaving such initiatives at the margins of health planning (Fanta & Pretorius, 2018). Also, the high cost of devices capable of supporting health applications further restricts access for disadvantaged populations. Unless addressed, these economic challenges will perpetuate inequities in mental health care access, particularly in under-resourced academic institutions.

Social Sustainability Challenges

The social dimension of sustainability involves user acceptance, digital health literacy, and equitable access. Considering that adoption rates are often shaped by users' perceptions of usefulness, their confidence in digital technologies, and their ability to engage with e-health platforms effectively (Sharifi & Simangan, 2021). However, digital health literacy among South Africans remains inconsistent and comparatively limited in rural and low-resource areas, weakening self-management and preventative engagement (Stormacq et al., 2019; Bantom et al., 2016). This can result in misinterpretation of medical information, delayed diagnoses, or ineffective care. Even in urban areas, poor digital health literacy limits people's ability to make informed mental health decisions (Positi & Cilliers, 2019).

Language issues introduce a further social barrier. Although South Africa has 12 official languages, most e-health tools are only available in English or other global languages. This excludes a significant portion of the population from accessing vital digital health services (Norris et al., 2013; Mbunge et al., 2022). This linguistic exclusivity reduces accessibility and reinforces inequities, particularly in underserved communities. Studies recommend translation services and localisation of digital platforms to ensure inclusivity (James & Versteeg, 2007).

Social media, although a powerful enabler of connectivity, can also be a conduit for misinformation. During the COVID-19 pandemic, conspiracy theories and anti-health narratives spread through digital platforms, undermining the credibility of interventions and complicating trust in DMHS (Mbunge et al., 2022). Apart from this, patient suitability is a concern: even though e-health interventions are highly effective for many mental health concerns, research shows that patients with severe mental disorders often require blended approaches or direct face-to-face interventions (Brenes et al., 2011). These social dimensions highlight the need for tailored services, culturally appropriate design, and patient-centred approaches if sustainable adoption is to be achieved.

Environmental Sustainability Challenges

The sustainable adoption of e-health tools depends on a supportive environment, including management commitment, government policy, and adequate infrastructure. A critical challenge is the lack of senior management support, which is essential for mobilising financial and human resources (Johnson & Diman, 2017). Effective leadership provides not only funding but also strategic vision, encouraging adoption and ensuring user satisfaction (Al-Mamary et al., 2014). Without it, initiatives risk underinvestment and failure. Furthermore, government policy adds complexity; regulatory gaps or restrictive laws can stifle innovation and hinder the scaling of e-health initiatives (Ramdani et al., 2020).

Beyond leadership, the availability of resources plays a decisive role in the delivery of DMHS. Sustained investment in financial capital, ICT infrastructure, skilled human resources, and reliable electricity is essential (Fanta & Pretorius, 2018). However, in many low-income contexts, these foundational requirements remain limited. Financial constraints restrict institutions' ability to develop, update, and maintain digital platforms while also absorbing high telecommunications costs (Hiran & Henten, 2020; Fagherazzi et al., 2020). Shortages of skilled human capital, particularly ICT expertise, disproportionately hinder smaller organisations, reducing their capacity to adopt and sustain e-health systems (Walker & Brown, 2020). Likewise, gaps in ICT infrastructure across South Africa continue to obstruct the scaling of digital health initiatives, stressing the need for targeted strategies to strengthen institutional capacity (Asah & Kaasbøll, 2023).

A stable electricity supply is fundamental to modern life and is a critical prerequisite for powering e-health tools, internet connectivity, and information communication technologies required. Without it, the provision of DMHS becomes severely constrained, limiting access to essential support for university staff. Unfortunately, Eskom, South Africa's biggest and main public energy company, has recently been unable to meet the nation's rising energy demands, which has resulted in the deployment of varying levels of rolling blackouts known as 'load shedding' (Laher et al., 2019). This has allegedly been attributed to poor management, corruption allegations, failure to properly implement new infrastructure, and inadequate maintenance of existing power plants (Niselow, 2023). As South Africa's energy constraints worsen, they are not only hindering its economic growth but are also affecting higher education institutions' daily operations, preventing e-health tools' adoption from becoming sustainable. Reports indicate that South Africa's living below the poverty line face significant challenges in affording safer electrical alternatives since they are living below the poverty line (Statistics South Africa, 2018). Due to a lack of resources, poor ICT infrastructure, and inconsistent electricity supplies, emerging nations such as South Africa are finding it difficult to effectively use e-health tools sustainably than developed economies (Fanta & Pretorius, 2018). Thus, addressing the digital divide is essential for universal healthcare access within SA HEIs.

Technological Sustainability Challenges

A fundamental challenge to technological sustainability lies in the inadequate digital infrastructure prevalent across South Africa. The effective delivery of digital mental healthcare through mobile health (m-health) and telehealth platforms necessitates reliable internet connectivity and appropriate technical equipment (Mbunge et al., 2022). However, research indicates that South Africa suffers from persistent shortages of technological resources, with many regions experiencing substandard internet connectivity that renders e-health tools impractical for mental health applications (Norris et al., 2013). These infrastructure deficiencies stem largely from budget constraints and limited funding allocations (Fagherazzi et al., 2020), which create a technological environment that is fundamentally incompatible with the requirements of sustainable DMHS implementation.

The historical inequalities that characterise South African society further compound these technological challenges. As researchers observe, the unequal distribution of digital devices and infrastructure across different population groups raises serious concerns about the equitable provision of DMHS through e-health tools (Mhlanga et al., 2022). Other scholars reinforce this perspective by highlighting how disparities in access to technology may exacerbate existing mental healthcare inequalities, particularly in rural areas with unstable internet connectivity (Mbunge et al., 2022). This digital divide not only limits the potential reach of e-health tools but also risks creating a two-tier mental health system where access to care becomes increasingly dependent on technological privilege.

Communication challenges present another significant challenge to the technological sustainability of e-health tools. Bauman and Rivers (2015) demonstrate how the absence of nonverbal cues in text-based, telephonic, or videoconferencing therapeutic sessions can lead to clinical misinterpretations and diagnostic inaccuracies. The asynchronous nature of email communication introduces additional complications, as time lags and a lack of immediacy may hinder the effective expression of empathy and emotional connection between practitioners and patients. These communication limitations suggest that e-health tools may be unsuitable for certain types of mental health interventions, thereby constraining their broader adoption and sustainability in comprehensive mental healthcare provision.

The sustainable implementation of e-health tools also faces challenges related to technical skill deficiencies among both practitioners and patients. Researchers stress that mental health professionals require not only the technical competence to operate e-health platforms but also the ability to troubleshoot system failures during clinical sessions (Regueiro et al., 2016). From the patient perspective, limited technical literacy may result in low adoption rates and ineffective utilisation of digital mental health resources (Reese et al., 2015). Technological difficulties during therapy sessions have been shown to cause significant disruption and frustration for patients, potentially undermining the therapeutic relationship and treatment outcomes.

Ethical concerns surrounding data privacy, confidentiality, and security represent some of the most complex technological sustainability challenges. These issues, as identified in the literature, are critical challenges to user acceptance of digital mental health interventions (Wies et al., 2021; Lal, 2019). The sensitive nature of mental health data creates particular vulnerabilities, as e-health platforms may be susceptible to unauthorised access, data breaches, or commercial exploitation of user information (Martinez-Martin & Kreitmair, 2018). These risks are compounded by the practices of some service providers who may share or sell user data for marketing purposes without adequate disclosure or consent from patients (Ajunwa, 2017). Such ethical violations not only jeopardise patient welfare but also erode trust in e-health tools, which limit their sustainable adoption.

The issue of informed consent in DMHS presents additional ethical complexities. Although the consent process is intended to ensure users understand the associated risks, benefits, and data management practices, research reveals substantial shortcomings in current implementation (Martinez-Martin & Kreitmair, 2018). Essential information is often obscured in lengthy terms and conditions or embedded within digital platforms, which users seldom read or fully comprehend (Perez Vallejos et al., 2019; Pywell et al., 2020). This lack of clear and accessible consent mechanisms increases users' vulnerability to privacy violations and data misuse, thereby undermining trust in e-health tools for mental healthcare among university staff.

In summary (see Table 2), the literature establishes that sustainable adoption of e-health tools for DMHS in SA HEIs faces economic, social, environmental, and technological sustainability challenges. Economically, high ICT costs, dependence on donor funding, and weak domestic investments undermine long-term viability. Socially, low digital health literacy, language barriers, misinformation, and limited user acceptance reduce their effectiveness. Environmentally, weak leadership, restrictive policies, resource shortages, and unreliable electricity inhibit the implementation. Technologically, unequal access, limited ICT skills, technical failures, communication constraints, and data security concerns further hinder trust and integration. Accordingly, addressing these interrelated challenges is critical for ensuring the sustainable and equitable adoption of e-health tools into DMHS within SA HEIs.

Table 2. Summary of challenges to the sustainable adoption of e-health tools

Sustainability challenge	Brief explanation
Economic Sustainability Challenges	• **High ICT and internet costs**: Internet access, data prices, and devices remain expensive, limiting equitable access to DMHS (Gillwald et al., 2018; Grzybowski, 2022). • **Dependence on donor funding**: Heavy reliance on donors (e.g., USAID, NPOs) creates vulnerability; withdrawal of aid destabilises programmes (Lewis et al., 2012; Wolthusen, 2025). • **Unstable domestic funding**: Insufficient government investment and reliance on external donors restrict long-term sustainability (Fanta & Pretorius, 2018; Kyalimpa, 2013). • **NPO financial instability**: NPOs face competition for limited donor resources; some scale down or shut down, disrupting DMHS delivery (Choto et al., 2022; Nhaitayi, 2014).
Social Sustainability Challenges	• **Low digital health literacy**: Limited skills hinder effective use and self-management of e-health tools (Stormacq et al., 2019; Positi & Cilliers, 2019). • **Language barriers**: Most platforms are in English/global languages, excluding many South African language speakers (Norris et al., 2013; Mbunge et al., 2022). • **Misinformation and distrust**: Social media spreads conspiracy theories, reducing the credibility of DMHS (Mbunge et al., 2022). • **User acceptance and suitability**: Some patients, particularly those with severe mental health disorders, require face-to-face or blended treatment (Brenes et al., 2011).
Environmental Sustainability Challenges	• **Lack of management support**: Weak institutional leadership undermines the allocation of financial and human resources (Johnson & Diman, 2017; Al-Mamary et al., 2014). • **Policy and regulatory limitations**: Inconsistent or restrictive policy frameworks constrain innovation and scaling (Ramdani et al., 2020). • **Resource constraints**: Limited funding, weak ICT infrastructure, and shortages in skilled personnel hinder adoption (Fagherazzi et al., 2020; Asah & Kaasbøll, 2023). • **Electricity instability**: Load-shedding and unreliable power supply disrupt ICT operations, undermining e-health service delivery (Laher et al., 2019; Niselow, 2023).
Technological Sustainability Challenges	• **Unequal access and digital divide**: Inequalities in ICT infrastructure and equipment exacerbate rural–urban and socio-economic disparities (Mhlanga et al., 2022). • **Technical failures and low skills**: Interruptions, lack of troubleshooting skills, and weak ICT competence frustrate adoption (Reese et al., 2015; Baniasadi et al., 2018). • **Communication limitations**: Absence of non-verbal cues in digital therapy can undermine empathy, diagnostic accuracy, and therapeutic outcomes (Bauman & Rivers, 2015; Van Wynsberghe & Gastmans, 2009). • **Privacy, confidentiality, and data security**: Concerns over breaches, misuse of sensitive data, and weak safeguards reduce trust (Borghouts et al., 2021; Martinez-Martin & Kreitmair, 2018). • **Informed consent issues**: Terms and conditions are often inaccessible, leading to inadequate user understanding of risks (Perez Vallejos et al., 2019; Pywell et al., 2020).

Source: Author's own creation based on the literature review

Strategic Pathways to Sustainably Adopt e-Health Tools

Notwithstanding the significant challenges outlined, SA HEIs can sustainably integrate e-health tools for DMHS by implementing strategic pathways aligned with the sustainability framework's economic, social, environmental, and technological pillars (Musakuro & Gie, 2025; Mensah, 2019; Fanta & Pretorius, 2018). Drawing on recent research, this section recommends practical interventions to address entrenched challenges and build long-term resilience. Aligning institutional priorities with these sustainability principles will enhance the accessibility and equity of mental health support while ensuring the long-term viability of e-health innovations.

Economic Sustainability Pathways

In the context of SA HEIs, economic sustainability pathways denote creating a financially viable model for DMHS that balances initial development costs with long-term operational expenses. The core idea is to ensure e-health tools remain accessible and effective without causing unsustainable financial strain on the institution (Mensah, 2019). Drawing on the work of Musakuro & Gie (2025), the pathway to achieving this involves strategic partnerships and smart infrastructure investment. This includes cultivating collaborations with government departments, private technology companies, and mental health NGOs to diversify funding sources, share costs, and access technical expertise. Moreover, a crucial strategy is to partner with Internet Service Providers (ISPs) to offer zero-rated access to the DMHS platforms, ensuring staff are not burdened by data costs, which could significantly improve equity and adoption rates (Musakuro & Gie, 2025; Mbunge et al., 2022). Also, SA HEIs are encouraged to consider offering financial incentives, such as stipends or other forms of recognition, to the university staff to promote the sustainable adoption of e-health tools in DMHS (Musakuro & Gie, 2025). Finally, a phased, scalable implementation starting with a pilot programme could allow for cost-effective testing and modifications, demonstrating value to secure further internal funding for a broader rollout.

Social Sustainability Pathways

For e-health tools to be sustainably adopted, social sustainability pathways must focus on services that are culturally appropriate, linguistically accessible, and destigmatising. Only then can they become trusted and adopted by the entire university community. To this end, e-health tools are useless if they are not used, which is why Musakuro & Gie (2025) emphasise that this pillar is achieved through in-depth stakeholder engagement and inclusive design. This process must involve co-creating the services with mental health practitioners and staff from the very beginning to ensure they address real needs and fit within the existing support ecosystem. Training programmes are also essential in cultivating digital literacy among both academic staff and health providers, thereby enhancing competency and confidence in the use of e-health tools (Mbunge et al., 2022). Given South Africa's diversity, DMHS content must be translated into multiple official languages and, more importantly, its examples and therapeutic approaches must be culturally contextualised (Musakuro & Gie, 2025; James & Versteeg, 2007). Complementary awareness campaigns can promote institutional understanding of digital mental health benefits, encouraging long-term usage (Stoll et al., 2020). Sustainability also requires comprehensive digital literacy training for staff and awareness campaigns for staff to combat stigma. Adopting a blended care model that integrates e-health tools with traditional, in-person counselling caters to varying user preferences and optimises the use of available resources (Musakuro & Gie, 2025). Finally, continuous feedback, evaluation, and system modification are further necessary to maintain social legitimacy and service quality (Balcombe & De Leo, 2021).

Environmental Sustainability Pathways

Environmental sustainability pathways depend on institutional leadership and resource security. Strong commitment from senior management is paramount, as executive support influences resource allocation and organisational adoption of e-health tools (Musakuro & Gie, 2025). In light of this, SA HEIs must prioritise securing additional resources, including reliable electricity supplies and robust ICT infrastructure, as these fundamental resources underpin the sustainable adoption of e-health tools (Fanta & Pretorius, 2018). Without stable energy and technological foundations, even well-designed e-health initiatives risk failure in South Africa's challenging operational environment.

Technological Sustainability Pathways

Technological sustainability pathways entail building e-health platforms that are not only secure and reliable at launch but are also maintainable, upgradable, and supported over the long term to adapt to evolving standards. Musakuro & Gie (2025) argue that this foundation should be built on rigorous data governance and continuous support. Given the sensitive nature of mental health data, implementing iron-clad security protocols and clear data governance policies that comply with South Africa's Protection of Personal Information Act (often called the POPI Act or POPIA) is non-negotiable for building and maintaining user trust (Musakuro & Gie, 2025; Botes, 2025). Furthermore, the technology should be interoperable, designed to integrate with existing university systems such as staff portals for a seamless experience (Fanta & Pretorius, 2018). A sustainable programme must also include dedicated and ongoing technical support, with staff available to assist users with troubleshooting. Finally, the platform must be viewed as a living product, with a plan and budget for regular updates, security patches, and feature improvements based on user feedback.

In summary, Table 3 synthesises the four core strategic pathways essential for the sustainable integration of e-health tools for DMHS, consistent with the four pillars of sustainability. Economic pathways focus on building financially viable models through partnerships, cost-sharing, and scalable pilots. Social pathways emphasise cultural and linguistic inclusivity, stakeholder co-design, digital literacy, and anti-stigma initiatives to secure uptake. Environmental pathways highlight the importance of institutional leadership, reliable energy, and ICT resilience in resource-constrained contexts. Technological pathways require secure, interoperable, and adaptable platforms underpinned by robust data governance and ongoing technical support. Collectively, these pathways provide a practical framework to strengthen accessibility, equity, and long-term viability of e-health interventions.

Table 3. Summary of strategic pathways for the sustainable adoption of e-health tools

Sustainability strategic pathway	Brief explanation
Economic sustainability pathways	• Develop financially viable e-health tools for DMHS through strategic partnerships (government, NGOs, ISPs), zero-rated access, scalable pilots, and university staff incentives to reduce costs and ensure long-term adoption (Musakuro & Gie, 2025; Mensah, 2019; Mbunge et al., 2022).
Social sustainability pathways	• Promote cultural relevance, linguistic accessibility, co-design with stakeholders, digital literacy training, awareness campaigns, blended care models, and continuous evaluation to build trust and reduce stigma (Musakuro & Gie, 2025; James & Versteeg, 2007; Stoll et al., 2020; Balcombe & De Leo, 2021).
Environmental sustainability pathways	• Secure institutional leadership commitment, reliable energy, and ICT infrastructure to ensure resilience in resource-constrained South African HEI contexts (Musakuro & Gie, 2025; Fanta & Pretorius, 2018).
Technological sustainability pathways	• Ensure secure, interoperable, and upgradable e-health platforms with strong data governance (POPIA compliance), continuous technical support, and regular updates to sustain trust and functionality (Musakuro & Gie, 2025; Botes, 2025; Fanta & Pretorius, 2018).

Source: Author's own creation based on the literature review

CONCLUSION

This study has explored the benefits, challenges, and strategic pathways for the sustainable adoption of e-health tools for DMHS within SA HEIs. The analysis confirms that although the benefits of e-health tools are substantial, including improved access, cost-effectiveness, and stigma reduction, their sustainable integration is constrained by a complex array of interconnected challenges. These challenges, categorised across economic, social, environmental, and technological pillars of sustainability, threaten to perpetuate existing inequities in mental healthcare access for university staff.

The findings carry significant implications. Theoretically, this study contributes a structured, sustainability-focused framework for analysing the adoption of e-health tools, moving beyond a purely technocentric view. For practitioners and institutional managers, the study provides a practical roadmap, emphasising the need for strategic partnerships, stakeholder co-design, leadership commitment, and robust data governance. From a policy perspective, it stresses the necessity for government action to stabilise funding, improve digital infrastructure, and develop supportive regulatory environments that encourage innovation while protecting users (university staff).

This study aligns directly with Sustainable Development Goal 3 (*Good Health and Well-being*) by addressing the challenges of resource constraints and inequitable access. SA HEIs and similar institutions are therefore uniquely positioned to not only enhance staff well-being and institutional resilience but also to serve as model implementers that contribute to the national and global attainment of SDG 3.

However, a limitation of this study is its reliance on a traditional literature review, which, even though it provides comprehensive qualitative and thematic insights, could be supplemented with primary empirical data. Future research should therefore investigate the lived experiences of university staff and practitioners through qualitative studies and test the proposed strategic pathways through quantitative methodologies and pilot projects. Finally, a concerted call to action is urgent: SA HEIs, policymakers, and private partners must collaborate proactively to translate these strategic pathways into tangible action. The mental well-being of the academic workforce, a critical national asset, depends on the sustainable and equitable adoption of e-health tools for digital mental health solutions.

REFERENCES

Ajunwa, I. (2017). Workplace Wellness Programs Could Be Putting Your Health Data at Risk. https://hbr.org/2017/01/workplace-wellness-programs-could-be-putting-your-health-data-at-risk

Al-Mamary, Y. H., Shamsuddin, A., & Aziati, N. (2014). Factors affecting successful adoption of management information systems in organizations towards enhancing organizational performance. *American Journal of Systems and Software*, *2*(5), 121–126.

Allen, J., Rowan, L., & Singh, P. (2020). Teaching and teacher education in the time of COVID-19. *Asia-Pacific Journal of Teacher Education*, *48*(3), 233–236. DOI: 10.1080/1359866X.2020.1752051

Andrews, G., Cuijpers, P., Craske, M. G., McEvoy, P., & Titov, N. (2010). Computer therapy for the anxiety and depressive disorders is effective, acceptable and practical health care: A meta-analysis. *PLoS One*, *5*(10), e13196. DOI: 10.1371/journal.pone.0013196 PMID: 20967242

Asah, F. N., & Kaasbøll, J. J. (2023). Challenges and strategies for enhancing eHealth capacity building programs in African Nations. *Journal of Personalized Medicine*, *13*(10), 1463. DOI: 10.3390/jpm13101463 PMID: 37888074

Asi, Y. M., & Williams, C. (2018). The role of digital health in making progress toward Sustainable Development Goal (SDG) 3 in conflict-affected populations. *International Journal of Medical Informatics*, *114*, 114–120. DOI: 10.1016/j.ijmedinf.2017.11.003 PMID: 29126701

Aungst, T. D., & Patel, R. (2020). Integrating Digital Health into the Curriculum—Considerations on the Current Landscape and Future Developments. *Journal of Medical Education and Curricular Development*, *7*, 1–7. DOI: 10.1177/2382120519901275 PMID: 32010795

Balcombe, L., & De Leo, D. (2021). Digital mental health challenges and the horizon ahead for solutions. *JMIR Mental Health*, *8*(3), e26811. DOI: 10.2196/26811 PMID: 33779570

Bantom, S. A., de la Harpe, R., & Ruxwana, N. (2016). September. Accessibility to patients' own health information: A case in rural Eastern Cape, South Africa. In *Proceedings of the Annual Conference of the South African Institute of Computer Scientists and Information Technologists* (pp. 1-9). DOI: 10.1145/2987491.2987505

Barkhuizen, N., Rothmann, S., & Van De Vijver, F. J. (2014). Burnout and work engagement of academics in higher education institutions: Effects of dispositional optimism. *Stress and Health, 30*(4), 322–332. DOI: 10.1002/smi.2520 PMID: 23949954

Barkway, P. (2006). Creating supportive environments for mental health promotion in the workplace. *Contemporary Nurse, 21*(1), 131–141. DOI: 10.5172/conu.2006.21.1.131 PMID: 16594890

Bauman, S., & Rivers, I. (2015). *Mental health in the digital age*. Palgrave Macmillan. DOI: 10.1057/9781137333179

Bengtsson, M. (2016). How to plan and perform a qualitative study using content analysis. *Nursing Plus Open, 2*, 8–14. DOI: 10.1016/j.npls.2016.01.001

Blair, J., & Abdullah, S. (2018). Supporting constructive mental health discourse in social media. *Proceedings of the 12th EAI International Conference on Pervasive Computing Technologies for Healthcare*, 299-303. DOI: 10.1145/3240925.3240930

Botes, M. (2025). Regulatory challenges of digital health: The case of mental health applications and personal data in South Africa. *Frontiers in Pharmacology, 16*, 1498600. DOI: 10.3389/fphar.2025.1498600 PMID: 40371347

Brenes, G. A., Ingram, C. W., & Danhauer, S. C. (2011). Benefits and challenges of conducting psychotherapy by telephone. *Professional Psychology, Research and Practice, 42*(6), 543–549. DOI: 10.1037/a0026135 PMID: 22247588

Bruwer, B., Sorsdahl, K., Harrison, J., Stein, D. J., Williams, D., & Seedat, S. (2011). Barriers to mental health care and predictors of treatment dropout in the South African Stress and Health Study. *Psychiatric Services (Washington, D.C.), 62*(7), 774–781. DOI: 10.1176/ps.62.7.pss6207_0774 PMID: 21724791

Choto, P., Musakuro, R. N., Iwu, G. I., & Tengeh, R. K. (2022). Marketing for improved sustainability in Non-Profit Organisations. In Bobek, V., & Horvat, T. (Eds.), *Non-government Organizations - New Perspectives*. IntechOpen., DOI: 10.5772/intechopen.105642

Christine, O., & Ernest, M. E. (2011). The effect of global economic crisis on service delivery in selected non-governmental organizations in Kenya. *Journal of Management and Strategy, 2*(4), 101–117. DOI: 10.5430/jms.v2n4p101

Fagherazzi, G., Goetzinger, C., Rashid, M. A., Aguayo, G. A., & Huiart, L. (2020). Digital Health Strategies to Fight COVID-19 Worldwide: Challenges, Recommendations, and a Call for Papers. *Journal of Medical Internet Research, 22*(6), 1–10. DOI: 10.2196/19284 PMID: 32501804

Fanta, G. B., & Pretorius, L. (2018). A conceptual framework for sustainable eHealth implementation in resource-constrained settings. *South African Journal of Industrial Engineering*, *29*(3), 132–147. DOI: 10.7166/29-3-2055

Gainsbury, S., & Blaszczynski, A. (2011). A systematic review of Internet-based therapy for the treatment of addictions. *Clinical Psychology Review*, *31*(3), 490–498. DOI: 10.1016/j.cpr.2010.11.007 PMID: 21146272

Garrido, S., Millington, C., Cheers, D., Boydell, K., Schubert, E., Meade, T., & Nguyen, Q. V. (2019). What works and what doesn't work? A systematic review of digital mental health interventions for depression and anxiety in young people. *Frontiers in Psychiatry*, *10*, 759. DOI: 10.3389/fpsyt.2019.00759 PMID: 31798468

Gillwald, A., Mothobi, O., & Rademan, B. (2018). The state of ICT in South Africa. Policy Paper no. 5, Series 5: After Access State of ICT in South Africa. Retrieved from https://www.africaportal.org/publications/state-ict-south-africa/

Grzybowski, L. 2022. *Disruptive Technologies in South Africa and Sub-Saharan Africa: The Case of Mobile Telecommunications Services*. Working Paper DT-005, African Economic Research Consortium.

Hiran, K. K., & Henten, A. (2020). An integrated TOE–DoI framework for cloud computing adoption in the higher education sector: Case study of Sub-Saharan Africa, Ethiopia. *International Journal of System Assurance Engineering and Management*, *11*(2), 441–449. DOI: 10.1007/s13198-019-00872-z

Howarth, A., Quesada, J., Silva, J., Judycki, S., & Mills, P. R. (2018). The impact of digital health interventions on health-related outcomes in the workplace: A systematic review. *Digital Health*, *4*, 1–8. DOI: 10.1177/2055207618770861 PMID: 29942631

James, J., & Versteeg, M. (2007). Mobile phones in Africa: How much do we really know? *Social Indicators Research*, *84*(1), 117–126. DOI: 10.1007/s11205-006-9079-x PMID: 20076776

Johnson, R. D., & Diman, K. (2017). An Investigation of the Factors Driving the Adoption of Cloud-Based Human Resource Information Systems by Small- and Medium-Sized Businesses. In Bondarouk, T., Ruël, H. J. M., & Parry, E. (Eds.), *Electronic HRM in the Smart Era (The Changing Context of Managing People)* (pp. 1–31). Emerald Publishing Limited., DOI: 10.1108/978-1-78714-315-920161001

Johnston, M. P. (2014). Secondary data analysis: A method of which the time has come. *Qualitative and Quantitative Methods in Libraries*, *3*, 619–626.

Kane, H., Baumgart, J. G., El-Hage, W., Deloyer, J., Maes, C., Lebas, M. C., Marazziti, D., Thome, J., Fond-Harmant, L., & Denis, F. (2022). Opportunities and Challenges for Professionals in Psychiatry and Mental Health Care Using Digital Technologies During the COVID-19 Pandemic: Systematic Review. *JMIR Human Factors*, *9*(1), e30359. DOI: 10.2196/30359 PMID: 34736224

Kyalimpa, P. (2013). *Leadership Competence and Sustainable Funding of Local Non-Governmental Organisations in Uganda*. Unpublished doctoral thesis. Mbarara University of Science and Technology.

Laher, A. E., Van Aardt, B. J., Craythorne, A. D., Van Welie, M., Malinga, D. M., & Madi, S. (2019). 'Getting out of the dark': Implications of load shedding on healthcare in South Africa and strategies to enhance preparedness. *South African Medical Journal*, *109*(12), 899–901. DOI: 10.7196/SAMJ.2019.v109i12.14322 PMID: 31865948

Lal, S. (2019). E-mental health: Promising advancements in policy, research, and practice. *Healthcare Management Forum*, *32*(2), 56–62. DOI: 10.1177/0840470418818583 PMID: 30739487

Lehtimaki, S., Martic, J., Wahl, B., Foster, K. T., & Schwalbe, N. (2021). Evidence on digital mental health interventions for adolescents and young people: Systematic overview. *JMIR Mental Health*, *8*(4), e25847. DOI: 10.2196/25847 PMID: 33913817

Lewis, T., Synowiec, C., Lagomarsino, G., & Schweitzer, J. (2012). E-health in low-and middle-income countries: Findings from the Center for Health Market Innovations. *Bulletin of the World Health Organization*, *90*(5), 332–340. DOI: 10.2471/BLT.11.099820 PMID: 22589566

Lund, C., Petersen, I., Kleintjes, S., & Bhana, A. (2012). Mental health services in South Africa: Taking stock. *The African Journal of Psychiatry*, *15*(6), 402–405. DOI: 10.4314/ajpsy.v15i6.48 PMID: 23160613

Maphalala, M. C., & Adigun, O. T. (2021). Academics' Experience of Implementing E-Learning in a SA Higher Education Institution. *International Journal of Higher Education*, *10*(1), 1–13. DOI: 10.5430/ijhe.v10n1p1

Martinez-Martin, N., & Kreitmair, K. (2018). Ethical issues for direct-to-consumer digital psychotherapy apps: Addressing accountability, data protection, and consent. *JMIR Mental Health*, *5*(2), e9423. DOI: 10.2196/mental.9423 PMID: 29685865

Mbunge, E., Batani, J., Gaobotse, G., & Muchemwa, B. (2022). Virtual healthcare services and digital health technologies deployed during coronavirus disease 2019 (COVID-19) pandemic in South Africa: A systematic review. *Global Health Journal (Amsterdam, Netherlands)*, *6*(2), 102–113. DOI: 10.1016/j.glohj.2022.03.001 PMID: 35282399

Mbunge, E., Muchemwa, B., & Batani, J. (2022). Are we there yet? Unbundling the potential adoption and integration of telemedicine to improve virtual healthcare services in African health systems. *Sensors International*, *3*, 100152. DOI: 10.1016/j.sintl.2021.100152 PMID: 34901894

Mensah, J. (2019). Sustainable development: Meaning, history, principles, pillars, and implications for human action: Literature review. *Cogent Social Sciences*, *5*(1), 1–21. DOI: 10.1080/23311886.2019.1653531

Mhlanga, D., Denhere, V., & Moloi, T. (2022). COVID-19 and the Key Digital Transformation Lessons for Higher Education Institutions in South Africa. *Education Sciences*, *12*(7), 1–17. DOI: 10.3390/educsci12070464

Moock, J. (2014). Support from the internet for individuals with mental disorders: Advantages and disadvantages of e-mental health service delivery. *Frontiers in Public Health*, *2*, 65. DOI: 10.3389/fpubh.2014.00065 PMID: 24967221

Mpofu, F. Y., Mpofu, A., Mantula, F., & Shava, G. N. (2024). Towards the Attainment of SDGs: The Contribution of Higher Education Institutions in Zimbabwe. *International Journal of Social Science Research and Review*, *7*(1), 474–493. DOI: 10.47814/ijssrr.v7i1.1719

Musakuro, R. N. (2025). The adoption of e-health tools for digital mental health services in a South African higher education institution. *International Journal of Research in Business & Social Science*, *14*(1), 47–57. DOI: 10.20525/ijrbs.v14i1.3841

Musakuro, R. N., & Gie, L. (2024). Exploring university staff experiences gained during COVID-19 in the provision of digital mental health services through e-health tools: A case of a selected South African University. *International Journal of Research in Business and Social Science*, *13*(7), 155–168. DOI: 10.20525/ijrbs.v13i7.3648

Musakuro, R. N., & Gie, L. (2025). Strategies for sustainable adoption of e-health tools for digital mental health services. *SA Journal of Human Resource Management*, *23*, 11. DOI: 10.4102/sajhrm.v23i0.3053

Neuendorf, K. A. (2018). Content analysis and thematic analysis. In Brough, P. (Ed.), *Advanced Research Methods for Applied Psychology Design - Analysis and Reporting* (pp. 211–223). Routledge., DOI: 10.4324/9781315517971

Nhaitayi, R. M. (2014). *Exploring staff perceptions of why selected development NPOs are able to deliver effective services.* Unpublished master's thesis. University of Cape Town.

Niselow, T. (2023). Sunday Read: Load shedding through the years and how Eskom has struggled to keep the lights on. https://www.news24.com/fin24/economy/eskom/sunday-read-load-shedding-through-the-years-and-how-eskom-has-struggled-to-keep-the-lights-on-20190324

Njenga, J. K. (2011). *eLearning adoption in Eastern and Southern African higher education institutions.* Unpublished Doctoral dissertation. University of the Western Cape.

Norris, L., Swartz, L., & Tomlinson, M. (2013). Mobile phone technology for improved mental health care in South Africa: Possibilities and challenges. *South African Journal of Psychology. Suid-Afrikaanse Tydskrif vir Sielkunde, 43*(3), 379–388. DOI: 10.1177/0081246313493376

O'Brien, A., Fahmy, R., & Singh, S. P. (2009). Disengagement from mental health services. *Social Psychiatry and Psychiatric Epidemiology, 44*(7), 558–568. DOI: 10.1007/s00127-008-0476-0 PMID: 19037573

Pagliari, C., Sloan, D., Gregor, P., Sullivan, F., Detmer, D., Kahan, J. P., Oortwijn, W., & MacGillivray, S. (2005). What is eHealth (4): A scoping exercise to map the field. *Journal of Medical Internet Research, 7*(1), e391. DOI: 10.2196/jmir.7.1.e9 PMID: 15829481

Perez Vallejos, E., Koene, A., Carter, C. J., Hunt, D., Woodard, C., Urquhart, L., Bergin, A., & Statache, R. (2019). Accessing online data for youth mental health research: Meeting the ethical challenges. *Philosophy & Technology, 32*(1), 87–110. DOI: 10.1007/s13347-017-0286-y

Philippe, T. J., Sikder, N., Jackson, A., Koblanski, M. E., Liow, E., Pilarinos, A., & Vasarhelyi, K. (2022). Digital health interventions for delivery of mental health care: Systematic and comprehensive meta-review. *JMIR Mental Health, 9*(5), e35159. DOI: 10.2196/35159 PMID: 35551058

Positiliti, D., & Cilliers, L. (2019). An Investigation of the Level of E-health Literacy in South Africa. *ICICIS, 12*, 261–271. DOI: 10.29007/jjrb

Pywell, J., Vijaykumar, S., Dodd, A., & Coventry, L. (2020). Barriers to older adults' uptake of mobile-based mental health interventions. *Digital Health, 6*, 2055207620905422. DOI: 10.1177/2055207620905422 PMID: 32110429

Ramdani, B., Duan, B., & Berrou, I. (2020). Exploring the Determinants of Mobile Health Adoption by Hospitals in China: Empirical Study. *JMIR Medical Informatics*, *8*(7), 1–17. DOI: 10.2196/14795 PMID: 32459630

Reese, R. J., Slone, N. C., Soares, N., & Sprang, R. (2015). Using telepsychology to provide a group parenting program: A preliminary evaluation of effectiveness. *Psychological Services*, *12*(3), 274–282. https://psycnet.apa.org/doi/10.1037/ser0000018. DOI: 10.1037/ser0000018 PMID: 25602503

Regueiro, V., McMartin, J., Schaefer, C., & Woody, J. M. (2016). Efficacy, efficiency, and ethics in the provision of telepsychology services: Emerging applications for international workers. *Journal of Psychology and Theology*, *44*(4), 290–302. https://psycnet.apa.org/doi/10.1177/009164711604400404. DOI: 10.1177/009164711604400404

Sharifi, A., & Simangan, D. (2021). Environmental Sustainability: The Missing Pillar of Positive Peace. *The Palgrave Handbook of Positive Peace*, 1-19. DOI: 10.1007/978-981-15-3877-3_35-1

Smoła, P., Młoźniak, I., Wojcieszko, M., Zwierczyk, U., Kobryn, M., Rzepecka, E., & Duplaga, M. (2024). The perception of facilitators and barriers to the use of e-health solutions in Poland: A qualitative study. *BMC Medical Informatics and Decision Making*, *24*(1), 381. DOI: 10.1186/s12911-024-02791-x PMID: 39695644

Snyder, H. (2019). Literature review as a research methodology: An overview and guidelines. *Journal of Business Research*, *104*, 333–339. DOI: 10.1016/j.jbusres.2019.07.039

Statistics South Africa. (2018). *National Poverty Lines*. https://www.statssa.gov.za/publications/P03101/P031012018.pdf

Stoll, J., Müller, J. A., & Trachsel, M. (2020). Ethical issues in online psychotherapy: A narrative review. *Frontiers in Psychiatry*, *10*, 993. DOI: 10.3389/fpsyt.2019.00993 PMID: 32116819

Stormacq, C., Van den Broucke, S., & Wosinski, J. (2019). Does health literacy mediate the relationship between socioeconomic status and health disparities? Integrative review. *Health Promotion International*, *34*(5), e1–e17. DOI: 10.1093/heapro/day062 PMID: 30107564

Theron, M., Barkhuizen, N., & Du Plessis, Y. (2014). Managing the academic talent void: Investigating factors in academic turnover and retention in South Africa. *SA Journal of Industrial Psychology*, *40*(1), 1–14. DOI: 10.4102/sajip.v40i1.1117

Titov, N., Hadjistavropoulos, H. D., Nielssen, O., Mohr, D. C., Andersson, G., & Dear, B. F. (2019). From research to practice: Ten lessons in delivering digital mental health services. *Journal of Clinical Medicine*, *8*(8), 1239. DOI: 10.3390/jcm8081239 PMID: 31426460

United Nations. (2020). *Policy Brief: COVID-19 and the Need for Action on Mental Health*. https://unsdg.un.org/sites/default/files/2020-05/UN-Policy-Brief-COVID-19-and-mental-health.pdf

Vally, Z. (2006). Cybertherapy: Development and usage in the South African context. *Psychology in Africa*, *14*(2), 151–165. DOI: 10.4314/ifep.v14i2.23716

Van Assche, E., Bonroy, B., Mertens, M., Van den Broeck, L., Desie, K., Bolinski, F., Amarti, K., Kleiboer, A., Riper, H., & Van Daele, T. (2022). E-mental health implementation in inpatient care: Exploring its potential and future challenges. *Frontiers in Digital Health*, *4*, 1027864. DOI: 10.3389/fdgth.2022.1027864 PMID: 36588747

Walker, R. S., & Brown, I. (2020). Big data analytics adoption: A case study in a large South African telecommunications organisation. *South African Journal of Information Management*, *21*(1), 1–10. DOI: 10.4102/sajim.v22i1.1180

Wies, B., Landers, C., & Ienca, M. (2021). Digital Mental Health for Young People: A Scoping Review of Ethical Promises and Challenges. *Frontiers in Digital Health*, *91*, 697072. Advance online publication. DOI: 10.3389/fdgth.2021.697072 PMID: 34713173

Willie, M. M. (2017). On Depression and Mental Disorder in South Africa. *Med Clin Rev*, *3*(4), 1–2. DOI: 10.21767/2471-299X.1000060

Wolthusen, R. (2025). Mental Health in Low-and Middle-Income Countries Amid USAID Funding Withdrawal. *Psychiatric News*, *60*(4), appi.pn.2025.04.4.35.a. Advance online publication. DOI: 10.1176/appi.pn.2025.04.4.35.a

World Commission on Environment & Development. (1987). *Our Common Future*. Oxford University Press.

World Health Organization. (2021). *Depression*. https://www.who.int/news-room/fact-sheets/detail/depression

Zhang, J., Wu, W., Zhao, X., & Zhang, W. (2020). Recommended psychological crisis intervention response to the 2019 novel coronavirus pneumonia outbreak in China: A model of West China Hospital. *Precision Clinical Medicine*, *3*(1), 3–8. DOI: 10.1093/pcmedi/pbaa006 PMID: 35960676

Zhou, L., Rudhumbu, N., Shumba, J., & Olumide, A. (2020). Role of Higher Education Institutions in the Implementation of Sustainable Development Goals. In Nhamo, G., & Mjimba, V. (Eds.), *Sustainable Development Goals and Institutions of Higher Education. Sustainable Development Goals Series*. Springer., DOI: 10.1007/978-3-030-26157-3_7

Compilation of References

Abd-alrazaq, A., Alajlani, M., Ahmad, R., AlSaad, R., Aziz, S., Ahmed, A., Alsahli, M., Damseh, R., & Sheikh, J. (2024). The performance of wearable AI in detecting stress among students: Systematic review and meta-analysis. *Journal of Medical Internet Research, 26*(1), e52622. DOI: 10.2196/52622 PMID: 38294846

Aboujaoude, E., & Gega, L. (2020). From digital mental health interventions to digital "addiction": Where the two fields converge. *Frontiers in Psychiatry, 10*, 1017. DOI: 10.3389/fpsyt.2019.01017 PMID: 32038336

Abura-Meerdink, G. A., & Albright, D. L. (2024). Effectiveness of adolescent school-based digital mental health interventions: A systematic review. *Research on Social Work Practice, 34*(6), 701–710. DOI: 10.1177/10497315231201140

Adu, M., Banire, B., Dockrill, M., Ilie, A., Lappin, E., McGrath, P., Munro, S., Myers, K., Obuobi-Donkor, G., Orji, R., Pillai Riddell, R., Wozney, L., & Yisa, V. (2024). Centering equity, diversity, and inclusion in youth digital mental health: Findings from a research, policy, and practice knowledge exchange workshop. *Frontiers in Digital Health, 6*, 1449129. DOI: 10.3389/fdgth.2024.1449129 PMID: 39544986

Afshar Jahanshahi, A., & Polas, M. R. H. (2023). Moving toward digital transformation by force: Students' preferences, happiness, and mental health. *Electronics (Basel), 12*(10), 2187. DOI: 10.3390/electronics12102187

Ajunwa, I. (2017). Workplace Wellness Programs Could Be Putting Your Health Data at Risk. https://hbr.org/2017/01/workplace-wellness-programs-could-be-putting-your-health-data-at-risk

Akbay, S., & Gizir, C. (2010). Cinsiyete göre üniversite öğrencilerinde akademik erteleme davranışı: Akademik güdülenme, akademik özyeterlik ve akademik yükleme stillerinin rolü [Academic procrastination behavior in university students by gender: The role of academic motivation, academic self-efficacy, and academic attribution styles]. *Mersin Üniversitesi Eğitim Fakültesi Dergisi, 6*(1), 60–78.

Allen, J., Rowan, L., & Singh, P. (2020). Teaching and teacher education in the time of COVID-19. *Asia-Pacific Journal of Teacher Education, 48*(3), 233–236. DOI: 10.1080/1359866X.2020.1752051

Al-Mamary, Y. H., Shamsuddin, A., & Aziati, N. (2014). Factors affecting successful adoption of management information systems in organizations towards enhancing organizational performance. *American Journal of Systems and Software, 2*(5), 121–126.

Amani, H., Habibi-Kaleybar, R., Farid, A., & Sheykhalizadeh, S. (2021). Meta-analysis of the effectiveness of interventions on test anxiety reduction. *Psychological Research, 45*, 56.

Amerson, R., Fisher, B. A., Bible, J., Burgess, L., Ravan, L., & Ward, L. D. (2021). Nursing education amid a pandemic. *Nurse Educator, 46*(5), 255–260. DOI: 10.1097/NNE.0000000000001039

Amin, O. B., Mishra, V., Tapera, T. M., Volpe, R., & Sathyanarayana, A. (2025). Extending stress detection reproducibility to consumer wearable sensors. *arXiv*. / arXiv.2505.05694DOI: 10.1109/EMBC58623.2025.11252853

Amin, A., Hong, Y., & Mazhar, B. (2025). Enhancing AI-Driven Mental Health Solutions: The Role of Social Support in Wysa's Effectiveness for Stress Management and Anxiety Reduction among International Medical Students in China. *International Journal of Human-Computer Interaction*, •••, 1–16. DOI: 10.1080/10447318.2025.2537788

Amin, R., Ara, S., & Imtiaz, M. (2022). Counselling during COVID-19. In *Education reform in the aftermath of the COVID-19 pandemic* (pp. 1–14). Springer. DOI: 10.4018/978-1-7998-8992-2.ch003

Andersson, G. (2018). Internet interventions: Past, present and future. *Internet Interventions : the Application of Information Technology in Mental and Behavioural Health, 12*, 181–188. DOI: 10.1016/j.invent.2018.03.008 PMID: 30135782

Andrews, B., Klein, B., Corboy, D., McLaren, S., & Watson, S. (2023). Therapist training in video chat technology for use in an adaptive digital mental health intervention: Challenges, facilitators and implications for training models. *Counselling & Psychotherapy Research, 23*(3), 818–829. DOI: 10.1002/capr.12667

Andrews, G., Cuijpers, P., Craske, M. G., McEvoy, P., & Titov, N. (2010). Computer therapy for the anxiety and depressive disorders is effective, acceptable and practical health care: A meta-analysis. *PLoS One, 5*(10), e13196. DOI: 10.1371/journal.pone.0013196 PMID: 20967242

Arnold, C., & Young, D. (2025). Wearable technology for student well-being: A pilot study in higher education. *Journal of Educational Technology, 21*(2), 45–61. DOI: 10.1016/j.jedutech.2025.01.003

Arnold, K. E., & Pistilli, M. D. (2012). Course signals at Purdue: Using learning analytics to increase student success. In *Proceedings of the 2nd International Conference on Learning Analytics and Knowledge (LAK '12)* (pp. 267–270). Association for Computing Machinery. DOI: 10.1145/2330601.2330666

Arora, A., & Srinivasan, R. (2021). Online mental health interventions during COVID-19: A review of teletherapy adoption in education. *Indian Journal of Psychological Medicine, 43*(5), 422–430. DOI: 10.1177/02537176211030150 PMID: 34584308

Asah, F. N., & Kaasbøll, J. J. (2023). Challenges and strategies for enhancing eHealth capacity building programs in African Nations. *Journal of Personalized Medicine, 13*(10), 1463. DOI: 10.3390/jpm13101463 PMID: 37888074

Asi, Y. M., & Williams, C. (2018). The role of digital health in making progress toward Sustainable Development Goal (SDG) 3 in conflict-affected populations. *International Journal of Medical Informatics, 114*, 114–120. DOI: 10.1016/j.ijmedinf.2017.11.003 PMID: 29126701

Auerbach, R. P., Mortier, P., Bruffaerts, R., Alonso, J., Benjet, C., Cuijpers, P., & Kessler, R. C. (2020). WHO World Mental Health Surveys International College Student Project: Prevalence and distribution of mental disorders. *Journal of Abnormal Psychology, 129*(1), 97–110. DOI: 10.1037/abn0000362 PMID: 30211576

Aungst, T. D., & Patel, R. (2020). Integrating Digital Health into the Curriculum—Considerations on the Current Landscape and Future Developments. *Journal of Medical Education and Curricular Development, 7*, 1–7. DOI: 10.1177/2382120519901275 PMID: 32010795

Ayobi, A., Grimes, A., Mackinnon, S., Soubutts, E., Eardley, R., Banks Gross, Z., & O'Kane, A. A. (2021, June). Designing visual cards for digital mental health research with ethnic minorities. In *Proceedings of the 2021 ACM Designing Interactive Systems Conference* (pp. 942-954). DOI: 10.1145/3461778.3462085

Azcona, D., Hsiao, I.-H., & Smeaton, A. F. (2018). Personalizing computer science education by leveraging multimodal learning analytics. In *2018 IEEE Frontiers in Education Conference (FIE)* [Conference session]. IEEE. DOI: 10.1109/FIE.2018.8658596

Aziz, N., Nordin, M. J., Abdulkadir, S. J., & Salih, M. M. M. (2021). Digital addiction: Systematic review of computer game addiction impact on adolescent physical health. *Electronics (Basel)*, *10*(9), 996. DOI: 10.3390/electronics10090996

Aznar-Díaz, I., Romero-Rodríguez, J.-M., García-González, A., & Ramírez-Montoya, M.-S. (2020). Mexican and Spanish university students' Internet addiction and academic procrastination: Correlation and potential factors. *PLoS One*, *15*(5), e0233655. DOI: 10.1371/journal.pone.0233655 PMID: 32442238

Badawi, E., Coursaris, C. K., Sénécal, S., & Léger, P. M. (2023). Facilitating engagement of universal school-based digital mental health solutions through user experience: A qualitative exploration. *Frontiers in Digital Health*, *5*, 1040739. DOI: 10.3389/fdgth.2023.1040739 PMID: 37035481

Badri Gargari, R., Sabouri, H., & Norzad, F. (2011). Academic procrastination: The relationship between causal attribution styles and behavioral postponement. *Iranian Journal of Psychiatry and Behavioral Sciences*, *5*(2), 76–72. PMID: 24644450

Bai, Y.-M., Lin, C.-C., & Chen, J.-Y. (2001). Internet addiction disorder among clients of a virtual clinic. *Psychiatric Services (Washington, D.C.)*, *52*(10), 1397. DOI: 10.1176/appi.ps.52.10.1397 PMID: 11585966

Baka, E., Tan, Y. R., Wong, B. L. H., Xing, Z., & Yap, P. (2025). A scoping review of digital interventions for the promotion of mental health and prevention of mental health conditions for young people. *Oxford Open Digital Health*, *3*, oqaf005. DOI: 10.1093/oodh/oqaf005 PMID: 40230873

Balcombe, L. (2023, October). AI chatbots in digital mental health. []. MDPI.]. *Informatics (MDPI)*, *10*(4), 82. DOI: 10.3390/informatics10040082

Balcombe, L., & De Leo, D. (2020). An integrated blueprint for digital mental health services amidst COVID-19. *JMIR Mental Health*, *7*(7), e21718. DOI: 10.2196/21718 PMID: 32668402

Balcombe, L., & De Leo, D. (2020). Psychological screening and tracking of athletes and digital mental health solutions in a hybrid model of care: Mini review. *JMIR Formative Research*, *4*(12), e22755. DOI: 10.2196/22755 PMID: 33271497

Balcombe, L., & De Leo, D. (2021). Athlete psychological resilience and integration with digital mental health implementation amid Covid-19. In *Anxiety, uncertainty, and resilience during the pandemic period-anthropological and psychological perspectives*. IntechOpen. DOI: 10.5772/intechopen.97799

Balcombe, L., & De Leo, D. (2021). Digital mental health challenges and the horizon ahead for solutions. *JMIR Mental Health*, *8*(3), e26811. DOI: 10.2196/26811 PMID: 33779570

Balcombe, L., & De Leo, D. (2022). Evaluation of the use of digital mental health platforms and interventions: Scoping review. *International Journal of Environmental Research and Public Health*, *20*(1), 362. DOI: 10.3390/ijerph20010362 PMID: 36612685

Balcombe, L., & De Leo, D. (2022, February). Human-computer interaction in digital mental health. [). MDPI.]. *Informatics (MDPI)*, *9*(1), 14. DOI: 10.3390/informatics9010014

Balcombe, L., De Leo, D., & Turner, M. J. (2022). Athlete psychological resilience and digital mental health implementation. *Frontiers in Psychology*, *13*, 1082998. DOI: 10.3389/fpsyg.2022.1082998 PMID: 36532980

Balkıs, M. (2007). Öğretmen adaylarındaki erteleme eğiliminin, karar verme stilleri ile ilişkisi [The relationship between preservice teachers' tendency to procrastinate and their decision-making styles]. *Pamukkale Üniversitesi Eğitim Fakültesi Dergisi*, *1*(21), 67–83.

Baneres, D. (2016). Towards a particular prediction system to evaluate student's success. In M. Reiff-Marganiec & S. Caballero (Eds.), *Proceedings of the 11th International Conference on P2P, Parallel, Grid, Cloud and Internet Computing (3PGCIC)* (pp. 935–945). Springer.

Baneres, D., & Serra, M. (2018). Predictive analytics: Another vision of the learning process. In Caballé, S., & Conesa, J. (Eds.), *Software data engineering for network eLearning environments* (pp. 1–25). Springer., DOI: 10.1007/978-3-319-68318-8_1

Bantom, S. A., de la Harpe, R., & Ruxwana, N. (2016). September. Accessibility to patients' own health information: A case in rural Eastern Cape, South Africa. In *Proceedings of the Annual Conference of the South African Institute of Computer Scientists and Information Technologists* (pp. 1-9). DOI: 10.1145/2987491.2987505

Barkhuizen, N., Rothmann, S., & Van De Vijver, F. J. (2014). Burnout and work engagement of academics in higher education institutions: Effects of dispositional optimism. *Stress and Health*, *30*(4), 322–332. DOI: 10.1002/smi.2520 PMID: 23949954

Barkway, P. (2006). Creating supportive environments for mental health promotion in the workplace. *Contemporary Nurse*, *21*(1), 131–141. DOI: 10.5172/conu.2006.21.1.131 PMID: 16594890

Bassi, E. M., Bright, K. S., Norman, L. G., Pintson, K., Daniel, S., Sidhu, S., Gondziola, J., Bradley, J., Fersovitch, M., Stamp, L., Moskovic, K., LaMonica, H. M., Iorfino, F., Gaskell, T., Tomlinson, S., Johnson, D. W., & Dimitropoulos, G. (2024). Perceptions of mental health providers of the barriers and facilitators of using and engaging youth in digital mental-health-enabled measurement based care. *Digital Health*, *10*, 20552076241253093. DOI: 10.1177/20552076241253093 PMID: 38726214

Bassilios, B., Ftanou, M., Tan, A., Morgan, A., Machlin, A., Mangelsdorf, S., & Pirkis, J. (2022). *Environmental scan of digital mental health services*. Australian Government Department of Health and Aged Care.

Bauman, S., & Rivers, I. (2015). *Mental health in the digital age*. Palgrave Macmillan. DOI: 10.1057/9781137333179

Beard, K. W. (2005). Internet addiction: A review of current assessment techniques and potential assessment questions. *Cyberpsychology & Behavior*, *8*(1), 7–14. DOI: 10.1089/cpb.2005.8.7 PMID: 15738688

Bengtsson, M. (2016). How to plan and perform a qualitative study using content analysis. *Nursing Plus Open*, *2*, 8–14. DOI: 10.1016/j.npls.2016.01.001

Bennett-Levy, J., Singer, J., Rotumah, D., Bernays, S., & Edwards, D. (2021). From digital mental health to digital social and emotional wellbeing: How Indigenous community-based participatory research influenced the Australian government's digital mental health agenda. *International Journal of Environmental Research and Public Health*, *18*(18), 9757. DOI: 10.3390/ijerph18189757 PMID: 34574678

Bergin, A. D., Vallejos, E. P., Davies, E. B., Daley, D., Ford, T., Harold, G., Hetrick, S., Kidner, M., Long, Y., Merry, S., Morriss, R., Sayal, K., Sonuga-Barke, E., Robinson, J., Torous, J., & Hollis, C. (2020). Preventive digital mental health interventions for children and young people: A review of the design and reporting of research. *NPJ Digital Medicine*, *3*(1), 133. DOI: 10.1038/s41746-020-00339-7 PMID: 33083568

Bernard, A., de Ossorno Garcia, S., Salhi, L., John, A., & DelPozo-Banos, M. (2023). Patterns of engagement in a digital mental health service during COVID-19: A cohort study for children and young people. *Frontiers in Psychiatry*, *14*, 1143272. DOI: 10.3389/fpsyt.2023.1143272 PMID: 37575580

Bevan Jones, R., Stallard, P., Agha, S. S., Rice, S., Werner-Seidler, A., Stasiak, K., Kahn, J., Simpson, S. A., Alvarez-Jimenez, M., Rice, F., Evans, R., & Merry, S. (2020). Practitioner review: Co-design of digital mental health technologies with children and young people. *Journal of Child Psychology and Psychiatry, and Allied Disciplines*, *61*(8), 928–940. DOI: 10.1111/jcpp.13258 PMID: 32572961

Bhatt, S. (2025). Digital mental health: Role of artificial intelligence in psychotherapy. *Annals of Neurosciences*, *32*(2), 117–127. DOI: 10.1177/09727531231221612 PMID: 39544658

Blair, J., & Abdullah, S. (2018). Supporting constructive mental health discourse in social media. *Proceedings of the 12th EAI International Conference on Pervasive Computing Technologies for Healthcare*, 299-303. DOI: 10.1145/3240925.3240930

Bloomfield, J., Koster, E., Li, H., & Patel, R. (2024). Wearable sensors for stress and cognitive workload in students: Evidence from classroom deployments. *Frontiers in Behavioral Neuroscience*, *18*, 110223. DOI: 10.3389/fnbeh.2024.110223

Bloomfield, L. S., Fudolig, M. I., Kim, J., Llorin, J., Lovato, J. L., McGinnis, E. W., McGinnis, R. S., Price, M., Ricketts, T. H., Dodds, P. S., Stanton, K., & Danforth, C. M. (2024). Predicting stress in first-year college students using sleep data from wearable devices. *PLOS Digital Health*, *3*(4), e0000473. DOI: 10.1371/journal.pdig.0000473 PMID: 38602898

Borenstein, M., Hedges, L. V., Higgins, J. P. T., & Rothstein, H. R. (2009). *Introduction to meta-analysis*. Wiley. DOI: 10.1002/9780470743386

Borghouts, J., Eikey, E., Mark, G., De Leon, C., Schueller, S. M., Schneider, M., Stadnick, N., Zheng, K., Mukamel, D., & Sorkin, D. H. (2021). Barriers to and facilitators of user engagement with digital mental health interventions: Systematic review. *Journal of Medical Internet Research*, *23*(3), e24387. DOI: 10.2196/24387 PMID: 33759801

Borghouts, J., Pretorius, C., Ayobi, A., Abdullah, S., & Eikey, E. V. (2023). Factors influencing user engagement with digital mental health interventions. *Frontiers in Digital Health*, *5*, 1197301. DOI: 10.3389/fdgth.2023.1197301 PMID: 37143934

Botes, M. (2025). Regulatory challenges of digital health: The case of mental health applications and personal data in South Africa. *Frontiers in Pharmacology*, *16*, 1498600. DOI: 10.3389/fphar.2025.1498600 PMID: 40371347

Boucher, E. M., & Raiker, J. S. (2024). Engagement and retention in digital mental health interventions: A narrative review. *BMC Digital Health*, *2*(1), 52. DOI: 10.1186/s44247-024-00105-9

Bourion-Bédès, S., Tarquinio, C., Batt, M., Tarquinio, P., Lebreuilly, R., Sorsana, C., & Baumann, C. (2021). Psychological impact of the COVID-19 crisis on French university students: Risk and protective factors. *European Journal of Health Psychology, 28*(2), 63–72. DOI: 10.1027/2512-8442/a000058

Braun, P., Schwientek, A. K., Angerer, P., Guthardt, L., Icks, A., Loerbroks, A., & Apolinário-Hagen, J. (2023). Investigating information needs and preferences regarding digital mental health services among medical and psychology students in Germany: A qualitative study. *Digital Health, 9*, 20552076231173568. DOI: 10.1177/20552076231173568 PMID: 37256006

Brenes, G. A., Ingram, C. W., & Danhauer, S. C. (2011). Benefits and challenges of conducting psychotherapy by telephone. *Professional Psychology, Research and Practice, 42*(6), 543–549. DOI: 10.1037/a0026135 PMID: 22247588

Brooks, H., Irmansyah, I., Syarif, A. K., Pedley, R., Renwick, L., Rahayu, A. P., Manik, C., Prawira, B., Hann, M., Brierley, H., Lovell, K., & Bee, P. (2023). Evaluating a prototype digital mental health literacy intervention for children and young people aged 11–15 in Java, Indonesia: A mixed methods, multi-site case study evaluation. *Child and Adolescent Psychiatry and Mental Health, 17*(1), 79. DOI: 10.1186/s13034-023-00608-9 PMID: 37365594

Brotherdale, R., Berry, K., Branitsky, A., & Bucci, S. (2024). Co-producing digital mental health interventions: A systematic review. *Digital Health, 10*, 20552076241239172. DOI: 10.1177/20552076241239172 PMID: 38665886

Brown, P., Prest, B., Miles, P., & Rossi, V. (2022). The development of national safety and quality digital mental health standards. *Australasian Psychiatry, 30*(2), 154–157. DOI: 10.1177/10398562211042361 PMID: 34569321

Bruwer, B., Sorsdahl, K., Harrison, J., Stein, D. J., Williams, D., & Seedat, S. (2011). Barriers to mental health care and predictors of treatment dropout in the South African Stress and Health Study. *Psychiatric Services (Washington, D.C.), 62*(7), 774–781. DOI: 10.1176/ps.62.7.pss6207_0774 PMID: 21724791

Bryant, B. R., Sisk, M. R., & McGuire, J. F. (2024). Efficacy of gamified digital mental-health interventions for pediatric populations: A systematic review and meta-analysis. *JAMA Pediatrics, 178*(11), 1136–1146. DOI: 10.1001/jamapediatrics.2024.3139 PMID: 39312259

Bryman, A. (2006). Integrating quantitative and qualitative research: How is it done? *Qualitative Research, 6*(1), 97–113. DOI: 10.1177/1468794106058877

Burchert, S., Alkneme, M. S., Alsaod, A., Cuijpers, P., Heim, E., Hessling, J., Hosny, N., Sijbrandij, M., van't Hof, E., Ventevogel, P., & Knaevelsrud, C.STRENGTHS Consortium. (2024). Effects of a self-guided digital mental health self-help intervention for Syrian refugees in Egypt: A pragmatic randomized controlled trial. *PLoS Medicine*, *21*(9), e1004460. DOI: 10.1371/journal.pmed.1004460 PMID: 39250521

Çakıcı, D. Ç. (2003). Lise ve üniversite öğrencilerinde genel erteleme ve akademik erteleme davranışının incelenmesi [An examination of the general procrastination behavior and academic procrastination behavior in high-school and university students] (Unpublished master's thesis). Ankara University, Ankara, Turkey.

Cameron, G., Mulvenna, M., Ennis, E., O'Neill, S., Bond, R., Cameron, D., & Bunting, A. (2025). Effectiveness of digital mental health interventions in the workplace: Umbrella review of systematic reviews. *JMIR Mental Health*, *12*(1), e67785. DOI: 10.2196/67785 PMID: 39854722

Cash, H., Rae, C. D., Steel, A. H., & Winkler, A. (2012). Internet addiction: A brief summary of research and practice. *Current Psychiatry Reviews*, *8*(4), 292–298. DOI: 10.2174/157340012803520513 PMID: 23125561

Cejudo, J., López-Delgado, M. L., & Losada, L. (2019). Effectiveness of the videogame "Spock" for the improvement of the emotional intelligence on psychosocial adjustment in adolescents. *Computers in Human Behavior*, *101*, 380–386. DOI: 10.1016/j.chb.2018.09.028

Charbonnier, E., Trémolière, B., Baussard, L., Goncalves, A., Lespiau, F., Philippe, A. G., & Le Vigouroux, S. (2021). Self-help cognitive behavioral therapy application for COVID-19-related mental health problems: A longitudinal trial. *Asian Journal of Psychiatry*, *60*, 102656. DOI: 10.1016/j.ajp.2021.102656 PMID: 33866282

Chaudhary, K. (2024). Impact of digital pedagogy on the psychological wellbeing of students during global pandemics: A narrative review. [SAPJ]. *South Asian Journal of Psychology*, *3*(1), 1–10. DOI: 10.9734/bpi/pller/v9/11861F

Chauhan, S.Sweta Sharadkumar Chauhan. (2015). Effectiveness of the Art of Living YES+ Programme on College Students. *International Journal of Indian Psychology*, *2*(4). Advance online publication. DOI: 10.25215/0204.070

Cheng, V. W. S., Davenport, T., Johnson, D., Vella, K., & Hickie, I. B. (2019). Gamification in apps and technologies for improving mental health and well-being: Systematic review. *JMIR Mental Health*, *6*(6), e13717. DOI: 10.2196/13717 PMID: 31244479

Chen, J., Yuan, D., Dong, R., Cai, J., Ai, Z., & Zhou, S. (2024). Artificial intelligence significantly facilitates development in the mental health of college students: A bibliometric analysis. *Frontiers in Psychology, 15*, 1375294. DOI: 10.3389/fpsyg.2024.1375294 PMID: 38515973

Chen, M., Ma, Y., Li, Y., Wu, D., Zhang, Y., & Youn, C. H. (2024). Wearable sensors and AI-based monitoring for student mental health in classroom settings: A review. *IEEE Access : Practical Innovations, Open Solutions, 12*, 34567–34583. DOI: 10.1109/ACCESS.2024.3456789

Chen, X., Chen, L., Song, D., Wang, Y., & Ryoo, J. (2025). *Digital mental health for young people: sustainably managing stress and anxiety*. Mental Health and Digital Technologies.

Cherewick, M., Lebu, S., Su, C., Richards, L., Njau, P. F., & Dahl, R. E. (2021). Study protocol of a distance learning intervention to support social emotional learning and identity development for adolescents using interactive mobile technology. *Frontiers in Education, 6*, 625–640. PMID: 33585394

Cho, H. N., Jung, K., Eisenberg, D., King, C. A., & Zheng, K. (2025). Barriers to digital mental health services among college students. *arXiv preprint arXiv:2507.21093*. DOI: 10.3233/SHTI251041

Choto, P., Musakuro, R. N., Iwu, G. I., & Tengeh, R. K. (2022). Marketing for improved sustainability in Non-Profit Organisations. In Bobek, V., & Horvat, T. (Eds.), *Non-government Organizations - New Perspectives*. IntechOpen., DOI: 10.5772/intechopen.105642

Christine, O., & Ernest, M. E. (2011). The effect of global economic crisis on service delivery in selected non-governmental organizations in Kenya. *Journal of Management and Strategy, 2*(4), 101–117. DOI: 10.5430/jms.v2n4p101

Cohen, K. A., & Schleider, J. L. (2022). Adolescent dropout from brief digital mental health interventions within and beyond randomized trials. *Internet Interventions : the Application of Information Technology in Mental and Behavioural Health, 27*, 100496. DOI: 10.1016/j.invent.2022.100496 PMID: 35257001

Costardi, C. G., D'agostini, A. C. C., Pan, P. M., & Bressan, R. A. (2023). Digital mental health interventions for school teachers–A narrative review. *Early Intervention in Psychiatry, 17*(8), 749–758. DOI: 10.1111/eip.13431 PMID: 37041728

Costescu, C., Podina, I. R., & Voinescu, A. (2022). Digital mental health: Interventions and assessment. *Frontiers in Psychology, 13*, 1014527. DOI: 10.3389/fpsyg.2022.1014527 PMID: 36506981

Creswell, J. W., & Plano Clark, V. L. (2018). *Designing and conducting mixed methods research* (3rd ed.). SAGE Publications.

Creswell, J. W., & Poth, C. N. (2018). *Qualitative inquiry and research design: Choosing among five approaches* (4th ed.). SAGE Publications.

Cross, S. P., & Alvarez-Jimenez, M. (2024). The digital cumulative complexity model: A framework for improving engagement in digital mental health interventions. *Frontiers in Psychiatry, 15*, 1382726. DOI: 10.3389/fpsyt.2024.1382726 PMID: 39290300

Cross, S. P., Karin, E., Staples, L. G., Bisby, M. A., Ryan, K., Duke, G., Nielssen, O., Kayrouz, R., Fisher, A., Dear, B. F., & Titov, N. (2022). Factors associated with treatment uptake, completion, and subsequent symptom improvement in a national digital mental health service. *Internet Interventions : the Application of Information Technology in Mental and Behavioural Health, 27*, 100506. DOI: 10.1016/j.invent.2022.100506 PMID: 35242587

Cross, S. P., Nicholas, J., Bell, I. H., Mangelsdorf, S., Valentine, L., Thompson, A., Gleeson, J. F., & Alvarez-Jimenez, M. (2023). Integrating digital interventions with clinical practice in youth mental health services. *Australasian Psychiatry, 31*(3), 302–305. DOI: 10.1177/10398562231169365 PMID: 37072342

Daisy, A. (2025). Digital mental health education: alleviating stigma and enhancing well-being in schools. In *Advancing sustainable development goals with educational technology* (pp. 143–180). IGI Global Scientific Publishing.

Dallinger, V. C., Krishnamoorthy, G., du Plessis, C., Pillai-Sasidharan, A., Ayres, A., Waters, L., Groom, Y., Alston, O., Anderson, L., & Burton, L. (2022). Utilisation of digital applications for personal recovery amongst youth with mental health concerns. *International Journal of Environmental Research and Public Health, 19*(24), 16818. DOI: 10.3390/ijerph192416818 PMID: 36554700

Dambi, J., Norman, C., Doukani, A., Potgieter, S., Turner, J., Musesengwa, R., Verhey, R., & Chibanda, D. (2022). A digital mental health intervention (Inuka) for common mental health disorders in Zimbabwean adults in response to the COVID-19 pandemic: Feasibility and acceptability pilot study. *JMIR Mental Health, 9*(10), e37968. DOI: 10.2196/37968 PMID: 35960595

Das, P. J., Kyndait, P., Jamir, S. I., Baishya, D., Kalita, J. K., & Komu, L. T. (2024). The role of technology in mental health: Evaluating digital interventions for psychological well-being. *International Journal of Scientific Research in Science and Technology, 11*(6), 366–386. DOI: 10.32628/IJSRST24116186

Davies, S. M., Jardine, J., Gutridge, K., Bernard, Z., Park, S., Dawson, T., Abel, K. M., & Whelan, P. (2021). Preventive digital mental health for children in primary schools: Acceptability and feasibility study. *JMIR Formative Research, 5*(12), e30668. DOI: 10.2196/30668 PMID: 34898446

Dayal, S., & Pratibha, . (2023). Roadblocks in education amidst global crisis—A study based in India. *PLoS One, 18*(10), e0285128. DOI: 10.1371/journal.pone.0292465

Dederichs, M., Weber, J., Pischke, C. R., Angerer, P., & Apolinário-Hagen, J. (2021). Exploring medical students' views on digital mental health interventions: A qualitative study. *Internet Interventions : the Application of Information Technology in Mental and Behavioural Health, 25*, 100398. DOI: 10.1016/j.invent.2021.100398 PMID: 34026567

Demir, B. (2025). The Effect of Well-Being Interventions on English Language Pre-Service Teachers' Ability to Cope with the Challenges During Their School Practicum. In G. Sönmez (Ed), *Challenges in Teacher Education: Pedagogy, Management, and Materials* (pp. 87-113). IGI Global Scientific Publishing. https://doi.org/10.4018/979-8-3693-7342-2

Demir, B., & Lüta, K. (2026). The mediating role of AI literacy in the relationship between technostress and cognitive load in higher education. In *Impacts of artificial intelligence on educational psychology and cognitive development* (pp. 1–26). IGI Global. https://doi.org/10.4018/979-8-3373-6375-2.ch007

Deng, C.-H., Wang, J.-Q., Zhu, L.-M., Liu, H.-W., Guo, Y., Peng, X.-H., Shao, J.-B., & Xia, W. (2020). Association of web-based physical education with mental health of college students in Wuhan during the COVID-19 outbreak: Cross-sectional survey study. *Journal of Medical Internet Research, 22*(10), e21301. DOI: 10.2196/21301 PMID: 32997639

Dias, A., Mikkelsen, S., & Schou, M. (2024). Wearable neurofeedback acceptance model for students' stress and anxiety management in academic settings (mSense). *Behavioral Sciences*. https://pubmed.ncbi.nlm.nih.gov/39446926/

Digital 2023 Global Overview Report. (2023). Retrieved May 28, 2024, from https://wearesocial.com/wp-content/uploads/2023/03/Digital-2023-Global-Overview-Report.pdf

Dolev-Cohen, M., & Barak, A. (2013). Effects of virtual communication on adolescent mental health: A randomized controlled trial. *Computers in Human Behavior, 29*(4), 1532–1539.

Dupuy, L., Sevin, E. D., Micoulaud-Franchi, J., & Philip, P. (2021). Factors associated with acceptance of a virtual companion providing screening and advice for sleep problems during the COVID-19 crisis. In *Proceedings of the 21st ACM International Conference on Intelligent Virtual Agents* (pp. 1–3). ACM. DOI: 10.1145/3472306.3478334

Duraku, Z. H., Davis, H., Arënliu, A., Uka, F., & Behluli, V. (2024). *Overcoming mental health challenges in higher education: A narrative review.* Frontiers in Psychology. onlinelibrary.wiley.com±2frontiersin.org±2pubmed.ncbi.nlm.nih.gov±2arxiv.orgfrontiersin.orgnews-medical.net±5bristol.ac.uk±5thetimes.co.uk±5pubmed.ncbi.nlm.nih.gov

Eisenberg, D., Gollust, S. E., Golberstein, E., & Hefner, J. L. (2007). Prevalence and correlates of depression, anxiety, and suicidality among university students. *The American Journal of Orthopsychiatry*, *77*(4), 534–542. DOI: 10.1037/0002-9432.77.4.534 PMID: 18194033

Eisen, S., Lin, N., Lyons, M., Scherrer, J., Griffith, K., & True, W.. (1998). Familial influences on gambling behavior: An analysis of 3359 twin pairs. *Addiction (Abingdon, England)*, *93*(9), 1375–1384. DOI: 10.1046/j.1360-0443.1998.93913758.x PMID: 9926543

Ellis, D. M., Draheim, A. A., & Anderson, P. L. (2022). Culturally adapted digital mental health interventions for ethnic/racial minorities: A systematic review and meta-analysis. *Journal of Consulting and Clinical Psychology*, *90*(10), 717–733. DOI: 10.1037/ccp0000759 PMID: 36227330

Elo, S., & Kyngäs, H. (2008). The qualitative content analysis process. *Journal of Advanced Nursing*, *62*(1), 107–115. DOI: 10.1111/j.1365-2648.2007.04569.x PMID: 18352969

Fabian, K. E., Foster, K. T., Chwastiak, L., Turner, M., & Wagenaar, B. H. (2023). Adapting a transdiagnostic digital mental health intervention for use among immigrant and refugee youth in Seattle: A human-centered design approach. *Translational Behavioral Medicine*, *13*(11), 867–875. DOI: 10.1093/tbm/ibad041 PMID: 37418614

Fagherazzi, G., Goetzinger, C., Rashid, M. A., Aguayo, G. A., & Huiart, L. (2020). Digital Health Strategies to Fight COVID-19 Worldwide: Challenges, Recommendations, and a Call for Papers. *Journal of Medical Internet Research*, *22*(6), 1–10. DOI: 10.2196/19284 PMID: 32501804

Fanta, G. B., & Pretorius, L. (2018). A conceptual framework for sustainable eHealth implementation in resource-constrained settings. *South African Journal of Industrial Engineering*, *29*(3), 132–147. DOI: 10.7166/29-3-2055

Faria, M., Zin, S. T. P., Chestnov, R., Novak, A. M., Lev-Ari, S., & Snyder, M. (2023). Mental health for all: The case for investing in digital mental health to improve global outcomes, access, and innovation in low-resource settings. *Journal of Clinical Medicine*, *12*(21), 6735. DOI: 10.3390/jcm12216735 PMID: 37959201

Ferrari, J. R. (2001). Procrastination as self-regulation failure of performance: Effects of cognitive load, self-awareness, and time limits on "working best under pressure.". *European Journal of Personality*, *15*(5), 391–406. DOI: 10.1002/per.413

Ferrari, J. R., Johnson, J. L., & McCown, W. G. (1995). *Procrastination and task avoidance: Theory, research, and treatment*. Springer. DOI: 10.1007/978-1-4899-0227-6

Fleming, T., Poppelaars, M., & Thabrew, H. (2023). The role of gamification in digital mental health. *World Psychiatry; Official Journal of the World Psychiatric Association (WPA)*, *22*(1), 46–47. DOI: 10.1002/wps.21041 PMID: 36640378

Fortuna, K. L., Myers, A. L., Walsh, D., Walker, R., Mois, G. D., & Brooks, J. M. (2020). Strategies to increase peer support specialists' capacity to use digital technology in the era of COVID-19: Pre–post study. *JMIR Mental Health*, *7*(7), e20429. DOI: 10.2196/20429

Foster, J., & Upsher, R. (2024, January). A systematic review of peer support interventions for student mental health and well-being in higher education, *Published online by Cambridge University Press. BJPsych Open*, *10*(1), e12. DOI: 10.1192/bjo.2023.603 PMID: 39721952

Ftanou, M., Machlin, A., Mangelsdorf, S. N., Morgan, A., & Bassilios, B. (2025). Australian digital mental health services: Consumer perceptions of their usability and acceptability. *Journal of Technology in Behavioral Science*, *10*(2), 320–335. DOI: 10.1007/s41347-024-00431-9

Gainsbury, S., & Blaszczynski, A. (2011). A systematic review of Internet-based therapy for the treatment of addictions. *Clinical Psychology Review*, *31*(3), 490–498. DOI: 10.1016/j.cpr.2010.11.007 PMID: 21146272

Gallagher, R. P. (2014). *National survey of college counseling centers 2014*. International Association of Counseling Services.

Gan, D. Z., McGillivray, L., Larsen, M. E., Christensen, H., & Torok, M. (2022). Technology-supported strategies for promoting user engagement with digital mental health interventions: A systematic review. *Digital Health*, *8*, 20552076221098268. DOI: 10.1177/20552076221098268 PMID: 35677785

Gander, F., ... (2023). *The Effects of an Online Positive Psychology Course on Happiness, Health, and Well-Being. Psychol Well-Being*, as described in PubMed pubmed.ncbi.nlm.nih.gov

Gao, Y. (2025). The impact and application of artificial intelligence technology on mental health counseling services for college students. *Journal of Computational Methods in Sciences and Engineering*, *25*(2), 1686–1701. DOI: 10.1177/14727978241302641

Garrido, S., Millington, C., Cheers, D., Boydell, K., Schubert, E., Meade, T., & Nguyen, Q. V. (2019). What works and what doesn't: A systematic review of digital mental health interventions for young people. *Frontiers in Psychiatry*, *10*, 759. DOI: 10.3389/fpsyt.2019.00759 PMID: 31798468

Gbollie, E. F., Bantjes, J., Jarvis, L., Swandevelder, S., Du Plessis, J., Shadwell, R., Davids, C., Gerber, R., Holland, N., & Hunt, X. (2023). Intention to use digital mental health solutions: A cross-sectional survey of university students attitudes and perceptions toward online therapy, mental health apps, and chatbots. *Digital Health*, *9*, 20552076231216559. DOI: 10.1177/20552076231216559 PMID: 38047161

George, A. S. (2024). Exam season stress and student mental health: An international epidemic. *Partners Universal International Research Journal*, *3*(1), 138–149.

Giannopoulou, I., Efstathiou, V., Triantafyllou, G., Korkoliakou, P., & Douzenis, A. (2021). Adding stress to the stressed: Senior high school students' mental health amidst the COVID-19 nationwide lockdown in Greece. *Psychiatry Research*, *295*, 113560. DOI: 10.1016/j.psychres.2020.113560 PMID: 33187723

Gibson, K., Trnka, S., Jonas, M., Pomare, P., Thompson, S., Tiatia-Siau, J., Aimiti Ma'ia'i, K. D., Aoake, M., Bouttier-Esprit, T., Spray, I., & Vyas, S. (2024). Digital mental health strategies used by young people in Aotearoa New Zealand during the COVID-19 pandemic:'Just do it yourself, DIY'. *Digital Health*, *10*, 20552076241260116. DOI: 10.1177/20552076241260116 PMID: 39070892

Gillinov, M., & Soltesz, E. G. (2020). Commentary: Atrial fibrillation after aortic valve replacement: Predict, prevent, protect. *The Journal of Thoracic and Cardiovascular Surgery*, *160*(5), 1261–1262. DOI: 10.1016/j.jtcvs.2019.05.080

Gillwald, A., Mothobi, O., & Rademan, B. (2018). The state of ICT in South Africa. Policy Paper no. 5, Series 5: After Access State of ICT in South Africa. Retrieved from https://www.africaportal.org/publications/state-ict-south-africa/

Glasserman-Morales, D., Carlos-Arroyo, R., Ruiz-Ramirez, R., & Alcantar-Nieblas, M. (2023). Real-time stress monitoring in educational settings using wearable technology. *Sensory Systems*, *12*(4), 231–248. DOI: 10.3390/systems12040231

Gomes, P., Pato, R., Lourenço, A., & Datia, V. (2023). *Wearable biosensors for enhancing student well-being and engagement: Insights from global case studies.* PubMed Central. https://pubmed.ncbi.nlm.nih.gov/38676053/

Gomes, F., Pato, L., Lourenço, J., & Datia, N. (2023). Multi-sensor wearables for student mental health: Opportunities and challenges. *International Journal of Human-Computer Interaction, 39*(12), 1234–1250. DOI: 10.1080/10447318.2023.2198741

Gómez Bergin, A. D., Valentine, A. Z., Rennick-Egglestone, S., Slade, M., Hollis, C., & Hall, C. L. (2023). Identifying and categorizing adverse events in trials of digital mental health interventions: Narrative scoping review of trials in the international standard randomized controlled trial number registry. *JMIR Mental Health, 10*, e42501. DOI: 10.2196/42501 PMID: 36811940

Gonsalves, P. P., Ansari, S., Berry, C., Gonsalves, F., Iyengar, S., Kashyap, P., Mittal, D., Pal, S., Razdan, E., & Michelson, D. (2025). Co-designing digital mental health interventions with young people: 10 recommendations from lessons learned in low-and-middle-income countries. *Health Education Journal, 84*(4), 373–384. DOI: 10.1177/00178969241297821

González-Brignardello, M. P., Sánchez-Elvira Paniagua, A., & López-González, M. Á. (2023). Academic procrastination in children and adolescents: A scoping review. *Children (Basel, Switzerland), 10*(6), 1016. DOI: 10.3390/children10061016 PMID: 37371248

Good, S. (2020). *Evaluating the Effectiveness of a Digital Mental Health Literacy Intervention for Children and Young People Within a School Setting* (Doctoral dissertation, Royal Holloway, University of London).

Goodman-Casanova, J. M., Dura-Perez, E., Guzman-Parra, J., Cuesta-Vargas, A., & Mayoral-Cleries, F. (2020). Telehealth home support during COVID-19 confinement for community-dwelling older adults with mild cognitive impairment or mild dementia: Survey study. *Journal of Medical Internet Research, 22*(5), e19434. DOI: 10.2196/19434 PMID: 32401215

Gopalakrishnan, A., Venkataraman, R., Gururajan, R., Zhou, X., & Genrich, R. (2022). Mobile phone enabled mental health monitoring to enhance diagnosis for severity assessment of behaviours: A review. *PeerJ. Computer Science, 8*, e1042. DOI: 10.7717/peerj-cs.1042 PMID: 36092018

Government of India. (2020). *National Education Policy 2020.* Ministry of Education. https://www.education.gov.in/nep2020

Government of Kerala. (2023). *Teacher-as-counsellor program: Mental health training for school educators*. Centre for Child Development. https://www.kerala.gov.in/education

Graham, A. K., Greene, C. J., Powell, T., Lieponis, P., Lunsford, A., Peralta, C. D., Orr, L. C., Kaiser, S. M., Alam, N., Berhane, H., Kalan, O., & Mohr, D. C. (2020). Lessons learned from service design of a trial of a digital mental health service: Informing implementation in primary care clinics. *Translational Behavioral Medicine*, *10*(3), 598–605. DOI: 10.1093/tbm/ibz140 PMID: 32766862

Graham, A. K., Lattie, E. G., Powell, B. J., Lyon, A. R., Smith, J. D., Schueller, S. M., Stadnick, N. A., Brown, C. H., & Mohr, D. C. (2020). Implementation strategies for digital mental health interventions in health care settings. *The American Psychologist*, *75*(8), 1080–1092. DOI: 10.1037/amp0000686 PMID: 33252946

Grant, J. E., Brewer, J. A., & Potenza, M. N. (2006). The neurobiology of substance and behavioral addictions. *CNS Spectrums*, *11*(12), 924–930. DOI: 10.1017/S109285290001511X PMID: 17146406

Gratzer, D., Torous, J., Lam, R. W., Patten, S. B., Kutcher, S., Chan, S., Vigo, D., Pajer, K., & Yatham, L. N. (2021). Our digital moment: Innovations and opportunities in digital mental health care. *Canadian Journal of Psychiatry*, *66*(1), 5–8. DOI: 10.1177/0706743720937833 PMID: 32603188

Grzybowski, L. 2022. *Disruptive Technologies in South Africa and Sub-Saharan Africa: The Case of Mobile Telecommunications Services*. Working Paper DT-005, African Economic Research Consortium.

Guo, T., Zhao, W., Alrashoud, M., Tolba, A., Firmin, S., & Xia, F. (2022). Multimodal educational data fusion for students' mental health detection. *IEEE Access : Practical Innovations, Open Solutions*, *10*, 70370–70382. DOI: 10.1109/ACCESS.2022.3187502

Gupta, N., & Ahuja, K. (2021). Effectiveness and perceptions of online counseling services among Indian university students during COVID-19: A mixed-methods study. *Journal of Psychosomatic Research*, *16*(2), 207–218. DOI: 10.32381/JPR.2021.16.02.9

Gupta, S., Gupta, S., & Kumar, S. (2024). Influence of internet addiction and academic procrastination on academic achievement of secondary & senior secondary school students. *International Journal of Indian Psychology*, *12*(2), 1293–1308. DOI: 10.25215/1202.115

Haikalis, M., Doucette, H., Meisel, M. K., Birch, K., & Barnett, N. P. (2022). Changes in college student anxiety and depression from pre-to during-COVID-19: Perceived stress, academic challenges, loneliness, and positive perceptions. *Emerging Adulthood, 10*(2), 534–545. DOI: 10.1177/21676968211058516 PMID: 35382515

Hair, J. F., Black, W. C., Babin, B. J., Anderson, R. E., & Tatham, R. L. (2013). *Multivariate data analysis* (8th ed.). Pearson Education Limited.

Hamdoun, S., Monteleone, R., Bookman, T., & Michael, K. (2023). AI-based and digital mental health apps: Balancing need and risk. *IEEE Technology and Society Magazine, 42*(1), 25–36. DOI: 10.1109/MTS.2023.3241309

Hands, A. S., & Shankar, S. (2025). Back from crisis mode: Exploring care-centred approaches to teaching in LIS. *Journal of Education for Library and Information Science, 66*(1), 85–93. DOI: 10.3138/jelis-2024-0052

Han, S. Y. S., Tomasik, J., Rustogi, N., Lago, S. G., Barton-Owen, G., Eljasz, P., Cooper, J. D., Ozcan, S., Olmert, T., Farrag, L. P., Friend, L. V., Bell, E., Cowell, D., Thomas, G., Tuytten, R., & Bahn, S. (2020). Diagnostic prediction model development using data from dried blood spot proteomics and a digital mental health assessment to identify major depressive disorder among individuals presenting with low mood. *Brain, Behavior, and Immunity, 90*, 184–195. DOI: 10.1016/j.bbi.2020.08.011 PMID: 32861718

Harith, S., Backhaus, I., Mohbin, N., Ngo, H. T., & Khoo, S. (2022). Effectiveness of digital mental health interventions for university students: An umbrella review. *PeerJ, 10*, e13111. DOI: 10.7717/peerj.13111 PMID: 35382010

Hayat, A., Kojuri, J., & Amini, M. (2020). Academic procrastination of medical students: The role of Internet addiction. *Journal of Advances in Medical Education & Professionalism, 8*(2), 83–89. DOI: 10.30476/JAMP.2020.85000.1159 PMID: 32426392

He, L., Chen, Y., Wang, W., He, S., & Hu, X. (2024). Wearable device-based real-time monitoring of physiological signals: Evaluating cognitive load across different tasks. *arXiv*. https://doi.org//arXiv.2406.07147DOI: 10.48550

Headspace National Youth Mental Health Foundation. (2023). *Mental health education program: Headspace schools & communities*. https://headspace.org.au/schools/mental-health-education-program/

Henderson, B., Kirby, K., McCann, A., McCay, D., Leeann, M., Mulvenna, M., . . . Quigley, T. (2014, September). Designing social prescription services to support people with long-term conditions. In *ENoLL Open Living Lab Days 2014 Conference Proceedings* (pp. 158-170). European Network of Living Labs.

Hickey, B. A., Chalmers, T., Newton, P., Lin, C. T., Sibbritt, D., McLachlan, C. S., Clifton-Bligh, R., Morley, J., & Lal, S. (2021). Smart devices and wearable technologies to detect and monitor mental health conditions and stress: A systematic review. *Sensors (Basel)*, *21*(10), 3461. DOI: 10.3390/s21103461 PMID: 34065620

Hicks, L. J., Toombs, E., Lund, J., Kowatch, K. R., Hopkins, C., & Mushquash, C. J. (2025). Expanding our understanding of digital mental health interventions for Indigenous youth: An updated systematic review. *Journal of Telemedicine and Telecare*, *31*(7), 919–960. DOI: 10.1177/1357633X241239715 PMID: 38584397

Himle, J. A., Weaver, A., Zhang, A., & Xiang, X. (2022). Digital mental health interventions for depression. *Cognitive and Behavioral Practice*, *29*(1), 50–59. DOI: 10.1016/j.cbpra.2020.12.009

Hiran, K. K., & Henten, A. (2020). An integrated TOE–DoI framework for cloud computing adoption in the higher education sector: Case study of Sub-Saharan Africa, Ethiopia. *International Journal of System Assurance Engineering and Management*, *11*(2), 441–449. DOI: 10.1007/s13198-019-00872-z

Hobbs, C., Jelbert, S., Santos, L. R., & Hood, B. (2024). Long-term analysis of a psychoeducational course on university students' mental well-being. *Higher Education*, *2*(6), 2093–2105. bristol.ac.uk. DOI: 10.1007/s10734-024-01202-4

Hollis, C., Morriss, R., Martin, J., Amani, S., Cotton, R., Denis, M., & Lewis, S. (2015). Technological innovations in mental healthcare: Harnessing the digital revolution. *The British Journal of Psychiatry*, *206*(4), 263–265. DOI: 10.1192/bjp.bp.113.142612 PMID: 25833865

Hopkin, G., Branson, R., Campbell, P., Coole, H., Cooper, S., Edelmann, F., & Salmon, M. (2024). Considerations for regulation and evaluation of digital mental health technologies. *Digital Health*, *10*, 20552076241293313. DOI: 10.1177/20552076241293313 PMID: 39502489

Hornstein, S., Forman-Hoffman, V., Nazander, A., Ranta, K., & Hilbert, K. (2021). Predicting therapy outcome in a digital mental health intervention for depression and anxiety: A machine learning approach. *Digital Health*, *7*, 20552076211060659. DOI: 10.1177/20552076211060659 PMID: 34868624

Hornstein, S., Zantvoort, K., Lueken, U., Funk, B., & Hilbert, K. (2023). Personalization strategies in digital mental health interventions: A systematic review and conceptual framework for depressive symptoms. *Frontiers in Digital Health*, *5*, 1170002. DOI: 10.3389/fdgth.2023.1170002 PMID: 37283721

Howarth, A., Quesada, J., Silva, J., Judycki, S., & Mills, P. R. (2018). The impact of digital health interventions on health-related outcomes in the workplace: A systematic review. *Digital Health*, *4*, 1–8. DOI: 10.1177/2055207618770861 PMID: 29942631

Hsieh, H. F., & Shannon, S. E. (2005). Three approaches to qualitative content analysis. *Qualitative Health Research*, *15*(9), 1277–1288. DOI: 10.1177/1049732305276687 PMID: 16204405

Hugh-Jones, S., Pert, K., Kendal, S., Eltringham, S., Skelton, C., Yaziji, N., & West, R. (2022). Adolescents accept digital mental health support in schools: A co-design and feasibility study of a school-based app for UK adolescents. *Mental Health & Prevention*, *27*, 200241. DOI: 10.1016/j.mhp.2022.200241

Hung, J. L., Wang, M. C., Wang, S., Abdelrasoul, M., Lo, Y., & He, W. (2017). Identifying at-risk students for early interventions—A time-series clustering approach. *IEEE Transactions on Emerging Topics in Computing*, *5*(1), 44–55. DOI: 10.1109/TETC.2015.2504239

Hunt, J., & Eisenberg, D. (2010). Mental health problems and help-seeking behavior among college students. *The Journal of Adolescent Health*, *46*(1), 3–10. DOI: 10.1016/j.jadohealth.2009.08.008 PMID: 20123251

Huntley, C. D., Young, B., Temple, J., Longworth, M., Smith, C. T., Jha, V., & Fisher, P. L. (2019). The efficacy of interventions for test-anxious university students: A meta-analysis of randomized controlled trials. *Journal of Anxiety Disorders*, *63*, 36–50. DOI: 10.1016/j.janxdis.2019.01.007 PMID: 30826687

Inkster, B., Sarda, S., & Subramanian, V. (2018). An empathy-driven, conversational artificial intelligence agent (Wysa) for digital mental well-being: Real-world data evaluation. *JMIR mHealth and uHealth*, *6*(11), e12106. DOI: 10.2196/12106 PMID: 30470676

Jackson, H. M., Gulliver, A., Hasking, P., Leach, L., Batterham, P. J., Calear, A. L., & Farrer, L. M. (2024). Exploring student preferences for implementing a digital mental health intervention in a university setting: Qualitative study within a randomised controlled trial. *Digital Health*, *10*, 20552076241277175. DOI: 10.1177/20552076241277175 PMID: 39224795

James, J., & Versteeg, M. (2007). Mobile phones in Africa: How much do we really know? *Social Indicators Research*, *84*(1), 117–126. DOI: 10.1007/s11205-006-9079-x PMID: 20076776

Janahi, Y., & Obeidat, M. (2025). Predictive analytics and AI in education: A systematic literature review on identifying and supporting at-risk students [Preprint]. *SSRN*. DOI: 10.2139/ssrn.5240920

Jiménez Zapata, R., Sánchez Castillo, V., & Pérez Gamboa, A. J. (2023). Health, education and pandemic: An analysis of their relationship. *Health Leadership and Quality of Life*, *1*(1), 14–26. DOI: 10.56294/hl2023195

Johnson, R. D., & Diman, K. (2017). An Investigation of the Factors Driving the Adoption of Cloud-Based Human Resource Information Systems by Small- and Medium-Sized Businesses. In Bondarouk, T., Ruël, H. J. M., & Parry, E. (Eds.), *Electronic HRM in the Smart Era (The Changing Context of Managing People)* (pp. 1–31). Emerald Publishing Limited., DOI: 10.1108/978-1-78714-315-920161001

Johnston, M. P. (2014). Secondary data analysis: A method of which the time has come. *Qualitative and Quantitative Methods in Libraries*, *3*, 619–626.

Kachgal, M. M., Hansen, L. S., & Nutter, K. J. (2001). Academic procrastination prevention/intervention: Strategies and recommendations. *Journal of Developmental Education*, *25*(1), 14–24.

Kaliisa, R., Misiejuk, K., López-Pernas, S., Khalil, M., & Saqr, M. (2023). Have learning analytics dashboards lived up to the hype? A systematic review of impact on students' achievement, motivation, participation and attitude [Preprint]. arXiv. https://arxiv.org/abs/2312.15042

Kane, H., Baumgart, J. G., El-Hage, W., Deloyer, J., Maes, C., Lebas, M. C., Marazziti, D., Thome, J., Fond-Harmant, L., & Denis, F. (2022). Opportunities and Challenges for Professionals in Psychiatry and Mental Health Care Using Digital Technologies During the COVID-19 Pandemic: Systematic Review. *JMIR Human Factors*, *9*(1), e30359. DOI: 10.2196/30359 PMID: 34736224

Kanuri, N., Arora, P., Talluru, S., Colaco, B., Dutta, R., Rawat, A., Taylor, B. C., Manjula, M., & Newman, M. G. (2020). Examining the initial usability, acceptability and feasibility of a digital mental health intervention for college students in India. *International Journal of Psychology*, *55*(4), 657–673. DOI: 10.1002/ijop.12640 PMID: 31867730

Karakaya, K., & Altınsoy, F. (2023). Academic procrastination of university students: The role of problematic internet use, self-regulated online learning, and academic self-efficacy. *MOJET, 11*(1), 77–93. DOI: 10.52380/mojet.2023.11.1.459

Karataş, H., & Bademcioglu, M. (2015). The explanation of the academic procrastination behaviour of pre-service teachers with five factor personality traits. *The International Journal of Research in Teacher Education, 6*(2), 11–25.

Karyotaki, E., Ebert, D. D., Donkin, L., Riper, H., Twisk, J., Burger, S., Rozental, A., Lange, A., Williams, A. D., Zarski, A. C., Geraedts, A., van Straten, A., Kleiboer, A., Meyer, B., Ünlü Ince, B. B., Buntrock, C., Lehr, D., Snoek, F. J., Andrews, G., & Cuijpers, P. (2019). Do guided internet-based interventions result in clinically relevant changes for patients with depression? An individual participant data meta-analysis. *Clinical Psychology Review, 63*, 80–92. DOI: 10.1016/j.cpr.2018.06.007 PMID: 29940401

Kassim, F., Azmi, N. F., Rahman, N. A. A., & Zainal, N. R. (2022). Gender difference in procrastination among university students. *Asian Journal of Research in Education and Social Sciences, 4*(3), 11–22. DOI: 10.55057/ajress.2022.4.3.2

Kauer, S. D., Mangan, C., & Sanci, L. (2014). Do online mental health services improve help-seeking for young people? *Journal of Medical Internet Research, 16*(3), e66. DOI: 10.2196/jmir.3103 PMID: 24594922

Kaur, I., Kamel, R., Sultanik, E., Tan, J., Mazefsky, C. A., Brookman-Frazee, L., McPartland, J. C., Goodwin, M. S., Pennington, J., Beidas, R. S., Mandell, D. S., & Nuske, H. J. (2025). Supporting emotion regulation in children on the autism spectrum: Co-developing a digital mental health application for school-based settings with community partners. *Journal of Pediatric Psychology, 50*(1), 129–140. DOI: 10.1093/jpepsy/jsae078 PMID: 39441712

Kealy, C., & Potts, C. (2025, March 3). Digital Mental Health Interventions for University Students With Mental Health Difficulties: A Systematic Review and Meta-Analysis. *Early Intervention in Psychiatry, 19*(3), e70017. DOI: 10.1111/eip.70017 PMID: 40033658

Kessler, R. C., Berglund, P., Demler, O., Jin, R., Merikangas, K. R., & Walters, E. E. (2005). Lifetime prevalence and age-of-onset distributions of DSM-IV disorders in the National Comorbidity Survey Replication. *Archives of General Psychiatry, 62*(6), 593–602. DOI: 10.1001/archpsyc.62.6.593 PMID: 15939837

Khai Lin, C., Abdul, N., Faizatul, A., & Peh, W. (2021). Factor contributing to internet addiction and its influence on academic procrastination behavior among UUM students. *Journal of Governance and Development*, *17*(2), 61–75. DOI: 10.32890/jgd2021.17.2.4

Khanna, M. S., & Carper, M. (2022). Digital mental health interventions for child and adolescent anxiety. *Cognitive and Behavioral Practice*, *29*(1), 60–68. DOI: 10.1016/j.cbpra.2021.05.003

Khatib, A., Abo-Rass, F., & Gelkopf, M. (2022). Theory of planned behavior: Exploring the use of digital mental health interventions in Israel. *The Journal of Nervous and Mental Disease*, *210*(7), 504–509. DOI: 10.1097/NMD.0000000000001459 PMID: 34966111

Kim, J., Aryee, L. M., Bang, H., Prajogo, S., Choi, Y. K., Hoch, J. S., & Prado, E. L. (2023). Effectiveness of digital mental health tools to reduce depressive and anxiety symptoms in low-and middle-income countries: Systematic review and meta-analysis. *JMIR Mental Health*, *10*, e43066. DOI: 10.2196/43066 PMID: 36939820

Kim, K. R., & Seo, E. H. (2015). The relationship between procrastination and academic performance: A meta-analysis. *Personality and Individual Differences*, *82*, 26–33. DOI: 10.1016/j.paid.2015.02.038

Klingsieck, K. B. (2013). Procrastination. *European Psychologist*, *18*(1), 24–34. DOI: 10.1027/1016-9040/a000138

Knapp, A. A., Hersch, E., Wijaya, C., Herrera, M. A., Kruzan, K. P., Carroll, A. J., Lee, S., Baker, A., Gray, A., Harris, V., Simmons, R., Kour Sodhi, D., Hannah, N., Reddy, M., Karnik, N. S., Smith, J. D., Brown, C. H., & Mohr, D. C. (2023). "The library is so much more than books": Considerations for the design and implementation of teen digital mental health services in public libraries. *Frontiers in Digital Health*, *5*, 1183319. DOI: 10.3389/fdgth.2023.1183319 PMID: 37560198

Ko, C.-H., Liu, G.-C., Hsiao, S., Yen, J.-Y., Yang, M.-J., Lin, W.-C., Yen, C.-F., & Chen, C.-S. (2009). Brain activities associated with gaming urge of online gaming addiction. *Journal of Psychiatric Research*, *43*(7), 739–747. DOI: 10.1016/j.jpsychires.2008.09.012 PMID: 18996542

Kodish, T., Schueller, S. M., & Lau, A. S. (2023). Barriers and strategies to improve digital mental health intervention uptake among college students of color: A modified Delphi study. *Journal of Behavioral and Cognitive Therapy*, *33*(1), 10–23. DOI: 10.1016/j.jbct.2022.12.002

Kozelka, E. E., Acquilano, S. C., Al-Abdulmunem, M., Guarino, S., Elwyn, G., Drake, R. E., & Carpenter-Song, E. (2023). Documenting the digital divide: Identifying barriers to digital mental health access among people with serious mental illness in community settings. *SSM. Mental Health*, *4*, 100241. DOI: 10.1016/j.ssmmh.2023.100241

Kozelka, E. E., Acquilano, S. C., Al-Abdulmunem, M., Guarino, S., Elwyn, G., Drake, R. E., & Carpenter-Song, E. (2024). Digital mental health and its discontents: Assumptions about technology that create barriers to equitable access. *Psychiatric Services (Washington, D.C.)*, *75*(3), 299–302. DOI: 10.1176/appi.ps.20230238 PMID: 38050440

Krisher, L., Boeldt, D. L., Sigmon, C. A. N., Rimel, S. E., & Newman, L. S. (2024). Pragmatic approach to the assessment and use of digital mental health interventions for health workers. *American Journal of Public Health*, *114*(S2), 171–179. DOI: 10.2105/AJPH.2023.307505 PMID: 38354345

Kumar, V. V., & Tankha, G. (2021). Nurturing spiritual intelligence in the classroom. In *Leading schools with social, emotional, and academic development (SEAD)* (pp. 187-201). IGI Global. DOI: 10.4018/978-1-7998-6728-9.ch010

Kumar, M., Macharia, P., Nyongesa, V., Kathono, J., Yator, O., Mwaniga, S., McKay, M., Huang, K. Y., Shidhaye, R., Njuguna, S., & Saxena, S. (2022). Human-centered design exploration with Kenyan health workers on proposed digital mental health screening and intervention training development: Thematic analysis of user preferences and needs. *Digital Health*, *8*, 20552076221090035. DOI: 10.1177/20552076221090035 PMID: 35444811

Kumar, M., & Sharma, A. (2020). Effectiveness of peer support counseling in Indian higher education: A psychological well-being perspective. *Asian Journal of Psychiatry*, *54*, 102203. DOI: 10.1016/j.ajp.2020.102203

Kumar, R., Singh, P., & Agarwal, S. (2025). Implementing wearable technology for student stress tracking and engagement in higher education: Case insights. *Education and Information Technologies*, *30*, 1021–1045. DOI: 10.1007/s10639-025-11500-x

Kunanti, N., Putri, S. A., & Fahmi, M. (2025). "Record, spread, judge": A short video reflecting the crisis of digital morality and media manipulation in modern society. *Action Research Literate*, *1*(1), 20–29. DOI: 10.46799/arl.v9i6.2971

Kurki, M., Gilbert, S., Mishina, K., Lempinen, L., Luntamo, T., Hinkka-Yli-Salomäki, S., Sinokki, A., Upadhyaya, S., Wei, Y., & Sourander, A. (2021). Digital mental health literacy-program for the first-year medical students' wellbeing: A one group quasi-experimental study. *BMC Medical Education, 21*(1), 563. DOI: 10.1186/s12909-021-02990-4 PMID: 34742258

Kuzilek, J., Hlosta, M., Herrmannova, D., Zdrahal, Z., Vaclavek, J., & Wolff, A. (2015). *OU Analyse: Analysing at-risk students at The Open University* (Learning Analytics Review No. LAK15-1). LACE Project. http://www.laceproject.eu/learning-analytics-review

Kvale, S., & Brinkmann, S. (2015). *InterViews: Learning the craft of qualitative research interviewing* (3rd ed.). SAGE Publications.

Kyalimpa, P. (2013). *Leadership Competence and Sustainable Funding of Local Non-Governmental Organisations in Uganda.* Unpublished doctoral thesis. Mbarara University of Science and Technology.

Laher, A. E., Van Aardt, B. J., Craythorne, A. D., Van Welie, M., Malinga, D. M., & Madi, S. (2019). 'Getting out of the dark': Implications of load shedding on healthcare in South Africa and strategies to enhance preparedness. *South African Medical Journal, 109*(12), 899–901. DOI: 10.7196/SAMJ.2019.v109i12.14322 PMID: 31865948

Lai, J., Rahmani, A., Yunusova, A., Rivera, A. P., Labbaf, S., Hu, S., Dutt, N., Jain, R., & Borelli, J. L. (2021). Using multimodal assessments to capture personalized contexts of college student well-being in 2020: Case study. *JMIR Formative Research, 5*(5), e26186. DOI: 10.2196/26186 PMID: 33882022

Lal, S. (2019). E-mental health: Promising advancements in policy, research, and practice. *Healthcare Management Forum, 32*(2), 56–62. DOI: 10.1177/0840470418818583 PMID: 30739487

Lal, S., Gleeson, J. F., D'Alfonso, S., Lepage, M., Joober, R., Lee, H., Abdel-Baki, A., Lecomte, T., & Alvarez-Jimenez, M. (2024). Digital mental health intervention for schizophrenia spectrum and psychotic disorders: Protocol for a pragmatic feasibility study of Horyzons-Canada. *Digital Health, 10*, 20552076241282231. DOI: 10.1177/20552076241282231 PMID: 39372808

Lattie, E. G., Stiles-Shields, C., & Graham, A. K. (2022). An overview of and recommendations for more accessible digital mental health services. *Nature Reviews Psychology, 1*(2), 87–100. DOI: 10.1038/s44159-021-00003-1 PMID: 38515434

Lehtimaki, S., Martic, J., Wahl, B., Foster, K. T., & Schwalbe, N. (2021). Evidence on digital mental health interventions for adolescents and young people: Systematic overview. *JMIR Mental Health*, *8*(4), e25847. DOI: 10.2196/25847 PMID: 33913817

Leo, A. J., Schuelke, M. J., Hunt, D. M., Metzler, J. P., Miller, J. P., Areán, P. A., Armbrecht, M. A., & Cheng, A. L. (2022). A digital mental health intervention in an orthopedic setting for patients with symptoms of depression and/or anxiety: Feasibility prospective cohort study. *JMIR Formative Research*, *6*(2), e34889. DOI: 10.2196/34889 PMID: 35039278

Leo, A. J., Schuelke, M. J., Hunt, D. M., Miller, J. P., Areán, P. A., & Cheng, A. L. (2022). Digital mental health intervention plus usual care compared with usual care only and usual care plus in-person psychological counseling for orthopedic patients with symptoms of depression or anxiety: Cohort study. *JMIR Formative Research*, *6*(5), e36203. DOI: 10.2196/36203 PMID: 35507387

Leuzzi, G., Job, M., Scafoglieri, A., & Testa, M. (2025). Smartphone apps and wearables for health parameters in young adulthood: Cross-sectional study. *JMIR Human Factors*, *12*, e64629. DOI: 10.2196/64629 PMID: 40902119

Lewis, T., Synowiec, C., Lagomarsino, G., & Schweitzer, J. (2012). E-health in low-and middle-income countries: Findings from the Center for Health Market Innovations. *Bulletin of the World Health Organization*, *90*(5), 332–340. DOI: 10.2471/BLT.11.099820 PMID: 22589566

Li, B., Friston, K. J., Liu, J., Liu, Y., Zhang, G., Cao, F., Su, L., Yao, S., Lu, H., & Hu, D. (2014). Impaired frontal-basal ganglia connectivity in adolescents with internet addiction. *Scientific Reports*, *4*(1), 5027. DOI: 10.1038/srep05027 PMID: 24848380

Lim, C. T., Fuchs, C., & Torous, J. (2024). Integrated digital mental health care: A vision for addressing population mental health needs. *International Journal of General Medicine*, *17*, 359–365. DOI: 10.2147/IJGM.S449474 PMID: 38318335

Linardon, J., Westrupp, E. M., Macdonald, J. A., Mikocka-Walus, A., Stokes, M. A., Greenwood, C. J., Youssef, G. J., Teague, S., Hutchinson, D., Sciberras, E., & Fuller-Tyszkiewicz, M. (2022). Monitoring Australian parents' shifting receptiveness to digital mental health interventions during the COVID-19 pandemic. *The Australian and New Zealand Journal of Psychiatry*, *56*(11), 1503–1514. DOI: 10.1177/00048674211065985 PMID: 34963330

Lincoln, Y. S., & Guba, E. G. (1985). *Naturalistic inquiry*. SAGE Publications. DOI: 10.1016/0147-1767(85)90062-8

Linden, B., Boyes, R., & Stuart, H. (2021). Cross-sectional trend analysis of the NCHA II survey data on Canadian post-secondary student mental health and well-being from 2013 to 2019. *BMC Public Health*, *21*(1), 590. DOI: 10.1186/s12889-021-10622-1 PMID: 33765965

Linden, D. J. (2011). *The compass of pleasure: How our brains make fatty foods, orgasm, exercise, marijuana, generosity, vodka, learning, and gambling feel so good*. Viking Adult.

Lipschitz, J. M., Pike, C. K., Hogan, T. P., Murphy, S. A., & Burdick, K. E. (2023). The engagement problem: A review of engagement with digital mental health interventions and recommendations for a path forward. *Current Treatment Options in Psychiatry*, *10*(3), 119–135. DOI: 10.1007/s40501-023-00297-3 PMID: 38390026

Liu, M., & Schueller, S. M. (2023). Moving evidence-based mental health interventions into practice: Implementation of digital mental health interventions. *Current Treatment Options in Psychiatry*, *10*(4), 333–345. DOI: 10.1007/s40501-023-00298-2

Liu, Q., & Khalil, M. (2023). Understanding privacy and data protection issues in learning analytics using a systematic review. *British Journal of Educational Technology*, *54*(6), 1715–1747. DOI: 10.1111/bjet.13388

Liverpool, S., Mota, C. P., Sales, C. M., Čuš, A., Carletto, S., Hancheva, C., Sousa, S., Cerón, S. C., Moreno-Peral, P., Pietrabissa, G., Moltrecht, B., Ulberg, R., Ferreira, N., & Edbrooke-Childs, J. (2020). Engaging children and young people in digital mental health interventions: Systematic review of modes of delivery, facilitators, and barriers. *Journal of Medical Internet Research*, *22*(6), e16317. DOI: 10.2196/16317 PMID: 32442160

Li, X., Zhang, Y., & Wang, L. (2025). Physiological and behavioral monitoring of students using wearables for personalized learning interventions. *Computers & Education*, *208*, 104379. DOI: 10.1016/j.compedu.2024.104379

Li, Y. (2023). Application of machine learning to predict mental health disorders and interpret feature importance. In *Proceedings of the 3rd International Symposium on Computer Technology and Information Science (ISCTIS 2023)* (pp. 257–261). IEEE. DOI: 10.1109/ISCTIS58954.2023.10213032

Lo, B., Pham, Q., Sockalingam, S., Wiljer, D., & Strudwick, G. (2022). Identifying essential factors that influence user engagement with digital mental health tools in clinical care settings: Protocol for a Delphi study. *Digital Health*, *8*, 20552076221129059. DOI: 10.1177/20552076221129059 PMID: 36249478

Loda, T., Löffler, T., Erschens, R., Zipfel, S., & Herrmann-Werner, A. (2020). Medical education in times of COVID-19: German students' expectations—A cross-sectional study. *PLoS One*, *15*(11), e0241660. DOI: 10.1371/journal.pone.0241660

Lolla, A. (2018). Mantras help the general psychological well-being of college students: A pilot study. *Journal of Religion and Health*, *57*(1), 110–119. DOI: 10.1007/s10943-017-0371-7 PMID: 28271341

Ludlow, K., March, S., Russell, J. K., Ryan, B., Brown, R. L., Hides, L., Donovan, C., Spence, S. H., Saxby, J., & Cobham, V. E. (2024). Co-designing a new digital mental health platform,'momentum', with caregivers of young people aged 7–17. *Digital Health*, *10*, 20552076241263693. DOI: 10.1177/20552076241263693

Ludlow, K., Russell, J. K., Ryan, B., Brown, R. L., Joynt, T., Uhlmann, L. R., Smith, G. E., Donovan, C., Hides, L., Spence, S. H., March, S., & Cobham, V. E. (2023). Co-designing a digital mental health platform,"Momentum", with young people aged 7–17: A qualitative study. *Digital Health*, *9*, 20552076231216410. DOI: 10.1177/20552076231216410 PMID: 38033517

Lukka, L., & Palva, J. M. (2023). The development of game-based digital mental health interventions: Bridging the paradigms of health care and entertainment. *JMIR Serious Games*, *11*(1), e42173. DOI: 10.2196/42173 PMID: 37665624

Lukka, L., Salonen, A., Vesterinen, M., Karhulahti, V. M., Palva, S., & Palva, J. M. (2023). The qualities of patients interested in using a game-based digital mental health intervention for depression: A sequential mixed methods study. *BMC Digital Health*, *1*(1), 37. DOI: 10.1186/s44247-023-00037-w

Lund, C., Petersen, I., Kleintjes, S., & Bhana, A. (2012). Mental health services in South Africa: Taking stock. *The African Journal of Psychiatry*, *15*(6), 402–405. DOI: 10.4314/ajpsy.v15i6.48 PMID: 23160613

Lyon, A. R., Dopp, A. R., Brewer, S. K., Kientz, J. A., & Munson, S. A. (2020). Designing the future of children's mental health services. *Administration and Policy in Mental Health*, *47*(5), 735–751. DOI: 10.1007/s10488-020-01038-x PMID: 32253634

Mabil-Atem, J. M., Gumuskaya, O., & Wilson, R. L. (2024). Digital mental health interventions for the mental health care of refugees and asylum seekers: Integrative literature review. *International Journal of Mental Health Nursing*, *33*(4), 760–780. DOI: 10.1111/inm.13283 PMID: 38291740

Machado, A. S., Ferreira, B., Pereira, C. Y., Carrola, C., de Melo, B. B. V., & Campos, C. (2024). Digital mental health interventions for children and youth. In *Handbook of Research on Advances in Digital Technologies to Promote Rehabilitation and Community Participation* (pp. 20–47). IGI Global Scientific Publishing.

Magomedova, A., & Fatima, G. (2025). Mental health and well-being in the modern era: A comprehensive review of challenges and interventions. *Cureus*, *17*(1). Advance online publication. DOI: 10.7759/cureus.77683 PMID: 39974249

Malla, A., & Joober, R. (2021). COVID-19 and the future with digital mental health: Need for attention to complexities. *Canadian Journal of Psychiatry*, *66*(1), 14–16. DOI: 10.1177/0706743720957824 PMID: 32885686

Manap, A., Rizzo, A., Yıldırmaz, A., Dilekçi, Ü., & Yıldırım, M. (2023). The mediating role of procrastination in the relationship between fear of missing out and internet addiction in university students. *International Journal of Environmental Research and Public Health*, *21*(1), 49. DOI: 10.3390/ijerph21010049 PMID: 38248514

Maphalala, M. C., & Adigun, O. T. (2021). Academics' Experience of Implementing E-Learning in a SA Higher Education Institution. *International Journal of Higher Education*, *10*(1), 1–13. DOI: 10.5430/ijhe.v10n1p1

Maqsood, A., Gul, S., Zahra, T., Noureen, N., & Khattak, A. (2024). From face-to-face to screen-to-screen: Exploring the multifaceted dimensions of digital mental health care. *Frontiers in Psychiatry*, *15*, 1413127. DOI: 10.3389/fpsyt.2024.1413127 PMID: 39564463

Marbouti, F., Diefes-Dux, H. A., & Madhavan, K. (2016). Models for early prediction of at-risk students in a course using standards-based grading. *Computers & Education*, *103*, 1–15. DOI: 10.1016/j.compedu.2016.09.005

Margolis, K., Kelsay, K., Talmi, A., McMillan, H., Fraley, M. C., & Thomas, J. F. F. (2018). A multidisciplinary, team-based teleconsultation approach to enhance child mental health services in rural pediatrics. *Journal of Educational & Psychological Consultation*, *28*(3), 342–367. DOI: 10.1080/10474412.2018.1431549

Martinez-Martin, N., Dasgupta, I., Carter, A., Chandler, J. A., Kellmeyer, P., Kreitmair, K., Weiss, A., & Cabrera, L. Y. (2020). Ethics of digital mental health during COVID-19: Crisis and opportunities. *JMIR Mental Health*, *7*(12), e23776. DOI: 10.2196/23776 PMID: 33156811

Martinez-Martin, N., & Kreitmair, K. (2018). Ethical issues for direct-to-consumer digital psychotherapy apps: Addressing accountability, data protection, and consent. *JMIR Mental Health*, *5*(2), e9423. DOI: 10.2196/mental.9423 PMID: 29685865

Masri, D., Jaber, L., Mashal, R., Albourini, F., Alsaoud, M. A., & Al-Tarawneh, A. M. (2024, February). The Role of Wearables & Technology in Mental Health. In *2024 2nd International Conference on Cyber Resilience (ICCR)* (pp. 1-5). IEEE. DOI: 10.1109/ICCR61006.2024.10532880

Maxwell, J. A. (2012). *A realist approach for qualitative research*. SAGE Publications.

Mayring, P. (2014). *Qualitative content analysis: Theoretical foundation, basic procedures and software solution*. Beltz.

Mbunge, E., Batani, J., Gaobotse, G., & Muchemwa, B. (2022). Virtual healthcare services and digital health technologies deployed during coronavirus disease 2019 (COVID-19) pandemic in South Africa: A systematic review. *Global Health Journal (Amsterdam, Netherlands)*, *6*(2), 102–113. DOI: 10.1016/j.glohj.2022.03.001 PMID: 35282399

Mbunge, E., Muchemwa, B., & Batani, J. (2022). Are we there yet? Unbundling the potential adoption and integration of telemedicine to improve virtual healthcare services in African health systems. *Sensors International*, *3*, 100152. DOI: 10.1016/j.sintl.2021.100152 PMID: 34901894

McBain, R. K., Schuler, M. S., Qureshi, N., Matthews, S., Kofner, A., Breslau, J. H. C., & Cantor, J. H. (2023). Expansion of telehealth availability for mental health care after state-level policy changes, 2019–2022. *JAMA Network Open*, *6*(6), e2318045. DOI: 10.1001/jamanetworkopen.2023.18045 PMID: 37310741

Mehra, A., & Kapoor, R. (2021). Online mental health support for college students during COVID-19: A qualitative study. *Journal of Affective Disorders*, *284*, 42–49. DOI: 10.1016/j.jad.2021.02.012

Mendes-Santos, C., Nunes, F., Weiderpass, E., Santana, R., & Andersson, G. (2022). Understanding mental health professionals' perspectives and practices regarding the implementation of digital mental health: Qualitative study. *JMIR Formative Research*, *6*(4), e32558. DOI: 10.2196/32558 PMID: 35412459

Mensah, J. (2019). Sustainable development: Meaning, history, principles, pillars, and implications for human action: Literature review. *Cogent Social Sciences*, *5*(1), 1–21. DOI: 10.1080/23311886.2019.1653531

Merry, S. N., Cargo, T., Christie, G., Donkin, L., Hetrick, S., Fleming, T., Holt-Quick, C., Hopkins, S., Stasiak, K., & Warren, J. (2020). Debate: Supporting the mental health of school students in the COVID-19 pandemic in New Zealand–a digital ecosystem approach. *Child and Adolescent Mental Health*, *25*(4), 267–269. DOI: 10.1111/camh.12429 PMID: 33025729

Meyerhoff, J., Kornfield, R., Lattie, E. G., Knapp, A. A., Kruzan, K. P., Jacobs, M., Stamatis, C. A., Taple, B. J., Beltzer, M. L., Berry, A. B. L., Reddy, M., Mohr, D. C., & Graham, A. K. (2023). From formative design to service-ready therapeutic: A pragmatic approach to designing digital mental health interventions across domains. *Internet Interventions : the Application of Information Technology in Mental and Behavioural Health, 34*, 100677. DOI: 10.1016/j.invent.2023.100677 PMID: 37808416

Mhlanga, D., Denhere, V., & Moloi, T. (2022). COVID-19 and the Key Digital Transformation Lessons for Higher Education Institutions in South Africa. *Education Sciences, 12*(7), 1–17. DOI: 10.3390/educsci12070464

Milková, E., Kaliba, M., & Ambrozova, P. (2022). Internet addiction in university students: Czech study. *Journal on Efficiency and Responsibility in Education and Science, 15*(2), 94–102. DOI: 10.7160/eriesj.2022.150204

Mindu, T., Mutero, I. T., Ngcobo, W. B., Musesengwa, R., & Chimbari, M. J. (2023). Digital mental health interventions for young people in rural South Africa: Prospects and challenges for implementation. *International Journal of Environmental Research and Public Health, 20*(2), 1453. DOI: 10.3390/ijerph20021453 PMID: 36674209

Ministry of Education. (2021). *Manodarpan – Psychosocial support for mental health and well-being of students*. Government of India. https://manodarpan.education.gov.in/

Ministry of Education. (2021). *School wellness programmes in India: Annual report*. Government of India.

Ministry of Education. India. (2020). *MANODARPAN: Psycho-social support for mental health & well-being during the COVID-19 outbreak and beyond*. https://www.education.gov.in/manodarpan/

Ministry of Human Resource Development, Government of India. (n.d.). *National Education Policy 2020*. https://www.education.gov.in/sites/upload_files/mhrd/files/NEP_Final_English_0.pdf

Min, W., Jun, G., & Feng, L. (2022). How psychological wellbeing and digital mental health services intervene the role of self-efficacy and affective commitment of university students in their performance? *Frontiers in Psychiatry, 13*, 946793. DOI: 10.3389/fpsyt.2022.946793 PMID: 35873249

Mishara, B. L., Chagnon, F., Daigle, M., Balan, B., Raymond, S., Marcoux, I., & Turecki, G. (2007). Helper behaviors and intervention styles related to short-term outcomes in telephone crisis intervention. *Suicide & Life-Threatening Behavior, 37*(3), 308–321. DOI: 10.1521/suli.2007.37.3.308 PMID: 17579543

Mitra, U., & Rehman, S. U. (2025)a. Significance of AI/ML Wearable Technologies for Education and Teaching. In *Wearable Devices and Smart Technology for Educational Teaching Assistance* (pp. 1-26). IGI Global Scientific Publishing.

Mitra, U., & Rehman, S. U. (2025)b. Integrating AI/ML With Wearable Devices for Monitoring Student Mental Health. In *Wearable Devices and Smart Technology for Educational Teaching Assistance* (pp. 257-284). IGI Global Scientific Publishing.

Mitra, U., & Rehman, S. U. (2025b). Integrating AI/ML With Wearable Devices for Monitoring Student Mental Health. In Wearable Devices and Smart Technology for Educational Teaching Assistance (pp. 257-284). IGI Global Scientific Publishing. Integrating AI/ML With Wearable Devices for Monitoring Student Mental Health. In Wearable Devices and Smart Technology for Educational Teaching Assistance (pp. 257-284). IGI Global Scientific Publishing.

Mitra, U., & Rehman, S. U. (2025a). Significance of AI/ML Wearable Technologies for Education and Teaching. In *Wearable Devices and Smart Technology for Educational Teaching Assistance* (pp. 1–26). IGI Global Scientific Publishing.

Mohr, D. C., Kwasny, M. J., Meyerhoff, J., Graham, A. K., & Lattie, E. G. (2021). The effect of depression and anxiety symptom severity on clinical outcomes and app use in digital mental health treatments: Meta-regression of three trials. *Behaviour Research and Therapy, 147*, 103972. DOI: 10.1016/j.brat.2021.103972 PMID: 34600398

Montagni, I., & Christophe, T. (2020). Mental Health-Related Digital Use by University Students: A Systematic Review. *Telemedicine Journal and e-Health, 26*(2), 131–146. Advance online publication. DOI: 10.1089/tmj.2018.0316 PMID: 30888256

Moock, J. (2014). Support from the internet for individuals with mental disorders: Advantages and disadvantages of e-mental health service delivery. *Frontiers in Public Health, 2*, 65. DOI: 10.3389/fpubh.2014.00065 PMID: 24967221

Moonaghi, H. K., & Beydokhti, T. B. (2017). Academic procrastination and its characteristics: A narrative review. *Future of Medical Education Journal, 7*(2), 43–50.

Mota, N. B., Pimenta, J., Tavares, M., Palmeira, L., Loch, A. A., Hedin-Pereira, C., & Dias, E. C. (2022). A Brazilian bottom-up strategy to address mental health in a diverse population over a large territorial area–an inspiration for the use of digital mental health. *Psychiatry Research*, *311*, 114477. DOI: 10.1016/j.psychres.2022.114477 PMID: 35245744

Mpofu, F. Y., Mpofu, A., Mantula, F., & Shava, G. N. (2024). Towards the Attainment of SDGs: The Contribution of Higher Education Institutions in Zimbabwe. *International Journal of Social Science Research and Review*, *7*(1), 474–493. DOI: 10.47814/ijssrr.v7i1.1719

Muchamore, I., Karanikolas, P., & Gooding, P. M. (2024). How lived experience expertise shapes research and development in digital mental health. *Available at SSRN* 4932039. DOI: 10.2139/ssrn.4932039

Musakuro, R. N. (2025). The adoption of e-health tools for digital mental health services in a South African higher education institution. *International Journal of Research in Business & Social Science*, *14*(1), 47–57. DOI: 10.20525/ijrbs.v14i1.3841

Musakuro, R. N., & Gie, L. (2024). Exploring university staff experiences gained during COVID-19 in the provision of digital mental health services through e-health tools: A case of a selected South African University. *International Journal of Research in Business and Social Science*, *13*(7), 155–168. DOI: 10.20525/ijrbs.v13i7.3648

Musakuro, R. N., & Gie, L. (2025). Strategies for sustainable adoption of e-health tools for digital mental health services. *SA Journal of Human Resource Management*, *23*, 11. DOI: 10.4102/sajhrm.v23i0.3053

Nadarajan, S., Hengudomsub, P., & Wacharasin, C. (2023). The role of academic procrastination on Internet addiction among Thai university students: A cross-sectional study. *Belitung Nursing Journal*, *9*(4), 384–390. DOI: 10.33546/bnj.2755 PMID: 37645572

Najdi, L., & Er-Raha, B. (2016). A novel predictive modeling system to analyze students at risk of academic failure. *International Journal of Computer Applications*, *156*(6), 25–30. DOI: 10.5120/ijca2016912482

Naslund, J. A., Aschbrenner, K. A., Araya, R., Marsch, L. A., Unützer, J., Patel, V., & Bartels, S. J. (2022). Digital technology for treating and preventing mental disorders in low-income and middle-income countries: A narrative review of the literature. *The Lancet. Psychiatry*, *9*(2), 123–136. DOI: 10.1016/S2215-0366(21)00301-1 PMID: 28433615

Naslund, J. A., & Deng, D. (2021). Addressing mental health stigma in low-income and middle-income countries: A new frontier for digital mental health. *Ethics, Medicine, and Public Health, 19*, 100719. DOI: 10.1016/j.jemep.2021.100719 PMID: 35083375

National Crime Records Bureau. (2022). [Ministry of Home Affairs, Government of India. https://ncrb.gov.in]. *Accidental Deaths and Suicides in India, 2021*, •••.

Navarro, A., Ortega, M., & López, J. (2024). Smartwatch-based monitoring of stress and attention in secondary school students: Implications for educational strategies. *Journal of Learning Analytics, 11*(3), 56–73. DOI: 10.18608/jla.2024.1134

Neuendorf, K. A. (2018). Content analysis and thematic analysis. In Brough, P. (Ed.), *Advanced Research Methods for Applied Psychology Design - Analysis and Reporting* (pp. 211–223). Routledge., DOI: 10.4324/9781315517971

Neuroscience News. (2024, March 11). *Happiness Takes Practice - Neuroscience News*. Neuroscience News. https://neurosciencenews.com/happiness-practice-25736/?utm_source=chatgpt.com

Nhaitayi, R. M. (2014). *Exploring staff perceptions of why selected development NPOs are able to deliver effective services*. Unpublished master's thesis. University of Cape Town.

Niemi, H., & Kumpulainen, K. (2022). Digital well-being in the Finnish education system: Integrating mental health and media literacy. *Nordic Journal of Digital Literacy, 17*(3), 145–160. DOI: 10.18261/njdl.17.3.2

Niselow, T. (2023). Sunday Read: Load shedding through the years and how Eskom has struggled to keep the lights on. https://www.news24.com/fin24/economy/eskom/sunday-read-load-shedding-through-the-years-and-how-eskom-has-struggled-to-keep-the-lights-on-20190324

Nishimura, T., Wakuta, M., Osuka, Y., Tsukui, N., Hirata, I., Takahashi, M., Adachi, M., Katayama, T., Aizaki, K., Sumiya, M., Kawakami, S., Iwabuchi, T., & Senju, A. (2024). Early detection of students' mental health issues from a traditional daily health observation scheme in Japanese schools and its digitalization. *Frontiers in Public Health, 12*, 1430011. DOI: 10.3389/fpubh.2024.1430011 PMID: 39314787

Njenga, J. K. (2011). *eLearning adoption in Eastern and Southern African higher education institutions*. Unpublished Doctoral dissertation. University of the Western Cape.

Nogueira-Leite, D., Marques-Cruz, M., & Cruz-Correia, R. (2024). Individuals' attitudes toward digital mental health apps and implications for adoption in Portugal: Web-based survey. *BMC Medical Informatics and Decision Making*, *24*(1), 99. DOI: 10.1186/s12911-024-02488-1 PMID: 38637866

Norris, L., Swartz, L., & Tomlinson, M. (2013). Mobile phone technology for improved mental health care in South Africa: Possibilities and challenges. *South African Journal of Psychology. Suid-Afrikaanse Tydskrif vir Sielkunde*, *43*(3), 379–388. DOI: 10.1177/0081246313493376

Nowell, L. S., Norris, J. M., White, D. E., & Moules, N. J. (2017). Thematic analysis: Striving to meet the trustworthiness criteria. *International Journal of Qualitative Methods*, *16*(1), 1–13. DOI: 10.1177/1609406917733847

Nuryana, Z., Xu, W., Kurniawan, L., Sutanti, N., Makruf, S. A., & Nurcahyati, I. (2023). Student stress and mental health during online learning: Potential for post-COVID-19 school curriculum development. *Comprehensive Psychoneuroendocrinology*, *14*, 100184. DOI: 10.1016/j.cpnec.2023.100184 PMID: 37038597

Nwaogu, J. M., Chan, A. P., Naslund, J. A., Hon, C. K., Belonwu, C., & Yang, J. (2021). Exploring the barriers to and motivators for using digital mental health interventions among construction personnel in Nigeria: Qualitative study. *JMIR Formative Research*, *5*(11), e18969. DOI: 10.2196/18969 PMID: 34751652

O'Brien, A., Fahmy, R., & Singh, S. P. (2009). Disengagement from mental health services. *Social Psychiatry and Psychiatric Epidemiology*, *44*(7), 558–568. DOI: 10.1007/s00127-008-0476-0 PMID: 19037573

O'Dea, B., King, C., Achilles, M. R., Calear, A. L., & Subotic-Kerry, M. (2021). Delivering a digital mental health service in Australian secondary schools: Understanding school counsellors' and parents' experiences. *Health Services Insights*, *14*, 11786329211017689. DOI: 10.1177/11786329211017689 PMID: 34045867

O'Leary, A., Lahey, T., Lovato, J., Loftness, B., Douglas, A., Skelton, J., Cohen, J. G., Copeland, W. E., McGinnis, R. S., & McGinnis, E. W. (2024). Using wearable digital devices to screen children for mental health conditions: Ethical promises and challenges. *Sensors (Basel)*, *24*(10), 3214. DOI: 10.3390/s24103214 PMID: 38794067

Obikane, E., Sasaki, N., Imamura, K., Nozawa, K., Vedanthan, R., Cuijpers, P., Shimazu, T., Kamada, M., Kawakami, N., & Nishi, D. (2022). Usefulness of Implementation Outcome Scales for Digital Mental Health (iOSDMH): Experiences from six randomized controlled trials. *International Journal of Environmental Research and Public Health*, *19*(23), 15792. DOI: 10.3390/ijerph192315792 PMID: 36497867

Ocak, G., & Bulut, R. (2015). The scale of academic procrastination: Validity and reliability study. *International Journal of Social Sciences and Education Research, 1*(2), 709–726.

OECD. (2021). *The impact of COVID-19 on student well-being.*

Olsson, T. M., Broberg, M., Frisk, S., Wackenhut, A. F., Kjellin, D., Gullstrand, S., Rost, S., & Skoog, T. (2024). Health-promoting learning environments in higher education: A scoping review of structural interventions to protect student mental health. *European Journal of Education, 59*(4), e12772. DOI: 10.1111/ejed.12772

Oluwafunmi A. E. (2024).Reviewing employee well-being and mental health initiatives in contemporary HR Practices, International Journal of Science and Research Archive, 2024, 11(01), 828–840. Article DOI: https://doi.org/.DOI: 10.30574/ijsra.2024.11.1.0153

Opie, J. E., Vuong, A., Welsh, E. T., Gray, R., Pearce, N., Marchionda, S., Mutch, R., & Khalil, H. (2024). Outcomes of best-practice guided digital mental health interventions for youth and young adults with emerging symptoms: Part I. A systematic review of socioemotional outcomes and recommendations. *Clinical Child and Family Psychology Review, 27*(2), 424–475. DOI: 10.1007/s10567-024-00469-4 PMID: 38489101

Orben, A., & Przybylski, A. K. (2019). Screens, teens, and psychological well-being: Evidence from three time-use-diary studies. *Psychological Science, 30*(5), 682–696. DOI: 10.1177/0956797619830329 PMID: 30939250

Orlowski, S., Lawn, S., Matthews, B., Venning, A., Wyld, K., Jones, G., Winsall, M., Antezana, G., Schrader, G., & Bidargaddi, N. (2016). The promise and the reality: A mental health workforce perspective on technology-enhanced youth mental health service delivery. *BMC Health Services Research, 16*(1), 562. DOI: 10.1186/s12913-016-1790-y PMID: 27724951

Owen, J. E., Kuhn, E., Jamison, A. L., Ramsey, K. M., Taylor, K., Heinz, A., ... & Rosen, C. S. (2025). The National Center for PTSD Model for Digital Mental Health: A public sector approach to development, evaluation, implementation, and optimization of resources for helping trauma survivors. *Psychological Trauma: Theory, Research, Practice, and Policy.*

Pagliari, C., Sloan, D., Gregor, P., Sullivan, F., Detmer, D., Kahan, J. P., Oortwijn, W., & MacGillivray, S. (2005). What is eHealth (4): A scoping exercise to map the field. *Journal of Medical Internet Research, 7*(1), e391. DOI: 10.2196/jmir.7.1.e9 PMID: 15829481

Palermo, E. H., Young, A. V., Deswert, S., Brown, A., Goldberg, M., Sultanik, E., Tan, J., Mazefsky, C. A., Brookman-Frazee, L., McPartland, J. C., Goodwin, M. S., Pennington, J., Marcus, S. C., Beidas, R. S., Mandell, D. S., & Nuske, H. J. (2023). A digital mental health app incorporating wearable biosensing for teachers of children on the autism spectrum to support emotion regulation: Protocol for a pilot randomized controlled trial. *JMIR Research Protocols, 12*(1), e45852. DOI: 10.2196/45852 PMID: 37358908

Panek, E. (2014). Left to their own devices: College students' "guilty pleasure" media use and time management. *Communication Research, 41*(4), 561–577. DOI: 10.1177/0093650213499657

Pardo, A., Bartimote, K., Buckingham Shum, S., Dawson, S., Gao, J., Gašević, D., Leichtweis, S., Liu, D., Martínez-Maldonado, R., Mirriahi, N., Moskal, A. C. M., Schulte, J., Siemens, G., & Vigentini, L. (2018). OnTask: Delivering data-informed, personalized learning support actions. *Journal of Learning Analytics, 5*(3), 235–249. DOI: 10.18608/jla.2018.53.15

Park, S. Y., Sigmon, C. N., Boeldt, D., & Sigmon, C. A. N. (2022). A framework for the implementation of digital mental health interventions: The importance of feasibility and acceptability research. *Cureus, 14*(9). Advance online publication. DOI: 10.7759/cureus.29329 PMID: 36277565

Patel, D., & Joshi, V. (2023). Integrated counseling and academic guidance services in Indian universities: An outcome-based evaluation. *International Journal of Educational Development, 98*, 102734. DOI: 10.1016/j.ijedudev.2023.102734

Patel, V., Saxena, S., Lund, C., Thornicroft, G., Baingana, F., Bolton, P., Chisholm, D., Collins, P. Y., Cooper, J. L., Eaton, J., Herrman, H., Herzallah, M. M., Huang, Y., Jordans, M. J. D., Kleinman, A., Medina-Mora, M. E., Morgan, E., Niaz, U., Omigbodun, O., & UnÜtzer, J. Ü. (2018). The Lancet Commission on global mental health and sustainable development. *Lancet, 392*(10157), 1553–1598. DOI: 10.1016/S0140-6736(18)31612-X PMID: 30314863

Patton, M. Q. (2002). *Qualitative Research and Evaluation Methods* (3rd ed.). Sage Publications.

Patton, M. Q. (2015). *Qualitative research & evaluation methods: Integrating theory and practice* (4th ed.). SAGE Publications.

Pendse, S. R., Nkemelu, D., Bidwell, N. J., Jadhav, S., Pathare, S., De Choudhury, M., & Kumar, N. (2022, April). From treatment to healing: envisioning a decolonial digital mental health. In *Proceedings of the 2022 CHI Conference on Human Factors in Computing Systems* (pp. 1-23).

Perez Vallejos, E., Koene, A., Carter, C. J., Hunt, D., Woodard, C., Urquhart, L., Bergin, A., & Statache, R. (2019). Accessing online data for youth mental health research: Meeting the ethical challenges. *Philosophy & Technology*, *32*(1), 87–110. DOI: 10.1007/s13347-017-0286-y

Petrovic, M., & Gaggioli, A. (2020). Digital mental health tools for caregivers of older adults—A scoping review. *Frontiers in Public Health*, *8*, 128. DOI: 10.3389/fpubh.2020.00128 PMID: 32411643

Pew Research Center. (2023). *Teens, social media & technology 2023*. https://www.pewresearch.org/internet/2023/

Phang, Y. S., Heaukulani, C., Martanto, W., Morris, R., Tong, M. M., & Ho, R. (2023). Perceptions of a Digital Mental Health platform among participants with depressive disorder, anxiety disorder, and other clinically diagnosed Mental disorders in Singapore: Usability and acceptability study. *JMIR Human Factors*, *10*, e42167. DOI: 10.2196/42167 PMID: 36989020

Philippe, T. J., Sikder, N., Jackson, A., Koblanski, M. E., Liow, E., Pilarinos, A., & Vasarhelyi, K. (2022). Digital health interventions for delivery of mental health care: Systematic and comprehensive meta-review. *JMIR Mental Health*, *9*(5), e35159. DOI: 10.2196/35159 PMID: 35551058

Pine, R. (2021). Teachers' and health professionals' attitudes towards adolescent mental health and digital mental health interventions. *Advances in Mental Health*, *19*(3), 295–305. DOI: 10.1080/18387357.2020.1814160

Pinge, A., Gad, V., Jaisighani, D., Ghosh, S., & Sen, S. (2024). Detection and monitoring of stress using wearables: A systematic review. *Frontiers of Computer Science*, *6*, 1478851. Advance online publication. DOI: 10.3389/fcomp.2024.1478851

Pistilli, M. D., & Arnold, K. E. (2012). In practice: Purdue's signals project. In *Proceedings of the 2nd International Conference on Learning Analytics and Knowledge (LAK '12)* (pp. 2–5).

Pithara, C., Farr, M., Sullivan, S. A., Edwards, H. B., Hall, W., & Gadd, C., & Authors. (2020). Implementing a digital tool to support shared care planning in community-based mental health services: Qualitative evaluation. *JMIR Mental Health*, *7*(3), e14868. PMID: 32191210

Plessen, C. Y., Panagiotopoulou, O. M., Tong, L., Cuijpers, P., & Karyotaki, E. (2024). Digital mental-health interventions for depression: A multiverse meta-analysis. *Journal of Affective Disorders*, *369*, 1031–1044. DOI: 10.1016/j.jad.2024.10.018 PMID: 39419189

Porche, M. V., Folk, J. B., Tolou-Shams, M., & Fortuna, L. R. (2022). Researchers' perspectives on digital mental health intervention co-design with marginalized community stakeholder youth and families. *Frontiers in Psychiatry*, *13*, 867460. DOI: 10.3389/fpsyt.2022.867460 PMID: 35530032

Porru, F., Schuring, M., Bültmann, U., Portoghese, I., Burdorf, A., & Robroek, S. J. (2022). Associations of university student life challenges with mental health and self-rated health: A longitudinal study with 6 months follow-up. *Journal of Affective Disorders*, *296*, 250–257. DOI: 10.1016/j.jad.2021.09.057 PMID: 34624809

Posiliti, D., & Cilliers, L. (2019). An Investigation of the Level of E-health Literacy in South Africa. *ICICIS*, *12*, 261–271. DOI: 10.29007/jjrb

Potts, C., Lindström, F., Bond, R., Mulvenna, M., Booth, F., Ennis, E., Parding, K., Kostenius, C., Broderick, T., Boyd, K., Vartiainen, A.-K., Nieminen, H., Burns, C., Bickerdike, A., Kuosmanen, L., Dhanapala, I., Vakaloudis, A., Cahill, B., MacInnes, M., & O'Neill, S. (2023). A multilingual digital mental health and well-being Chatbot (ChatPal): Pre-post multicenter intervention study. *Journal of Medical Internet Research*, *25*, e43051. DOI: 10.2196/43051 PMID: 37410537

Prensky, M. (2001). Digital natives, digital immigrants part 2: Do they really think differently? *On the Horizon*, *9*(6), 1–6. DOI: 10.1108/10748120110424843

Putera, M. D. A. (2024). Mental health impacts by elevated digital screen time during COVID-19 pandemic. *Journal of Psychiatry Psychology and Behavioral Research.*

Pychyl, T. A., Morin, R. W., & Salmon, B. R. (2000). Procrastination and the planning fallacy: An examination of the study habits of university students. *Journal of Social Behavior and Personality*, *15*(5), 135–150.

Pywell, J., Vijaykumar, S., Dodd, A., & Coventry, L. (2020). Barriers to older adults' uptake of mobile-based mental health interventions. *Digital Health*, *6*, 2055207620905422. DOI: 10.1177/2055207620905422 PMID: 32110429

Radeef, A., Ghazi, G., & Musa, R. (2018). Translation and validation study of the Chen Internet Addiction Scale (CIAS) among Malaysian college students. *Journal of International Dental and Medical Research*, *11*, 32–37.

Rahman, S. N. A., Mahmud, M. I., & Johari, K. S. K. (2024). Exploring of Expressive Art Therapy in Counselling: A Recent Systematic Review. *Qubahan Academic Journal*, *4*(2), 430–457. DOI: 10.48161/qaj.v4n2a479

Rajkishan, S. S., Meitei, A. J., & Singh, A. (2024). Role of AI/ML in the study of mental health problems of the students: A bibliometric study. *International Journal of System Assurance Engineering and Management, 15*(5), 1615–1637. DOI: 10.1007/s13198-023-02052-6

Ramdani, B., Duan, B., & Berrou, I. (2020). Exploring the Determinants of Mobile Health Adoption by Hospitals in China: Empirical Study. *JMIR Medical Informatics, 8*(7), 1–17. DOI: 10.2196/14795 PMID: 32459630

Rathakrishnan, B., Hamzah, H. M., & Arokiasamy, L. (2022). Resilience training to improve mental well-being among university students: A Malaysian perspective. *International Journal of Environmental Research and Public Health, 19*(17), 10751. DOI: 10.3390/ijerph191710751 PMID: 36078463

Ratheesh, A., & Alvarez-Jimenez, M. (2022). The future of digital mental health in the post-pandemic world: Evidence-based, blended, responsive and implementable. *The Australian and New Zealand Journal of Psychiatry, 56*(2), 107–109. DOI: 10.1177/00048674211070984 PMID: 34996319

Ratten, V. (2020). Coronavirus (Covid-19) and the entrepreneurship education community Available to Purchase. *Journal of Enterprising Communities: People and Places in the Global Economy, 14*(5), 753–764. DOI: 10.1108/JEC-06-2020-0121

Reddy, R. (2020). Barriers to mental health service utilization in Indian college students: A cultural and systemic review. *The International Journal of Social Psychiatry, 66*(5), 457–465. DOI: 10.1177/0020764020931844

Reese, R. J., Slone, N. C., Soares, N., & Sprang, R. (2015). Using telepsychology to provide a group parenting program: A preliminary evaluation of effectiveness. *Psychological Services, 12*(3), 274–282. https://psycnet.apa.org/doi/10.1037/ser0000018. DOI: 10.1037/ser0000018 PMID: 25602503

Reetha, V., & Kamble, S. V. (2025). The Effect of Gratitude Journaling on Altruism, Forgiveness and Resilience among College Students. *International Journal of Indian Psychology, 13*(1).

Regueiro, V., McMartin, J., Schaefer, C., & Woody, J. M. (2016). Efficacy, efficiency, and ethics in the provision of telepsychology services: Emerging applications for international workers. *Journal of Psychology and Theology, 44*(4), 290–302. https://psycnet.apa.org/doi/10.1177/009164711604400404. DOI: 10.1177/009164711604400404

Renfrew, M. E., Morton, D. P., Morton, J. K., & Przybylko, G. (2021). The influence of human support on the effectiveness of digital mental health promotion interventions for the general population. *Frontiers in Psychology, 12*, 716106. DOI: 10.3389/fpsyg.2021.716106 PMID: 34489818

Rezapour, M., & Elmshaeuser, S. K. (2022). *AI-based analysis of COVID-19 impact on student mental health.* ArXiv frontiersin.org+2arxiv.org+2pubmed.ncbi.nlm.nih.gov+2

Rheinberger, D., Baffsky, R., McGillivray, L., Zbukvic, I., Dadich, A., Larsen, M. E., Lin, P.-I., Gan, D. Z. Q., Kaplun, C., Wilcox, H. C., Eapen, V., Middleton, P. M., & Torok, M. (2023). Examining the feasibility of implementing digital mental health innovations into hospitals to support youth in suicide crisis: Interview study with young people and health professionals. *JMIR Formative Research, 7*, e51398. DOI: 10.2196/51398 PMID: 37971790

Riboldi, I., Cavaleri, D., Calabrese, A., Capogrosso, C. A., Piacenti, S., Bartoli, F., Crocamo, C., & Carrà, G. (2023). Digital mental health interventions for anxiety and depressive symptoms in university students during the COVID-19 pandemic: A systematic review of randomized controlled trials. *Revista de Psiquiatría y Salud Mental, 16*, 47–58. DOI: 10.1016/j.rpsm.2022.04.005 PMID: 35755491

Rickwood, D., Telford, N., Parker, A., Tanti, C., & McGorry, P. (2019). Headspace—Australia's innovation in youth mental health: Who are the clients and why are they presenting? *The Medical Journal of Australia, 200*(2), 108–111. DOI: 10.5694/mja13.11235 PMID: 24484115

Ridout, B., Forsyth, R., Amon, K. L., Navarro, P., & Campbell, A. J. (2024). The Urgent Need for an Evidence-Based Digital Mental Health Practice Model of Care for Youth. *JMIR Mental Health, 11*, e48441. DOI: 10.2196/48441 PMID: 38534006

Rodriguez-Villa, E., Rozatkar, A. R., Kumar, M., Patel, V., Bondre, A., Naik, S. S., Dutt, S., Mehta, U. M., Nagendra, S., Tugnawat, D., Shrivastava, R., Raghuram, H., Khan, A., Naslund, J. A., Gupta, S., Bhan, A., Thirthall, J., Chand, P. K., Lakhtakia, T., & Torous, J. (2021). Cross cultural and global uses of a digital mental health app: Results of focus groups with clinicians, patients and family members in India and the United States. *Global Mental Health (Cambridge, England), 8*, e30. DOI: 10.1017/gmh.2021.28 PMID: 34512999

Rojnic Kuzman, M. (2023). Digital transcultural psychiatry in times of crisis: The Help for Helpers webinar series. *European Psychiatry : the Journal of the Association of European Psychiatrists, 66*(S1), S7. DOI: 10.1192/j.eurpsy.2023.39

Romero, C., & Ventura, S. (2013). Data mining in education. *Wiley Interdisciplinary Reviews. Data Mining and Knowledge Discovery*, *3*(1), 12–27. DOI: 10.1002/widm.1075

Rosenberg, B. M., Kodish, T., Cohen, Z. D., Gong-Guy, E., & Craske, M. G. (2022). A novel peer-to-peer coaching program to support digital mental health: Design and implementation. *JMIR Mental Health*, *9*(1), e32430. DOI: 10.2196/32430 PMID: 35080504

Rothblum, E. D., Solomon, L. J., & Murakami, J. (1986). Affective, cognitive, and behavioral differences between high and low procrastinators. *Journal of Counseling Psychology*, *33*(4), 387–394. DOI: 10.1037/0022-0167.33.4.387

Rozgonjuk, D., Sindermann, C., Elhai, J. D., & Montag, C. (2020). Individual differences in fear of missing out (FoMO): Age, gender, and the Big Five personality trait domains, facets, and items. *Personality and Individual Differences*, *171*, 110546. DOI: 10.1016/j.paid.2020.110546

Rudd, B. N., & Beidas, R. S. (2020). Digital mental health: The answer to the global mental health crisis? *JMIR Mental Health*, *7*(6), e18472. DOI: 10.2196/18472 PMID: 32484445

Ruzek, J. I., Sadeh-Sharvit, S., Bunge, E. L., Sheperis, D. S., Fitzsimmons-Craft, E., Guinn, V., Joseph, R., Cameron, E., & Taylor, C. B. (2024). Training the psychologist of the future in the use of digital mental health technologies. *Professional Psychology, Research and Practice*, *55*(5), 395–404. DOI: 10.1037/pro0000567

Rygaard, N. P. (2020). Improving the mental health of abandoned children: Experiences from a global online intervention. *The American Psychologist*, *75*(9), 1376–1388. DOI: 10.1037/amp0000726

Sakellari, E., Notara, V., Lagiou, A., Fatkulina, N., Ivanova, S., Korhonen, J., Kregar Velikonja, N., Lalova, V., Laaksonen, C., Petrova, G., & Lahti, M. (2021). Mental health and wellbeing at schools: Health promotion in primary schools with the use of digital methods. *Children (Basel, Switzerland)*, *8*(5), 345. DOI: 10.3390/children8050345 PMID: 33925744

Salimi, N., Gere, B., Talley, W., & Irioogbe, B. (2023). College students mental health challenges: Concerns and considerations in the COVID-19 pandemic. *Journal of College Student Psychotherapy*, *37*(1), 39–51. DOI: 10.1080/87568225.2021.1890298

Sarfo, J. O., Amoadu, M., & Ansah, E. (2023). Internet addiction among college students from 20 countries: Scoping review of risk factors and impact on academic procrastination and sleep quality. *International Journal of Media and Information Literacy*, *8*(2), 382–400. DOI: 10.13187/ijmil.2023.2.382

Sarif, N., & Vandana. (2021). Digital learning, students' mental health and role of psychological capital amidst COVID-19 pandemic in India. *Ensemble: A Journal of the Department of Education, 1*(Special Issue), 108–119.

Sasaki, N., Obikane, E., Vedanthan, R., Imamura, K., Cuijpers, P., Shimazu, T., Kamada, M., Kawakami, N., & Nishi, D. (2021). Implementation Outcome Scales for Digital Mental Health (iOSDMH): Scale development and cross-sectional study. *JMIR Formative Research*, *5*(11), e24332. DOI: 10.2196/24332 PMID: 34817391

Schenzle, S., & Schultz, J. H. (2024). "Students are bringing the revolution into the classroom!" teachers' and counselors' perceptions of the need for psychosocial support in crisis-affected classrooms in Lebanon. *Teaching and Teacher Education*, *139*, 104416. DOI: 10.1016/j.tate.2023.104416

Schneider, M. L., Cha, B. S., Borghouts, J., Eikey, E. V., Schueller, S. M., Stadnick, N. A., & Sorkin, D. H. (2024). Individual and organizational outcomes of engaging peers in the cocreation of digital mental health interventions. *Psychological Services*. PMID: 39172398

Schueller, S. M., & Torous, J. (2020). Scaling evidence-based treatments through digital mental health. *The American Psychologist*, *75*(8), 1093–1104. DOI: 10.1037/amp0000654 PMID: 33252947

Schuler, B. R., & Raknes, S. (2022). Does group size and blending matter? Impact of a digital mental health game implemented with refugees in various settings. *International Journal of Migration, Health and Social Care*, *18*(1), 83–94. DOI: 10.1108/IJMHSC-07-2021-0060

Senecal, C., Koestner, R., & Vallerand, R. J. (1995). Self-regulation and academic procrastination. *The Journal of Social Psychology*, *135*(5), 607–619. DOI: 10.1080/00224545.1995.9712234

Şenormancı, Ö., Şenormancı, G., Güçlü, O., & Konkan, R. (2014). Attachment and family functioning in patients with internet addiction. *General Hospital Psychiatry*, *36*(2), 203–207. DOI: 10.1016/j.genhosppsych.2013.10.012 PMID: 24262601

Severes, B., Barreto, M., & Esteves, A. (2025). Designing for mental health in higher education: A collaborative approach to digital interventions. *Behaviour & Information Technology*, *44*(10), 2474–2492. DOI: 10.1080/0144929X.2024.2436503

Shan, X., Ou, Y., Ding, Y., Yan, H., Chen, J., Zhao, J., & Guo, W. (2021). Associations between internet addiction and gender, anxiety, coping styles and acceptance in university freshmen in South China. *Frontiers in Psychiatry, 12*, 558080. Advance online publication. DOI: 10.3389/fpsyt.2021.558080 PMID: 34135779

Shapiro, S. S., & Wilk, M. B. (1965). An analysis of variance test for normality (complete samples). *Biometrika, 52*(3/4), 591–611. DOI: 10.2307/2333709

Sharifi, A., & Simangan, D. (2021). Environmental Sustainability: The Missing Pillar of Positive Peace. *The Palgrave Handbook of Positive Peace*, 1-19. DOI: 10.1007/978-981-15-3877-3_35-1

Sharma, A., & Sharma, R. (2021). Digital mental health services in higher education: Challenges and opportunities in India. *Indian Journal of Psychological Medicine, 43*(3), 233–239. DOI: 10.1177/02537176211001548

Sharma, S., & Iyer, P. (2018). Group counseling as a strategy to reduce academic stress among undergraduates. *Journal of College Student Psychotherapy, 32*(4), 303–317. DOI: 10.1080/87568225.2018.1438477

Shaw, M., & Black, D. W. (2008). Internet addiction: Definition, assessment, epidemiology, and clinical management. *CNS Drugs, 22*(5), 353–365. DOI: 10.2165/00023210-200822050-00001 PMID: 18399706

Shen, N., Kassam, I., Chen, S., Ma, C., Wang, W., Boparai, N., Jankowicz, D., & Strudwick, G. (2022). Canadian perspectives of digital mental health supports: Findings from a national survey conducted during the COVID-19 pandemic. *Digital Health, 8*, 20552076221102253. DOI: 10.1177/20552076221102253 PMID: 35646379

Shohel, M. M. C., Mahmud, A., Urmee, M. A., Anwar, M. N., Rahman, M. M., Acharya, D., & Ashrafuzzaman, M. (2022). Education in emergencies, mental wellbeing and e-learning. In Shohel, M. M. C. (Ed.), *E-learning and digital education in the twenty-first century* (pp. 1–22). IntechOpen. DOI: 10.5772/intechopen.97425

Simpson, W., & Pychyl, T. (2009). In search of the arousal procrastinator: Investigating the relation between procrastination, arousal-based personality traits, and beliefs about procrastination motivations. *Personality and Individual Differences, 47*(8), 906–911. DOI: 10.1016/j.paid.2009.07.013

Singh, D., Mehta, R., & Choudhary, A. (2024). Integrating wearable devices and predictive analytics for academic risk management in universities. *Interactive Learning Environments, 32*(7), 1020–1038. DOI: 10.1080/10494820.2024.2345678

Singh, R., Menon, V., & Arora, P. (2021). Efficacy of mobile apps in managing student anxiety and depression: A review of randomized controlled trials. *Computers in Human Behavior*, *122*, 106834. DOI: 10.1016/j.chb.2021.106834

Singh, S., Roy, D., Sinha, K., Parveen, S., Sharma, G., & Joshi, G. (2020). Impact of COVID-19 and lockdown on mental health of children and adolescents: A narrative review with recommendations. *Psychiatry Research*, *293*, 113429. DOI: 10.1016/j.psychres.2020.113429 PMID: 32882598

Sirois, F. (2007). "I'll look after my health, later": A replication and extension of the procrastination–health model with community-dwelling adults. *Personality and Individual Differences*, *43*(1), 15–26. DOI: 10.1016/j.paid.2006.11.003

Sirois, F. M. (2013). Procrastination and stress: Exploring the role of self-compassion. *Self and Identity*, *13*(2), 128–145. DOI: 10.1080/15298868.2013.763404

Sirois, F. M. (2023). Procrastination and stress: A conceptual review of why context matters. *International Journal of Environmental Research and Public Health*, *20*(6), 5031. DOI: 10.3390/ijerph20065031 PMID: 36981941

Sirois, F. M., & Pychyl, T. A. (2013). Procrastination and the priority of short-term mood regulation: Consequences for future self. *Social and Personality Psychology Compass*, *7*(2), 115–127. DOI: 10.1111/spc3.12011

Sirois, F. M., & Pychyl, T. A. (2016). *Procrastination, health, and well-being*. Academic Press.

Sit, H. F., Hong, I. W., Burchert, S., Sou, E. K. L., Wong, M., Chen, W., Lam, A. I. F., & Hall, B. J. (2022). A feasibility study of the WHO digital mental health intervention step-by-step to address depression among Chinese young adults. *Frontiers in Psychiatry*, *12*, 812667. DOI: 10.3389/fpsyt.2021.812667 PMID: 35069297

Slade, S., & Prinsloo, P. (2013). Learning analytics: Ethical issues and dilemmas. *The American Behavioral Scientist*, *57*(10), 1510–1529. DOI: 10.1177/0002764213479366

Slimmen, S., Timmermans, O., Mikolajczak-Degrauwe, K., & Oenema, A. (2022). How stress-related factors affect mental wellbeing of university students A cross-sectional study to explore the associations between stressors, perceived stress, and mental wellbeing. *PLoS One*, *17*(11), e0275925. DOI: 10.1371/journal.pone.0275925 PMID: 36342914

Smith, K. A., Blease, C., Faurholt-Jepsen, M., Firth, J., Van Daele, T., Moreno, C., Carlbring, P., Ebner-Priemer, U. W., Koutsouleris, N., Riper, H., Mouchabac, S., Torous, J., & Cipriani, A. (2023). Digital mental health: Challenges and next steps. *BMJ Mental Health*, *26*(1), e300670. DOI: 10.1136/bmjment-2023-300670 PMID: 37197797

Smith, K. A., Hardy, A., Vinnikova, A., Blease, C., Milligan, L., Hidalgo-Mazzei, D., Lambe, S., Marzano, L., Uhlhaas, P. J., Ostinelli, E. G., Anmella, G., Zangani, C., Aronica, R., Dwyer, B., Torous, J., & Cipriani, A. (2024). Digital mental health for schizophrenia and other severe mental illnesses: An international consensus on current challenges and potential solutions. *JMIR Mental Health*, *11*, e57155. DOI: 10.2196/57155 PMID: 38717799

Smoła, P., Młoźniak, I., Wojcieszko, M., Zwierczyk, U., Kobryn, M., Rzepecka, E., & Duplaga, M. (2024). The perception of facilitators and barriers to the use of e-health solutions in Poland: A qualitative study. *BMC Medical Informatics and Decision Making*, *24*(1), 381. DOI: 10.1186/s12911-024-02791-x PMID: 39695644

Snyder, H. (2019). Literature review as a research methodology: An overview and guidelines. *Journal of Business Research*, *104*, 333–339. DOI: 10.1016/j.jbusres.2019.07.039

Soneson, E., Fazel, M., Goli, P. S., & White, S. R. (2025). Are Adolescents Sensitive About Sensitive Data? Exploring Student Concerns About Privacy, Confidentiality, and Data Use in Health Research. *The Journal of Adolescent Health*, *76*(6), 1008–1017. DOI: 10.1016/j.jadohealth.2025.03.004 PMID: 40372302

Song, M., & Song, Y. M. (2023). Randomized controlled trials of digital mental health interventions on patients with schizophrenia spectrum disorder: A systematic review. *Telemedicine Journal and e-Health*, *29*(6), 798–812. DOI: 10.1089/tmj.2022.0135 PMID: 36264184

Song, S., Seo, Y., Hwang, S., Kim, H. Y., & Kim, J. (2024). Digital phenotyping of geriatric depression using a community-based digital mental health monitoring platform for socially vulnerable older adults and their community caregivers: 6-week living lab single-arm pilot study. *JMIR mHealth and uHealth*, *12*(1), e55842. DOI: 10.2196/55842 PMID: 38885033

Soubutts, E., Shrestha, P., Davidson, B. I., Qu, C., Mindel, C., Sefi, A., & McNaney, R. (2024, May). Challenges and opportunities for the design of inclusive digital mental health tools: understanding culturally diverse young people's experiences. In *Proceedings of the 2024 CHI Conference on Human Factors in Computing Systems* (pp. 1-16). DOI: 10.1145/3613904.3642641

Srivastava, S., & Kumar, C. (2024). Adjustment, academic procrastination, and internet addiction among school students: A correlation study. *International Journal of Indian Psychology*, *12*(2), 74. DOI: 10.25215/1202.074

Stamou, P., Tsoli, K., & Babalis, T. (2024, May). The role of counseling for non-traditional students in formal higher education: A scoping review. []. Frontiers Media SA.]. *Frontiers in Education*, *9*, 1361410. DOI: 10.3389/feduc.2024.1361410

Stanger, S. B., & Lucas, S. J. (2024). Using indirect service-learning to promote evidence-based digital mental health tools on college campuses. *Teaching of Psychology*, *51*(2), 240–247. DOI: 10.1177/00986283221084005

Staples, L. G., Nielssen, O., Dear, B. F., Bisby, M. A., Fisher, A., Kayrouz, R., & Titov, N. (2023). Prevalence and predictors of long COVID in patients accessing a national digital mental health service. *International Journal of Environmental Research and Public Health*, *20*(18), 6756. DOI: 10.3390/ijerph20186756 PMID: 37754615

Statistics South Africa. (2018). *National Poverty Lines*. https://www.statssa.gov.za/publications/P03101/P031012018.pdf

Steel, P. (2007). The nature of procrastination: A meta-analytic and theoretical review of quintessential self-regulatory failure. *Psychological Bulletin*, *133*(1), 65–94. DOI: 10.1037/0033-2909.133.1.65 PMID: 17201571

Stein, D. J., Fineberg, N. A., & Chamberlain, S. R. (Eds.). (2021). *Mental health in a digital world*. Academic Press.

Stern, E., Micoulaud Franchi, J. A., Dumas, G., Moreira, J., Mouchabac, S., Maruani, J., Philip, P., Lejoyeux, M., & Geoffroy, P. A. (2023). How can digital mental health enhance psychiatry? *The Neuroscientist*, *29*(6), 681–693. DOI: 10.1177/10738584221098603 PMID: 35658666

Stevic, A., Schmuck, D., Koemets, A., Hirsch, M., Karsay, K., Thomas, M. F., & Matthes, J. (2022). Privacy concerns can stress you out: Investigating the reciprocal relationship between mobile social media privacy concerns and perceived stress. *Communications*, *47*(3), 327–349. DOI: 10.1515/commun-2020-0037

Stiles-Shields, C., Ramos, G., Ortega, A., & Psihogios, A. M. (2024). Increasing digital mental health reach and uptake via youth partnerships. *npj Mental Health Research, 3*, 12.

Stiles-Shields, C., Gustafson, E. L., Lim, P. S., Bobadilla, G., Thorpe, D., Summersett Williams, F. C., Donenberg, G. R., Julion, W. A., & Karnik, N. S. (2025). Pre-implementation determinants for digital mental health integration in Chicago pediatric primary care. *Journal of Pediatric Psychology*, *50*(1), 86–95. DOI: 10.1093/jpepsy/jsae058 PMID: 39101560

Stiles-Shields, C., Ramos, G., Ortega, A., & Psihogios, A. M. (2023). Increasing digital mental health reach and uptake via youth partnerships. *Npj Mental Health Research*, *2*(1), 9. DOI: 10.1038/s44184-023-00030-1 PMID: 37483392

Stoll, J., Müller, J. A., & Trachsel, M. (2020). Ethical issues in online psychotherapy: A narrative review. *Frontiers in Psychiatry*, *10*, 993. DOI: 10.3389/fpsyt.2019.00993 PMID: 32116819

Stormacq, C., Van den Broucke, S., & Wosinski, J. (2019). Does health literacy mediate the relationship between socioeconomic status and health disparities? Integrative review. *Health Promotion International*, *34*(5), e1–e17. DOI: 10.1093/heapro/day062 PMID: 30107564

Subramaniam, S., Tan, J. Y., & Lim, R. B. (2023). Institutional preparedness in fostering mental well-being: Case studies from Asian higher education. *Asia Pacific Education Review*, *24*(1), 1–15. DOI: 10.1007/s12564-023-09782-4

Subroto, S., & Chowdhury, N. (2025). Dimensions and barriers for digital (in) equity and digital divide: A systematic integrative review. *Digital Transformation and Society*, *4*(2), 111–127. DOI: 10.1108/DTS-04-2024-0054

Sucala, M., Schnur, J. B., Constantino, M. J., Miller, S. J., Brackman, E. H., & Montgomery, G. H. (2012). Virtual reality and computer-based interventions for anxiety: A meta-analysis. *Journal of Anxiety Disorders*, *26*(1), 74–84. DOI: 10.1016/j.janxdis.2011.09.005

Susnjak, T., Ramaswami, G. S., & Mathrani, A. (2022). Learning analytics dashboard: A tool for providing actionable insights to learners. *International Journal of Educational Technology in Higher Education*, *19*(1), 12. Advance online publication. DOI: 10.1186/s41239-021-00313-7 PMID: 35194560

Svartdal, F., Dahl, T. I., Gamst-Klaussen, T., Koppenborg, M., & Klingsieck, K. B. (2020). How study environments foster academic procrastination: Overview and recommendations. *Frontiers in Psychology*, *11*, 540910. DOI: 10.3389/fpsyg.2020.540910 PMID: 33224046

Ta, A., Salgin, N., Demir, M., Reindel, K. P., Mehta, R. K., McDonald, A., . . . Sasangohar, F. (2025). Real-time stress monitoring, detection, and management in college students: A wearable technology and machine-learning approach. *arXiv preprint arXiv:2505.15974*.

Taher, R., Hall, C. L., Bergin, A. D. G., Gupta, N., Heaysman, C., Jacobsen, P., Kabir, T., Kalnad, N., Keppens, J., Hsu, C.-W., McGuire, P., Peters, E., Shergill, S., Stahl, D., Stock, B. W., & Yiend, J. (2024). Developing a process for assessing the safety of a digital mental health intervention and gaining regulatory approval: A case study and academic's guide. *Trials*, *25*(1), 604. DOI: 10.1186/s13063-024-08421-1 PMID: 39252100

Taher, R., Hsu, C. W., Hampshire, C., Fialho, C., Heaysman, C., Stahl, D., Shergill, S., & Yiend, J. (2023). The safety of digital mental health interventions: Systematic review and recommendations. *JMIR Mental Health*, *10*(1), e47433. DOI: 10.2196/47433 PMID: 37812471

Tariq, M. U. (2025a). AI-Driven Innovations: Transforming Healthcare, Agriculture, and Environmental Science. In Emara, T., Hassan, E., Trinh, T., Li, G., & Saber, A. (Eds.), *The Role of Artificial Intelligence in Advancing Applied Life Sciences* (pp. 87–118). IGI Global Scientific Publishing., DOI: 10.4018/979-8-3693-9208-9.ch003

Tariq, M. U. (2025b). Navigating Cancer Care: The Crucial Role of Educators and Healthcare Providers in Supporting Patients of Color. In Clarke, K., & Moffett, N. (Eds.), *Cancer Diagnosis, Treatment and Care: Reflections for the Education of Survivors and Healthcare Providers* (pp. 405–424). IGI Global Scientific Publishing., DOI: 10.4018/979-8-3693-5400-1.ch021

Tariq, M. U. (2025c). Empowering Patients With AI-Ethical Digital Tools for Health Data Management and Decision. In Pesqueira, A., & de Bem Machado, A. (Eds.), *Navigating Privacy, Innovation, and Patient Empowerment Through Ethical Healthcare Technology* (pp. 197–216). IGI Global Scientific Publishing., DOI: 10.4018/979-8-3693-7630-0.ch008

Tariq, M. U. (2025d). Navigating the Convergence of IoMT and Generative AI in Global Healthcare: Opportunities, Challenges, and Ethical Considerations. In Kumar, V., Katina, P., & Zhao, J. (Eds.), *Convergence of Internet of Medical Things (IoMT) and Generative AI* (pp. 513–534). IGI Global Scientific Publishing., DOI: 10.4018/979-8-3693-6180-1.ch022

Tariq, M. U. (2025e). Enhancing Pandemic Preparedness With AI-Driven Risk Prediction Models. In Shah, I., Sial, Q., & Fateh, S. (Eds.), *Generative AI Techniques for Sustainability in Healthcare Security* (pp. 77–94). IGI Global Scientific Publishing., DOI: 10.4018/979-8-3693-6577-9.ch005

Taubman, D. S., Heininger, W., Salazar, S., Salazar, L., Riba, M., Greden, J. F., & Parikh, S. V. (2022). Depression on college campuses conference: Addressing an evolving crisis. *Academic Psychiatry*, *46*(3), 359–363. DOI: 10.1007/s40596-021-01575-z

Taylor, K. V., Garchitorena, L., Scaramutti-Gladfelter, C., Wyrick, M., Grill, K. B., & Seixas, A. A. (2024). A digital mental health solution to improve social, emotional, and learning skills for youth: Protocol for an efficacy and usability study. *JMIR Research Protocols*, *13*(1), e59372. DOI: 10.2196/59372 PMID: 39701588

Taylor, M. E., Liu, M., Abelson, S., Eisenberg, D., Lipson, S. K., & Schueller, S. M. (2024). The reach, effectiveness, adoption, implementation, and maintenance of digital mental health interventions for college students: A systematic review. *Current Psychiatry Reports*, *26*(12), 683–693. DOI: 10.1007/s11920-024-01545-w PMID: 39392547

Telles, S., Maharana, K., Balrana, B., & Balkrishna, A. (2011A). Effects of high-frequency yoga breathing called kapalabhati compared with breath awareness on the degree of optical illusion perceived. *Perceptual and Motor Skills*, *112*(3), 981–990. DOI: 10.2466/02.20.22.PMS.112.3.981-990 PMID: 21853784

Telles, S., Sharma, S. K., & Balkrishna, A. (2011B). Blood pressure and heart rate variability during yoga-based alternate nostril breathing. *Journal of Alternative and Complementary Medicine (New York, N.Y.)*, *17*(2), 109–117. DOI: 10.1089/acm.2010.0140 PMID: 21303197

Theron, M., Barkhuizen, N., & Du Plessis, Y. (2014). Managing the academic talent void: Investigating factors in academic turnover and retention in South Africa. *SA Journal of Industrial Psychology*, *40*(1), 1–14. DOI: 10.4102/sajip.v40i1.1117

Thomas, R., & George, L. (2019). Mental health literacy and help-seeking behavior among youth: A meta-analytical study. *Children and Youth Services Review*, *100*, 104–112. DOI: 10.1016/j.childyouth.2019.02.035

Thomson, M., Henderson, G., Rogers, T., Locke, B., Vines, J., & MacBeth, A. (2024). Digital mental health and peer support: Building a Theory of Change informed by stakeholders' perspectives. *PLOS Digital Health*, *3*(5), e0000522. DOI: 10.1371/journal.pdig.0000522 PMID: 38814923

Titov, N., Hadjistavropoulos, H. D., Nielssen, O., Mohr, D. C., Andersson, G., & Dear, B. F. (2019). From research to practice: Ten lessons in delivering digital mental health services. *Journal of Clinical Medicine*, *8*(8), 1239. DOI: 10.3390/jcm8081239 PMID: 31426460

Tokunaga, R. S. (2017). A meta-analysis of the relationships between psychosocial problems and internet habits: Synthesizing internet addiction, problematic internet use, and deficient self-regulation research. *Communication Monographs*, *84*(4), 423–446. DOI: 10.1080/03637751.2017.1332419

Tomičić, A., & Gjorgjioska, M. A. (2024). Epistemic inequality in the digital era: Unpacking biases in digital mental health. *Theory & Psychology*, *34*(6), 777–797. DOI: 10.1177/09593543241279131

Topooco, N., Fowler, L. A., Fitzsimmons-Craft, E. E., DePietro, B., Vázquez, M. M., Firebaugh, M. L., Ceglarek, P., Monterubio, G., Newman, M. G., Eisenberg, D., Wilfley, D. E., & Taylor, C. B. (2022). Digital interventions to address mental health needs in colleges: Perspectives of student stakeholders. *Internet Interventions : the Application of Information Technology in Mental and Behavioural Health*, *28*, 100528. DOI: 10.1016/j.invent.2022.100528 PMID: 35378846

Torous, J., Linardon, J., Goldberg, S. B., Sun, S., Bell, I., Nicholas, J., Hassan, L., Hua, Y., Milton, A., & Firth, J. (2025). The evolving field of digital mental health: Current evidence and implementation issues for smartphone apps, generative artificial intelligence, and virtual reality. *World Psychiatry; Official Journal of the World Psychiatric Association (WPA)*, *24*(2), 156–174. DOI: 10.1002/wps.21299 PMID: 40371757

Torous, J., Wisniewski, H., Gorrindo, T., Rauseo-Ricupero, N., & Hilty, D. (2020). The role of digital navigators in promoting clinical care and technology integration into practice. *Digital Biomarkers*, *4*(Suppl. 1), 119–135. DOI: 10.1159/000510144 PMID: 33442585

Tracy, S. J. (2010). Qualitative quality: Eight "big-tent" criteria for excellent qualitative research. *Qualitative Inquiry*, *16*(10), 837–851. DOI: 10.1177/1077800410383121

Tremain, H., McEnery, C., Fletcher, K., & Murray, G. (2020). The therapeutic alliance in digital mental health interventions for serious mental illnesses: Narrative review. *JMIR Mental Health*, *7*(8), e17204. DOI: 10.2196/17204 PMID: 32763881

Tuckman, B. W. (1991). The development and concurrent validity of the Procrastination Scale. *Educational and Psychological Measurement*, *51*(2), 473–480. DOI: 10.1177/0013164491512022

Türkiye İstatistik Kurumu. (2023). *Hanehalkı Bilişim Teknolojileri (BT) Kullanım Araştırması, 2023.* Retrieved June 24, 2024, from https://data.tuik.gov.tr/Bulten/Index?p=Hanehalki-Bilisim-Teknolojileri-%28BT%29-Kullanim-Arastirmasi-2023-49407

Turmaine, K., Jeannic, A.-L., Dumas, A., & Chevreul, K. (2021). Lessons learned from an e-mental health intervention: The promotion of StopBlues in 41 French cities. *European Psychiatry : the Journal of the Association of European Psychiatrists, 64*(S1), S110–S111. DOI: 10.1192/j.eurpsy.2021.318

Twenge, J. M., Martin, G. N., & Campbell, W. K. (2019). Decreases in psychological well-being among American adolescents after 2012 and links to screen time during the rise of smartphone technology. *Journal of Abnormal Psychology, 128*(2), 119–133. DOI: 10.1037/abn0000410 PMID: 30570269

UNESCO International Institute for Higher Education in Latin America and the Caribbean et al. (2024). *Supporting Student Mental Health and Well-being in Higher Education*, UNESCO: United Nations Educational, Scientific and Cultural Organisation. Venezuela (Bolivarian Republic of). Retrieved from https://coilink.org/20.500.12592/40ycqb3 on 21 Nov 2025. COI: 20.500.12592/40ycqb3.

UNESCO. (2018). *Digital literacy global framework.* UNESCO Publishing.

UNESCO. (2021). *Mental health and education: Global initiatives.* UNESCO.

United Nations. (2015). *Transforming our world: The 2030 Agenda for Sustainable Development.* https://sdgs.un.org/2030agenda

United Nations. (2020). *Policy Brief: COVID-19 and the Need for Action on Mental Health.* https://unsdg.un.org/sites/default/files/2020-05/UN-Policy-Brief-COVID-19-and-mental-health.pdf

University Grants Commission. (2019). *Guidelines for promotion of mental health and well-being of students.* UGC.

Uzun, A., Unal, E., & Tokel, S. (2014). Exploring internet addiction, academic procrastination, and general procrastination among pre-service ICT teachers. *Mevlana International Journal of Education, 4*(1), 189–201. DOI: 10.13054/mije.14.18.4.1

Vacek, J., & Vondrackova, P. (2014). Behavioural addictions: Classification, phenomenology, prevalence and therapy. *Česká a Slovenská, 110*(3), 144–150.

Vally, Z. (2006). Cybertherapy: Development and usage in the South African context. *Psychology in Africa, 14*(2), 151–165. DOI: 10.4314/ifep.v14i2.23716

Van Assche, E., Bonroy, B., Mertens, M., Van den Broeck, L., Desie, K., Bolinski, F., Amarti, K., Kleiboer, A., Riper, H., & Van Daele, T. (2022). E-mental health implementation in inpatient care: Exploring its potential and future challenges. *Frontiers in Digital Health*, *4*, 1027864. DOI: 10.3389/fdgth.2022.1027864 PMID: 36588747

van Grunsven, J. (2021). Perceptual breakdown during a global pandemic: Introducing phenomenological insights for digital mental health purposes. *Ethics and Information Technology*, *23*(S1, Suppl 1), 91–98. DOI: 10.1007/s10676-020-09554-y PMID: 32905100

Venning, A., Herd, M. C., Oswald, T. K., Razmi, S., Glover, F., Hawke, T., Quartermain, V., & Redpath, P. (2021). Exploring the acceptability of a digital mental health platform incorporating a virtual coach: The good, the bad, and the opportunities. *Health Informatics Journal*, *27*(1), 1460458221994873. DOI: 10.1177/1460458221994873 PMID: 33601947

Verger, P., Combes, J. B., Kovess-Masfety, V., Choquet, M., Guagliardo, V., Rouillon, F., & Peretti-Watel, P. (2009). Psychological distress in first year university students: Socioeconomic and academic stressors, mastery and social support in young men and women. *Social Psychiatry and Psychiatric Epidemiology*, *44*(8), 643–650. DOI: 10.1007/s00127-008-0486-y PMID: 19096741

Verma, S., Nair, A., & Das, M. (2022). Trauma-informed educational practices and student well-being: Evidence from higher education settings. *Teaching and Teacher Education*, *112*, 103638. DOI: 10.1016/j.tate.2022.103638

Vial, S., Boudhraâ, S., & Dumont, M. (2022). Human-centered design approaches in digital mental health interventions: Exploratory mapping review. *JMIR Mental Health*, *9*(6), e35591. DOI: 10.2196/35591 PMID: 35671081

Vicary, E., Brierley, H., Wilkinson, J., Adesina, M., Bee, P., Lovell, K., Uzun, N., Bee, E., & Brooks, H. (2025). Bridging the Gap in Mental Health Literacy: Co-adapting and feasibility testing a digital intervention to improve mental health literacy amongst young people aged 12-14 in the UK. *Frontiers in Psychiatry*, *16*, 1546109. DOI: 10.3389/fpsyt.2025.1546109 PMID: 40761590

Vij, R., & Narula, A. (2026). Fostering Effective Feedback and Mental Well-Being: Overcoming Challenges in Digital Education. In *Digital Tools and Platforms for Effective and Personalized Learning* (pp. 437-462). IGI Global Scientific Publishing. DOI: 10.4018/979-8-3373-6013-3.ch016

Visier-Alfonso, M. E., Sarabia-Cobo, C., Cobo-Cuenca, A. I., Nieto-López, M., López-Honrubia, R., Bartolomé-Gutiérrez, R., Alconero-Camarero, A. R., & González-López, J. R. (2024). Stress, mental health, and protective factors in nursing students: An observational study. *Nurse Education Today*, *139*, 106258. DOI: 10.1016/j.nedt.2024.106258 PMID: 38781822

Walker, R. S., & Brown, I. (2020). Big data analytics adoption: A case study in a large South African telecommunications organisation. *South African Journal of Information Management*, *21*(1), 1–10. DOI: 10.4102/sajim.v22i1.1180

Wang, X., Jiang, F., Luo, L., Li, H., Jiang, W., & Shen, X. (2025). Digital Transformation of College Students' Mental Health Education in the Intelligent Era: Model Innovation and Practical Exploration. *health education, 7*(5), 8-18.

Wang, Y., & Liu, H. (2025). *Using physiological measures to enhance learning and engagement in digital classrooms: A conference study*. SCITEPRESS – Science and Technology Publications, 134384. https://www.scitepress.org/Papers/2025/134384/134384.pdf

Wang, C., Pan, R., Wan, X., Tan, Y., Xu, L., Ho, C. S., & Ho, R. C. (2020). Immediate psychological responses and associated factors during the initial stage of the COVID-19 epidemic among the general population in China. *International Journal of Environmental Research and Public Health*, *17*(5), 1729. DOI: 10.3390/ijerph17051729 PMID: 32155789

Wani, C., McCann, L., Lennon, M., & Radu, C. (2024). Digital mental health interventions for adolescents in low-and middle-income countries: Scoping review. *Journal of Medical Internet Research*, *26*, e51376. DOI: 10.2196/51376 PMID: 39471371

Weinstein, A., & Lejoyeux, M. (2010). Internet addiction or excessive internet use. *The American Journal of Drug and Alcohol Abuse*, *36*(5), 277–283. DOI: 10.3109/00952990.2010.491880 PMID: 20545603

Wies, B., Landers, C., & Ienca, M. (2021). Digital mental health for young people: A scoping review of ethical promises and challenges. *Frontiers in Digital Health*, *3*, 697072. DOI: 10.3389/fdgth.2021.697072 PMID: 34713173

Willie, M. M. (2017). On Depression and Mental Disorder in South Africa. *Med Clin Rev*, *3*(4), 1–2. DOI: 10.21767/2471-299X.1000060

Wolthusen, R. (2025). Mental Health in Low-and Middle-Income Countries Amid USAID Funding Withdrawal. *Psychiatric News*, *60*(4), appi.pn.2025.04.4.35.a. Advance online publication. DOI: 10.1176/appi.pn.2025.04.4.35.a

World Commission on Environment & Development. (1987). *Our Common Future*. Oxford University Press.

World Health Organization. (2021). *Adolescent mental health.* https://www.who.int/news-room/fact-sheets/detail/adolescent-mental-health

World Health Organization. (2021). *Depression.* https://www.who.int/news-room/fact-sheets/detail/depression

World Health Organization. (2021). *Global strategy on digital health 2020–2025.* https://www.who.int/health-topics/digital-health

World Health Organization. (2024, September 25). *Teens, screens and mental health* [Media release]. https://www.who.int/news/item/[insert full URL]

Worthington, E. L., & Aten, J. D. (2009). Psychotherapy with religious and spiritual clients: An introduction. *Journal of Clinical Psychology, 65*(2), 123–130. DOI: 10.1002/jclp.20561 PMID: 19090533

Xiao, R., & Liu, X. (2021). Analysis of the architecture of the mental health education system for college students based on the Internet of Things and privacy security. *IEEE Access : Practical Innovations, Open Solutions, 9*, 81089–81096. DOI: 10.1109/ACCESS.2021.3084208

Xi, Y., Paracha, S., Hands, C., & Angelakis, I. (2025). *Still looking for new ways of promoting children's mental health education through digital technologies: a systematic review*. Mental Health and Digital Technologies.

Xu, Y., Yang, H., Jin, Z., Xiang, J., Xu, H., Pokay, Y. H., Mao, H., Cai, X., Wu, Y., & Wang, D. B. (2023). Application of a Digital Mental Health Clinic in secondary schools: Functionality and effectiveness evaluation. *JMIR Formative Research, 7*(1), e46494. DOI: 10.2196/46494 PMID: 37883144

Yeo, G., Reich, S. M., Liaw, N. A., & Chia, E. Y. M. (2024). The effect of digital mental health literacy interventions on mental health: Systematic review and meta-analysis. *Journal of Medical Internet Research, 26*, e51268. DOI: 10.2196/51268 PMID: 38421687

Yi, Z., Min, T., Chong, L., & Yani, S. (2024). Research on practical pathways for digital technology-empowered mental health education for rural children in central and western China. *Applied & Educational Psychology, 5*, Article 12766.

Yin, R., Martinengo, L., Smith, H. E., Subramaniam, M., Griva, K., & Car, L. T. (2024). The views and experiences of older adults regarding digital mental health interventions: A systematic review ofqualitative studies. *The Lancet. Healthy Longevity*, *5*(11), 100638. DOI: 10.1016/j.lanhl.2024.08.007 PMID: 39491881

Young, K. S. (1999). Internet addiction: Symptoms, evaluation, and treatment. *Innovations in Clinical Practice*, *17*, 19–31.

Zainal, N. H., Wang, V., Garthwaite, B., & Curtiss, J. E. (2025). What factors are related to engagement with digital mental health interventions (DMHIs)? A meta-analysis of 117 trials. *Health Psychology Review*, •••, 1–21. DOI: 10.1080/17437199.2025.2547610 PMID: 40857362

Zhang, J., Wu, W., Zhao, X., & Zhang, W. (2020). Recommended psychological crisis intervention response to the 2019 novel coronavirus pneumonia outbreak in China: A model of West China Hospital. *Precision Clinical Medicine*, *3*(1), 3–8. DOI: 10.1093/pcmedi/pbaa006 PMID: 35960676

Zhang, X., Lewis, S., Chen, X., Berry, N., & Bucci, S. (2022). Mental health professionals views and the impact of COVID-19 pandemic on implementing digital mental health in China: A nationwide survey study. *Internet Interventions : the Application of Information Technology in Mental and Behavioural Health*, *30*, 100576. DOI: 10.1016/j.invent.2022.100576 PMID: 36185346

Zhang, X., Lewis, S., Firth, J., Chen, X., & Bucci, S. (2021). Digital mental health in China: A systematic review. *Psychological Medicine*, *51*(15), 2552–2570. DOI: 10.1017/S0033291721003731 PMID: 34581263

Zhao, X., Stadnick, N. A., Ceballos-Corro, E., Castro, J.Jr, Mallard-Swanson, K., Palomares, K. J., Eikey, E., Schneider, M., Zheng, K., Mukamel, D. B., Schueller, S. M., & Sorkin, D. H. (2023). Facilitators of and barriers to integrating digital mental health into county mental health services: Qualitative interview analyses. *JMIR Formative Research*, *7*(1), e45718. DOI: 10.2196/45718 PMID: 37191975

Zhou, L., Rudhumbu, N., Shumba, J., & Olumide, A. (2020). Role of Higher Education Institutions in the Implementation of Sustainable Development Goals. In Nhamo, G., & Mjimba, V. (Eds.), *Sustainable Development Goals and Institutions of Higher Education. Sustainable Development Goals Series*. Springer., DOI: 10.1007/978-3-030-26157-3_7

Zhou, S., & Eisenberg, D. (2022). College student mental health: Current trends and implications for higher education. In *Research handbook on society and mental health* (pp. 325–347). Edward Elgar Publishing. DOI: 10.4337/9781800378483.00024

Zhu, S., Wang, Y., & Hu, Y. (2025). Facilitators and Barriers to Digital Mental Health Interventions for Depression, Anxiety, and Stress in Adolescents and Young Adults: Scoping Review. *Journal of Medical Internet Research*, *27*, e62870. DOI: 10.2196/62870 PMID: 40127430

Zhu, Y. (2025). Crisis and countermeasures of digital transformation in American higher education: Based on the perspective of students' subjectivity. *International Journal of Education. Humanities and Social Sciences*, *2*(1), 14–23.

Zope, S. A., & Zope, R. A. (2013). Sudarshan kriya yoga: Breathing for health. *International Journal of Yoga*, *6*(1), 4–10. DOI: 10.4103/0973-6131.105935 PMID: 23440614

Zou, Z., Wang, H., d'Oleire Uquillas, F., Wang, X., Ding, J., & Chen, H. (2017). Definition of substance and non-substance addiction. In Zhang, X., Shi, J., & Tao, R. (Eds.), *Substance and Non-substance Addiction* (pp. 21–41). Springer Singapore., DOI: 10.1007/978-981-10-5562-1_2

About the Contributors

Shafiq Ul Rehman is an experienced educator and professional consultant with a background in curriculum development and educational technology. His teaching and research experience spans more than 11 years. Dr. Shafiq is working with various educational institutions to implement sustainable practices and innovative teaching strategies. Dr. Shafiq received his Ph.D. degree from Universiti Sains Malaysia (USM), Malaysia, in 2017. He was a Postdoctoral Research Fellow at Singapore University of Technology and Design (SUTD), Singapore, from 2017 to 2020. He is currently Acting Dean, College of Information Technology and Chairman Department of Computer Science, Kingdom University, Bahrain. He is also a Senior Assistant Professor with research interests in cybersecurity, artificial intelligence, and the latest emerging IT technologies. He lectures in various Computer Science and IT courses, including developing curriculum and courseware in tandem with current technology trends. In addition to editing 5 books, he has authored over 70 international research publications in the fields of cybersecurity, artificial intelligence, healthcare, IoT, and other emerging technologies. His expertise in these fields extends to academic and industrial consulting, as well as speaking and training at a variety of international organizations, conferences, and seminars.

***

Ashraf Alam currently holds the position of Research Faculty at the Centre of Excellence in Public Policy, Sustainability and ESG Research, housed within the Faculty of Law and Policy Studies at Alliance University, Bangalore. Renowned for his transdisciplinary acumen spanning education, technology, and policy studies, Dr. Ashraf has been distinguished as one of the World's Top 2% Scientists by Stanford University and Elsevier, an accolade that highlights the breadth and depth of his scholarly impact. His prolific academic output includes over fifty SCOPUS-indexed publications and more than one hundred conference presentations at esteemed national and international academic forums. His educational trajectory reflects both depth and versatility: a Ph.D. in Education from the Indian Institute of Technology (IIT) Kharagpur, an M.Ed. with a concentration in Mathematics Education, and a B.S. in Computer Science from the University of Delhi. He also holds postgraduate degrees in Public Administration (M.A.) and Mathematics (M.Sc.), supplemented by a suite of postgraduate diplomas in Higher Education, Guidance and Counselling, Educational Technology, Criminology and Police Administration, and Value Education. Dr. Ashraf is an active participant in global scholarly discourse. As Associate Editor of Frontiers in Education, he plays a pivotal role in curating and guiding intellectual contributions across the Educational, Pedagogical, and Learning Sciences. Concurrently, he serves as Founder and Director of Academic Chronicles Private Limited, where he orchestrates editorial board formation and develops strategic frameworks for peer-reviewed publishing in the Social, Behavioural, and Humanistic Sciences. His research has been disseminated through elite academic platforms, including Elsevier, Springer, Taylor & Francis, Wiley, Routledge, Sage, Emerald, and IEEE, and addresses a remarkably diverse array of topics such as pedagogical theories, educational administration, educational psychology, educational sociology, educational policy, technology-integrated learning, mathematics education, educational philosophy, educational technology, teacher education, and AI/ML in learning environments. Dr. Ashraf's scholarly rigor is further demonstrated by his success in qualifying multiple prestigious examinations including UGC-NET-JRF in both Education and Adult and Continuing Education, UGC- NET in Public Administration, and GATE in Humanities and Social Sciences. At the heart of Dr. Ashraf's intellectual ethos lies a steadfast belief in education as a catalytic and emancipatory force capable of engendering social justice, human flourishing, societal progress, and sustainable transformation. His recent explorations into 'Happiness Engineering' and holistic well- being in school ecosystems articulate a vision of education that transcends instrumentalist paradigms, prioritizing emotional intelligence, global consciousness, empathy, and psychosocial resilience among learners. His research agenda seeks to conceive educational praxis through the affordances of inclusive digital learning, gamified instructional design, and artificial intelligence (AIEd), thereby constructing robust, ethically grounded frameworks for 21st century education. At Alliance University, Dr. Ashraf remains committed to architecting pedagogical models that not only cultivate intellectual dexterity and cognitive excellence but also prepare learners for morally responsive leadership, intellectual nimbleness, and responsible global citizenship in an increasingly volatile, uncertain, complex, and ambiguous (VUCA) world.

Nneoma Andrew-Vitalis is a Scholarly, data-driven data scientist/Machine Learning Engineer with 5+ years of experience in data science, machine learning, statistical modelling, and predictive modelling. Proficient in Python, SQL, LLM, PySpark, Power BI, and cloud computing, with a track record of transforming raw data into actionable insights. Strong expertise in building monitoring systems, developing scalable frameworks, optimising algorithms, and developing machine learning solutions to enhance business decision-making. Passionate about leveraging AI for business intelligence, automation, and product innovation.

Rohit Banerjee is currently pursuing a Bachelor of Technology in Computer Science and Engineering at JIS College of Engineering, India. His academic interests include Artificial Intelligence, Database Management Systems, Compiler Design, Operating Systems, and Software Engineering. In addition to his coursework, he is actively engaged in research and innovation, with a patent in progress for a Wireless Detachable Bluetooth Microphone Speaker. He has worked on diverse projects that integrate technology with real-world problem solving, including the development of "HealthTrackr," a MERN-based personal health and fitness tracker with advanced analytics, and an AI-powered navigation bot designed for national-level hackathons. His work also extends to smart automation systems, such as an automatic floor-cleaning machine with intelligent sensing capabilities. Rohit's research and project experiences reflect his dedication to bridging theory with practice and leveraging computer science for innovation. His long-term vision is to contribute to both academic research and industry by advancing technologies that create meaningful societal impact while fostering global collaboration in knowledge and innovation.

Selin Cengiz is an MA student in the field of English language teaching. She has been working as an English language instructor since August 2024. Her current research interest is the psychological aspect of language learning. Orcid ID: 0009-0008-9967-6938

Bora Demir after graduating from English Language Teaching department of Çanakkale Onsekiz Mart University, he got his MA degree from the same university. He earned his PhD from Yeditepe University on English Language Teacher Education. He has become an associate professor in 2023. He is currently a member of the School of Foreign Languages in Çanakkale Onsekiz Mart University. He has participated and presented his research at various reputable international conferences, and published articles in national and international journals/books with research interests in various aspects of language teaching and language teacher education. He is the founder and the Editor-in-Chief of the academic journal "Innovational Research in ELT" since 2019.He also edits the journal of "ELT-

Turkey" which is a publication of the AELTE.More recently, he has edited three reference books to be used in ELT departments namely, "Interculturality in English Language Learning and Teaching", "Discourse Analysis and Language Teaching" and "Language Teaching Approaches and Methods". His research interests include technology assisted language teaching, cognitive aspects of language learning, and psychological aspect of language learning and teaching.

Deepa Sharma holds PhD, MBA in Human Resource Management, currently working as Assistant Professor at MMIM, Maharishi Markandeshwar (Deemed to be University), a NAAC accredited Grade 'A++' University, Mullana, Ambala (Haryana). She has more than 9 years of experience in academics. She has written 80+ research papers for various Scopus and UGC listed refereed national and international journals and 27 research papers are appearing on Scopus Preview. There are 94 citations on Research Gate and 814 citations on Google Scholar (h-index - 16, i16-index-23). She has also presented papers in 60 conferences and seminars. Her area of interest includes Human resource management, Human relations, organizational behavior, digital marketing, and customer engagement.

Rhodrick Nyasha Musakuro is a Lecturer in International Human Resource Management (HRM) at the University of Sunderland (UK), a role he assumed in October 2023, following 7+ years of teaching at Cape Peninsula University of Technology (CPUT) in South Africa. Complementing his academic career, he possesses 3 years of HR Consulting experience from Joubert & Monty. Dr. Musakuro earned a PhD in HRM, with his thesis focusing on the sustainable adoption of e-health tools for digital mental health services within the South African higher education context. He also holds Master's, Bachelor's, and National Diploma in HRM from CPUT, all awarded cum laude (with distinction). As an early career researcher, Dr. Musakuro has contributed several peer-reviewed articles, book chapters, to the field and has several manuscripts under review. He has presented his research findings at 5+ international conferences and supervised 9 MSc HRM students to completion. He actively enhances the academic community by reviewing for the SA Journal of Human Resource Management and the South African Journal of Information Management. Beyond teaching and research, his expertise extends to curriculum design, accreditation processes, and community engagement initiatives. Dr. Musakuro is a professional member of the South African Board of People Practices (SABPP). His research interests include Technology Adoption, Digital Mental Health Services, Sustainability, and Talent Management.

Obinna Emmanuel Obi-Akwari is a Lawyer and Software Developer, currently working as a Front-End Developer. He specializes in Javascript, TypeScript,

React, and Node.js, building scalable, user-friendly applications. Passionate about technology and innovation, he is a future founder driven to create impactful software solutions. He is also an avid researcher in software development and AI, exploring advancements in automation, machine learning,and software testing. With extensive experience in API integrations, full-stack development, and quality assurance, he strives to enhance performance, efficiencyy, and user experience in dynamic environments. His interdisciplinary background in law and technology enables him to approach problem-solving with a unique perspective.

Ene Ojaide is an accomplished data scientist and AI researcher with a strong background in machine learning, predictive analytics, and data driven problem-solving. Holding an MSc in Data Science from Nottingham Trent University, UK, she is a dedicated contributor to the field, Ene is a scholar who actively bridges the gap between theoretical research and real-world applications, strongly focusing on leveraging machine learning and AI for societal impact, interpretability, ethical AI, and data-driven decision-making. Beyond research, Ene plays a key role in fostering knowledge exchange and upholding high academic standards. She contributes to industry discussions, mentors aspiring data scientists, and promotes diversity in tech.

Sabyasachi Pramanik is a professional IEEE member. He obtained a PhD in Computer Science and Engineering from Sri Satya Sai University of Technology and Medical Sciences, Bhopal, India. Presently, he is an Associate Professor, Department of Computer Science and Engineering, Haldia Institute of Technology, India. He has many publications in various reputed international conferences, journals, and book chapters (Indexed by SCIE, Scopus, ESCI, etc). He is doing research in the fields of Artificial Intelligence, Data Privacy, Cybersecurity, Network Security, and Machine Learning. He also serves on the editorial boards of several international journals. He is a reviewer of journal articles from IEEE, Springer, Elsevier, Inderscience, IET and IGI Global. He has reviewed many conference papers, has been a keynote speaker, session chair, and technical program committee member at many international conferences. He has authored a book on Wireless Sensor Network. He has edited 8 books from IGI Global, CRC Press, Springer and Wiley Publications.

Deepa Sharma has done Ph.D., MBA in Human Resource Management, currently working as Assistant Professor at MMIM, Maharishi Markandeshwar (Deemed to be University), NAAC Accredited Grade 'A++' University, Mullana, Ambala (Haryana). She has more than 9 years of experience in academics. She has written 61+ research papers for various Scopus and UGC listed referred National & International Journals and 13 papers appear on SCOPUS Preview.

Muhammad Usman Tariq is a strategic higher education leader and scholar with more than 17 years of international experience across academia, research, and industry. He holds dual doctorates, a PhD in Artificial Intelligence and a Doctorate in Business Administration and has published extensively as the author of research articles, case studies, book chapters, and academic texts. His contributions also include several patents, reflecting his applied research in technology, business, and education. He is the Founder and CEO of TheCaseHQ.com, a global hub for professional certification programmes, narrative and video case studies, and digital learning innovation. In addition, he serves as President of the Gulf Higher Education Network (Gulf HE), an initiative dedicated to advancing academic practice, faculty development, and institutional collaboration across the region. He is a Principal Fellow of Advance HE (UK), Chartered Fellow of the CIPD (UK), Senior Fellow of SEDA (UK), and a Senior Member of IEEE, reflecting his standing as both an academic innovator and a global professional leader.

Renu Vij has been mentoring spanning over 13 years, she has established herself as a seasoned educator, mentor, and a prominent figure in the corporate arena. Her multifaceted journey encompasses teaching, mentoring, and conducting impactful corporate sessions, all underpinned by her remarkable expertise as a certified psychometric

Index

A

C

D

E

H

I

L

M

www.ingramcontent.com/pod-product-compliance
Lightning Source LLC
LaVergne TN
LVHW060007031026
849161LV00025B/1543

* 9 7 9 8 3 3 7 3 5 0 0 7 3 *